Recast All under Heaven

D1528883

RECAST ALL UNDER HEAVEN

Revolution, War, Diplomacy, and Frontier China in the 20th century

Xiaoyuan Liu

NEW YORK • LONDON

2010

The Continuum International Publishing Group
80 Maiden Lane, New York, NY 10038
The Tower Building, 11 York Road, London SE1 7NX

www.continuumbooks.com

Copyright © 2010 by Xiaoyuan Liu

All rights reserved. No part of this book may be reproduced, stored in a retrieval system, or transmitted, in any form or by any means, electronic, mechanical, photocopying, recording, or otherwise, without the written permission of the publishers.

Library of Congress Cataloging-in-Publication Data
Liu, Xiaoyuan, 1952–
Recast all under heaven : revolution, war, diplomacy, and frontier China in the 20th century / Xiaoyuan Liu.
p. cm.
Includes bibliographical references and index.
ISBN-13: 978-1-4411-6220-5 (alk. paper)
ISBN-10: 1-4411-6220-8 (alk. paper)
ISBN-13: 978-1-4411-3489-9 (pbk. : alk. paper)
ISBN-10: 1-4411-3489-1 (pbk. : alk. paper)
1. China–History–20th century. 2. China–Territorial expansion–History–20th century. 3. China–Ethnic relations–History–20th century. 4. China–Foreign relations. I. Title.

DS774.5.L569 2010
951.05–dc22

2010004648

ISBN: 978-1-4411-6220-5 (hardback)
978-1-4411-3489-9 (paperback)

Typeset by Newgen Imaging Systems Pvt Ltd, Chennai, India
Printed in the United States of America by Sheridan Books, Inc

Contents

List of Maps

Preface

The chapters in this volume are based on essays written over a considerable time period. Some of these have been published in various forms before. Although focusing on different geographic areas, all construct their narratives and analyses around the same historical theme—modern transformation of Chinese territoriality. As China shed its imperial tradition and took on a new national persona, its tributary and territorial dependencies went in different directions. This book is about these stories in the twentieth century. These chapters are part of my ongoing effort to give the concept of Chinese territoriality a niche in the historiography about twentieth-century China. The concept necessarily brings "frontier China" to the center of scholarly attention and unapologetically demolishes the disciplinary barrier between studies of China's domestic and foreign affairs. "Frontier China" has received adequate scholarly attention for China's premodern periods but remained marginal or even been forgotten for China's modern era, especially for the twentieth century. Although there are studies of modern conditions of frontier regions such as Mongolia, Xinjiang, and Tibet, these are works by a small number of highly specialized scholars whose erudition and expertise concentrate on these non-Chinese areas and rarely take a frontier perspective of Chinese history per se. This book intends to bring "frontier China" back into the mainstream of Chinese studies. Such an approach is not only scholarly sound but also timely for the twenty-first century when the rest of the world is observing and wanting to understand China's seemingly nonstop wrestling with two basic questions of modern nationhood, territoriality and ethnicity, both involving "frontier China."

Yet there is a particular reason for putting these previously exposed essays together here. It is to make factual findings and interpretations of the twentieth-century Chinese frontier history readily available to college-level students. The original essays were therefore subjected to some not too radical re-tailoring for this purpose. Since these essays were written at different times and for different venues, the most difficult part of the revision was to make them into coherent chapters of a book. From the author's point of view, I hope that even if these chapters turn out not working together like a spotlight, they can at least illuminate as individual candles.

To highlight the interpretative aspect of these essays, the overall structure of the book is organized thematically while the chapters in each section are arranged chronologically.

Part I includes two chapters that present separately the paradigm of territoriality transformation and the perception of China as both an East Asian and a Center Asian entity in terms of its geopolitical identity. Part two contains three chapters on the Chinese Nationalist experience during a decisive moment for Chinese territoriality, World War II. They highlight the imaginary character of the Chinese designs and policies during the Republic period for renewing or updating the relations between the Chinese central authorities and certain dependencies of the late Qing Empire. Although the cases discussed, Korea, Vietnam, and Inner Mongolia, belonged differently to the categories of "foreign" and "domestic" affairs of China, they really reflected the externalizing and internalizing effects of the same process of China's territoriality transformation. Part III copes with what used to be a puzzling phenomenon in the Cold War era, Chinese Communist as intensified Chinese Nationalism. The three chapters trace separately the historical processes in which the Chinese Communists reconciled their internationalist ideology with their nationalist political drive, reined in Mongolian separatism with Communist revolution, and overcame the Tibetan theocracy with patient application alternately of suasion and force. These chapters show that either as a challenger or as the holder of the central power of China, the Chinese Communists never diverged from the direction of modern transformation of Chinese territoriality and worked similarly as the Nationalists for recasting China in a national mould. The three chapters in last part of the book consider the international aspect of China's nation-building odyssey. They show that always an international enterprise, the attainment of modern Chinese territoriality shaped great powers' conceptions about the international politics of Asia, affected other Asian countries' national identity and security, and sowed seeds of prolonged misgivings between China and its neighbors. In conclusion, the Epilogue serves as a reminder that Chinese territoriality continues to be a dynamic process rather than a static new status quo.

I wish to express my heart-felt gratitude to Angela Kao and Marie-Claire Antoine, two editors at Continuum Books. Angela Kao first discussed the project with me and helped initiate the book into the list of the press. As the project progressed, however, she left Continuum Books. Then Marie-Claire Antoine graciously took over and provided me with valuable advice throughout the project. The publication of the book also gives me an opportunity to thank friends and colleagues who helped in various ways with the preparations and publications of the original essays. They are Uradyn E. Bulag, Warren I. Cohen, Lowell Dittmer, Hao Yufan, Michael H. Hunt, William C. Kirby, Julia Lee, Li Xiaobing, Tian Xiansheng, Ezra Vogel, George Wei, and Yang Kuisong. Steven Levine, one who evaluated the project for Continuum Books and revealed his identity, and another anonymous reader offered many excellent suggestions for revising the essays into a coherent book. Hopefully the final result is not too far from their standard. It goes without saying that I am alone responsible for all remaining errors and defects in the book.

A number of chapters in the book originally appeared in different forms and under different titles. Chapter One was published in Li Xiaobing and Tian Xiansheng, eds., *Xifang Shixue Qianyan Yanjiu Pingxi* (New historiography in the contemporary West) (Shanghai Cishu Chubanshe, 2008. In Chinese), Chapter Two as *Occasional Paper #78 of The Asia Program* (Woodrow Wilson International Center for Scholars, Washington, D.C., 1998), Chapter Three in *Journal of American–East Asian Relations*, volume 1, number 2 (summer 1992), Chapter Four in *Modern Asian Studies*, volume 33, number 2 (May 1999), Chapter Five in *Inner Asia*, volume 1, number 2 (August 1999), Chapter Six in George Wei and Xiaoyuan Liu, eds., *Chinese Nationalism: Historical and Recent Cases* (Greenwood Publishing Group, 2001), Chapter Eight in *Harvard Asian Quarterly*, volume 11 (2–3) (Spring/Summer 2008),

Chapter Ten as "The Shadow of Mongolia over the Negotiations for the Sino–Soviet Alliance, 1949–1950" (in Chinese) at the official website of the Center for Cold War International History Studies, East China Normal University, Shanghai, China, http://www.coldwarchina.com, in January 2005, and Chapter Eleven in Yufan Hao, George Wei, and Lowell Dittmer, eds., *Challenges to China's Foreign Policy: Diplomacy, Globalization, and the Next World Power* (University Press of Kentucky, 2008). The subjects of Chapters Seven and Ten have received much detailed treatment in several chapters of my book, *Reins of Liberation: An Entangled History of Mongolian Independence, Chinese Territoriality, and Great Power Hegemony, 1911–1950* (Stanford University Press and Woodrow Wilson Center Press, 2006). The contents of Chapter Nine and the Epilogue were presented to several international symposiums in 2009. I am grateful to these publishers for permitting me to use the essays here.

PART I

A Territorial Perception of Modern China

CHAPTER ONE

Modern Transformation of Chinese Territoriality

When entering the twentieth century, the Manchu rule in China disintegrated rapidly. Han Chinese-centered nationalist politics emerged to become the new frame of reference of China's state affairs, including China's inter-ethnic and frontier relations. Such development would soon affect the writing of twentieth-century Chinese history. Two tendencies seem to have been present in what we read about twentieth-century China. One is marginalization of historical subjects concerning frontier affairs. The frontiers, which played a key role in structuring the Chinese Empire before the twentieth century, have lost prominence in historiography on twentieth-century, "national" China. While studies of China in the past century are overwhelmingly about the histories of revolutions, wars, reforms, socioeconomic conditions, and intellectual developments in the eastern provinces of China, topics about China's Central Asian frontiers become rarities attended to by a small group of specialists. Another is antagonization of China's interethnic relations. The twentieth-century alienation of Mongolia, Tibet, and Xinjiang from China proper has been a principal concern of the scholarships in the field, but rarely is it illustrated how the rivalries in these frontiers contributed to the vitality of China as a "nation." In different ways, the Inner Asian frontiers were similarly vital to the Qing Empire and to the Chinese national state of the twentieth century. By no means a harmonious family for various ethnic groups, the Qing Empire founded by the small ruling caste of the Manchus could not have continued without multiethnic collaboration. The state of the "Chinese nation" would not have existed without interethnic contests, for the new nation began with its Han-Chinese core's centralizing effort to overcome the separatist tendencies of the non-Han frontiers. The question is how the earlier collaboration was replaced by the conflicts of the twentieth century and how the frontiers have remained relevant to this date.[1]

To answer these questions is to restore the importance of the frontiers to the history of twentieth-century China. The rest of the book will tackle the task. This chapter leads the discussion by clarifying a number of key conceptions.

Territoriality

In a proposition to reconsider the meaning of the twentieth century, the historian Charles Maier points out that historians of the past century have been obsessed with ideological conflicts, massive political persecutions, genocides, and destruction of civilian lives by wars. They have overlooked one of the fundamental developments of the human societies, which involves the genesis, growth, and resultant crises of "territoriality." He defines territoriality this way:

> Territoriality means simply the properties, including power, provided by the control of bordered political space, which until recently at least created by the framework for national and often ethnic identity. Despite our taking it as a given for so long, territoriality has not

"Gu Jin Hua Yi Quyu Zongyao Tu" (Essential Map of Ancient and Present China and the Barbarian States), a map produced between 1098 and 1100 in the Northern Song Dynasty showing the cartographic tradition of China in making political maps. Note that the map was consistent with the imperial practice of China of not using borderlines. In this map the meaning of the Great Wall was ambiguous for the Chinese influence during the Han and Tang Dynasties, as indicated in the map, went beyond the Great Wall.

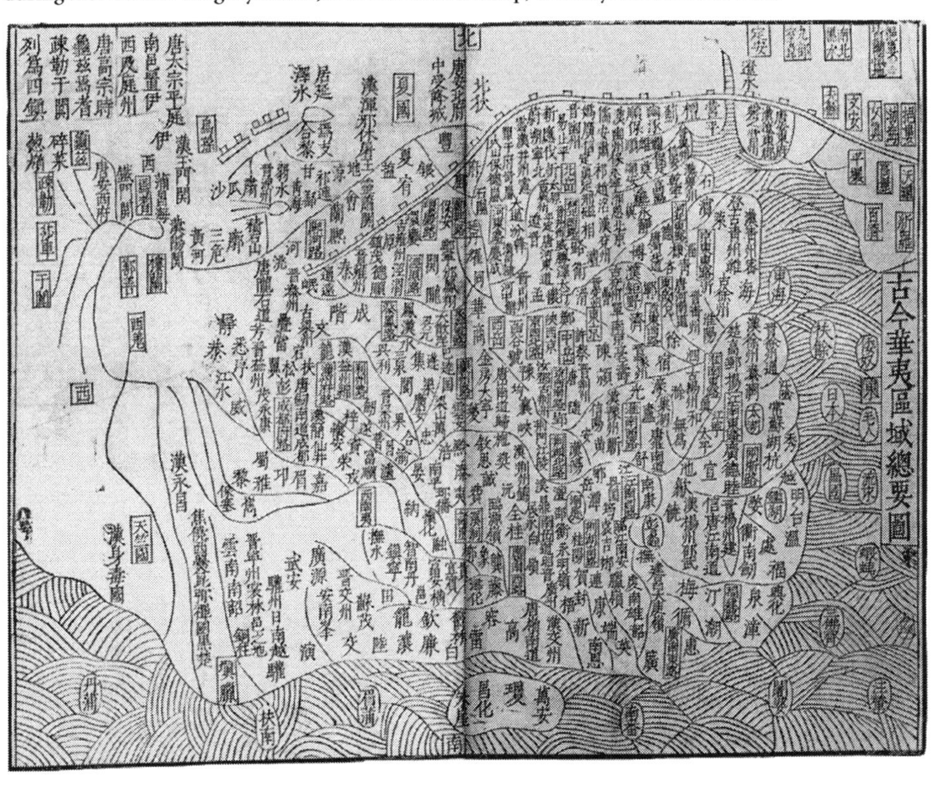

Source: "Ancient Maps of China," Department of Geography at Hong Kong Baptist University and National Geomatics Centre of China, http: //geog.hkbu.edu.hk/geog1150/Chinese/. The original is housed in Beijing Library, Beijing, China.

"Da Ming Hun Yi Tu" (Amalgamated Map of the Great Ming Empire). Probably made around 1389, the map continued Chinese cartographic tradition. The left part of the map shows locations of Africa.

Source: "Ancient Maps of China," Department of Geography at Hong Kong Baptist University and National Geomatics Centre of China, http://geog.hkbu.edu.hk/geog1150/Chinese/. The original is housed in the First Historical Archives of China, Beijing, China.

> been a timeless attribute of human societies. It is a historical formation, and its political form was also historical, that is, it has a beginning and an end. But it has not followed the trajectory of the century through time, providing rather the spatially anchored structures for politics and economics that were taken for granted from about 1860 to about 1970 or 1980 but that have since begun to decompose.[2]

This conception has not often appeared in analyses of modern Chinese history. A closely related term, extraterritoriality, is however one of the key words in studies of modern Chinese history. After the Qing Empire lost its first war ever with a Western power, the Opium War with Great Britain between 1840 and 1842, Western countries gained various privileges in China under the legal umbrella of extraterritoriality. The legal term therefore summarizes "all the properties including power" possessed by Western powers in China until their "unequal treaties" with China were abolished in World War II. In this long period, extraterritoriality was not a rigid legal conception but a mechanism that facilitated foreign powers' and their nationals' activities in China and a symbol that allowed foreign powers to identify with one another vis-à-vis China. Detrimental as it was to the Qing Empire, extraterritoriality served as a negative indicator that modern transformation of Chinese territoriality began.

The evolvement of territoriality has coincided neither with the turns of centuries in world history nor with changes of dynasties in Chinese history. Important steps in formation and transformation of territoriality are landmarks of epochal significance by themselves. A fundamental indicator of modern territoriality is congruence between the state entity and its legally demarcated territory. Modern territoriality requires clearly established international boundaries and state sovereignty based on such boundaries; it also prescribes organization of the society, administration of population, and utilization of natural resources informed by unequivocal consciousness of a nation-state. At least in the case of Chinese history, territoriality had existed before modern times in forms molded by different phases of the Chinese civilization. Its modern incarnation, however, unquestionably followed the norms of the international community.

Historical China

In considering China's modern transformation, one cannot avoid dealing with a term, "historical China." Scholars in China tend to view the domain of the Qing Empire as the ultimate geographic area of "historical China." The main stream of the Qing scholarship in the West in contrary separates the Qing Empire and "historical China" as two different conceptions. An objection to modern "territorialism" has been clearly voiced. According to this opinion, delimiting premodern human activities with modern national maps is to read history backward, "like a primitive archaeologist ripping artifacts out context to store neatly in a museum."[3]

The debate about "historical China" can easily fall into the trap of a-historical contentions. Actually, no matter how the territorial domain of the Qing Empire is defined, an indisputable fact is that the Qing Dynasty was the parent of modern China. To investigate the modern transformation of Chinese territoriality is to study the changes of the state organization, social relations, and territorial features of China that began during the Qing Dynasty. Chinese history fostered its own tradition of territorialism. For instance, the ancient conception *bantu*, which may be loosely translated into "households and maps," indicates a long practice of administering people in relation to the territories of their residence. The rigidity demonstrated by ancient Chinese dynasties in guarding their territorial domains could be as severe as modern nation-states. In its spatial and temporal existence, China is like an ageless river ebbing and flowing. The Qing Dynasty has continually received historians' special attention long after its demise not only because it was the parent of modern China but also because the river of China was vast in the time of the Qing.

Emperor Yongzheng bragged about the vastness of the Qing Empire this way: "China's unification began with the Qin [Dynasty], and its unification with the area beyond the Great Wall began with the Yuan but completed during our dynasty. Since the ancient time our dynasty has been the only one that combines China and the outer realm into one family and possesses an enormous territory." The first premier of the People's Republic of China (PRC) Zhou Enlai agreed, attributing the size of the PRC to the territorial achievements of the Manchu rulers before the twentieth century.[4]

Yet, the matter of territoriality concerns more than the size of territory and is not limited to frontier affairs. Instead, the conditions and any modification of territoriality are immediately relevant to the fundamentals of statehood. In the twentieth century the nationalist lamenting about the shape of China being reduced from that of a begonia leaf to that of a rooster employed vivid images to incite the Chinese people's anti-imperialist indignation. Whereas these images can convey the most obvious change of China's territory, they tell little about the transformation of Chinese territoriality. Modern transformation of Chinese territoriality not only set new standards for measuring state sovereignty, territorial integrity, and administrative authority but also altered the operations of the central government in managing civil affairs and utilizing land and other natural resources. For instance, the Qing government inherited the ancient *yizhan* system (postal carriage through horse riders' relay) but expanded and perfected the system to guarantee smooth communications and effective governance during the Qing Empire's westward advance. In the nineteenth century the Western impact brought about the old system's replacement by the modern postal service. Such structural and functional changes occurred at different levels and in various aspects of the Qing Empire, reflecting developments necessitated by modern transformation of Chinese territoriality. The significance of such changes cannot be explicated by China's nationalist historiography focusing on China's fall to a semi-colonial predicament after the Opium War. These have to be understood as part of a history about the reconstruction of China into a "national state" after the mid-nineteenth century.[5]

"Historical China" is by no means unique in world history. As comparative history shows, Europe and China achieved unification respectively in the time of the Roman Empire and that of the Qin-Han dynasties, but then they followed different paths. In Europe a multistate system emerged to pave the way for the era of nation-states; China by contrast maintained its unitary tradition to this date.[6] Unity vis-à-vis plurality is just one way to compare China and Europe. After the Roman Empire collapsed, it took a long time for nation-states to achieve normative dominance in Europe. Until the mid-seventeenth century, European states and China continued to share certain common features as far as territoriality was concerned, such as imprecise interstate boundaries, ambiguous conceptions about state territories, and lack of differentiation between domestic and foreign affairs.

Not until 1648 did these shared features begin to fade away as the inter-state behaviors in the East and the West became increasingly different. In the year the Peace of Westphalia marked a decisive victory of independence by secular monarchies over universality of imperial and religious authorities in Europe. Bilateral diplomacy began to demarcate international boundaries among European states. As the seventeenth century came to the end, however, Louis XIV of France still could not have a clear idea bout the size and shape of the French territory, and he only had several rather different rough estimates. Other European states were even worse in this regard. When the eighteenth century began, principal European countries did make important advance in differentiating domestic from foreign affairs and conducting diplomacy with specialized government agencies. At the eve of the French Revolution, England and France completed respectively the mapping of their state territories with modern cartographic technique.[7]

Whereas European states were completing the modern cartographic images of their territorial domains, the Qing Dynasty was consolidating its newly achieved mastery of China and thereby continuing and even aggrandizing China's grand-unity tradition. This is not to say that parallel developments between multi-state Europe and unitary Qing China ceased completely. In the seventeenth century and up to the first half of the eighteenth century, the Qing Empire matched Europe in mapping territories and even took the lead briefly. In 1646 the Manchu conqueror Dorgon ordered a comprehensive survey of land and population in the empire. In 1689, in concluding the Treaty of Nerchinsk with Russia, Emperor Kangxi set a precedent for the Qing Dynasty of demarcating borders with bilateral diplomacy. Then Kangxi ordered the making of the "Confidential Map of the Qing Empire" by employing the cartographic skill of Jesuit missionaries serving in his court. The making of the map took a decade and completed in 1718, and the final product marked China's leading position in the world in mapping state territories with modern cartographic technique.[8]

Yet, China's cartographic achievements under Emperor Kangxi and his two immediate successors did not reflect or initiate modern transformation of Chinese territoriality. The inter-state behavior of the Qing Empire differed normatively from that of the European nation-states not because the two models did not share any single practice but because their state systems were informed by completely different conceptions. Whereas modern European states demarcated borders and mapped their territories as necessary steps in the context of international competitions with one another, the cartographic endeavor of the Qing, though a political act for consolidating the Manchu rule in China, was intended as a showcase of the vast celestial dynasty and an image record of the imperial orthodoxy.[9]

Thus, during the two hundred years from the Manchu conquest of China and the Opium War, China and Europe followed their respective paths in consolidating or fostering two interstate systems. When the Qing Dynasty made painstaking efforts to preside over the imperial sphere and to enrich the frontier management of the ageless China, the West employed legal pacts and lethal power to define "state sovereignty" and promote "national interests." By the end of the eighteenth century, as the Qing Empire reached its high peak, the West was set to introduce its modern international order to the rest of the world via imperialism and colonialism.

Sovereignty

Obviously, the crux of territoriality is sovereignty, involving its delimitation and execution. In the view of international laws, sovereignty is about "ultimate authority," over which three types of political entities have competed in history—universal, national, and local.[10] China before the Opium War may well be defined as a "feudal sovereign state" possessing "integral territorial and maritime sovereignty." As such, at the time China held "ultimate authority" and "absolute power" over its inner and outer dependencies.[11] The problem is, the meaning of any conception has to be understood within context. From today's point of view, the so-called absolute feudal sovereignty itself was relative by nature. The sovereignty conception of ancient China was universalistic, as expressed in the Chinese term *tianxia* (all under heaven). It had little in common with modern theory on sovereignty that centers on nation-state. "Chinese sovereignty," if sovereignty can be used at all to describe Chinese imperial power, tolerated relative or "sub-sovereignty" held by various political entities (dependencies, tributary states, guest states, peer states, and so on) within the Sino-centric celestial domain or all under heaven. At least in theory, "Chinese sovereignty" provided a benevolent umbrella for a stratified, deferential order of big and smaller states. By contrast, modern sovereignty entails pursuit of absolute sovereignty by individual nation-states and makes anarchy a normal condition among them who, in theory, are all "equal."

The merit of the traditional East Asia inter-state order informed by "Chinese sovereignty" and the reasons for the order's demise in modern times are yet to be fully investigated by historians. Since the nineteenth century, history has unmistakably favored sovereignty of the European origin, enthroning it as "international" norm and making it the starting point of modern international laws. An authoritative definition of state sovereignty considers the conception in four aspects: (1) interdependent sovereignty, or state right to control cross-border personnel, materials, and ideas; (2) domestic sovereignty, or effectiveness of state power and authority at home; (3) international legal sovereignty, or recognition of territorial state by the international society; (4) Westphalian sovereignty, or state power free of direct or indirect interference from external forces.[12] Comparable functions or elements can probably be found in premodern and non-Western interstate systems. In any historical era or cultural context, the actual function of state power cannot be separated from authority and control, but in different historical context the connotation of authority may vary and the criterion of control may change. What separates the traditional East Asian inter-state order and the modern international system is their fundamentally different construing of "authority" and "control."

The first phase of the East–West encounter took place long before the Opium War. Between the sixteenth and the eighteenth centuries, European missionaries, merchants, and adventurers of various types came to the Sino-centric world of East Asia, fitting into the socio-cultural environment to pursue their undertakings. The rulers of the Ming and the Qing Empires accommodated these new comers as men from afar drawn toward the wealth and civilization of the celestial dynasty, and their countries as tributary or trading states into the realm of "all under heaven." Under Emperors Kangxi (1661–1722) and Yongzheng (1722–1735), a so-called rites controversy between the Qing court and the Papacy ended the successful story of the Jesuit mission in China, reflecting confrontation between two types of universalistic authorities. The next monarch, Qianlong (1736–1799), kept China's traditional institutions and practices intact in arrogantly rejecting the requests by the Macartney Embassy from England (1793) for relaxing trade restrictions and for establishing a permanent diplomatic relationship. This was the last time the West presented the relational norms among equal states to China in a gentlemanly manner, and this was also the last time a Qing ruler, with confidence and conviction about China's centrality in the world, could counter the Western norms with China's own.[13] When the second long scene of this inter-systemic encounter began, the curtain was raised by the Opium War. The authority and power of the Qing Empire now faced unprecedented challenge. Modern transformation of territoriality was forced upon China.

Transformation

China was the center of the traditional East Asian inter-state order, and the transformation of Chinese territoriality inevitably meant the order's disintegration. Under the Western impact, the East Asian countries shared a common experience of becoming "national" but they followed different paths. Situating at the margin of the Sino-centric world, Japan soon learned a lesson from its abortive resistance against the West and started a swift process, known in history as the Meiji Restoration, of emulating the West in reorganizing the Japanese state and society. At the turn of the nineteenth and twentieth centuries, Japan became the first modernized Asian country and the only imperialist power among its Asian peers. In the meantime, An Nam (Annan to the Chinese and predecessor of modern Vietnam), Burma (predecessor of Union of Myanmar), Nanzhang (predecessor of the Laos), Korea, and the Liuchiu Kingdom (today's Okinawa of Japan) went from the tributary dependencies of the Qing Empire to the colonies of Western powers and Japan. In the late nineteenth century, to maintain influence over its "outer dependencies," the Qing Dynasty fought France and Japan respectively over An Nam and Korea. The results of the Sino-French War of 1884–1885 and the Sino-Japanese War of 1894–1895 were China's acceptance of An Nam's status as a "state by itself" (*zi wei yi guo*) and relinquishment of its long relationship with Korea characterized by the two sides' mutual obligations of "fostering the small and serving the great" (*zixiao shida*).[14] Not until after World War II could China partially renew its close relationship with these two neighbors. When communist revolutions took over successively China and the northern halves of Vietnam and Korea, these countries became "brotherly states" to one another in the "socialist camp."

Among Asian countries, Siam's modern transformation is a fascinating case comparable to China. The modern experience of Siam differed from Japan's imperialist mischief as well as the colonial fate of Korea, An Nam, and Burma. Similar to Burma and An Nam, premodern Siam, while deferring to China as an "upper state," was one of the major power centers of the tributary system, called "mandala" or circles, among Southeast Asian countries. The states within this system were not separated by clearly demarcated borderlines and engaged one another frequently in competition over dependency states. To survive, the small and weak often had to submit themselves simultaneously to two or more strong neighbors. Cambodia, for instance, served Siam as "father" and An Nam as "mother," maintaining its "independence" with dual "submission." After British influence entered Burma in the 1820s, the ambiguous buffer zones among Southeast Asian countries began to be replaced by clear divides between Western powers' spheres of influence. In maneuvering with the intruding Western powers, Siam managed to gain its own "geo-body" defined with modern conceptions and practices of sovereignty and stepped into the modern era by renewing its statehood as a "nation-state."[15]

Apparently, the traditional inter-state order of East Asia contained many galactic centers around the mega-center of China. These overlapped and penetrated one another, and the so-called hegemony by those relatively strong power centers over the relatively weak peripheries was expressed mainly through symbolic tributary gestures rather than actual domination. The so-called feudal centralization of the traditional Chinese Empire was in reality a bifurcated polity with intensive power centralization in the imperial core area—China proper, and extensive diffusion of power and influence along the imperial peripheries. Similar to Siam, the modern transformation of Chinese territoriality meant a dual process of losing relative "feudal sovereignty" in one type of territorial realm and establishing absolute modern sovereignty in another. In the process the state behavior and the functions of the state power in many important aspects changed. The following are the most important indicators of China's regeneration from a falling traditional empire into a rising modern national state.

First, establishment of international boundaries. Inter-state borders were by no means unheard of in premodern China. For instance the Song Dynasty used rivers as borderlines between itself and the powerful non-Chinese Liao and Jin Dynasties. The Qing Dynasty also used tablets to mark the divides between its imperial territories and neighboring states like Burma, Korea, Sikkim, and Nepal.[16] In 1793, when the British envoy George Macartney came to the Qing court requesting trade and diplomatic relations with China, Emperor Qianlong retorted: "The borders of the celestial dynasty are strictly enforced and outsiders are never allowed to cross and mingle with the locals. Therefore the demand by your state to establish a place in the capital must not be permitted." He also told the visitor: "Every feet of land of the celestial dynasty is registered and incorporated into the map. The border locations are inviolable. Even small islands and sandbars are demarcated and administered separately." Qianlong's predecessor, Emperor Yongzheng, seems to have adopted a different attitude toward borders and territories. In 1728 the king of An Nam asked Yongzheng to concede 120 *li* of disputed territories between the two states. Yongzheng agreed to concede 80 *li*. But the An Nam king still persisted in getting the 40 *li* left. Yongzheng became angry at first but then decided to humor the king in the south. He laid out his rationale this way: "I am reigning over the universe and all submissive states are included in my domain. An Nam is ranked among the invested dependencies, and every feet of its land belongs to me. There is no need to be so concerned about these insignificant 40 *li*. . . . These 40 *li* is my interior land if assigned to Yunnan, and my outer territory if to An Nam. There is really no difference. I will bestow this piece of land to the king and let him guard it for me."[17]

Actually, the father's and the son's respective stances on territories and borders are not contradictory to each other. Both talked about the divides between the "interiors of the celestial dynasty" and the "outer dependencies," but not international boundaries of modern significance. In their eyes, the interiors, inner dependencies, and outer dependencies of the celestial dynasty were all included in the imperial "registry and maps" (*banji*), and the distinction between the interiors and the latter two was rather elastic. As for the divides beyond the outer dependencies, they were not the direct responsibilities of the celestial dynasty. In the time of the Qing this center-tilted, layered perception about the relationship between China proper and the borderlands was likened with the layout of traditional Chinese residence: China proper was the central hall, the inner dependencies were the doors and windows, and the outer dependencies the fences or walls of the yard.[18] In such a perception, the celestial dynasty did not have neighboring states as we understand today. If we take the "dependency borders" of the Qing time for international borders of the modern times, Emperor Yongzhen would become the first sovereign of the Qing Dynasty who "gave away land carelessly to foreigners and foreign countries."[19] This, of course, is to read history backwardly.

It was under great powers' pressure that the Qing Dynasty changed its "dependency borders" into modern international borders. As pointed out by Maier, a feature of modern territoriality is that the bordered space is no longer "construed as a passive enclosure to be policed and kept orderly" but becomes "a source of resources, livelihood, output, and energy." It is no longer a "security buffer" but a "decisive means of power and rule."[20] As Western colonialism extended competition over territories of such modern significance to Asia, the traditional conceptions, institutions, mode of behavior, and policies of Chinese power faced a comprehensive crisis. During the few decades following the Opium War of 1840–1842, Western powers not only demolished the "fences and walls" of the "celestial dynasty" but also broke the "doors and windows" of China and entered the "central hall." Wielding superior military power and protected by the legal armor of the newly created treaties with China, Western powers inserted their interests and influence into China, partitioned China into spheres of influence, and took China's natural resources as their own. Consequently, the Qing government not only lost completely its relative authority over "outer dependencies" but was also about to lose its absolute control over the "interiors."

In general, it is not wrong to suggest that the modern territory of China was the result of Western powers' nibbling away the territories of "historical China" of the Qing version. This statement is however incomplete in presenting the historical process of Chinese territoriality. Although China of the Qing Dynasty was weak and conservative in dealing with the Western challenge, it managed to stage a rather stubborn resistance. The directions of the modern boundaries of China had therefore to be determined by the balance of power between the Qing Empire and those Western powers concerned and that among all interested Western powers. Once a borderline was demarcated, it was based on international agreements. Outside such a borderline, China lost permanently its relative "feudal sovereignty." Inside it, China established its absolute modern sovereignty recognized by international laws. Without seeing the other, "gaining," side of the coin, any discussion of the modern changes of Chinese territories could only point out the quantitative reduction of China's size but not understand the qualitative transformation of Chinese territoriality. Only by noting what happened on both sides of the borderline can we explain why after reduced in size, the territory of "historical China" became "modern."

Second, differentiation between domestic and foreign affairs. To Chinese rulers, the layered relationship of the Chinese Empire, involving "all under heaven," was about the distinctions between the superior and the inferior, the esteemed and the humble, the intimate and the estranged, and the close and the distant. If a relationship could be meaningfully defined as one between the "internal" (*nei*) and the "external" (*wai*), the definition had to be based on the distinctions listed above. The ancient maxim about "internalize all the Chinese and externalize all the barbarians" (*nei zhuxia er wai yidi*) ran through the statecraft of China's dynastic history. The Manchus relocated their Qing Dynasty from Manchuria to the Central Plain of China, added several important territories to the imperial domain bequeathed from the Ming Dynasty, and used Lifan Yuan (Office of Dependency Management) to administer the imperial frontiers. As a ruling ethnic minority from Inner Asia, the Manchu rulers were more conscious than their Ming predecessors of the significance of the various "dependencies" at the peripheries of the empire.[21] Since the "fan," or dependencies, was manageable, Lifan Yuan can almost be equated to an office in charge of internal affairs in our own times. Such historical conversion however cannot be done because Lifan Yuan was also in charge of the Qing Empire's relations with Russia. The office cannot be viewed as a "foreign office" either because the Mongolian and Tibetan affairs in its charge were not foreign affairs to the Qing emperors. From the antiquity China's dynastic governments always had an official position named *dahonglu* (grand receptionist of all visitors), or similar function with various names. Its responsibility was to arrange appropriate protocols for visiting dignities or tributary missions from "states within the realm" (*yunei*) that "leaned inwardly" (*xianghua*). This kind of offices also cannot fit into "domestic" or "foreign" affairs as we understand today. When the Qing Dynasty reached its high peak in Emperor Qianlong's time, the Qing government officially put Holland, France, and the United States, Korea, Japan, and the Liuchiu Kingdom into the same category as "eastern barbarians" (*dongyi*), indicating an enlarged "realm" of the "celestial dynasty" in the eyes of the Qing rulers. Before the Opium War, the Department of Rites of the Qing government listed "various western ocean countries," Korea, and An Nam as "guest states" (*keguo*), differentiating the former from the latter two only in terms of the frequencies and regularities of their "tributary" missions to China.[22] Under such circumstances differentiation between "domestic" and "foreign" affairs in government functions could hardly happen.

After the Opium War, the uninvited guests from the West invalidated the Chinese conception of "all under heaven is one family" and the Qing rulers' devices of "reigning over the universal realm." Inside China the Western powers eventually acted as if they were the masters. Li Hongzhang, one of the most important officials of the Qing Empire during the second half of the nineteenth century, characterized the situation as an "unprecedented grand upheaval in several thousand years."[23] Shocked by the upheaval, rulers of the Qing Dynasty realized gradually that the Western system of equal states could restrain Western powers' activities in China better than the Sino-centric order for "all under heaven." In 1861, defeated again in the second opium war (or the *Arrow* war) and still fighting the Taiping rebels, the Qing government opened its first specialized office in charge of its relations with Western countries, Zongli Yamen (Office of the General Management of Various States' Affairs). The office was not only the forerunner for China's ministry of foreign affairs in the twentieth century but also one of the indicators of modern Chinese territoriality that differentiated administrative function for foreign affairs from that for domestic matters. Western powers were now all "foreign states" equal to the Qing Dynasty, and those outer dependencies such as An Nam, Burma, Korea, and Liuchiu also became "foreign" to China by falling into the hands of the great powers. The good old days when the "celestial dynasty" had no neighbors were irreversibly gone. As the Qing government started to modernize its diplomacy, powerful colonial empires already surrounded China from all directions. Such Western encirclement of China would not end until the tide of colonialism began to retreat from Asia after World War II.

Third, expansion of domestic authority. "Ancient nine prefectures, reformed institutions today, named as provinces, twenty-two in total." These words were the new additions to the classic *San Zi Jing* (three-character canons) made by the scholar Zhang Binglin in 1928.[24] At the time *San Zi Jing* had modern competitors as a textbook for elementary education, but Zhang Binglin's revision certainly reflected the contemporary consciousness of the Chinese state. The history of China's administrative divisions and establishments is long and rich. An epochal change nevertheless occurred simultaneously with the demarcation of China's modern boundaries. Administrative divisions and establishments are direct indicators of the scopes, forms, and intensities of the actual control exercised by the central authority. Such authority, or domestic sovereignty, of modern states in the West did not go beyond their international borders but left no hollow pockets within these borders. In contrast, the administrative establishment of the traditional Chinese empire was a concentric structure and the actually control decreased progressively away from the ruling center. As China lost its outer dependencies and pressured by powerful new neighbors, the ruling center could no longer use the old "loose rein" and "hollow frontier" approaches to manage the inner dependencies on the imperial frontiers. Starting with the late nineteenth century, the Qing government acted as any sovereign "nation-state" would and adopted a series of measures to solidify its control over territories, especially those along the frontiers.

Resultantly, modern ethnopolitics in China's frontiers happened and became one of the thorniest issues in the political life of twentieth-century China. The late Qing government and its successors in the twentieth century pushed frontier administrative reform in various forms. These were intended to achieve the same goal, which was to enhance the central authority and control in the frontiers to the same level as in China's interior provinces. In other words, as China's relations with former outer dependencies became matters of foreign diplomacy, China's central governments endeavored to turn those inner dependencies along the frontiers into matters of domestic administration. In late Qing, the old ethnic segregation policy and the old approach of managing different frontier regions with different types of offices were suspended. The new policy was to extend the Chinese province system, station central government's army, and move Han-Chinese into the frontier regions. These measures continued during the republic period. When the People's Republic of China was established in 1949, the Chinese Communist government installed a system of "regional nationality autonomy" and took various steps for radical social changes in the frontiers. These "domestic" measures caused upheavals in the local societies as effectively as penetrations by foreign influence. As results, the so-called Mongolia question, Tibet question, and Xiniang question have continued to this date.

Fourth, establishment of international sovereignty. Without a supreme authority to provide order to the international arena, modern European states followed a set of precedents and reached a series of agreements derived from their competitions. These became international laws. This historical process is comparable to the Spring and Autumn period and the Warring States period of Chinese history when numerous Chinese states fought one another yet followed a set of norms in their mutual relations. The rules of the game were however internal to the Chinese states, applied only to "states of courtesy and propriety" but not to "barbarians beyond the pale." For a considerable period, while extending world wide, modern international laws were also rules of the privileged Western club and discriminated against non-Western countries. During the eighteenth and nineteenth centuries, when intruding into Asia, the international system based on equality among nation-states produced a set of unequal treaties and scores of colonies. In the mid-nineteenth century, the mismatch of cultural behavior and the gap of material power between Confucian China and industrial England decided the result of the clash between the Eastern and Western interstate systems these countries represented respectively. From the center of the ageless, Sino-centric "all under heaven," China fell to the periphery of the rising international order of the Europe-centered world. During the next hundred years, China tried to rid itself of a repressive treaty system imposed on it by Western powers while reentering the international community. China became a state beyond the pale.[25]

China's international struggle bore significant results during World War II. In 1943, China was able to abrogate the "unequal treaty system," and, two years later, it stood among the founding states of the United Nations as one of the "Big Four." These landmark events indicated China's attainment of complete sovereignty in the modern sense. It should be pointed out however that, unlike Japan and many other Asian countries, China's modern experience went beyond transformation into a "national state" and attaining a full-fledged sovereign status among the world's states. China chose a revolutionary path and, during the second half of the twentieth century, joined the Soviet Union in challenging the prevalent international system.[26] The so-called brotherly relationship among members of the "socialist camp" after World War II appeared contradictory conceptually and practically to the norms of international relations. The long-term impact of the "socialist" international relations is beyond this investigation. One thing is clear: the Chinese revolution of the twentieth century was one of the political movements in non-Western countries that made the modern international system truly global by contributing to the retreat of Western and Japanese colonialism from Asia and shattering the Western monopoly of modern international-relation culture.[27]

* * *

The four aspects discussed above are the most obvious indicators of the modern transformation of Chinese territoriality. They however cannot show the whole picture of the long and intricate historical process. The process began during the final decades of the Qing and certain threads have continued to this date. As a matter of fact, every facet of China's modernization is related in a certain way with transformation of territoriality. Transformation of Chinese territoriality has been a regional phenomenon as well. During the nineteenth and twentieth centuries, a galaxy of "national states" burst into East Asia and superceded the Sino-centric world of the region. Yet, not every Asian country has achieved its final form of national state. For instance, the issue of Korean reunification has still suspended in mid-air an integral peninsular state.

Even China remains suspensory. One of the oldest states in world history but also one of the youngest national states of the modern times, China has gone through a most complicated and twisted path of territoriality transformation. During the first half of the twentieth century, continuous civil wars and the devastating war of resistance against Japan brought the Chinese nation into an age of great uncertainty. The very shape of China's geo-body was in question again. During World War II, the Chinese Nationalist Government strived hard in the stage of inter-allied diplomacy to assure a bright future for Chinese territoriality, painfully conscious of the distance between China's "great power" status and its actually weakness.

That is history now, but a contradiction between China's perceived status and its actual conditions has persisted. China's reforms and resultant developments in the past three decades have left little doubt that we are witnessing a new cycle of China's re-rise in a unprecedented scale. Yet, in the future of China still lie unsettled, thorny questions concerning territoriality. After China regained its "lost territories" and thus solved one of the core items of China's political agenda in the twentieth century, in the twenty-first century China continues to face the challenging question about "national unification." Taiwan remains outside the PRC, Hong Kong and Macau are still in transition termed "one country, two systems," and Tibet and Xinjiang, though internal to China's national boundaries, continue to generate separatist forces. If China's national agenda continues to lag behind its international agenda, the world will likely witness a precedent: a leading world power without a settled geo-body.

Notes

1. Scholarly works on China's Inner Asian frontiers and ethnic affairs of the twentieth century are not abundant. Recent studies of Mongolia, in the order of publication dates, include Uradyn E. Bulag, *Nationalism and Hybridity in Mongolia* (Oxford: Oxford University Press, 1998); Sechin Jagchid, *The Last Mongol Prince: The Life and Times of Demchugdongrob, 1902–1966* (Bellingham: Western Washington University Press, 1999); Christopher P. Atwood, *Young Mongols and Vigilantes in Inner Mongolia's Interregnum*

Decades, 1911–1931 (Leiden: Brill, 2002); and Xiaoyuan Liu, *Reins of Liberation: An Entangled History of Mongolian Independence, Chinese Territoriality, and Great Power Hegemony, 1911–1950* (Stanford and Washington, DC: Stanford University Press and Wilson Center Press, 2006). Noticeable works on modern Tibet are Melvyn Goldstein, *A History of Modern Tibet, 1913–1951: The Demise of the Lamaist State* (Berkeley: University of California Press, 1989) and *A History of Modern Tibet, 1952–1956: Gathering of Storms* (Berkeley: University of California Press, 2007); A. Tom Grunfeld, *The Making of Modern Tibet* (Armonk: M.E. Sharpe, 1996); Tsering Shakya, *The Dragon in the Land of Snow: A History of Modern Tibet Since 1947* (London: Pimlico, 1999); John Kenneth Knaus, *Orphans of the Cold War: America and the Tibetan Struggle for Survival* (New York: Public Affairs, 1999); Kenneth Conboy and James Morrison, *The CIA's Secret War in Tibet* (Lawrence: University Press of Kansas, 2002); Alexandre Andreyev, *Soviet Russia and Tibet: The Debacle of Secret Diplomacy, 1918–1930s* (Leiden: Brill, 2003), Gray Tuttle, *Tibetan Buddhists in the Making of Modern China* (New York: Columbia University Press, 2005); and Hsiao-ting Lin, *Tibet and Nationalist China's Frontier: Intrigues ad Ethnopolitics, 1928–1949* (Vancouver: British Columbia University Press, 2006). Xinjiang is the subject of Linda Benson, *The Ili Rebellion: The Moslem Challenge to Chinese Authority in Xinjiang, 1944–1949* (Armonk: M.E. Sharpe, 1990); Andrew Forbes, *Warlords and Muslims in Chinese Central Asia: A Political History of Republican Xinjiang, 1911–1949* (New York: Cambridge University Press, 1996); and David Wang, *Under the Soviet Shadow: The Yining Incident, Ethnic Conflict and International Rivalry in Xinjiang, 1944–1949* (Hong Kong: Chinese University Press, 1999). In addition, M.E. Sharpe, the publisher, has published three collaborative volumes, Stephen Kotkin and Bruce Elleman, eds., *Mongolia in the Twentieth Century: Landlocked Cosmopolitan* (1999); S. Frederick Starr, ed., *Xinjiang: China's Muslim Borderland* (2004); and Barry Santman and June Teufel Dreyer, eds., *Contemporary Tibet: Politics, Development, and Society in a Disputed Region* (2006).

2. Charles S. Maier, "Consigning the Twentieth Century to History: Alternatives for the Modern Era," *American Historical Review*, 105 (3) (June 2000): 807–831.
3. David Ludden, "Presidential Address: Maps in the Mind and the Mobility of Asia," *Journal of Asian Studies*, 62 (4) (November 2003): 1057–1078. Representative works by Chinese scholars in this regard are Ma Manli, *Zhongguo Xibei Bianjiang Fazhanshi Yanjiu* (A study of the developmental history of China's northwestern frontiers) (Heilongjiang Jiaoyu Chubanshe, 2001); Ge Jianxiong, *Tongyi yu Fenlie: Zhongguo Lishi de Qishi* (Unity and division: revelation of Chinese history) (Beijing: Sanlian Shudian, 1994); and Ma Dazheng and Liu Di, *Ershi Shji Zhongguo Bianjiang Yanjiu* (Frontier studies in twentieth-century China) (Harbin: Heilongjiang Jiaoyu Chubanshe, 1998).
4. Ma Dazheng, 256; Zhou Enlai, *Zhou Enlai Xuanji* (Selected works of Zhou Enlai) (Beijing: Renmin Chubanshe, 1984), 2: 262.
5. Liu Wenpeng, *Qingdai Yichuan yu Jiangyu Xingcheng zhi Guanxi Yanjiu* (A study of the relationship between the courier system of the Qing Dynasty and the formation of territories) (Beijing: Zhongguo Renmin Daxue Chubanshe, 2004).
6. R. Bin Wong, *China Transformed: Historical Change and the Limits of European Experience* (Ithaca: Cornell University Press, 1997), 76–77.
7. Martin van Creveld, *The Rise and Decline of the State* (Cambridge: Cambridge University Press, 1999), 86, 133–134, 143–144.

8. Laura Hostether, *Qing Colonial Enterprise: Ethnography and Cartography in Early Modern China* (Chicago: University of Chicago, 2001), 70, 75–76; Jin Ergang and Su Hua, *Zhifang Biandi: Zhongguo Kanjie Baogaoshu* (Administered frontiers: a report on the investigation of Chinese boundaries) (Beijing: Shangwu Yinshuguan, 2000), 11–17.
9. Jin Zhe, *Kang Yong Qian Shiqi Yutu Huizhi yu Jiangyu Xingcheng Yanjiu* (A study of map making during the periods of Kangxi, Yongzheng, and Qianlong and the formation of territories) (Beijing: Zhonguo Renmin Daxue Chubanshe, 2003), 55, 58.
10. John Boli, "Sovereignty from a World Polity Perspective," in Stephen D. Krasner, ed., *Problematic Sovereignty: Contested Rules and Political Possibilities* (New York: Columbia University Press, 2001), 55.
11. Ma Dazheng, 349–350; Shao Xunzheng, *Zhong Fa Yuenan Guanxi Shimo* (History of Chinese–French–Vietnamese relations) (Shijiazhuang: Hebei Jiaoyu Chubanshe, 2000), 48–49.
12. Stephen D. Krasner, "Problematic Sovereignty," in Krasner, ed., 2.
13. For insightful discussions of these events, see Liam Matthew Brocky, *Journey to the East: The Jesuits Mission to China, 1579–1724* (Cambridge: The Belknap Press of Harvard University Press, 2008) and James Hevia, *Cherishing Men from Afar* (Durham: Duke University Press, 1995).
14. Wang Zhichun, *Qingchao Rouyuan Ji* (Qing records of pacifying the remote) (Beijing: Zhonghua Shuju, 1989), 374–376; Shao Xunzheng, 117.
15. Thongchai Winichakul, *Siam Mapped: A History of the Geo-Body of a Nation* (Honolulu: University of Hawaii Press, 1994), 77, 82, 88–89, 101.
16. Gu Jigang and Shi Nianhai, *Zhongguo Jiangyu Yange Shi* (History of China's changing territories) (Beijing: Shangwu Yinshuguan, 2000), 161, 168; Wang Zhichun, 135; Liu Yongzhi, *Zhong Chao Guanxi Shi Yanjiu* (Zhengzhou: Zhongzhou Guji Chubanshe, 1994), 256–257; Academia Sinica, *Zhohua Minguo Shi Dili Zhi (Chugao)* (Historical geography of the Republic of China [first draft]) (Taipei: Academia Sinica, 1980), 40–52.
17. Wang Zhichun, 142–143, 68–69.
18. Ma Dazheng, 398.
19. Jin Ergang and Su Hua, 21.
20. Maier, 818.
21. For insightful discussions of the Manchu governance and territorial management, see Pamela Kyle Crossley, *A Translucent Mirror: History and Identity in Qing Imperial Ideology* (Berkeley: University of California Press, 1999); Mark Elliott, *The Manchu Way: The Eight Banners and Ethnic Identity in Late Imperial China* (Stanford: Stanford University Press, 2001); and Peter C. Perdue, *China Marches West: The Qing Conquest of Central Eurasia* (Cambridge, MA: The Belknap Press of Harvard University, 2005).
22. Fan Xiuchuan, *Zhongguo Bianjiang Guji Tijie* (Annotated bibliography of ancient works on Chinese frontiers) (Urumuqi: Xinjiang Renmin Chubanshe, 1995), 216–218; Mao Haijian, *Tianchao de Bengkui* (Disintegration of the celestial dynasty) (Beijing: Sanlian Shudian, 1995), 28, note 15.
23. Liang Qichao, *Li Hongzhang Zhuan* (Biography of Li Hongzhang) (Xian: Shanxi Daxue Chubanshe, 2009).
24. *San Zi Jing, Bai Jia Xing, Qian Zi Wen* (Three-character canons, a hundred family names, and thousand-character text) (Shanghai: Shanghai Guji Chubanshe, 1988), 100.

25. Zhang Yongjin, *China in the International System, 1918–1920: The Middle Kingdom at the Periphery* (London: Macmillan, 1991), contends that after 1840 China was incorporated into the Euro-centric international system but was not accepted as a member of the international community until the end of World War II.
26. Akira Iriye suggests in his *Power and Culture: The Japanese-American War, 1941–1945* (Cambridge: Harvard University Press, 1981) that Japan's "co-prosperity sphere for greater East Asia" during World War II was a copy of the Anglo-American hegemony but not a fundamental challenge to the Western system and conceptions of international relations.
27. Mlada Bukovansky, *Legitimacy and Power Politics: The American and French Revolutions in International Political Culture* (Princeton: Princeton University Press, 2002); David Armstrong, *Revolution and World Order: The Revolutionary State in International Society* (Oxford: Clarendon Press, 1993) are fascinating studies of how "revolutionary states" between the eighteenth and the twentieth centuries impacted the international system.

CHAPTER TWO

China's Central Asian Identity

A common practice in the field of Chinese study is to identify China as an East Asian country. Written histories of twentieth-century China tend to cover only the eastern half of the country, and Chinese foreign policy is considered principally as a subject of East Asian international relations.[1] A. Doak Barnett's last book reminds us, however, that China also has a less familiar part, the "Far West."[2] The peoples and cultures of the Far West cannot be defined as Chinese, or Han, and the region's geopolitical location is in Central Asia.[3] In other words, today's China has two geopolitical identities: it is an East Asian power and a Central Asian power. China's Central Asian identity owes much to its Mongolian, Tibetan, and Xinjiang frontiers, a region in combination constituting more than a half of China's territory, establishing China's inland boundaries, and determining China's geopolitical position that bridges East, South, and Central Asian regions. The region's multinational population enriches China's cultural life, shapes China's administrative system, and affects China's social stability. For China, the economic and strategic importance of the region cannot be exaggerated. After the disintegration of the Soviet Union, Central Asia has emerged as a new and dynamic region of the world. To China, the long-term meaning of this new condition is by no means clear. China's own economic and political reforms have also added to the instability of the region. Ethnic unrests in Xinjiang, Inner Mongolia, and Tibet since the reforms began seem to have indicated that Chinese Central Asia may change from an asset into a liability for China. No matter what China will become in this century, its East Asian identity will never change. But there is no consensus among commentators about China's Central Asian identity in the future.

This chapter offers an overview about how China's current Central Asian position was secured sixty years ago, focussing on events that led to consolidation of Chinese authority in Inner Mongolia, Xinjiang, and Tibet.[4] The process was far from a natural one, but neither was it as simple as one of military conquest. There is nothing historically inevitable about the process and its consequences. These were contingent on the interplay of several historical conditions. The most important of these are Chinese nationalism, frontier nationalities' separatist movements, and the peculiar international environment in the post-World War II years.

Chinese Nationalism

Chinese nationalism is a multifaceted historical phenomenon. In the early decades of the twentieth century, Chinese nationalists were faced with two closely related questions. First, should the "Chinese nation" be a unitary ethnic entity of the Han people or an inclusive political identity for all the subjects of the former Qing Empire? Secondly, should modern China, defined as a national state, include only the eastern provinces of China where the Han people concentrated, or should it also encompass the vast non-Han territories in the west where the "original domain" of the Qing Empire reached its limit? Chinese nationalists'

"Zhonghua Minguo Wai Menggu" (Chinese Republic and Outer Mongolia), a map published in China in 1947. The red stamp in the area of Outer Mongolia says: "Outer Mongolian independence has been recognized by our state and detailed and accurate border is yet to be demarcated."

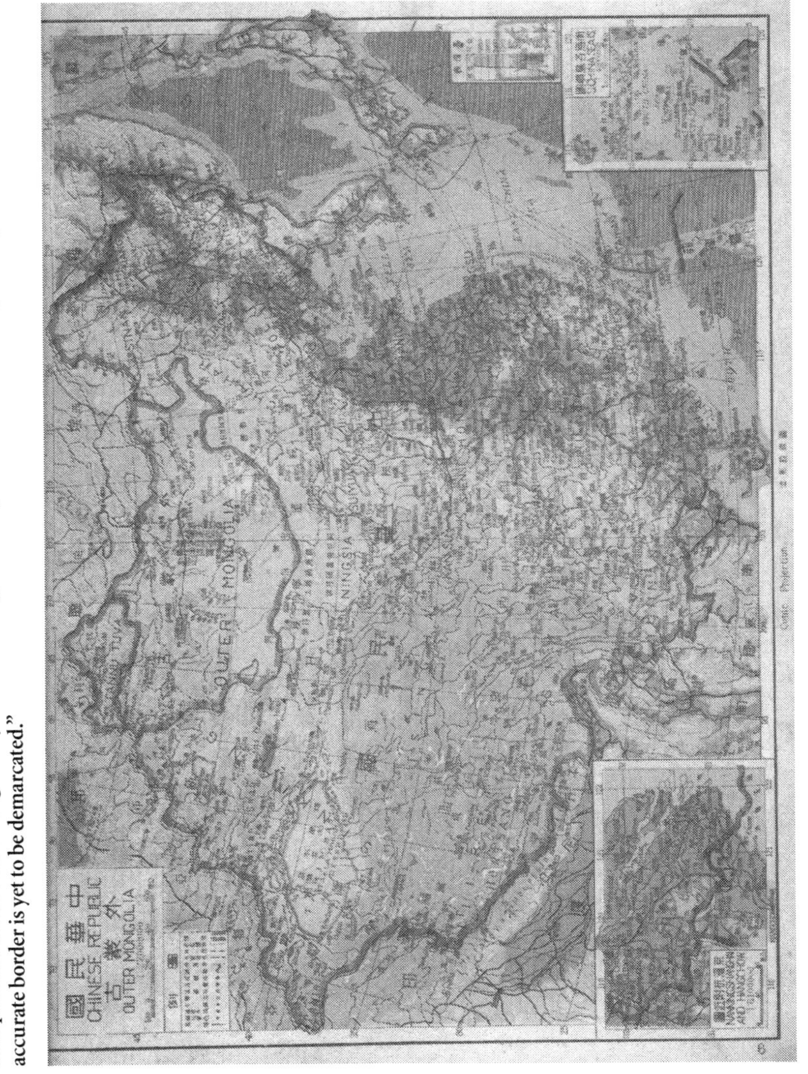

Source: http://commons.wikimedia.org/wiki/file:1947_zhonghua_minguo_quantu.png#filehistory. The original publisher cannot be verified.

"Xinjiang Wei'u'er Zizhiqu Ditu" (Map of Xinjiang Uygur Autonomous Region) (English added). The three highlighted areas, Ili, Tacheng, and Altai were the three rebellious districts between 1944 and 1949.

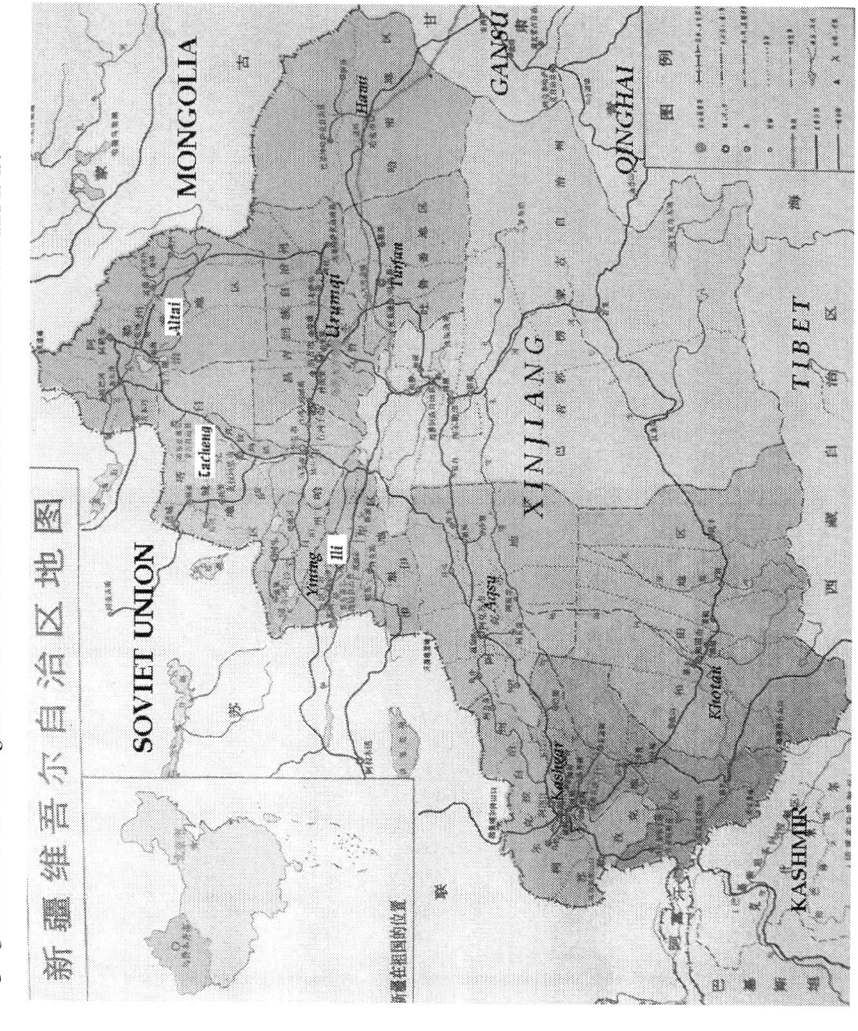

Source: Dangdai Zhongguo de Xinjiang (Xinjiang of contemporary China) (Beijing: Dangdai Zhongguo Chubanshe, 1991).

answer to these questions constituted none less than a redefinition of the outer boundaries and inner character of the Chinese state. In China's dynastic history, similar tasks had been handled by the founding generations of each dynasty. Yet Nationalist leaders of the twentieth-century China performed their duty in an unprecedented way—they reinvented China as a national state.

The nationalists' official definitions of the new China can be found in Sun Yet-sen's "Three People's Principles" and Chiang Kai-shek's book, *China's Destiny.* These Chinese leaders inherited the imperial domain of the bygone Qing state as the geo-body of the Chinese Republic and reclassified all the peoples in that domain, Han and non-Han, with one common identity, "Chinese Nation" (*zhonghua minzu*). Chiang's book actually changed Sun's creed on "five-race republic" into a one-race theory in which China's numerous non-Han ethnic groups were depicted as mere "clans."[5] These doctrines set the agenda for Chinese nationalism: not only the "lost territories" in eastern China must be recovered, Chinese authority in the northern and western borderlands, such as Mongolia, Tibet, and Xinjiang, must also be restored. During the entire republican period, these borderlands were "grey areas" in state affairs: although not lost to China in legal sense, they were practically beyond the central government's control. The Chinese government always insisted that the status of these areas was an issue of China's internal affairs. Yet, in practice, Chinese sovereignty in these territories had to be brought up time and again by Chinese diplomacy with certain foreign powers.

After assuming central authority and claiming reunification of China in 1928, the Chinese Nationalist Government could exercise effective control only in a small number of provinces in eastern and southern China. Its authority over the vast territories in the northeast and the west was either nonexistent or just a ceremonial cover for arrangements that allowed local regimes to retain their semi-independent status. Such a weak position of the Nationalist Government actually made the Chinese Republic very close to the classic definition of nation-state as a single-nation entity.[6]

The situation however did not persuade the Kuomintang (Nationalist Party or KMT) leadership to modify its official nationalism. Rather, Nationalist leaders' ambitions about China's economic growth, concerns with frontier defence, longing for the traditional Chinese ideal of "grand unity" *(da yitong)*, and antiforeign imperialist proclivity kept them in a tenacious effort. This, to borrow Benedick Anderson's expression, was to stretch the "short, tight, skin" of Chinese nation "over the gigantic body" of the Qing empire.[7] The other side of the story is that the constant physical separation between the KMT and the remote frontier regions kept its leaders ignorant about and insensitive toward the cultures and aspirations of the non-Han peoples. Throughout the republican period, the KMT approach to these peoples remained rigid and condescending. The combination between a persistent territorial drive and Han-centric nationalist doctrines created a policy contradiction for the KMT itself and also presented an object of ridicule for foreign governments. During World War II, officials in the British Foreign Office pointed out that the frenzied Han nationalism promoted by the KMT regime could actually deprive China of any right to claim sovereignty over Tibet, a non-Han territory.[8]

That the KMT was more interested in competing with foreign powers for control over the frontiers than in establishing legitimacy with the non-Han peoples proved beneficial to the Chinese Communist Party (CCP) on two counts. First, in the long run, the KMT's dogged diplomatic effort to maintain at least a nominal Chinese sovereignty in the ethnic borderlands preserved these areas in legal terms for the CCP's People's Republic. Secondly, the KMT's negligence in devising a constructive policy toward the frontier ethnic groups provided an opportunity to the CCP to create a "new Han person (*xin hanren*)" image for itself among non-Han peoples. This afforded the CCP a significant edge in competing with the KMT for support from the non-Han peoples of China.

The CCP's relationship with Chinese nationalism is more complicated. It has been said that nationalism is neither the politics of the right nor that of the left, for it is solely concerned with the fulfilment of self-determination, not with any other ideologies.[9] This assertion can be applied to the case of China in the sense that ultimately the KMT and the CCP agreed on the most basic items of China's national agenda. Otherwise, the two parties' respective ideological convictions did contaminate their nation-making and state-building programs. A close examination of the CCP's experience with the "national question" or China's ethnic frontiers will be made in a later chapter. Suffice it to say here to the frontier peoples Chinese Communism offered an alternative only in a limited sense.

Frontier Nationalism

It has been said that China's war with Japan was a "fortunate catastrophe" for the CCP.[10] The same could be said about the Tibetans, Mongols, and Xinjiang's Muslim peoples. Although China's ethnic frontiers in the north and west had been in an estranged relationship with the Chinese government ever since the establishment of the Chinese Republic, it was during China's war with Japan that these frontiers made headways in solidifying their separation from Chinese sovereignty. In taking advantage of the Chinese government's preoccupation with Japan in the east, the Tibetan government escalated its activities to gain international support. While Outer Mongolia, in the name of the Mongolian People's Republic, was fortified against both China and Japan under the protection of the Soviet Union, a Mongolian government under Prince De (Demchugdongrub) emerged in Inner Mongolia under Japan's direct protection. By 1944, an "Eastern Turkestan Republic" emerged in Xinjiang and thus fundamentally changed the struggle in the region from one between local warlords and the central government to one between Uygur and Kazak nationalists and Chinese Nationalist authorities.

The war years therefore saw not only an upsurge of Han nationalism in China proper, but also a rise of separatist movements in the ethnic frontiers. The KMT and the CCP encountered tremendous difficulties in convincing the frontier nationalists that Japan, not the Han government, was their true enemy. After Japan's defeat, however, these frontier movements and regimes unravelled one after another. Why did not the KMT–CCP civil war of 1945–1949 become another opportunity for the frontier movements? An answer can be found on the Chinese side. Briefly, unlike the earlier civil conflicts in twentieth-century China, the 1945–1949 civil war was a military process leading to state consolidation, not to further state and social disintegration. Another factor is the changed international atmosphere in the postwar period, which will be discussed later. But these frontier movements' internal conditions and characters must also be held responsible for their eventual fate.

It has been suggested that the Tibetan question in the twentieth century was one of national self-determination.[11] Before the Tibetan theocracy succumbed to Beijing's pressure and signed an agreement with the Chinese authorities in 1951 to end its separation from China, self-determination was indeed sought by the Tibetan government. But it is difficult to define the Tibetan cause before that point as a "national" one. Until 1951, in its relationship with China, Lhasa's objective can be more properly defined as "civilizational self-preservation" than as national self-determination. Here lies a fundamental reason for Tibet's failure: the Tibetan government sought to preserve the Tibetan way of life but was convinced that this could be done only if Tibet continued to isolate itself from the rest of the world. This stand ran into direct conflict with the requirements of the political reality of the time: to resist modern China effectively, Tibet needed either to modernize itself or open up itself to foreign influence. Melvyn Goldstein's study shows that during the first half of the twentieth century when Tibet seemed to have a chance to hold its ground, Tibetan leaders were reluctant to do either.[12] The mentality of the Tibetan elites in the first half of the twentieth century can be compared with that of the Qing rulers in the first half of the nineteenth century. The difference is that too many powers were interested in opening China to allow it to keep its old ways.

It is also illuminating to compare Tibet with Outer Mongolia. Until the Sino-Soviet treaty of 1945, the Chinese government regarded both as "special territories."[13] The two areas, however, were similar only in one sense: the Chinese government held no control over either of them. Then the two were drastically different in their domestic and foreign affairs. During World War II, officials of the British Foreign Office wondered why the British policy in Tibet could not follow the Soviet precedent in Outer Mongolia. They concluded that (1) Britain was a democratic country that must be accountable to international public opinions, and (2) the British government relied on American support in the war and Washington did not want to see anything to happen to Tibet that might offend the Chinese ally.[14] British officials should have included in their answers Lhasa's own attitude: the British did not have a willing recipient of external influence in Lhasa whereas the Russians did in Ulaanbaatar. The Tibetan government wanted just enough British presence in order to counterbalance the Chinese, which was limited to a commissioner's office, a small hospital, and a short-lived English school. In 1942, a discussion took place in the British government about opening a bank in Lhasa simply because of a rumor that the Chinese might do so. The idea bore no result because the Tibetan government wanted neither the British nor the Chinese to expand their influence.[15]

In addition, it may be asked whether or not Lhasa wanted to separate itself completely from China. To the Tibetan authorities, if the Chinese government was a self-appointed boss, the British an uninvited guest. Lhasa's balancing game between the two could continue only if the eastern connection was kept in place. Such a functional intention was further strengthened by an institutional need to legitimize the theocratic system of Tibet through traditional rituals involving the central authorities of China. Thus, the republican period saw the continuation of the ceremonial relationship between China and Tibet inherited from the Qing Dynasty, which involved the Chinese central government's conferring of titles upon top Tibetan officials and acknowledging of important Tibetan lamas' reincarnations. In 1940, attempting to politicize this relationship, the KMT government even managed to reopen an office in Lhasa.

The question is how to interpret the relationship. Lhasa insisted that these arrangements be viewed religiously, or a patron–priest relationship in which the Chinese government served as a *tanyue* (almsgiver) but not a superior authority. This was already a privileged position reserved for China that the British could not compete. Yet Chinese Nationalist leaders interpreted the position in political terms and viewed it an evidence of Republican China's sovereignty over Tibet and Lhasa's continual allegiance to the central government of China. Interestingly, although endeavouring to weaken Chinese influence in Tibet, in this

Tibetan–Chinese dispute the British government actually took the Chinese side. Throughout the republican period, the British government was consistent in recognizing China's "suzerainty" over Tibet while disputing the Chinese government's claim for "sovereignty."

During World War II, the Chinese Nationalist Government's relocation to Sichuan, a province close to Tibet, also helped enhance Chinese interest in Tibet. Chinese officials viewed Tibet as a rear area for China' resistance against Japan. The Chinese authorities made several attempts to open a route through Tibet for getting allied aid materials.[16] In the name of the common war effort against Japan, from time to time the Chinese government urged its Western allies to adopt a stand on the Tibetan question in favor of China. The Tibetan–Chinese relationship during the republican period can be described with a Chinese metaphor, *ou duan si lian*, or "after the lotus root snaps, its fibres stay connected."[17]

In contrast, the radical social and political changes in Outer Mongolia under Moscow's aegis did not leave even symbolic evidence of continued Chinese influence in the territory.[18] The matter was completely relegated to Sino–Soviet diplomacy. Although the Chinese government never stopped claiming sovereignty over Outer Mongolia before the end of World War II, in practical matters, such as frontier defence and border control, the Chinese authorities treated Outer Mongolia as if it was a foreign country.[19] In 1944, when border incidents took place between Xinjiang and Outer Mongolia, the Chinese government carefully reiterated its sovereign claim over Outer Mongolia yet treated the affair as one with the Soviet government.[20] Outer Mongolia had been "Sovietized" since the 1920s and was physically very close to the CCP region in the northwest. Moscow's intentions aside, KMT leaders had to consider what they could gain from recovering Outer Mongolia in terms of China's domestic politics.[21] In the summer of 1945, when negotiating with Moscow about Soviet entry into the war against Japan and general Sino–Soviet relations, the KMT leadership made a decision to bargain Outer Mongolia away in exchange for Soviet cooperation in the CCP issue.[22]

The Mongolian story, however, did not end with the Sino–Soviet treaty of 1945. The treaty just set a new environment for events to unfold in Inner Mongolia. Details of the situation in postwar Inner Mongolia will be considered in a couple of chapters later. The main features of relevant events are highlighted here.

During the republican period, Mongols of Inner Mongolia were divided into several provinces. The division effectively prevented the Mongols from organizing a unified political movement. During the war, Prince De's regime under Japanese protection maintained limited influence in a number of banners in western Inner Mongolia. After Japan's defeat, although Prince De was discredited, political autonomy remained a strong and popular demand among the Inner Mongols. In September 1945, a "Provisional Government of Inner Mongolian People's Republic" was established in western Inner Mongolia (Silingol League, Chahar), and in January 1946 an "Eastern Mongolian People's Autonomous Government" appeared in the east (Xing'an League, Liaobei). These regimes despatched delegations to Outer Mongolia and approached the Soviet–Mongolian military commands in Inner Mongolia and Manchuria for assistance. Thus, in Inner Mongolia and Manchuria, the CCP–KMT rivalry, Chinese–Soviet diplomatic struggle, and Mongol–Han ethnopolitics became intertwined in a perplexing tangle. In May 1947, when a unified "Inner Mongolian Autonomous Government" was established in Wangyemiao (currently Ulanhot, Xing'an League), the CCP emerged a victor from this multisided contest.[23]

Several factors may explain this development. First, the CCP was in a better position than the KMT to manipulate the Mongolian movement. Geographically the CCP bases were much closer to Inner Mongolia than the KMT government, and organizationally the CCP could adapt itself easily to the mass movement in Inner Mongolia. In contrast, the KMT government remained a southern regime and continued its old approach of dealing mainly with the traditional elites of the Mongolian society. At the time, Chiang Kai-shek decided not to classify Prince De as a "Mongolian traitor" (*Mengjian*) but received him in Chongqing in the hope that Prince De could be used to control the situation in Inner Mongolia. The KMT establishment included several Mongolian members who had collaborated with the Chinese Nationalists for years. Their long-term sojourning in KMT-controlled areas however had reduced their influence in Inner Mongolia to the minimum.

In the postwar years, the most active elements in Inner Mongolia's autonomous movement were Mongolian youth. The CCP's mass work, reformist social programs, and relatively sensitive policies toward ethnic minorities were rather appealing to these people. Yun Ze (Ulanfu), an Inner Mongolian cadre of the CCP, who spoke Chinese and Russian but not Mongolian, emerged in this period as the CCP's most important organizer in Inner Mongolia. He and some other Mongolian CCP members played the key role in bringing many big and small Mongolian autonomous parties and organizations into the fold of the CCP.

Another factor was lack of unity among the Mongols. Inner Mongolia's postwar autonomous movement included radical youth, ordinary farmers and herdsmen, Mongol princes, former members of Prince De's collaborative government, and KMT, CCP, and Outer Mongolian agents. These people pursued different agendas and the divisive condition provided Yun Ze and his associates with an opportunity to use a coherent and well-thought program to enlist followers. At a time when the KMT government was still the legitimate central government of China and the CCP's support of minority nationalities' right to self-determination was still fresh on record, alliance with the CCP, the most effective anti-government force in China, might indeed be considered by many Mongols as an attractive strategy to win freedom from the KMT regime, the symbol of Han oppression.

But this was so only when the Inner Mongols realized that immediate independence or unification with Outer Mongolia could not be achieved. Here the Soviet and Outer Mongolian policies played an important role of suasion. According to one of Yun Ze's reports to the CCP Central Committee, before October 1945, the government of Outer Mongolia summoned Inner Mongolian notables and princes to a conference across the border; the Soviet–Mongolian military command in Inner Mongolia also helped organize an independent government. But, in November, those delegates returned with an unexpected advice from the Outer Mongolian government: "national autonomy with the CCP's help was as good as national independence."[24] This development pushed Inner Mongolian nationalists closer to the CCP.

Soviet influence played a key role in restraining the Pan-Mongol tendency in Inner Mongolia. In the postwar years, seeing the KMT as an American ally, Moscow wanted a clear divide between its Mongolian buffer and China. A Pan-Mongol movement would have kept the borderline between Outer and Inner Mongolia "soft" and would therefore have left the question of Outer Mongolia open. Yet, Moscow's policy preference may have been affected by another factor. That is, the CCP, not the KMT, had stronger influence in Inner Mongolia in the immediate postwar years. Had it been the other way around, it cannot be ruled out that Moscow might have fostered an Inner Mongolian regime to enlarge its Mongolian buffer against the KMT.

This was exactly the situation in Xinjiang during the better part of the Chinese Civil War. During World War II, the turns and twists of events in Xinjiang kept outside observers mystified. In 1942, the Xinjiang warlord Sheng Shicai suddenly turned against his Soviet protector and rallied to the KMT government. Moscow's reaction to the development was even more puzzling: the Soviet government withdrew its troops and other personnel from Xinjiang and thus gave up a long-term sphere of influence too easily.[25] At the beginning, the KMT government appeared to be the winner from these events, but its gains were limited. After the Soviet departure, Chiang Kai-shek was able to maneuver Sheng Shicai out of Xinjiang and thereby ended the last of a series of warlord regimes in the province. The KMT authority, however, was not fully established afterwards. In 1944, a rebellion broke out in the northwestern corner of Xinjiang and a different game followed. Now the warlord politics of Xinjiang was replaced by an ethnopolitical confrontation between the Han central government and a Muslim "Eastern Turkestan Republic" (ETR). One thing did not change, though: the Soviets again became the pivotal influence in the region.

Studies of the ETR are few and rarely agree with one another. Because the Soviet and ETR archival materials remain closed to scholarly examination, many questions raised in the literature cannot be answered with certainty. Neither has the existent literature asked all the relevant questions. The most debated question in the literature is about the Soviet involvement in the ETR.[26] Only recently some inside information began to emerge from Xinjiang.[27] Now we know that from the very beginning the Soviet government was involved in the planning and preparations for the rebellion. Not only Soviet consulate officers in Xinjiang were active, the Soviet government also despatched a military advisory group to Ashan, one of the three rebellious districts, as early as in June 1944. After the ETR was formally launched in mid-November, more Soviet advisers arrived in Yining, the site of the ETR government, and helped plan new military offensives against KMT garrisons in Xinjiang. When peace talks between the KMT government and the ETR began in 1946, Soviet advisers left temporarily for about a year and then returned again in August 1947. The Soviet advisory group was finally withdrawn in August 1949, just a few days before a secret CCP delegation arrived in Yining.[28]

Soviet military aid to the ETR was vitally important for the regime's survival. By August 1949, the ETR had more than fourteen thousand troops whose equipment included antiaircraft guns, fourteen aeroplanes, thirty-one tanks and armed vehicles, and other types of motor vehicles. But the most controversial and speculated issue at the time was whether or not Soviet troops participated directly in the ETR's military operations. According to new information from Xinjiang, at least seven of the ETR's military operations involved Soviet or Outer Mongolian troops. Six of these took place in 1944 and 1945, before the peace talks began. An example was the battle of Wusu, a county city of the Tacheng district. In early September 1945, the Chinese garrison defending the city managed to fend off a joint ETR–Soviet attack for five days. The defence finally collapsed in the last day when three Soviet fighters, several armed vehicles, and an artillery unit joined the fight. In the battle the ETR captured more than a thousand Chinese troops. Together with some other offensives in Ili and Ashan undertaken at the same time, the battle of Wusu helped clear the KMT influence out of northwestern Xinjiang and consolidated the ETR's position.[29] These facts were not known at the time even by the suspicious Chinese government. Soviet military involvement in the ETR was one of the worst examples of Moscow's cynical international behavior: when secretly helping the ETR undermine the Chinese authority in Xinjiang, the Soviet government was becoming a formal ally of the KMT government through the Sino–Soviet treaty of 1945.

The ETR affair indicated that to Moscow, China's ethnic politics was as useful as warlord politics for maintaining its influence in Xinjiang. But Soviet involvement did not change the fact that the Ili rebellion had deep roots in the Muslim population's antagonism against the

Chinese authorities. The debate about whether the ETR was a Soviet puppet or a genuinely indigenous nationalist movement misses the point. It is more useful to ask why the movement became associated with the Soviet Union and what were the consequences of such association. It would simplify history to assert that any anti-central government movement in Xinjiang would have to rely on Soviet assistance. In the 1930s, for instance, a rebellion occurred in southern Xiniang that created a short-lived "Eastern Turkestan Islamic Republic." Leaders of this rebellion sought assistance from the British and Afghan governments, not Moscow.

Therefore, although geographic proximity made the ETR–Soviet association possible, there were other factors that made such an association necessary. Like the Chinese Communist Party that was not merely another peasants uprising in China's dynastic cycles, the ETR was also not just one more Muslim rebellion in China's troubled northwestern frontier. The movement's social-political content requires careful examination. When trying to decide the characters of the ETR regime, contemporary Western observers tried to find out whether or not its policies showed any tendency of Sovietization. Unequivocal evidence of such a tendency was not found at the time. The inquiry into "Sovietization" is understandable for the time but is simple-minded in retrospect. Again the CCP can serve as an example: if the CCP could develop a "Yan'an way" of Chinese Communist revolution, the ETR's need for survival and other political considerations also induced its leaders to cater to the most popular and immediate demands of their constituencies, leaving more radical social programs to the future. As a matter of fact, when the ETR leadership and the CCP Central Committee started direct communications in late summer of 1949, this was exactly how the former explained to the latter the lack of revolutionary content in the ETR programs.[30]

The ETR movement had an influential leftist wing from the very beginning. Never a monolithic movement, the change of the ETR leadership in mid-1946 secured the leftists' predominant position. Before, the movement's most influential leader was a religious figure (Ali Han Tore) whose principal messages included Islamism and Pan-Turkism. In this period the movement showed a very strong anti-Han tendency that led to ethnic massacres in certain places. Yet, even in this period, leftist partisans played a significant role in organizing the uprising. In 1946, as the peace talks with the KMT government proceeded, the leadership shifted into the hands of a group of secular-minded partisans, such as Ahmet Jan Kasimi, Abdul Kerim Abbas, and Izhak Han Mura Haji, who were either educated in the Soviet Union or had previous contacts with the CCP. Although the new leadership continued to maintain the Islamic facet of the movement for the purpose of internal unity, its main messages were about democracy, liberty, and national liberation. The new leadership also adopted a "correct" policy toward the Han residents in its area and focussed its attack on the KMT government.[31] Not only its sympathy with the Soviet Union was openly announced, the new leadership also made secret contact with the CCP as early as December 1946. During the rest of the Chinese Civil War, the organs of the ETR publicly praised the CCP and showed enthusiasm about the CCP's military advance. Then, in August 1949, with Moscow's assistance, a secret CCP delegation arrived in Yining and started direct communications between the ETR leadership and the CCP Central Committee.[32]

Studies of modern Xinjiang disagree why in late 1949 the ETR dissolved itself and joined the PRC.[33] Because the ETR's most important leaders perished in an air-plane crash in late August when they were flying to Beijing, we cannot know how these leaders would have got along with the CCP in the long run. A few questions need to be considered here: What did the ETR leaders intend to discuss with the CCP? How did the CCP leadership view the ETR's status? And what was discussed between the CCP and Moscow about the ETR in 1949?[34]

Available information may not provide satisfactory answers to all these questions. But, in 1949, the Soviet Union, the CCP, and the ETR leadership seemed to agree that their common as well as separate interests could be better served by ending the ETR.[35]

Failure of Containment

It appears that in post-World War II China, in the entangled ethnopolitical, partisan, and international struggles, there were no rigid lines between enemies and allies. Such identities were changeable according to situations. To those participants in these struggles, including frontier forces, Chinese parties, and foreign powers, loyalties to one's ethnic group, state, and ideological principles were not always congruent with one another, and none of these was predominant in policy making all the time. Yet these seemingly chaotic contests finally came to a confluence that produced the People's Republic of China.

changeable identities

Cold War conceptions such as "China's fall to Communism" or "Communist conquest of China" indicate that Western powers', especially America's, attempt to contain Communism failed in China. These conceptions obscure other significant historical developments and their complex interactions. In post-World War II China, there were two closely related political-military movements on the march. The obvious one was the CCP's advance from the north to the south, and another, less visible and often misunderstood, was the expansion of Chinese, or Han, power from the east to the west. Against these two movements, there were also two kinds of containment. One was the U.S.–KMT partnership in eastern China to stop the CCP, and another involved the British and Soviet governments' separate collaborations with non-Han regimes in western China to keep the Chinese at bay.

While these foreign powers' relationships with the southward CCP movement were relatively steady, their relationships with the westward Chinese movement were fluid. Moscow first modified its policy in Inner Mongolia to accommodate the CCP, and then, in Xinjiang, the Soviet government subordinated its partnership with the ETR to its alliance with the PRC. In Tibet, the British retreat from India in 1947 pulled the rug from under Lhasa's balancing stratagem against Chinese power. The Tibetan government watched the development of the Chinese Civil War nervously, preying that the KMT eventually emerge as the winner.[36] Ironically, the KMT government's intention to use military force to solve the Tibetan question and even its idea of "liberating" Tibetan people from their supposedly "inhumane" system were in fundamental agreement with the CCP's.[37] History cannot reveal how a victorious KMT would have substantiated its claim of sovereignty over Tibet. What we know is that after 1949, the antagonism between the People's Republic of China and the West provided the CCP with a convenient justification to solve the Tibetan question forcefully.

A remaining question is what role the United States played in the western containment. In the last stage of the Chinese Civil War, to a certain degree CCP leaders' deliberation of their strategies toward the frontier regions was influenced by a Moscow-inspired theory about U.S. conspiracies along China's western frontiers. The historical literature in the PRC today continues to contend that there were indeed such conspiracies. For instance, U.S. consulate officers' involvement in Xinjiang politics in the late 1940s has been used as evidence. In mid-1947, in coordination with the Chinese authorities in Xinjiang, Douglas S. Mackiernan, U.S. vice-consul at Tihwa (Urumqi), made contact with Osman Batur, an anti-ETR Kazak leader in the Ashan area. The connection was maintained to September 1949, the eve of the CCP takeover. In April 1950, when leaving Xinjiang via Tibet, Mackiernan was killed by Tibetan border guards.[38]

The significance of the Mackiernan affair to Washington's China policy might be marginal. In the Cold War atmosphere of the late 1940s, however, the episode was enough to cause concerns in Moscow and Beijing. Interestingly, the Mackiernan entanglement was not an act of the western containment defined above. It was part of the U.S.–KMT partnership to contain communist influence in the northwest. In other words, in the context of Xinjiang's ethnic confrontation, the Americans were on the Chinese side.

In the late 1940s and early 1950s, U.S. policy makers found it difficult to position China's ethnic-frontier politics in their foreign policy agenda. The difficulty arose from a few factors. First, America's geostrategic focus had always been on the East Asian–Pacific region. Without tangible interests in and necessary knowledge about Chinese Central Asia, the U.S. government was neither willing nor able to play an active role in the region.[39] Secondly, America's traditional China policy was to maintain China's territorial integrity, which in World War II was amplified by President Franklin D. Roosevelt into one of "making China a great power." The policy not only helped evict Japan from Chinese territories but also put restraints on the other two territorial contenders in China, Britain, and the Soviet Union. To American leaders, their policy toward China was historically relevant and politically appropriate partially because they were in favor of China's ridding itself of those damaging consequences of its past encounter with the West. Never did they take it upon themselves to constrain Chinese nationalism, especially when Chinese nationalism was deemed useful in containing communism. Therefore, although frontier separatists often hoped that Washington could be true to its stated commitment to the principle of national self-determination and lend them a helping hand in their resistance against the Chinese, as long as China remained an American ally, the U.S. government did not want to act in any way that might be interpreted as harmful to China's sovereignty.

Thirdly, in the late 1940s and early 1950s, even when the defeat of the KMT became inevitable and America's China policy began a difficult transition, the policy continued to be Chinese-, or Han-, centric. On the one hand, the KMT, though ousted from the mainland, did not alter its stand on Chinese territories, and, on the other, U.S. policy makers harbored a hope that the CCP's nationalist propensity could eventually turn the PRC against the Soviet Union.[40] In 1947, George Kennan predicted:

> I have a feeling that should they [the CCP] ever expand to a point where they could command the majority of the resources of China and where they could represent a major military force in their own right, the men in the Kremlin would suddenly discover that this fluid subtle oriental movement which they thought they held in the palm of their hand had quietly oozed away between their fingers and that there was nothing left there but a ceremonious Chinese bow and a polite and inscrutable Chinese giggle.[41]

When the Beijing–Moscow split did come years later, it was neither subtle nor polite on both sides. Yet in the initial years of the Cold War, American policy makers' high expectation in Chinese nationalism kept their government on the Chinese, or Han, side in both China's international and ethnopolitical struggles.

* * *

The repeated cycles of political unification and division in Chinese history may easily lead to a view that the republican period was another period of disintegration, or an interregnum between two centralized empires.[42] This approach tends to overlook constructive elements in those "disintegrative" phases and to underestimate qualitative changes when a new unification occurred. The republican phase of modern Chinese history is one of intensive state building, in which Chinese political parties, frontier regimes and forces, and foreign powers all played significant roles. When the PRC was established, the centralized Chinese state did not merely repeat the Qing Empire but was formed in accordance with doctrines of Chinese nationalism and Chinese communism. The Inner Asian frontiers were incorporated into the PRC not as a trophy of the traditional imperial "great game," but as an integral part of the modern Chinese "nation-state." For the first time in Chinese history, China's Central Asian affairs became internalized not only in name but also in practice. When this huge piece of the Chinese jigsaw puzzle fell into place, the emerging picture of Chinese power was astounding.

In the process, the two Chinese parties, the KMT and the CCP, worked like teammates in a relay race. From a Chinese-centric point of view, the KMT was better qualified to run the first section and the CCP to charge toward the finish line. Between the two, the KMT adhered to the traditional Chinese ideal of "grand unity" more closely and consistently. Yet the KMT's principal contribution was to articulate the ideal with the vocabulary of the time of nation-states and to implant, though often theoretically, a modern identity of the Chinese state into international politics. Throughout the republican period, the KMT remained a political force of southern China. This southern character explains both the KMT's deft diplomacy in dealing with Western powers and its arrogant, ineffectual approach to the ethnic frontiers. By contrast, between the 1920s and 1940s, the Chinese Communists were forced to move from their southern bases to the northwest. In the process they put in abeyance the doctrinal stance on minority nationalities borrowed from Moscow and adopted a pragmatic approach toward the frontier peoples. During the last round of the KMT–CCP power struggle, the CCP took over from the KMT the cause of national unification and carried out political-military operations in the borderlands. These operations were facilitated by its newly acquired proficiency in ethnic politics and its alliance with the Soviet Union.

Although the three frontier movements under discussion differed from one another in significant aspects, they shared certain common weakness in confronting the centralizing Chinese nationalism. To avoid being "nationalized" into the modern Chinese state, these movements had to take internal and external balancing actions. On both counts, however, they proved inadequate. Internally, the Tibetan government failed to act to modernize its society and state apparatus, Inner Mongolians never achieved coherence among themselves, and the ETR was led by its own leftist propensities into the Communist, yet nonetheless Chinese, camp. External isolation was another reason for these frontier peoples to become "minority nationalities" of the PRC. Much weaker than the robust Chinese power, these "state-seeking" peoples felt necessary to rely on foreign support. Yet, historical and geopolitical factors accorded them only a single-power contact, Tibet with Britain, Xinjiang with the Soviet Union, and Inner Mongolia with Japan first and the Soviet Union later. Thus, in the international scene of the time, the Tibetan, Mongolian, and ETR questions existed only as appendages of these powers' "private" foreign policies but not in the agenda of the postwar international community. During and after World War II, the time-honored conception of state sovereignty and the rigid differentiation between "internal" and "external" affairs in international practices allowed the Chinese government to champion passionately Asian peoples' anticolonial cause yet at the same time to defend its own internal ethnopolitics. Once the interested foreign powers became unable to maintain the same degree of involvement in or opted for a different orientation toward Chinese Central Asia, frontier nationalists or establishments immediately lost their leverage of balancing the Chinese state externally.

In the immediate postwar years, the emerging Cold War international politics proved highly unfavorable to the frontier peoples' causes. In the bi-polarized confrontation, states identified with one another according to universalistic ideologies more than traditional interests. When competing with each other to win China over to their own sides, the Soviet Union and the United States identified separately with the CCP and the KMT. Gone was the old entente between the British in Tibet and Russians in Mongolia and Xinjiang that had kept the Chinese in check. In its place was a new axis among the Americans, the Soviets, and the Chinese to make China a valid Asian power. Such an unspoken collaboration among the giants was too overwhelming for the small frontier forces to bear.

In sum, during the decade preceding the PRC, at work in Chinese Central Asia were some intricately intertwined national, international, and transnational forces. Their forms, temperament, and interrelationships have since then changed drastically. Yet in the mid-twentieth century, together these forces cemented the connection between the Central and East Asian halves of today's China.

Notes

1. John King Fairbank's *China: A New History* (Harvard, 1992) calls for broadening our sights in order to view Inner Asia peoples as a "critical part of the history of the Chinese people" (p. 25). Yet among the book's eight references of Tibet only one is in the twentieth-century period; and Xinjiang and Mongolia are mentioned several times, all in nineteenth-century or still earlier contexts. Immanuel Hsu's *The Rise of Modern China* (Oxford, 1995) pays more attention to the questions of Xinjiang and Mongolia but only in the context of the Sino–Soviet relations.
2. A. Doak Barnett, *China's Far West: Four Decades of Change* (Westview Press, 1993).
3. The current usage of "Central Asia" in both Western and Chinese literatures usually includes only the five CIS republics east of the Caspian Sea. In this discussion the conception is used in an older historical context when China's Inner Asian frontiers appeared still open. It is therefore interchangeable with "Inner Asia" as used in Owen Lattimore's pioneer studies of Chinese frontiers.
4. The Tibetans, Mongols, and Uigurs are not the only "territorial minorities" of China. These are discussed here together because (1) they are frontier nationalities in Chinese Central Asia, and (2) they are the only ones that developed strong separatist movements before the People's Republic was established in 1949.
5. Chiang Kai-shek, *China's Destiny* (New York: Roy Publishers, 1947), 30. The "five-race republic" idea includes the Han, Manchus, Mongols, Tibetans, and "Hui," a name for the Muslim peoples of Xinjiang.
6. For an insightful discussion of the myth that the nation-state is a single-nation entity, see Walker Connor, *Ethnonationalism: The Quest for Understanding* (Princeton University Press, 1994), especially 40–41, 70–71, 95–97.
7. Benedict Anderson, *Imagined Communities: Reflections on the Origin and Spread of Nationalism* (Verso, 1996), 86.
8. Foreign Research and Press Service to Mr. Ashley Clark, November 2, 1942, FO 371/31700, Public Record Office.

9. Elie Kedourie, *Nationalism* (Blackwell, 1966), 84–86.
10. Anderson, 158, note 6.
11. Warren W. Smith, Jr., *Tibetan Nation: A History of Tibetan Nationalism and Sino-Tibetan Relations* (Westview, 1996). The "Tibetan nation" conception is not clearly defined in the book. Melvyn C. Goldstein's more careful and original study of the pre-1951 history of Tibet, *A History of Modern Tibet, 1913–1951*, avoids using the conception altogether and properly discusses Tibetan policies as behaviors of the "lamaist state."
12. Goldstein, *A History of Modern Tibet.*
13. Chinese Ministry of Information, *China Handbook, 1937–1945* (New York: The MacMillan Company, 1947), 3.
14. "Russian methods in Mongolia compared with British methods in Tibet," March 3, 1945, FO 371/46121.
15. Sir H. Seymour to Foreign Office, July 25, 1942, and R. Peel to O. K. Caroe, August 26, 1942, L/P&S/12/4205, Oriental and India Office Collections (OIOC), the British Library.
16. Memos from Ministry of Foreign Affairs to Mongolian and Tibetan Affairs Commission, August 13, 1942, and September 1944, Quanzong Hao (general record number) 141: 2623 and 141: 3220.
17. Hsiao-ting Lin, *Tibet and Nationalist China's Frontier: Intrigues and Ethnopolitics, 1911–1949* (Vancouver: British Columbia University Press, 2006), and Gray Tuttle, *Tibetan Buddhists in the Making of Modern China* (New York: Columbia University Press, 2005) are two insightful studies of the Nationalist effort to maintain political and nonpolitical relations with Tibet.
18. Peter S. H. Tang, *Russian and Soviet Policy in Manchuria and Outer Mongolia, 1911–1931* (Duke University Press, 1959), 271–398.
19. Military Council, "Procedures for Treating Outer Mongolians [*waimengren*] Who Entered the Chinese Territory," July 11, 1940, QH 141: 1202; Alashan Banner to the Mongolian and Tibetan Affairs Commission, April 21, 1942, QH 141: 1783.
20. *Zhonghua Minguo Zhongyao Shiliao Chubian, Dui Ri Kangzhan Shiqi: Disanbian, Zhanshi Waijiao* (Priliminary compilation of important historical records of the Republic of China, the period of the War of Resistance against Japan: volume 3, wartime diplomacy) (Taipei: Kuomintang Dangshi Weiyuanhui, 1981), 1: 165–167, 2: 458–459.
21. Memo, "Restoration of Our Country's Territorial Integrity," June 7, 1943, box 3, Victor Hoo papers, reflects the thinking of the KMT Ministry of Foreign Affairs about the difference between Tibet and Outer Mongolia during World War II. The document proposed a few steps for reining Tibet in, but it pointed out frankly that Outer Mongolia had already become an independent state and its recovery by China would not be easy and would have to be preceded with de-Sovietization of the land.
22. Xiaoyuan Liu, *A Partnership for Disorder: China, the United States, and Their Policies for the Postwar Disposition of the Japanese Empire, 1941–1945* (Cambridge University Press, 1996), 258–286.
23. The Archives of Inner Mongolian Autonomous Region, *Nei Monggu Zizhi Yundong Lianhehui: Dang'an Shiliao Xuanbian* (Selected archival materials on the League of Inner Mongolia Autonomous Movement) (Beijing: Dang'an Chubanshe, 1989).
24. *Neimenggu Zizhi Yundong Lianhehui*, 3–5.
25. These events caused different speculations in U.S. State Department and British Foreign Office. According to a British source, L/P&S/12/2376, OIOC, in one of the conversations between the two agencies, the British participants were taken aback by the fact that

Stanley Hornback, the State Department's leading China hand, had nothing to offer on the Xinjiang situation. John W. Garver, *Chinese–Soviet Relations, 1937–1945: The Diplomacy of Chinese Nationalism* (Oxford University Press, 1988), 164–174 discusses these events in Xinjiang.

26. For different views, see Linda Benson, *The Ili Rebellion: The Moslem Challenge to Chinese Authority in Xinjiang, 1944–1949* (M.E. Sharpe, Inc., 1990); Andrew D. Forbes, *Warlords and Muslims in Chinese Central Asia: A Political History of Republican Sinking, 1911–1949* (Cambridge University Press, 1986); David D. Wang, *Under the Soviet Shadow: The Yining Incident: Ethnic Conflict and International Rivalry in Xinjiang, 1944–1949* (Hong Kong: Chinese University Press, 1999); and James A. Millward, *Eurasian Crossroad: A History of Xinjiang* (New York: Columbia University, 2007).
27. By far the most informative publication is Compilation Committee on the History of the Three-District Revolution of Xinjiang, *Xinjiang Sanqu Geming Dashiji* (Chronicle of events of the three-district revolution of Xinjiang) (Urumqi: Xinjiang Renmin Chubanshe, 1994).
28. *Xinjiang Sanqu Geming Dashiji*, 12, 44, 78, 171, 247, 304.
29. *Sanqu Geming Dashiji*, 12–13, 31, 46, 57, 78, 93, 102–103, 126, 149, 171, 247, 253, 309.
30. *Sanqu Geming Dashiji*, 312–313.
31. Benson, *The Ili Rebellion*, 32; Compilation Committee on the History of the Three-District Revolution of Xinjiang, *Xinjiang Sanqu Geming Lingdaoren Xiang Zhonggong Zhongyang de Paogao ji Wenxuan* (Reports to the Central Committee of the Chinese Communist Party and other writings by leaders of the three-district revolution of Xinjiang) (Urumqi: Xinjiang Renmin Chubanshe, 1995).
32. *Xinjiang Sanqu Geming Dashiji*, 206–208, 302, 305–306.
33. Benson, *The Ili Rebellion*, does not address this question directly. The omission is a major defect of the otherwise informative study. But, indirectly, Benson makes a connection between the ETR's dissolution with the accidental death of its most important leaders in August 1949 (p. 176). Forbs' *Warlords and Muslim in Chinese Central Asia*, 221, speculates that ETR leaders' expressed allegiance to the PRC might be a political ploy to open the door for future negotiations under Moscow's support. The official line of interpretation in China treats the ETR movement as part of the Chinese revolution and accordingly its incorporation into the PRC in 1949 came naturally.
34. There are some interesting facts relevant to these questions. Before leaving for Beijing, Ahmet Jan Asimi cautioned the CCP that the nationalist and Islamic tendencies in Xinjiang politics had to be coped with patience, making effort at the same time to constrain these tendencies within the ETR. Initially, the CCP invited ETR leaders to come to Beijing as representatives of entire Xinjiang. This was before the KMT authorities in Xinjiang rallied to the CCP. After Xinjiang was "liberated" peacefully, however, former KMT officials in the new Xinjiang government occupied more prominent positions than ETR leaders. On at least two occasions CCP and Soviet leaders discussed the Xinjiang issue. In the early months of 1949, Mao Zedong talked with Anastas Mikoyan in Xibaipo, Hebei, and then in July and August Liu Shaoqi meet with Stalin in Moscow. In these conversations Soviet leaders suggested that the CCP speed up its advance toward Xinjiang and also offered advice about how to deal with national minorities.
35. Moscow's assistance to the CCP's military advance into Xinjiang was significant, which among other things, included two divisions of air units with more than seventy airplanes transporting CCP troops in November 1949. See Chen Haihan, *Zai Peng Zong Zhihui*

Xia (Under commander-general Peng [Dehuai]) (Beijing: Jiefangjun Chubanshe, 1984), 249, 257.

36. Weekly letter from the Indian Mission, Lhasa, March 21, 1948, FO 371/70042.
37. "Questions and Answers about the Conditions of Tibet," 1941, QH 141: 3636, the Second Historical Archives of China, Nanjing; Wu Zhongxin to Chiang Kai-shek, December 26, 1943 and enclosure, "Propaganda Outline for Tibet," QH 141: 2374; "Plan for Tibet during the Period of Rebellion Suppression," November 19, 1949, QH 141: 3702; "Ten Programs for Liberating Slaves in Tibet and Xikang," August 13, 1939, QH 141: 3136.
38. *Xinjiang Sanqu Geming Dashiji*, 237. Records of the Office of Chinese Affairs, 1945–1950: Top Secret Subject Files, 1945–1950, box 17, contains information about the State Department's handling of the Mackiernan case after the vice-consul was killed. Osman's anti-CCP military activities continued to March 1951, when he was captured in Gansu province. Thomas Laird, *Into Tibet: The CIA's First Atomic Spy and His Secret Expedition to Lhasa* (New York: Grove Press, 2002), is a detailed account of the Mackiernan affair.
39. U.S. consulate was first opened in Tihwa in April 1943. From August 1944, American land-lease materials for China began to pass through Xinjiang. But this can hardly be viewed as an expansion of U.S. influence because the transportation from India to Lanzhou was a Chinese operation. During the final stage of the Chinese Civil War, a "Chennault plan" for American support of a northwestern resistance against the CCP was circulated in the State Department but it was not considered seriously.
40. The difficulty for the U.S. government to switch sides in China's ethnic politics can be seen in the Tibetan case. In late 1950, when the Tibetan issue was brought up in the United Nations, the KMT delegation's reaction was that the issue should be included in its own protest against the Soviet Union's aggression in China but should not be considered separately. At the time, George Kennan's prescription for U.S. policy toward the prospect of CCP control of Tibet was that "our only concern need be to make sure that no one thinks our prestige is engaged in it." Top secret memo, "Estimate: possible further danger points in light of Korean situation," June 30, 1950, George F. Kennan papers, box 24.
41. "Russian–American Relations," a lecture at University of Virginia, February 20, 1947, George F. Kennan Papers, box 16. At the time Kennan was three months from becoming the first director of the State Department's Policy Planning Staff. For American effort to split the CCP and Moscow, see David Allan Mayers, *Cracking the Monolith: U.S. Policy against the Sino-Soviet Alliance, 1949–1955* (Louisiana State University Press, 1986).
42. James E. Sheridan, *China in Disintegration: The Republican Era in Chinese History, 1912–1949* (New York, 1975).

PART II

Chinese Nationalist Experiences

CHAPTER THREE

Resume China's Korean Connection

As our understanding of the republic period of modern Chinese history deepens and broadens, it becomes increasingly difficult to uphold a conventional view that the period was an insignificant "interregnum" between the enduring Qing Dynasty and the rising People's Republic of China.[1] In the trajectory of modern transformation of Chinese territoriality, the Republic of China continued those threads that had started in the last few decades of the Qing, and, when the right historical moment appeared, took decisive steps to finalize China's geo-body as we know today. The right historical moment was China's eight-year war with Japan, which, albeit its horrendous toll to China, turned China's international environment around and reopened territorial issues in several directions for settlement to China's advantage. In a balance sheet on the war's territorial consequences to China, the most obvious items may include Taiwan and Manchuria that were regained from Japan and Outer Mongolia that was lost to the Soviet sphere. There were also some obscured items that continued to beg answers after the end of World War II: Would China want to reassert influence in its former "tributary dependencies" like Korea, Vietnam, and the Liuchius (Ryukyu)? Could China keep its sovereign claims over the Inner Asian frontiers such as Tibet, Xinjiang, and even Inner Mongolia after Outer Mongolia gained decisive independence? This and the next two chapters consider some of the items in the obscured category. The Chinese Nationalist Government's efforts regarding these territories during and after World War II, though failing to achieve intended goals, were historical specimens typically illustrating the nationalist thread of thinking and policies on these matters. Call it traditional Chinese mentality about centrality, or geopolitical concern about security, or internationalist projection of Chinese responsibility, the Chinese Nationalists and the Chinese Communists had much to share despite the commonly accepted periodization of twentieth-century Chinese history with the year of 1949. We turn first to Korea, a model tributary dependency of the Chinese Empire for centuries before its colonization by Japan at the turn of the twentieth century, and a country that entangled China and the United States in World War II and after.

Illusive Greatness

Leaders in Chongqing welcomed the beginning of the American–Japanese war in the Pacific at the end of 1941. China had been fighting the Japanese military alone for years. In the long run, the Western Allies' participation in the Asian war was seen in Chongqing as an assurance of China's final victory over Japan. Even better, by fighting as an ally of the United States and Great Britain, the Chinese government could at last hope to be treated as an equal by the Western powers, a status that had been denied to China during the past century.[2]

As such an equal, the Chinese government was faced with some long-term policy issues. The most important was how to define China's new role and position in the world in general and in Asia in particular. Chongqing's definition was ambivalent. Chinese leaders were certainly pleased by the wartime American policy of treating China as a great power, but more often than not they felt that by acting as a spokesman on behalf of Asian nationalism the Chinese government could serve itself better. Chongqing tried to play such a role soon after Pearl Harbor. On January 7, 1942 Chiang Kai-shek sent a telegram to Roosevelt, urging the president to impress upon the British and the Dutch governments the need for acting in accordance with the spirit of the Atlantic Charter in their own colonial affairs. Liberalization of these governments' colonial policies, the Chinese leader reasoned, would help enlist the Asian people to the Allied war effort.[3] In the summer of 1942, the Chinese government began to contemplate guiding principles for restructuring the international relations in the Asian-Pacific region after the war. In a document entitled "The Pacific Charter," Chongqing sought to supplement the Atlantic Charter in three aspects: complete defeat of Japan, positive national self-government, and racial equality.[4] These ideas would eventually be carried by the Chinese delegation to a summit meeting with the Western Allies in Cairo in 1943.

The Western Allies were suspicious about Chongqing's anticolonial rhetoric. In a report to Washington dated June 17, 1942, American ambassador Clarence Gauss commented that Chinese leaders' statements on postwar freedom to Asian dependent areas reflected "[a] Chinese tendency to consider [that] China should be the leader of Asiatic peoples." About a month later, Lauchlin Currie, Roosevelt's personal envoy to Chongqing, conveyed a similar concern to Chiang. He told Chiang that some people in the United States were reluctant to support President Roosevelt's policy of aid to China due to their wariness of a militarist and antiwhite China. It would therefore be advisable, in Currie's opinion, for the Chinese government to improve China's internal democracy and especially avoid using anti-foreign expressions and phrases like "China as the leader of Asia" in its public statements. Chiang took the advice and afterwards cautioned Chinese officials against stating that China was the leader of Asia.[5]

At the time, Chiang was pragmatic about China's international prospects. In December 1942, when talking to Wellington Koo, then Chinese ambassador to London, Chiang professed: "China herself had no intention to dictate or dominate in Asia. Her policy of favoring the liberation of weak and small peoples was a fundamental one, but there was no intention on her part to take any active steps to realize it, [though] these countries would themselves look to China as a natural leader and her civilization as a great heritage for Asia." On a different occasion, Chiang commented to the effect that no one would accept China's leadership if China lacked sufficient strength and, for the present, although morally and spiritually deserving the status as a great power, China was actually ill-qualified in terms of material strength and progress.[6]

These are rare exposés of Chiang's thought. His discourse on China's natural superiority among Asian countries indicated that in heart Chiang was very much a traditionalist. He could not think of China's proper position in Asia without mentally traveling back to the old glorious days of the Confucian Chinese Empire. But Chiang was also a realist who would not even dream that "right" alone could overcome "might." Then how could a weak country like China hope to recover its presumed proper position in Asia? Should this goal be postponed until China obtained the necessary material strength? Chiang saw another alternative—support from friendly Western powers, especially the United States. Diplomacy therefore became the most important instrument for China to improve its international image and enhance its international status. Chiang imparted this idea emphatically to Chinese diplomats, whom he called China's "spiritual soldiers."[7] Chiang was also quite honest with Ambassador Koo when he admitted that the Chinese government had no intention of taking any active steps to free colonial Asia. The anti-imperialist oratory of Chongqing, therefore, was neither sustained by a strong foreign policy nor derived from a blind anti-Western antagonism. Instead, it was a calculated tactic originating from a weak position. Chongqing's moderate anticolonialism was designed not to alienate the Western powers but to strengthen its own bargaining position with them; not to cost any serious effort of China's to improve Asian colonial peoples' conditions but to reestablish its spiritual appeal among them.

The question of Korea was a vehicle for Chongqing to achieve these goals. China's traditional relationship with Korea before the Sino-Japanese War of 1894–1895 and Japan's colonization of Korea are familiar stories. What is important is how the KMT leadership in the war years interpreted this history and connected the interpretation to China's postwar position in Korea. In the spring of 1938, having lost the battle of Shanghai and also been forced out of Nanjing by Japanese troops, Chiang Kai-shek realized that a turning point in the history of Sino-Japanese relations had been reached. The dilapidated China could no longer coexist with the expanding Japan. The current struggle would decide whether China would be completely subjugated by Japan or Japan would be defeated and deprived of its empire. Chiang refused to accept China's subjugation. On April 1, a moment of military frustration, he talked to KMT party functionaries about recovering from Japan Taiwan, the Liuchiu (Ryukyu) Islands, and Korea. He told his audience that Dr. Sun Yat-sen, the founder of the KMT, bequeathed to the party a revolutionary strategy called "recover [*huifu*] Korea and Taiwan to strengthen China." This was designed as a countermeasure against Japan's continental expansion. Chiang said:

> Korea used to be a vassal state of China and Taiwan a Chinese territory. Geographically speaking, both are lifelines on which China's very existence and safety hinge. If China seeks to establish a substantial national defense and secure a lasting peace in East Asia, it must not allow the imperialist Japan to control Korea and Taiwan. The meaning of the Premier's [Sun's] policy is that only by helping our compatriots [*tongpao*] in Korea and Taiwan to regain their independence [d*uli*] and freedom, can the Republic of China strengthen its own defense and lay the foundation of peace in East Asia.[8]

Chiang's use of terms like *tongpao* and d*uli* for both Taiwan and Korea may sound confusing to an audience today, and he would indeed differentiate the two territories later. What was unmistakable at the time was his intense concern about China's postwar security.

On the eve of the Pacific war, Chiang called Roosevelt's attention to the Chinese government's stand on national defense. In a message to the president, Chiang stated that China would never give up Manchuria because its loss to China would be followed by Xinjiang and Tibet, and would also create a great difficulty for China to recover Outer Mongolia. Chiang's nightmare was a scramble for China proper by Britain, Japan, and Russia after they nipped away all China's peripheral areas.[9] At the moment, Chiang was too prudent to reveal to the president his intentions toward Korea and Taiwan, though in his mind these places were also among those peripheral areas vital to China's security. After the Pacific war began, the Chinese government no longer felt hindered in clarifying its new policy toward those territories and interests lost to Japan before the Mukden incident of 1931. On December 9, 1941, the Chinese declared war on Japan and at the same time invalidated all the existing treaties and agreements between China and Japan.[10]

Beginning in 1942, Chinese officials openly talked about restoring independence to Korea. Then, in November, T. V. Soong, Chinese foreign minister, made by far the most authoritative statement on the issue.[11] Although publicly encouraging Korea to separate itself from the Japanese empire, Chongqing was careful that this should become a common policy of the Allied powers. In the war years, Chongqing's Korea policy became a double-barreled undertaking. On the one hand, Chongqing cultivated a close relationship with Korean expatriates in China, mainly the groups working under the leadership of a "Korean Provisional Government" (KPG). On the other hand, it consulted with the Allies, principally the United States, for the sake of achieving their consent to Korean independence and agreement to accept the KPG as the legitimate leadership in postwar Korea.

The wartime relationship between the Chinese Nationalists and these Korean partisans had its roots in an earlier period. After the "March First Movement" of 1919 was suppressed by the Japanese in Korea, Korean revolutionaries in exile came to China and made contact with Sun Yat-sen. But, at that time, Sun was dismayed by his inability to provide the Koreans with the assistance they sought. In the 1920s, some Korean youths enrolled in the Whampoa Military Academy, of which Chiang Kai-shek was the president. Otherwise, the Korean revolutionaries received little help.

After Japan occupied Manchuria, the Chinese Nationalist Government began to pay close attention to Korean partisan activities in China because of some sensational assassinations by Korean patriots of Japanese high officials. In early 1933, Chiang Kai-shek received Kim Ku, a prominent figure of the KPG and organizer of those assassinations. At the meeting, Chiang suggested that Sun Yat-sen's "Three People's Principles" would be a good program for all Asian peoples. Kim agreed and offered that if the Chinese government could give the KPG substantial financial aid, it would be able to start uprisings in Japan, Korea, and Manchuria within two years. The next day, the Chinese side informed Kim that Chiang hoped the Koreans change their tactics from terrorist activities to long-term preparations for war of liberation. For this purpose, Chiang was willing to help the KPG train military cadets. The resultant training program, however, did not last due to Japan's protest.[12] About the same time, a left-wing Korean group under the leadership of Kim Won-bong, a graduate of the Whampoa Academy, also began to receive assistance from the Chinese government. The cooperation between the Chinese and the Koreans grew as Chinese–Japan relations deteriorated. Before Pearl Harbor, the Chinese authorities managed to bring the two Korean groups under Kim Ku and Kim Won-bong into a nominal unity and helped them organize a "Korean Restoration Army" (KRA).[13]

Inevitably, the Chongqing–KPG relationship was troubled with its innate inequality between the two sides and the continued infighting among Korean factions. The changed situation in the Pacific after Pearl Harbor nevertheless prompted the Chinese government to formalize its Korean policy. From July to December 1942, an ad hoc committee consisting of a half-dozen top Chinese officials reviewed the government's Korea policy. The working basis of the committee was a "Guiding Plan for Helping and Using the Korean Revolutionary Forces in China" drafted by the National Military Council. The document established Korea's "complete independence" as a fundamental objective of China's Korea policy, stipulated a close Chinese supervision over Koreans' military and political activities in China, and supported the KPG as the designated leadership of a unified Korean independence movement. Furthermore, the plan stated that China's policy toward Korea aimed at fostering a pro-Chinese attitude among the Korean nationalists in order to prevent them from falling under the influence of other foreign powers. The plan did not identify which foreign powers were meant. But, during their deliberation of the Korean question, Chinese officials were clearly troubled by Soviet intentions.[14]

Chiang was not satisfied with the plan. He wanted a clearly defined central authority responsible for the Korean affairs, which the plan failed to offer. Chiang also felt that the plan was too rigid in endorsing only one Korean group, the KPG. He wanted his government to have a more flexible policy that would be able to meet different contingencies and guarantee lasting Chinese influence on the Koreans. To be prepared for unpredictable developments within the Korean movement, the Chinese government must not close its door to other anti-Japanese Korean groups. At the same time, Chiang approved the notion that the KPG be the focus of China's Korea policy. It would remain the principal beneficiary of Chongqing, receiving the lion's share of the Chinese assistance and diplomatic recognition in due course.

A new guiding plan was produced accordingly. The plan proscribed China's leading role among the Allies in granting recognition to the KPG. The KMT party organization and the National Military Council would separately be responsible for financing the Koreans' political and military activities in China. In return, the Koreans were obliged to collect intelligence information for the Chinese government, to conduct psychological warfare within enemy's troops, and to enlarge their contact with and influence on Korean population both within Korea and abroad. The KPG was also required to put its military force, the KRA, under the direct control of the Chinese National Military Council.[15]

Implementation of the plan, however, failed to erase factional frictions among the Korean partisans. During the war years, the some six hundred Korean expatriates in the KMT region were divided into numerous organizations. From 1942 to 1945, the Chinese government interfered in the Korean infighting, trying to produce a monolithic Korean party absorbing all the existing Korean organizations. This was never achieved.[16] Throughout the war, Chongqing's Korea policy had only a narrow basis on the KPG, which was closely controlled by the Chinese government. Aside from putting the KPG under the KMT's ideological guidance, Chongqing set up strict regulations about the activities of the KRA. The chief of staff of the KRA was Yin Chengfu, a Chinese general appointed by Chiang. Important positions of the KRA, except commander in chief, were occupied by Chinese officers with Koreans serving as deputies. A "nine-point code" delimited the areas and set the conditions for the KRA to operate in China. Before either of the two following conditions happened, the Chinese authorities demanded, the KRA "ought only to accept orders from the supreme commander of the Chinese military forces but not from any other authorities": (1) the end of the war between China and Japan, and (2) the advance of the KPG into Korea. Noticeably, Allied diplomatic recognition of the KPG was not a contingency that would affect the attachment of the KRA to the Chinese army.[17] Under the Chinese regulations, the KRA became an auxiliary of the Chinese military, not an instrument of the Korean independence movement.

Actually, Chongqing was never enthusiastic about helping the Koreans develop an effective military force. The Chinese authorities endorsed the KRA principally as a political ploy to appease KPG leaders. Before the end of 1944, troops of the KRA had never exceeded six hundred. It began moderate expansion in 1945 when Korean soldiers serving in the Japanese Army started to desert. Chongqing considered a training program for the KRA but still did not want to use the Korean troops for combat purposes. Not until May 1945 did Chongqing agree to turn the command of the KRA over to the KPG. Deprived of actual control of the KRA and the chance for engaging the Japanese in real combat, the KPG remained a club for idle talk throughout the war. It is not surprising that in postwar years, with little exaggeration, Kim Ku would mock his own wartime sojourn in China with these words: "My life in Chongqing consisted in taking shelter [from Japanese air raids] with the members of the Provisional Government and eating and sleeping once in a while."[18]

The restrictive and occasionally mortifying sponsorship proffered by the Chinese government did lead the Koreans to consider moving the KPG from Chongqing to Washington. In late 1942 the KPG made such an overture to the American government to no avail.[19] The KPG leaders' agony was that, conscious of the limits of the Chinese patronage, they could not find any other government among the Allies willing to develop a de facto relationship with the KPG and to offer some assistance.

Chongking's restrictions on the KRA reflected the lack of intention on KMT leaders' part to use military means to achieve its goals in Korea. Instead, Chongqing based its long-term objectives in Korea completely on persuading the other Allied powers to receive the KPG as a legitimate representative of the Korean people.[20] In other words, although Korean independence constituted a fundamental goal in Chongqing's postwar programs, the KMT leadership was prepared at most to use diplomacy to maneuver the Western Allies into action. Neither the Chinese army nor the small Korean force under it would be used for the purpose of driving the Japanese out of Korea. Chiang's "spiritual soldiers," or the diplomats, had to take on the task of seducing the Allies into accepting the Chinese conceptions about Korean affairs.

The prospect of this diplomatic battle was not promising. The fact that the 1942 plan merely included a principle of China's first recognition of the KPG but not a timetable for this step reflected a dilemma that Chongqing faced. The dilemma, as viewed by a Chinese official, was that "a premature recognition [of the KPG by China] might cause displeasure on the part of Great Britain and therefore also affect America's attitude, but a delay of recognition would encourage a Soviet conspiracy regarding the Korean problem."[21] Throughout the war, the Chinese government strove in vain to find a way out of this predicament. Loathing the conservative British attitude toward Asian colonies and fearing Soviet intentions in East Asia, the KMT leadership could only see Washington as the potential cosponsor of its Korean program.

Abortive Partnership

Despite the foreseeable importance of the United States in the postwar settlement for Asia, during the first two years of the war U.S. government officials dealt with the Korean issue in a responsive manner. In April 1942, Chiang Kai-shek in Chongqing and T.V. Soong in Washington conducted a coordinate diplomatic maneuver seeking American endorsement of the KPG. President Roosevelt and the State Department demurred and also thwarted the Chinese attempt to grant recognition to the KPG with certain expedient arguments. The American position at the time was that in order to retain a freedom of action, it would be wise for Chongqing not to make a premature commitment. Chongqing should wait for progress in the Allied war effort in the Pacific and clarification of the Indian question. The Chinese heeded this advice reluctantly.[22]

But Chongqing could not set the issue aside for long. In early December of 1942, encouraged by Roosevelt's "personal diplomacy" with China earlier in the year, Chiang summoned his American adviser, Owen Lattimore, outlining for him a program for postwar territorial settlement in East Asia. Chiang was eager to transmit his program to Roosevelt as a basis for formal discussions between the two governments. Soon after his interview with Chiang, Lattimore returned to the United States and delivered Chiang's proposals to the president through Currie. The exchanges hereby initiated by Chiang were significant to

Chinese–American wartime diplomacy over both Korea and Indochina. The Indochina aspect will be discussed separately in the next chapter.

According to what was recorded by Lattimore, the Chinese leader wanted Taiwan to be returned to China "but with America having the privilege of having a naval and air base there." In Manchuria, joint Chinese–American naval and air bases should be established for the purpose of "protection against [a resurgent] Japan." Chiang was opposed to Indochina's restoration to France and proposed that China act as a "big brother" there for a time period. As for Korea, mindful of the proximity of the Soviet Union, Chiang suggested that Korea become a "semi-independent [state] under American and Chinese tutelage which, of course, means Chinese." What was important was to exclude Russian influence from that peninsula.[23]

President Roosevelt's response, also via Lattimore, was disheartening to Chiang. Although Lattimore and Currie advised the president to give Chiang some encouragement, Roosevelt was more cautious. He did not want to encourage any thought on the part of the Chinese government about an exclusive American–Chinese postwar responsibility for the western Pacific, neither was he anxious to grasp Chiang's invitation regarding American bases in Taiwan and in the Liaodong Peninsula. What the president wanted to get across to Chiang was the "four big policemen" idea. Roosevelt also promoted his favorite idea about a trusteeship system for the former colonies in southwestern Pacific that would presumably also be supported by the British. The president's disagreement with Chiang over Korea was explicit: "It would be undesirable to attempt to exclude Soviet Russia from such problems as the independence of Korea." Isolation of the Russians in the northern part of the Pacific would create, not solve, tensions.[24] Chongqing's anti-Soviet disposition was familiar to Washington, but this was the first time that the Chinese leaders learned about Washington's determination to include the Russians in postwar settlement in Northeast Asia.

The stance taken by Roosevelt was in concert with the deliberation of the Korean question within the State Department. Before the Roosevelt–Chiang communications, the State Department had an internal debate about Korea. Probes about American attitude toward Korea did not just come from Chongqing. Syngman Rhee, who supposedly represented the KPG in the United States, and some other Korean figures also frequented the State Department, and they had influential American friends.[25] In mid-February 1942, in an internal memo Assistant Secretary of State Adolph A. Berle expressed his concern about the building up of a "very considerable sentiment in the United States in respect of Korean independence." He was concerned that a continued passive attitude on the part of the government might invite public criticism. The Far Eastern Division of the State Department attributed Berle's memorandum to his ignorance and lack of sound judgment about both the nature of the Koreans' activities in America and the current policy of the State Department.[26]

According to the Far Eastern Division, due to the Japanese rule for thirty-seven years, the Korean people "have been emasculated politically" and therefore were not in a position to manage a state on their own. Consequently, after this war, "for a generation at least Korea would have to be protected, guided and aided to modern statehood by the great powers" before regaining complete independence. So far as Korean nationalists outside Korea were concerned, to qualify for American support, they first had to achieve internal unity and demonstrate their representativeness for the Korean people at home. In practice, this standard not only prevented U.S. recognition of "any shadow organization of Koreans" as a provisional government for Korea, but also opposed a de facto relationship between Washington and any Korean group during the war. As a matter of fact, the Far Eastern Division argued against Washington's public support to Korean independence, stressing the necessity of consultation among the leading Allies. China and the Soviet Union were identified as the two powers that had particular concerns about Korea, though the American military authorities must not attach too much importance to the "Korean volunteers" under the auspices of the Chinese government. In the eyes of State Department officials, "Koreans in China have been largely rascals and running dogs of the Japanese Army" and hence untrustworthy. This sweeping verdict set the State Department's evaluation of the KPG far apart from Chongqing's. As for the question about what stance the U.S. government should take on Korea's postwar status, deliberations in the State Department were inconclusive. There was however a strong opinion in the State Department that gave higher priority to postwar relationship among great powers than to Korean independence.[27]

In 1943, international supervision for Korea became official American policy after President Roosevelt committed himself to the idea. On February 22, fresh from his communications with Chiang, Roosevelt conferred with senior State Department officials and members of the department's research staff, expressing through generalities his views on postwar issues. For East Asia, the president said that Taiwan and Manchuria should be returned to China, a trusteeship should be arranged for Korea, and Indochina should not be returned to France but its disposition remained undecided. In the next month, when talking to British Foreign Secretary Anthony Eden, who was visiting in Washington, Roosevelt categorically suggested that Korea be placed under an *international* trusteeship, "with China, the United States and one or two other countries participating." Eden expressed his support.[28]

During World War II, the idea of decolonization saw its heyday in Washington. American officials considered trusteeship as a device to give former colonial powers a part in a peaceful burial of their empires, though reckoning some wartime allies', such as the British, interests, Washington would be willing to endorse trusteeships of different forms.[29] Roosevelt's suggestion about "international trusteeship" for Korea differentiated this territory from European colonies in Asia. A special arrangement for Korea was necessary because after the Japanese empire was destroyed and with the prospect of immediate Korean independence excluded, the peninsula would become a "public land," devoid of either a sovereign government or a suzerain owner and liable to international rivalry.

After the president made clear his intention, the State Department filled in the details. In May, at one of the department's planning meetings, Hugh Borton, a former Columbia professor in Japanese history, pointed out that as Korea's incompetence for self-government was generally accepted, then the problem of the disposition of Korea could be condensed by a "negative approach." If one of the victorious powers of the United Nations was to control Korea until Korea was ready for independence, the big question had to be which power would exercise such a role. Borton believed China and the Soviet Union would hate to see each other's predominant position in Korea and therefore the only feasible and safe course would be some mechanism for international control.[30]

Interestingly, State Department officials estimated Chongqing's intentions in Korea with similar terms as they defined America's postwar policy toward China. As Chongqing continued to perform poorly in the war, American officials' opinions were changing with regard to whether or not China in postwar Asia would be able to function as a principal stabilizing power. Nevertheless, a constant theme in the State Department's wartime papers on China was that America's interests in Asia would require the emergence of a unified, friendly, prosperous, strong, and progressively democratic China. Among these adjectives, only "democratic" was not used by American planners when they described Chongqing's objectives in Korea. The Chinese aspirations in the Korean Peninsula were viewed as non-expansionist and basically defensive. It was suggested that for historical, ideological, and security reasons, China would want Korea to be detached from the Japanese empire and to become an independent and friendly neighbor. China wanted Korea to be strong so that in the future it would not again serve as a stepping-stone for foreign invasions of China.[31] A "specialist" view in the State Department held that traditionally, China's foreign policy had been motivated by "a question of closeness and interest," but not "geographic proximity." In the postwar years, the current Chinese government would follow this tradition and seek opportunity for development in its own peripheral regions such as Xinjiang, Mongolia, and Manchuria, but not expansion into Korea. In addition, there was also the question of China's capability. It was pointed out that the Chinese were realistic, and they could see what a difficult situation would emerge for China if it attempted to assume unilateral control of Korea. The Chinese government was not capable of such a control, and Chinese officials would not insist upon it.[32]

The opinion above was an interesting, yet misjudged, case of anticipating China's international behavior through understanding China's historical traditions. The time was long past when China was the predominant power in East Asia and could determine its own way to handle external affairs. In seeing Chongqing's intentions in Korea in a mirror image of America's own, American officials overlooked a possibility that China's weakness and lack of security might be the very reasons for Chongqing to seek control over those geographically proximate territories such as Korea.[33] Surprisingly, the wartime relationship between the KMT and the KPG was not subject to a careful analysis in the State Department. Even if State Department officials might not immediately be privy to the content of the Chiang–Roosevelt communications on Korea, the U.S. embassy in Chongqing was effective enough to let the State Department know about the Chinese control of the KRA. The State Department was also conversant with Chongqng's jealousy against foreign powers' interference with Korean independence. Actually, Ambassador Gauss had warned in late 1942 that the wartime KMT–KRA relationship would have long-term effects in postwar Chinese–Korean relations. The misinterpretation of Chongqing's intentions in Korea led the State Department not to expect any difficulty from the Chinese side with regard to the trusteeship formula. On the eve of the Cairo Conference, the planning staff of the State Department was confident that international trusteeship over Korea "would be in harmony with the statement of the Chinese Government that 'Korea much be free and independent'."[34]

In the meantime, the State Department was worried about Soviet intentions in Korea. In 1943, a memorandum of the Far East Division maintained that no matter whether or not Russia would eventually enter the Pacific war, it would certainly want to move into the "political vacuum" in North China and Korea after the defeat of Japan. According to State Department planners, the attributes of Moscow's Korea policy would include, "to apply the Soviet conception of proper treatment of colonial peoples, to strengthen enormously the economic resources of the Soviet Far East, to acquire ice-free ports, and to occupy a dominating strategic position in relation both to China and to Japan." They predicted: "A Soviet occupation of Korea would create an entirely new strategic situation in the Far East, and its repercussions with China and Japan might be far-reaching." Exclusive Soviet influence in Korea would sever China's connection with the outside world in northeastern Asian and thus would not only "seriously undermine Chinese confidence in the postwar settlement, but would provoke China to undertake similarly unilateral action there and elsewhere."[35] Thus, as

President Roosevelt endeavored to quell Chiang Kai-shek's anti-Soviet zeal in Korean affairs, the State Department had its own fear of the unknown Soviet factor.

Moscow's intention was not the only problem. The British disposition was also worrisome. Korea per se was not a place that the British cared much about. About Korea, wartime British Prime Minister Winston Churchill once said: "I'd never heard of the bloody place till I was seventy-four." To the British what was important was the meaning of a Korean settlement to the general issue of colonialism. In October 1943, an informal exploration with the British Foreign Office and Colonial Office by American officials found out that the British did not want to make decisions on Korea for the present "as the situation at a later date might have radically changed." Neither did the British want to burden themselves with postwar responsibility in Korea.[36] At the time, the State Department's planning for Korea already began to consider a more active role for the United States. Such findings from London were therefore disappointing to Washington.

In light of American officials' suspicions about the Russians and wariness about the British, their trust of the Chinese in the matter of trusteeship for Korea was amazing. The reserved style of Chongqing's wartime diplomacy may have contributed to this. From March to September, T. V. Soong was in Washington and conversed with President Roosevelt and his principal aides on issues in postwar East Asia. A leading theme in these conversations that the Americans tried to impart to the Chinese was Washington's support of China as a great power in postwar Asia. Roosevelt was emphatic on this point, telling Soong that he wanted to "put China in the sun even before she has the economic power." Hopkins also predicted that although "the United States will be tremendously powerful after the war, particularly in the Pacific where it will play a big role, . . . China alone will count in the Pacific." Such flattering promise of support was conditional, though. Among other things, American leaders tried to persuade the Chinese to recognize the necessity for accommodating Soviet interests in Northeast Asia. American officials suggested to Soong that the Chinese government recognize Soviet Russia's "legitimate commercial interest" in Manchuria. President Roosevelt was specific in suggesting that the Chinese approach the Russians directly to settle "the questions of railways and other pending questions in Manchuria." The issue of Outer Mongolia was also mentioned in such a context.[37]

When Korea was discussed, Soong was unresponsive to his hosts' repeated references to international trusteeship. In view of Chiang Kai-shek's objection to including the Russians in Korean affairs and his private criticism of Washington's hesitation in making a commitment to Korean independence, Soong was too clever to express his view on this sensitive subject.[38] He felt obliged to make a statement on Korea only when being provoked by a question about Chinese "popular concept, from point of view geographically, historically and politically, regarding Korea." Apparently sensing a suspicion of China's territorial ambitions behind this line of inquiry, Soong rushed to assert:

> [The] Chinese in no sense think of Korea as a part, or a lost part, of an existing or a once having existed Chinese empire. Nor . . . do they so think of Indo-China . . . [The] prevalent Chinese opinion runs . . . to the idea that Korea should be put under an international trusteeship. Indo-China also, . . . the disposal of which would best be made in terms of a trusteeship.

This improvised response was the first and also the only support to the trusteeship solution in Korea expressed by a high-ranking Chinese official. It may have helped strengthen the American belief that the Chinese would not oppose the trusteeship formula. Yet the significance of Soong's statement was not more than a reluctant echo to his American hosts' chorus.[39]

On the eve of the Cairo Conference, a consensus in the U.S. government was that international trusteeship was the "preferred solution" of the Korean problem, and that the Chinese could be easily brought on board. From the American point of view, in postwar Korea, Chinese domination would be improbable, Soviet control undesirable, and Chinese–Soviet rivalry unacceptable. Although the feasibility of the international trusteeship formula remained questionable, it seemed the only way to preempt troubles in postwar Korea and thereby to keep intact the postwar cooperation among the "Big Four" in Asian as well as global affairs. After Cairo, although officials in the State Department complained about President Roosevelt's sidestepping the department during the conference, they were basically satisfied with the decisions reached at Cairo.[40]

The Chinese went to their first and only summit with the Western Allies with very different ideas about Korea. When making preparations for the Cairo Conference, the Chinese government set a goal that the Big Four should "at once recognize Korean independence by joint or parallel actions, or issue a declaration guaranteeing Korean independence after the war." To Chinese leaders, Korean independence and legitimacy of the KPG were identical. Their principal concern was still to establish Chongqing's predominant influence in Korean affairs and forestall any Soviet scheme regarding Korea. So far as trusteeship was concerned, the official Chinese programs did not even mention the term.[41]

The Cairo Conference of November 1943 was a turning point in China's century-long struggle to reestablish its international status since the Opium War. Chiang's sitting together with Roosevelt and Churchill symbolized China's great-power status, and the conferees' decisions on abolishing the Japanese Empire and returning Taiwan and Manchuria to China promised rearrangements of East Asian international relations in favor of China. Yet, as the historian Herbert Feis pointed out, in 1943, "a vision of the future was being used to redress the weakness of the present."[42] In other words, the Western leaders made these promises to boost the morale of the lethargic Chinese government and to keep it in the war. Since Feis wrote these lines, there have been scholarly efforts to balance the president's wartime concerns with his long-term objectives in East Asia. Feis' view on the American-Chinese agreement over postwar issues has nevertheless remained valid.[43]

As a matter of fact, the two governments' agreement on the eventual recovery by China of Manchuria, Taiwan, and the Pescadores only took the easiest step. Much more difficult issues would be when and under what conditions these territories should be restored to China. By the same token, the American–Chinese agreement at Cairo on Korea's independence actually concealed the two governments' serious disagreement about how the objective should be achieved. An even deeper divergence existed in Washington's and Chongqing's views about what new power relationship ought to be forged in postwar Northeast Asia.

The territorial decisions of Cairo were mainly results of a discussion between Roosevelt and Chiang on November 23, and the displeased British were notified only afterwards.[44] The American side did not keep records of the meeting. Until recently, historians could only base their studies on a "summary record" provided by the Kuomintang (KMT) government in Taiwan in 1957. Item (7) of the record, "On Korea, Indo-China and Thailand," reads:

> President Roosevelt advanced the opinion that China and the United States should reach a mutual understanding of the future status of Korea, Indo-China and other colonial areas as well as Thailand. Concurring, Generalissimo Chiang stressed on the necessity

> of granting independence to Korea. It was also his view that China and the United States should endeavor together and help Indo-China achieve independence after the war and that independent status should be restored to Thailand. The President expressed his agreement.[45]

The diplomatic volume of the *Zhonghua Minkuo Zhongyao Shiliao Chubian: Dui Ri Kangzhan Shihqi* (Important historical documents of the Republic of China, preliminary compilation: The period of the war resistance against Japan), published in Taipei in 1981, includes a "Daily Record of the Cairo Conference." This document was submitted to Chiang Kai-shek after the conference by Dr. Wang Ch'ung-hui, who accompanied Chiang to Cairo as secretary-general of the Supreme National Defense Council and director of Chongqing's postwar foreign policy planning agency. With regard to the November 23 meeting, the "record" indicates that Chiang's highest priority was to achieve "definite understanding" with the Allies on all the issues pertinent to "liquidation of Japan's aggressions." The results of the consultation are summarized as the following:

> The consultation achieved consummate agreement. The two sides agreed on these points: (1) all the Chinese territories seized by Japan should be returned to China; (2) all the Pacific islands under Japan's occupation should be taken away permanently; (3) Korea should be granted its independence after Japan's defeat. President Roosevelt also agreed that Japanese properties in China, public or private, should be confiscated by the Chinese government at the end of the war. *As for the method of helping Korea achieve freedom and independence, the two sides had an understanding that China and the United States should cooperate in assisting the Koreans* [italics added].[46]

Both "records" show the complete meeting of minds between Roosevelt and Chiang over Korea, but the second is more specific on two important points. One is the timing for Korea to regain independence—"after Japan's defeat," neither earlier nor later. The other is a bilateral American–Chinese partnership in assisting the Koreans. These two points accurately represented the Chinese government's policy toward Korea to the point of the conference, but the records certainly misinterpreted the American view and therefore the character of the November 23 meeting.

President Roosevelt went to Cairo without any expectation that he and Chiang would have difficulties over Korea. Among other things, he was preoccupied with the issue how to dispose the Japanese-mandated islands in the Central Pacific. Heading toward Cairo on board the U.S.S *Iowa*, Roosevelt told his aides that "trusteeship" would be "a very satisfactory solution of the government of ex-enemy territory" in the Pacific. For a period of time he had also held the view that trusteeship should be applied to Korea. Now, expecting the issue to be discussed with the Chinese, he was confident that "the Generalissimo [Chiang Kai-shek] desires a trusteeship over Korea, *administered by Russia, China, and the United States as trustees* [italics added]." After meeting with Chiang on November 23, Roosevelt realized that he had misread Chongqing's intentions massively. The next day, at a meeting of the Combined Chiefs of Staff, he told the participants: "There was no doubt that China had wide aspirations which included the re-occupation of Manchuria and Korea." According to hearsay that circulated within the State Department after Cairo, the president rebutted Chiang's whatever intentions toward Korea: "You may have Manchuria. You may have the Pescadores and you may have Formosa, but you may not have Korea, which is to be detached from Japan and is to be given its independence after a period of international supervision." It cannot be verified whether or not the president really said these words to Chiang, but they are consistent with what he had said to his aides aboard *Iowa*. Chiang Kai-shek's diary entry on the November 23 meeting also indicates the dissonant character of the discussion: "I cautioned him [Roosevelt] that judgment about Russia must be based on facts and its action in the future, and I also explicitly told him that I really dare not trust the Russians."[47]

Later, the Cairo decision on Korea was generally regarded as the basis of the Allied policy toward Korea. But, at best, that decision was ambiguous. Roosevelt and Chiang obviously disagreed on the timing and procedure for Korea to regain its independence. But the crux of their disagreement was about what power or powers should participate in the postwar politics of Northeast Asia. Although both leaders agreed on Korean independence, they hardly meant the same thing. Indeed, "the Cairo Declaration did not end the territorial questions; it intensified them."[48]

Elusive Contingencies

After Cairo, Chinese leaders realized that, given the American attitude toward the Korean issue, their formula for a Sino–American condominium over Korea was unrealistic. Some readjustments had to be made. At first, the long-standing policy calling for Chongqing's initiative in granting recognition to the KPG was abandoned. During American Vice President Henry A. Wallace's visit to China in the summer of 1944, the KPG intensified its diplomatic effort for gaining international recognition. Chiang Kai-shek became concerned and, on July 10, he ordered the Secretariat of the KMT Central Committee and the Waijiaobu (Ministry of Foreign Affairs) to study immediately the possibility of granting either formal or actual recognition to the KPG. The Waijiaobu concluded that, after the Cairo Conference, China could no longer act unilaterally on the Korea question. At Cairo, the two Western powers had expressed clearly their reluctance to rush into a premature commitment to Korea, as indicated in the "in due course" clause about Korea independence in the Cairo Declaration. It would be unwise for China to take any further action alone lest the Western Allies be caused to reconsider their promise at Cairo to support China's other postwar aspirations. This view also got support from the three-member guiding group on Korea, consisting of Zhu Jiahua, Wu Tiecheng, and Ho Yingqin. Consequently, in mid-September, Chiang made a decision against formal recognition of the KPG. To appease the disheartened Koreans, Chiang instructed the Waijiaobu that the Korean Restoration Army would be turned over to the KPG, and the KPG would in the future receive "favorite treatment" as a de facto government. The limit of Chongqing's wartime sponsorship of the KPG was thus reached.[49]

Chiang's decision was also affected by the Waijiaobu's observation that, without Soviet participation, a Chinese or even an American-British-Chinese recognition of the KPG might lead to misunderstanding and suspicions in Moscow. Such a consequence would be detrimental to the already fragile Chinese–Soviet relationship. During 1944 and 1945 Chongqing became increasingly fearful that Moscow might at first organize the Korean expatriates in Russian Siberia into a "Korean Lublin Government" and then extend its influence into the Korean Peninsula. The anxiety was intensified after the Yalta formula on the Polish question became known to Chongqing, which seemed to establish an ominous precedent to the Korean question. Occasionally, there were suggestions within the Chinese government favoring a direct discussion of Korea with Moscow, but this line of thinking did not prevail. The KMT leadership still preferred a common front with the Western Allies for curbing the Russians. Nevertheless, due to Washington's attitude, the Chinese government believed that its original plan had to be modified. The Soviets could be allowed an insignificant role in Korea provided that there would be an entente over Korea among China, the United States, and Britain.[50]

An opportunity for forging such a tripartite coalition regarding Korea seemed to come in September 1944, when the American and the British governments sent separate but identical "draft questionnaires on Korea" to the Chinese government, suggesting "studies of a factual nature be prepared and exchanged" between the Chinese and themselves. This invitation resulted in collaboration among staffs of the Supreme National Defense Council, the National Military Council, and the Waijiaobu for working out a response. Then, early in 1945, Yang Yunzhu, director of the Department of East Asian Affairs of the Waijiaobu, traveled to Washington to consult with State Department officials. From January 24 to February 14, the two sides held eleven meetings. Although the Americans and the Chinese could find agreement on a number of general principles, these discussions failed to clarify the key issue regarding the form and nature of an interim administration for Korea prior to its complete independence. The "in due course" clause of the Cairo Declaration remained a mysterious factor in the American–Chinese consultation. During the discussions the Americans only briefly outlined their trusteeship idea but were reluctant or unable to offer any detail. Still, Yang could sense the differences between the American formula and the Chinese plan in his pocket for an interim government in Korea. Yet, because Chiang Kai-shek permitted Yang to use the Chinese plan only as a counterproposal, Yang did not even show the plan to his American counterparts.[51]

The Chinese plan pocketed by Yang was revealing about the Chinese intentions after the Cairo Conference. Ever since the Cairo Conference, the Chinese government had tried to translate the "in due course" clause into tangible terms that could serve its interests. Militarily, this clause could mean a period of military occupation by Allied forces, which, in the opinion of the Waijiaobu, might last about five years. While Chinese ground forces would assume the responsibility for maintaining domestic order in Korea, the other Allies' air and naval forces would be deployed to defend Korea from external attack. By the time of Yang's mission to Washington, a political program had also been worked out as an alternative to Washington's trusteeship formula. This program, entitled "Plan for Assisting the Independence of Korea," contained an "ideal solution" of the Korean problem and a secondary choice. The most important components of the preferred solution were three: (1) Allied responsibility for maintaining Korea's domestic order and national defense during the initial military occupation period, (2) establishment of a Korean "provisional government" having full power in civil affairs in Korea right after Japan's defeat, and (3) recognition and guarantee by the Allies of complete Korean independence and a formal Korean government after the conclusion of the occupation period. For Chongqing, the key in this solution was the coexistence of a Korean government and an Allied military mechanism in Korea from the very beginning of the occupation period. This formula also identified "in due course" with the occupation period and therefore denied the trusteeship formula, which provided for post-occupation foreign supervision in Korea. The Korean "provisional government" in the occupation period could be no other but the KPG under Chongqing's patronage. In this way, the Cairo pledge for international guarantee for Korean independence would be readily translated into a clause for China's security in Northeast Asia.[52]

However, if the American government should insist that the Koreans would not be capable of immediate self-government, the Chinese plan would offer an alternative over the third point listed above. The Chinese government agreed to concede that *after* the independence and a formal government of Korea were recognized and guaranteed by the United Nations, a "temporary system of international assistance" could be established jointly by China, the United States, and Britain in Korea to help the new Korean government. But this "assistance" should be limited to three years. As a concession to Washington's "Big Four" formula, the plan agreed that all these steps should be discussed and agreed upon by China and the two Western powers, and, if the Soviet government was willing to join in, it should be welcomed.[53]

The details of this "assistance system" were not included in the plan that Yang brought to Washington, but responsible Chinese officials had a clear idea about how it should be structured. Through this system, China's leading influence in Korea should of course be maintained. The advisory responsibilities would be divided among the Big Four. China would be in charge of diplomatic and police affairs, the United States would guide financial and transportation matters, Britain would provide judicial advice, and the Soviet Union could help with the public health needs of the Korean government. It would be even better if the other three governments did not insist on appointing their advisors and be willing to accept appointees from lesser states. In Ambassador Wellington Koo's opinion, because China and Korea were "as close as lips to teeth," in this period China needed to act on Korea's behalf in international affairs and maintain military bases in the country. Such arrangements were necessary for China to discharge its international obligations at the end of the war as well as to strengthen its own national defense. At the same time, China's leading political responsibility in Korea must be supplemented by the Western Allies' major economic responsibility.[54]

During the last year of the war, Chinese leaders themselves became increasingly suspicious that even their modified Korea policy would be acceptable to Washington. Consequently, a question emerged as to whether the American trusteeship formula should be accepted as the last resort. Over this question, officials in Chongqing were divided. Some in the Waijiaobu believed that at the end of the war, China would be too weak to influence events in Korea. Therefore, America's interest and presence in Korea should be encouraged, and China should not resist intractably American's trusteeship plan. But some prominent KMT functionaries like Chen Lifu and Chen Guofu held that China as a revolutionary power had an obligation to support Korean independence and therefore should take decisive steps to recognize the KPG without too much anxiety about other countries' attitudes. Until the end of the war, Chongqing's Korea policy drifted without adopting either of these opposite positions.[55]

For the evolution of the U.S. policy toward Korea, the Cairo Conference concluded a period of exploring principles but did not initiate another for formulating operational policies. Early in April 1944, London unexpectedly urged Washington to translate the Cairo decision on Korea to tangible terms. The British embassy in Washington sent a questionnaire on Korea to the State Department, trying to hammer out an Anglo-American interpretation of the Cairo Declaration on Korea. But the Americans suggested that the Chinese ought also to be included in any further discussion of Korea. This led to the aforementioned Yang Yunzhu mission to Washington.[56]

The invitation extended to Chongqing was a ritual of Washington's policy of treating China as a great power and a tactic to tackle the British more than a serious call for Chinese opinion on Korea. Actually, the State Department believed that because of Cairo, Chongqing would be more manageable than before as far as the Korea question was concerned. In June 1944, when Vice President Wallace was on his way to China, the State Department expected that the Korean question might be stirred up in Chongqing. But its instruction to Ambassador Gauss confidently stated: "In the circumstances of the Cairo Declaration it would seem that the Chinese would hardly be likely to act in the matter of Korean recognition without prior consultation with the parties to that instrument." This judgment was verified by the Chinese themselves. In February 1945, Shao Yülin, an official of the Waijiaobu and personal advisor of Chiang Kai-shek, told American officials in Washington that his government had no official relation with any Korean group and was in complete agreement with the American government on withholding recognition of the KPG at present. Although Shao wanted this conversation to be on a "personal basis," the State Department took what he said as Chongqing's official position.[57] Yang Yunzhu's mission to Washington reveals the posture adopted by Chinese diplomacy on Korea: unless asked by Washington, the Chinese government would keep its thought to itself. After the encounter with President Roosevelt at Cairo, Chiang, worried about being construed as ambitious and expansionist, chose a policy of silent dissent in dealing with Washington. American officials however interpreted this as the Chinese government's acquiescence in the U.S. formula.

During the last two years of the war, the State Department's planning for Korea did result in itemizing the trusteeship formula to a certain degree. Two postwar periods were contemplated. One was the period of military government in Korea right after the Japanese surrender. It was to be followed by a trusteeship period preceding Korea's complete independence. Chinese participation in both was expected. Despite the unmistakable military weakness of Chongqing, State Department planning staff still assumed that at the end of the war Chinese troops would be able to reach some foreign areas connected with China by land, including Korea and Indochina. Therefore, in 1944, the policy planning in the State Department expected both China and Britain to participate in the invasion of Korea and contribute to the Allied military government in that country afterwards.[58]

The U.S. government's open pledge for Korean independence at Cairo served as a stimulus to the State Department's effort to match the means of policy with American objectives in Korea. A new element in the post-Cairo planning for Korea was a positive consideration about America's military role in reconquering the peninsula. To guarantee the implementation of U.S. policy in Korea, the State Department planning staff argued in early 1944 that American troops would have to constitute a substantial portion of the liberation forces in Korea, and the other powers' representation in the projected occupation authority should not "be so large as to prejudice the effectiveness of American participation in CAA [Allied civil affairs administration]." Such a projection did not have solid support from U.S. military strategy for the Pacific. In 1944, the issue of Soviet entry into the Pacific war was under consideration in Washington, but American strategists focused their attention on the Red Army's prospective actions in Manchuria and North China, which would be able to assist American's major effort to defeat Japan in the Pacific. Korea was either overlooked or left to uncertainty.[59] The evolution of the State Department planning was nevertheless significant. Before Cairo, the focus of the planning was on how the United States might prevent a rivalry between China and the Soviet Union, the two countries that would have greater influence and more interests than other powers in Korea. Now the idea was that the United States itself must become the leading influence in Korea.

With regard to the trusteeship period following the initial stage of the occupation, the State Department's planning did not make any substantial progress. Despite the omission of the trusteeship formula in the Cairo Declaration, the State Department interpreted that document as an endorsement of its standing preference for an interim international regime in Korea prior to its full independence. Never taking seriously Chongqing's passivity toward the trusteeship solution, American policy makers turned their attention to convincing the Russians of the advantage of their Korea Policy. This was achieved at Yalta by an oral understanding between President Roosevelt and Soviet leader Stalin. They agreed that the United States, China, the Soviet Union, and probably Great Britain should be included in the international supervision over Korea before its independence. They also made a special point that in this period no foreign troops should be stationed in Korea. Their opinions varied only over the length of the trusteeship. Roosevelt suggested a period of twenty to thirty years, but Stalin preferred a shorter one. Although again the State Department was not fully consulted in advance, Roosevelt once more got what the political strategists in the State Department wanted, that was, Soviet consent to international trusteeship in Korea. Yet the president also disappointed the State Department on one vital issue. Taking into account the prospect of Soviet entry into the war against Japan, planners in the State Department believed that it was important for the American and Soviet leaders to consider carefully "the question of which countries should participate in the military occupation of Korea." When agreeing on the *nonmilitary* nature of the international trusteeship, Roosevelt and Stalin somehow completely evaded the occupation period that would precede and influence the implementation of trusteeship for Korea.[60]

Discrepancy between political objectives and military means would prove a vital weakness in Washington's postwar policy regarding Korea. Although officials in the State Department recognized that U.S. military presence in Korea would be a sine qua non for the success of American policy, American military planning in the Pacific followed its own logic. Early in 1945, when American strategists did begin to consider the importance of Korea for future military operations, they saw it as one of the strategic links in a so-called Japanese citadel. In April 1945, the U.S. Joint Chiefs of Staff believed that, by controlling this "citadel" first, a campaign of bombardment and blockade against Japan should be conducted to pave the way for the final invasion. The disadvantage was that such a campaign in peripheral areas might prove time consuming and costly, and it might therefore delay the invasion of Japan proper. After the difficult conquest of Okinawa was completed in June, U.S. strategists believed that an adequate forward base was secured from which the invasion of the Japanese home islands could be launched. Consequently, the need for conquering Korea before the invasion disappeared.[61]

In June and early July, the State Department prepared a series of "briefing book papers" for the coming Potsdam Conference. With regard to Korea, these papers only restated the principle of international trusteeship, emphasizing that, to be successful, such an arrangement ought to be *preceded* with a joint military effort by the major Allies to liberate Korea. But American military leaders were not prepared for discussing such effort with the Russians at Potsdam. When questioned by the Russians about the timing of U.S. military operation against Korea, General George C. Marshall replied that the issue could not be decided until the early results of the American invasion of Japan were stabilized.[62]

During the war period of the Truman administration, despite the prospect of Soviet entry into the Pacific war and the deterioration of the U.S.–Soviet relationship, American policy makers stuck to the idea about an international trusteeship for Korea. The Korean issue in Asia did not seem to have such ominous implications to U.S.–Soviet relations as the Polish case in Europe. There was only one instance in which the prospective cooperation with Moscow in Korea was questioned. In May, Acting Secretary of State Joseph Grew put a question to Secretary of War Henry Stimson about whether the Yalta agreement on the Far East should still be supported by the U.S. government without adding some new conditions for the Russians to comply with. One of these was that Moscow must accept definitely a Big-Four trusteeship as the only authority to select a temporary Korean government. Later, at a meeting among the State, Navy, and War Secretaries, Ambassador Averell Harriman, as a participant in the Yalta discussions, testified that at Yalta President Roosevelt had already reached an oral agreement with Stalin on trusteeship for Korea.[63] The testimony made Grew's "new condition" unnecessary.

Grew's overture for revisiting the Yalta Agreement is nevertheless instructive. It points to the fixed conception about Korea among American policy makers. Also unchanged was Washington's determination not to allow Chongqing's anti-Soviet tendency in the Korean issue to grow. Observing the Soviet leaders at close range, even George Kennan believed that leaders in Chongqing were paranoid in fearing a Soviet conspiracy about Korea. He did not see any evidence suggesting that Moscow had the intention to organize a Korean movement in its territory as an instrument of expansion. Instead, Kennan suggested that the KMT leadership pay attention to the Korean group in the Chinese Communist region. In July, a planning committee of the State Department reiterated the standing conviction that it would be unwise for the United States to support the Chinese approach of using the KPG as a countervailing political force against the Soviet Union. If there should really be a danger of a Soviet-sponsored Korean government, the committee reasoned, the "best antidote" would not be the Chinese-sponsored KPG but cooperation between the other three Allies and Moscow.[64]

At the same time, the Russians began to retreat from the Yalta understanding on trusteeship in Korea. During the Sino-Soviet negotiations at Moscow from July to August, which was held as a corollary of the Yalta Agreement, Stalin complained to T.V. Soong that although he and Roosevelt had agreed on trusteeship in Korea as a prelude to independence, the current American leadership was more receptive to the British view, seeing trusteeship as a step toward colonization. He also said that, at Yalta, no binding decision regarding Korea had been reached.[65]

Given the intensified U.S.–Soviet relations in Europe and the electrifying situation in East Asia during the final days of the Pacific war, Washington could no longer hope that a harmonious cooperation with the Soviet Union would emerge in postwar Korea. Trusteeship was not abandoned, however. It only changed from a vehicle for Big-Four cooperation into one of the thorny issues in the emerging Soviet–American competition. It also became clear to Washington that the policy had to be substantiated with military force. On August 10, angered by Soviet behavior during the Sino–Soviet negotiations in Moscow, Ambassador Harriman suggested to President Truman that American troops land at Dairen (Dalian) and Korea if Japan surrendered before the Russians could occupy these areas. "I cannot see," the ambassador remarked, "that we are under any obligation to the Soviets to respect any zone of Soviet military operation." With the president's approval, the Joint Chiefs of Staff treated this proposal as a "matter of urgency" and set a timetable for the race to Dairen and Korea. Also on August 10, the War Department instructed General Albert C. Wedemeyer in China that he direct American assistance to the Chinese government for the purposes of recapturing Chinese territories from Japanese occupation and sending Chinese troops to Korea and Japan. In an ensuing discussion between Wedemeyer and Chiang Kai-shek, the two agreed that China's timely control of Pusan, Korea, would be able to prevent the

Russians from establishing control by themselves or through a Korean communist regime in that peninsula.[66]

Chiang Kai-shek must have been delighted by the reorientation in Washington's Korea policy. But the idea of using Chinese troops in Korea to counter the Soviet Red Army proved a wild optimism about Chongqing's capability. One day before the Japanese surrender, the State-War-Navy Coordination Committee admitted that occupation of Korea had to begin without Chinese and British participation, but their forces should be introduced into the southern half of Korea whenever permitted by conditions. Thus, the last few days of the war saw a transformation of Washington's objective in Korea from Big-Four cooperation to an ABC entente confronting the Russians, which had been pursued by Chongqing for some time but rejected by the Americans. The State Department's expectation that the Soviets would be the predominant military influence in Korea was materialized when the Red Army poured into that peninsula during the second half of August 1945. Having committed to international trusteeship and having decided to play a leading role in postwar disposition of Korea, American policy makers now had to improvise a two-zone occupation arrangement for the purpose of containing the Russians in Korea. But the implementation of this scheme would have to rely on Moscow's willingness to contain its own military advance to the area north of the 38th Parallel.[67]

* * *

When the war ended in Asia and the Pacific in mid-August 1945, the wartime planning by both the American and Chinese governments for Korea proved futile. The American and Chinese policies toward Korea had some features in common. Both contained a paternalistic attitude of their own types, both took the Soviet Union as a potential threat to their objectives in Korea, and both relied heavily on diplomatic maneuver for committing the other Allied governments to their solutions for the Korean question. Otherwise the Americans and the Chinese pursued different objectives. In resuming China's relations with Korea that had been severed by Japan a half century before, Chongqing's policy was guided mainly by geostrategic interests, considering Korea as a key to China's postwar security. Washington's orientation was decided within a cosmopolitical framework, treating Korea as a testing ground for President Roosevelt's version of a new world orchestrated harmoniously by great powers. Both Chiang Kai-shek and Franklin D. Roosevelt practiced power politics but they followed different logics. From a weak country's position, Chiang resorted to the old, famed approach of Chinese diplomacy of playing one barbarian state (the United States) against another (the Soviet Union). From a big power's perspective, Roosevelt based his policy on a principle of equitable readjustment of interests, which had a precedent in Woodrow Wilson's "Fourteen Points." Neither proved effective. Even before the conclusion of the war, Chongqing and Washington could foresee that their policies for Korea were doomed for the reason that neither was well prepared to deal with Soviet military power in the region. But given their fixed military strategies and political objectives, neither government had much room to maneuver.

The ultimate lesson from the abortive Sino–American diplomacy over Korea is not that had the two government cooperated on one of their policies, the postwar history of Korea would have been different. Due to China's weakness, a change of Chongqing's attitude toward the trusteeship formula from one of silent dissent to one of positive support would not have reinforced the U.S. position in Korea vis-à-vis the Soviets; and Washington's endorsement of the KPG could also not have altered the military balance of power in Korea at the conclusion of the war. More important, political strategists in both Chongqing and Washington exaggerated their countries' ability to shape Korea's future. The postwar history of Korea was to be written principally by the Koreans themselves, albeit the severe interference from great powers.

Therefore, a more useful question about the meaning of the wartime Sino–American diplomacy over Korea should be in what manner this episode may have affected the U.S.–Chinese relations in the years to come. China and the United States emerged from World War II as two changed powers in East Asian international politics. The war years saw the two countries' search for their new identities and new roles in East Asia. The policy preparations for Korea and other East Asian territories in Chongqing and Washington were mental exercises of this nature. It proved that the Americans could not condone the Chinese nationalistic stance in world affairs nor could the Chinese accept the American globalist approach to Asian issues. Most interestingly, despite the turns and twists in postwar history of China and American–Chinese relations, this discrepancy persisted and finally resulted in a military confrontation between the two nations in the 1950s.

Notes

1. Revisionist works are trickling out in recent years. For instance, Jay Taylor's new biography, *The Generalissimo: Chiang Kai-shek and the Struggle for Modern China* (Cambridge: The Belknap Press of Harvard University Press, 2009) reevaluates one of the dominant figures of the era, and Frank Dikötter's *The Age of Openness: China before Mao* (Berkeley: University of California Press, 2008) considers the period as a "golden age of engagement with the world."
2. *Xian Zongtong Jiang Gong Sixiang Yanlun Zongji* (Complete works of the late President Chiang [Kai-shek]), 40 vols, Historical Commission of the Central Committee of the Kuomintang, comp. (Taipei: Guomindang Dangshi Weiyuanhui, 1984. Hereafter cited as *Zongji*), 18:410–416; *Jiang Zongtong Milu* (Secret records of President Chiang [Kai-shek]), 14 vols, Furuya Keiji, comp. (Taipei: Zhongyang Ribaoshe, 1974–1977. Hereafter cited as *Milu*), 13:3.
3. *Zhonghua Minguo Zhongyao SHILIAO Chubian: Dui Ri Kangzhan Shiqi* (Preliminary compilation of important historical records of the Republic of China: the period of the war of resistance against Japan), 7 vols, Historical Commission of the Central Committee of the Kuomintang, comp. (Taipei: Guomindang Dangshi Weiyuanhui, 1981. Hereafter cited as *ZZSC*), Pt. 3, 1:154–155.
4. *ZZSC*, Pt. 3, 3:796–798. By "positive national self-government" the Chinese government meant automatic relinquishment by the Allied powers of their own colonies, not merely the liberation of the enemies' colonial possessions.
5. U.S. Department of State, *Foreign Relations of the United States: Diplomatic Papers: China, 1942* (Washington, D.C.: G.P.O. 1956. Hereafter cited as *FRUS* plus subtitle), *732; Shihliao*, Pt. 3, 1:703; *Zongji*, 19:347.
6. Wellington Koo, "Reminiscences of Wellington Koo" (Chinese Oral History Project of the East Asian Institute of Columbia University, n.d.), V, Pt. A, 249; *Zongji*, 19:347.
7. *Zongji*, 19:162–618.

8. *Geming Wenxian* (Revolutionary documents), multivolume, Historical Commission of the Central Committee of the Kuomintang, comp. (Taipei: Guomindang Dangshi Weiyuanhui, 1976–), 76:370.
9. Wu Xiangxsiang, *Di Er Ci Zhong Ri Zhanzheng Shi* (History of the second Chinese-Japanese war) (Taipei: Zonghe Yuekanshe, 1973–1974), 2:775.
10. *ZZSC*, Pt. 3, 3:41–45; Chinese Ministry of Information, *China Handbook, 1937–1943* (New York, 1943), 143–144.
11. *FRUS: China*, 1942, 174.
12. Kim Ku, *Pai Fan Yizhi* (Reminiscences of Pai Fan) (Taipei, 1969), 187–189; Hu Chunhui, "Chen Guofu and the Korean independence movement," in Institute of Korean Studies of the Republic of China, comp., *Zhoung Han Guanxi Shi Guoji Taolunhui Lunwenji, 960–1949* (Collected essays of the International Conference on Sino-Korean Relations, 960–1949) (Taipei, 1983), 273–281.
13. Fan Tingjie, "Korean Revolution in China," *Zhuanji Wenxue*, 27.1 (July 1975): 36–41, 27.4 (October 1975): 84–86, and 28.2 (February 1976): 90, 28.4 (April 1976): 53, 82–83; Hu Chunhui, *Hanguo Duli Yundong zai Zhongguo* (Korean independence movement in China) (Taipei, 1976), 47–48, 153–154; Chong-sik Lee, *The Politics of Korean Nationalism* (Berkeley, Calif., 1965), 129, 185–186, 189–190, 209–210, 223–224.
14. Yang Daqing, "Between Lips and Teeth: Chinese-Korean Relations, 1910–1950," in Bruce Cumings, ed., *Chicago Occasional Papers on Korea* (Chicago, 1991), 72–73; Hu Songping, *Zhu Jiahua Nianpu* (Chronicle of Zhu Jiahua) (Taipei, 1969), 53; Hu, *Hanguo*, 97, 101–104.
15. Ibid., 105–107.
16. Ibid., 247–269, 273–277; Lee, *Korean Nationalism*, 202, 206, 210–212.
17. Hu, *Hanguo*, 108, 211–212.
18. Ibid., 165–167, 169–171, 182–185, 193; Lee, *Korean Nationalism*, 223–225, 230.
19. *FRUS, 1942*, 1:880–881.
20. This approach was in concert with Chongqing's general orientation toward Asian colonies, which was delineated by Chiang Kai-shek in his aforementioned conversation with Ambassador Koo at the end of 1942.
21. Hu, *Hanguo*, 306.
22. *FRUS, 1942*, 1:867–875; Hu, *Hanguo*, 310–311.
23. Memo on Chinese postwar aims, December 4, 1942, Lauchlin Currie Papers, Box 5. The "big brother" proposal for Indochina was perhaps the first information ever known to Washington about the Chinese intention on the Indochina question.
24. *ZZSC*, Pt. 3, 1:746–478; *FRUS: China, 1942*, 185–187.
25. Syngman Rhee to Hornbeck, November 29, 1941, Stanley K. Hornbeck Papers, Box 268; memo of conversation between John W. Staggers, attorney for the Korean Commission, and Hornbeck, March 27, 1942, ibid.; four letters between James H. R. Cromwell, president of the Korean-American Council, and Secretary of State Cordell Hull, May 5 and 20, 1942, June 3 and 23, 1942, Institute of Pacific Relations (IPR) Papers, Box 62; T-319, May 20, 1943, Harley A. Notter Records, Box 63. Also see Hong-kyu Park, "From Pearl Harbor to Cairo: America's Korean Diplomacy, 1941–1943," *Diplomatic History* 13 (Summer 1989).
26. A. A. Berle to Welles, February 17, 1942, Hornbeck Papers, Box 268; FE to Welles, February 20, 1942, ibid.

27. Memo by William R. Langdon, February 20, 1942, ibid.; S-minutes-10, August 12, 1942, Notter Records, Box 76; S-18a, October 2, 1942, ibid.; P-31, August 6, 1942, ibid., Box 54; Hornbeck to Welles, April 11, 1942, Hornbeck Papers, Box 269.
28. Memo, "Indications of Contact with President on Post-War Matters," n.d., idid.; Hull's memo on president's meeting with Eden, March 27, 1943, ibid., Box 19; Louis, *Imperialism at Bay*, 156–157.
29. P-118 (P-I.O.-95), October 21, 1942, Notter Records, Box 54; Robert E. Sherwood, *Roosevelt and Hopkins: An Intimate History* (New York, 1948), 718.
30. ST minutes-18, May 19, 1943, Notter Records, Box 79.
31. PG-34, October 4, 1943, ibid., Box 119; SR document, "China," n.d., ibid., Box 11; memo by Division of Chinese Affairs, "Outline of Long-range Objectives and Policies of the United States with Respect to China," January 12, 1845, Top Secret General Records of Chongqing Embassy, China, 1945, Box 1.
32. T minutes-51, June 25, 1943, Makoto Iokibe, ed., *The Occupation of Japan: U.S. Planning Documents, 1942–1945* (microfilm; hereafter cited as *OJ*) (Bethesda, Md., 1987), 1-C-1; ST minutes-18, May 19, 1943, Notter Records, Box 79.
33. A more proper precedent, therefore, can be Li Hongzhang's scheme about Korea before the first Sino–Japanese war of 1894–1895.
34. T-319, May 26, 1943, ibid., Box 63; PG-32, October 2, 1943, ibid., Box 119; Park, "From Pearl Harbor to Cairo," 355–356.
35. Memo, August 19, 1943, Hornbeck Papers, Box 369; Hornbeck to Secretary Hull, August 13, 1942, ibid., Box 269; PG-28, October 2, 1943, Notter Records, Box 119.
36. Charles Wilson, *Churchill; Taken from the Diaries of Lord Moran* (Boston, 1966), 451; memo of conversation on Hornbeck's recent trip to London, October 28, 1943, Notter Records, Box 79.
37. "Record of conversation with the president and Mr. Hopkins," July16, 1943, T.V.
38. Koo, "Reminiscences," V, Pt. A, 449–450, and Pt. B, 371.
39. *FRUS: China, 1943,* 133–137, 845–845.
40. PG-32, October 2, 1943, Notter Records, Box 119; PG-33, October 2, 1943, ibid.; T-319, May 26, 1943, ibid., Box 63; Hugh Borton, *American Presurrender Planning for Postwar Japan* (New York, 1967), 13.
41. *ZZSC,* Pt. 3, 3:503–506.
42. Feis, *China Tangle,* 108–109.
43. For instance, Robert Dallek, *Franklin D. Rooselvelt and American Foreign Policy, 1932–1945* (New York, 1979), 428–429.
44. Thorne, *Allies of a Kind,* 311–312.
45. *FRUS: Conferences at Cairo and Tehran,* 1943, 325.
46. *ZZSC,* Pt. 3, 3:527–528.
47. *FRUS: Cairo and Tehran, 1943, 197, 257, 334;* D (CDA) minutes-2, February 8, 1945, Records of Harley A. Notter, Box 134; *Milu,* 13:117.
48. Louis, *Imperialism at Bay,* 274.
49. Hu, *Hanguo,* 307, 308; Yang, "Between Lips and Teeth," 76.
50. Ibid., 122–123; Shao Yülin, *Shi Han Huiyilu* (My mission to Korea) (Taipei, 1980), 54–55, 66–67; "Plans for postwar disposition of Japan," June 7, 1944, Victor Hoo Papers, Box 3; "Report by the secretariat of the Supreme National Defense Council," November 6, 1944,

Koo Papers, Box 79; "Plan for assisting Korean independence," March 25, 1945, ibid., Box 81.

51. "Oral Statement," and "Draft Questionnaire on Korea," n.d., Koo Papers, Box 79; memo by YangYunzhu, "Report on the discussion of the Korean question with U.S. State Department," April 10, 1945, ibid.; "Report," November 6, 1944, ibid.; Chiang Kai-shek to Wang Chonghui, n.d., ibid.; *FRUS, 1945,* 6:1020–1022.
52. "Establishment of an international security zone on the Pacific," June 7, 1944, Hoo Papers, Box 3; "Plans for postwar disposition of Japan," June 7, 1944, ibid.; "Report," November 6, 1944, Koo Papers, Box 79.
53. Ibid.; "Plan for assisting Korean independence," March 25, 1945, ibid., Box 81.
54. Koo to the Waijiaobu, December 1, 1944, ibid., Box 54; The metaphor of "the lips to the teeth" is another example of how certain traditional Chinese conceptions of territorial security may have influenced modern Chinese diplomacy. The first use by a Chinese statesman of this metaphor probably occurred in 655 B.C. and the story is recorded in the Confucian classis, *Zuozhuan.*
55. Memo by Yang Yunzhu, "Problems regarding Korea, Japanese mandated territories, and China's lost territories," n.d., ibid., Box 79; Hu, "Chen Guofu," 9.
56. P. H. Gore-Booth to Harley A. Notter, April 4, 1944, Notter Records, Box 19; memo by Borton, "Consideration of the draft questionnaire on Korea," April 18, 1944, ibid.; G. B. Sansom to J. W. Ballantine, June 16 and 28, 1944, ibid.; memo of conversation between Gore-Booth and B. Gerig, 26 June 1944, ibid.; memo of conversation between Sir George Sansom and Ballantine and others, July 17, 1944, ibid.
57. *FRUS, 1944,* 5:1279; *FRUS, 1945,* 6:1018–1019, 1022.
58. CAC-128, March 29, 1944, Notter Records, Box 109.
59. CAC-66a, February 5, 1944, ibid.; U.S. Department of Defense, *The Entry of the Soviet Union into the War Against Japan: Military Plans, 1941–1945* (Washington, D.C., 1955), 28–45.
60. PWC-124a, May 4, 1944, Notter Records, Box 109; *FRUS: The Conferences at Malta and Yalta, 1945,* 358–361, 770.
61. Grace P. Hayes, *The History of the Joint Chiefs of Staff in World War II: The War against Japan* (Annapolis, Md., 1982), 551, 658, 702–703, 713; U.S. Department of Defense, *Entry of the Soviet Union,* 61–68.
62. *FRUS: The Conference of Berlin,* 1:311–313, 925–930: ibid., 2:351–352; Robert M. Slusser, "Soviet Far Eastern Policy, 1945–1950: Stalin's Goals in Korea," in Yonosuke Nagai and Akira Iriye, eds., *The Origins of the Cold War in Asia* (New York, 1977), 134–135, argues that this information may have encouraged the Russians to occupy all of Korea.
63. Grew to Stimson, May 12, 1945. *OJ,* 5-B-7; minutes of the Committee of Three meeting, May 15, 1845, ibid.; Stimson Diary, L1, 128.
64. *FRUS, 1945,* 6:1026–1027; meeting No. 215 of IDACFE, July 31, 1945, *OJ,* 2-B-196.
65. "Notes taken at Sino-Soviet conferences, Moscow, 1945": minutes of Sin-Soviet negotiations, July 2, 1945, Hoo Papers, Box 2.
66. *FRUS, 1945,* 7:967; U.S. Department of State, *State-War-Navy Coordination Committee Policy Files, 1944–1947* (Wilmington, Del., 1977; microfilm), JCS memo SM-3149, August 30, 1945, SWNCC 67; Albert C. Wedemeyer, *Wedemeyer Reports!* (New York,

1958), 344–345; Feis, *China Tangle*, 337; radio, Wedemeyer to Marshall, July 10, 1945, Wedemeyer Papers, Box 1539; Charles F. Romanus and Riley Sunderland, *United States Army in World War II; China-Burma-India Theater: Time Runs Out in CBI* (Washington, D.C., 1959), 389–391.

67. JCS 1467/1, August 13, 1945, SWNCC 21; *FRUS, 1945*, 6:1038–1039; JWPC 264/9, August 13, 1945, and JWPC 385/1, August 16, 1945, JCS Records, I, Japan; Michael C. Sandusky, *American's Parallel* (Alexander, Va., 1983), 226–227, 230, 246–247; William W. Stueck, Jr., *The Road to Confrontation: American Policy toward China and Korea, 1947–1950* (Chapel Hill, N.C., 1981), 21–22.

CHAPTER FOUR

Recast China's Role in Vietnam

Contrary to a conventional view that in the war years the Chinese government had no Indochina policy, the wartime Chinese diplomacy actively searched a role for China to play in postwar Indochina.[1] To Chongqing, the importance of an Indochina policy transcended any ordinary bilateral relationship with its southern neighbor. First, unlike Korea whose postwar settlement would be part of a policy in dealing with the defeated Japan, Indochina belonged to the Western colonial system in Asia, of which China's principal wartime allies were members. Secondly, the precolonial relationship between China and Vietnam had been conducted within the traditional framework of the Chinese Empire with Vietnam as a "tributary dependence" of the celestial court in Beijing. Thus any attempt by the Chinese government to challenge the French colonial rule in Indochina would also pose a challenge to itself in laying a new basis for China's modern relations with Southeast Asian countries. Thirdly, because President Franklin D. Roosevelt displayed a personal interest in the future of the French colony, more than any other issue concerning postwar Asia KMT leaders had to contemplate the matter in connection with their American alliance.

In coping with these issues, Chinese leaders had three options. They could follow American leadership and settle with the role of a junior partner to Washington's Asian policy; they could accept restoration of the prewar status quo in Southeast Asia and continue to be a weak country encircled by Western empires; or they could start assuming great-power responsibilities while taking the initiative in mustering international support for China's leading role in reorganizing the East Asian international order. Although Chinese Nationalist leaders always coveted the third position, the country's weakness severely restrained their ambitions. The resultant plot of Chinese diplomacy on Indochina thus had a grandiose beginning but a gloomy conclusion.

"Big-Brother"

By 1941, China had already fought Japan arduously for four lonely years. Therefore Japan's attack of Pearl Harbor on December 7 and the resultant American entry into World War II were welcoming developments in Chongqing. Chinese diplomacy was invigorated under the new circumstances. Soon, the Western Allies got the first glimpse of a renovated Chinese foreign policy. In early 1942, when talking to an American officer in Chongqing, Wang Chonghui, secretary-general of the Chinese Supreme Council of National Defense, identified Chinese nationals in Indochina, Burma, Thailand, Malaya, the Dutch East Indies, and the Philippines as the most important concern for China's Southeast Asian policy. According to Wang, three alternate solutions were then under consideration by the Chinese government: (1) China's direct control of these areas; (2) plebiscites in these territories to decide whether they would remain under their prewar colonial authorities or under some new political authority; and, (3), these areas to be put under the supervision of an international organization. Wang identified the first two as Chongqing's preferred solutions.[2]

Chinese nationals in Southeast Asia were an old concern of Chinese foreign policy, but Chongqing's projection of the three solutions unveiled a new audacity to alter the prewar status quo of the region. Apparently the sting in these propositions was directed more toward Western colonial powers than toward Japan. The origin of Chongqing's anticolonialism and claim for Chinese patronage over Southeast Asian countries can be traced back to Sun Yat-sen, founder of the Kuomintang (KMT). In his doctrine of Chinese nationalism, Sun not only advocated the emancipation of China from foreign imperialism but also embraced an ill-defined *wangdao* (kingly way) tradition of China, or imperial China's alleged benevolent overlordship over its lesser neighbors.[3] But not until now, when Japan's action of war in the Pacific shattered the Western empires and also drove China and the Western powers into alliance, did the KMT leadership see an opportunity to assert China's leading role in Southeast Asian affairs.

Especially, the KMT regime's recent alliance with the United States emboldened officials in Chongqing. Intending to place China under America's aegis, President Roosevelt pledged to help the Chinese government redefine China's "national standing." From the spring of 1942, he began to promote an idea among the allied powers that after the war China should act as one of the "four policemen" of the world.[4] So far as Asia's colonial issue was concerned, Roosevelt seemed to believe that he could easily persuade Chiang Kai-shek to follow his lead. In February, Roosevelt invited Chiang to join him in setting up a trusteeship for Southeast Asian territories after the war.[5]

This was Roosevelt's earliest disclosure to a foreign government of his trusteeship formula for Indochina and some other Southeast Asian countries. Three months later, however, when repeating the trusteeship idea to the visiting Soviet foreign minister V. M. Molotov, the president attributed the authorship of the idea to Chiang Kai-shek.[6] Chiang was oblivious of his own contribution to Roosevelt's trusteeship formula for Indochina. In August, after learning more about the formula from Lauchlin Currie, Roosevelt's personal envoy, Chiang was troubled by certain connotations of the proposed solution.[7]

To begin with, the trusteeship idea reflected American leaders' paternalism toward Asian peoples, which disturbed Chiang even further when he heard Currie describing the relationship between China and the Western powers as one "between an adolescent child and its parents." Chiang responded to his condescending guest by saying that the United States "often shows a 'superior complex' overweening toward everybody else."[8]

In a more practical sense, Chiang was apprehensive of the trusteeship formula's ominous implications for China's own borderlands, such as Manchuria, Mongolia, and Tibet. Currie seemed unaware of the connection here. When talking with Chiang about trusteeship in Indochina, Currie imprudently broached the thought that after the war Manchuria could be made a buffer zone to separate China, Russia, and Japan. Not surprisingly, Chiang fiercely resented this proposition.[9] Furthermore, the trusteeship solution as described by Currie would not confer on China a leading role in postwar settlement in Vietnam or other colonies in Southeast Asia. In 1942, still intoxicated by China's new alliance with the United States and hoping to gain valuable returns from the relationship, KMT leaders could not be satisfied with China's role as merely one of several trustees, especially when the formula itself represented a Western initiative.

Currie's visit did caution KMT leaders against any overt display of China's ambition to claim leadership in Asian affairs. Soon Chiang Kai-shek himself formulated an official rhetoric on the matter, which disclaimed China's "right" to lead Asia but reaffirmed its "responsibility" for assisting underprivileged Asian nations.[10] In an informal message to

Roosevelt in late 1942, Chiang outlined his vision about a new international order in postwar Asia. As far as Indochina was concerned, Chiang sidestepped the president's proposal for an international trusteeship and offered that China "act as big brother" for Indochina before it would be able to gain complete independence. "That would work out all right," Chiang reasoned, "because Indochina was far distant from Russia" and China had some "old ties" with the people there.[11]

Noteworthy in the message is an important distinction between Korea and Indochina. While encouraging the United States to join China in a "tutelage" for postwar Korea in order to hold the nearby Soviet power at bay, Chiang appeared confident that China could act alone in Indochina.[12] Indochina was beyond the reach of the USSR but close to the KMT bases in South China. From a geostrategic point of view, Chiang obviously believed that his government was positioned to assume control in Indochina at a certain point in the course of the war.[13] China's right to exercise such authority had been granted by an inter-Allied understanding reached at the end of 1941, which created a "China theatre of the United Nations" under Chiang's command to include China, Thailand, and Indochina.[14] In his message to Roosevelt, Chiang actually asked the president's agreement to expand his wartime military authority over Indochina into a postwar political responsibility that would allow China to supervise the territory *unilaterally.*

Although Chiang did not specify the attributes of "tutelage" for Korea and "big brotherhood" for Indochina, the explicit anti-Sovietism in the former and the implicit anti-Western tendency in the latter were enough to alarm U.S. policy makers. It was hard for them not to notice that Chiang's need for the presence of American influence in postwar Asia was proportional to the proximity of Soviet Russia and his fear of Soviet power. In Indochina, where Soviet influence seemed unlikely to reach, Chiang preferred a thorough de-Westernization of the local affairs, even if this would mean his rejection of a partnership with President Roosevelt.

Roosevelt cautiously avoided any overt contradiction with Chiang over these matters. What he did was to offer a soft rebuttal to Chiang's proposals via Owen Lattimore, his personal representative to Chiang. In a letter bearing Lattimore's signature, Chiang was told that excluding the Russians from Korean affairs would be harmful to postwar stability in Northeast Asia. As for China's big-brother role in Indochina, Lattimore's letter contained only a vague comment to the effect that in the South Pacific and Southeast Asia, Roosevelt would be willing to consider a single-nation trusteeship in certain areas but multinational supervision in others.[15]

The American president's resort to ambiguity did not deter Chongqing. For, in general, Roosevelt's China policy in 1943 retained the theme of "making China a great power." In the middle of the year, Roosevelt announced to T. V. Soong, Chinese foreign minister and Chiang's brother-in-law: "I want to put China in the sun even before she has the economic power."[16] The problem was that Chiang Kai-shek wanted to sunbathe wearing his own garb and marking out his own beach. In the spring of 1943, Chiang Kai-shek published his notorious book, *China's Destiny,* in which he made a sweeping claim to China's "original territories." Chiang listed the Ryukyu Islands, Hong Kong, Taiwan, the Pescadores, Vietnam, and Burma as the first group of territories that China had lost to foreign powers. Although Chiang did not mean that China should necessarily retake all these areas, he did want to see China again exercising tremendous sway over them. As he told Wellington Koo (Gu Weijun), Chinese ambassador to London, "it was not necessary to say that China had no particular view" on territories in Southeast Asia. Soon the Waijiaobu (Chinese Ministry of Foreign Affairs) would begin to contemplate measures for implementing China's foreign policy objectives as outlined in

Chiang's book.[17] In public, KMT officials propagated the so-called ties of blood between the Chinese and Vietnamese peoples, alluding to China's special position in Vietnam. After Chongqing broke diplomatic relationship with the French Vichy regime in August, for the first time during the war the KMT's official organ, *Zhongyang Ribao* (Central daily), began to editorialize China's interests in Vietnam as a matter solely between China and the Vietnamese people. The French factor was eradicated.[18]

A truism about China's wartime diplomacy is that given Chongqing's reliance on U.S. support, its thrust for an independent foreign policy could not go far. Chiang Kai-shek and his associates were painfully aware of this fact. China's "big brother" position in Indochina would not take shape if Chongqing could not overcome French and British opposition diplomatically and sustain an occupation operation in the territory materially. On both counts, Washington's support was essential. Having failed to win President Roosevelt's sympathy with his initial proposals, in 1943 Chiang tried once again at his summit meeting with Roosevelt at Cairo.

A Chinese "summary record" of the Roosevelt–Chiang political dialogue at Cairo, which took place on November 23, indicates that the two only reached a vague understanding about their governments' cooperation in helping Indochina achieve independence after the war. Nothing is mentioned in the record about either Roosevelt's trusteeship formula or Chiang's big-brother proposition.[19] The final document of the conference, the Cairo Communique, while containing an ambiguous promise for Korea to gain independence "in due course," did not mention Vietnam at all. After the summit, Chiang told his associates that at Cairo he had invited Roosevelt to join him in making declaration to support independence for Vietnam. But the president, according to Chiang, cavalierly dismissed the idea with a laugh.[20]

The American side kept no minutes of the discussion. After the conference, President Roosevelt claimed that Chiang "whole-heartedly supported" his Indochina policy.[21] He would repeat the same story many times. Roosevelt's most vivid description of his discussion with Chiang was given to a group of reporters aboard the U.S.S. *Quincy*, on February 23, 1945, when he was on his way back to the United States from the Yalta Conference. But when Roosevelt supposedly recited verbatim Chiang's reproach of French colonialism, he was in reality repeating word for word his own speech delivered at a Pacific War Council meeting that took place a few months before the Cairo Conference.[22]

The fact is that at Cairo, neither Roosevelt nor Chiang had the other's "whole hearted" support. What available evidence does reveal is that the two leaders' accord concerning Indochina was limited to two matters. The first was their opposition to the restoration of French sovereignty in Indochina. The second was that the people in the area would not be able to gain independence without tangible assistance from the outside. Roosevelt and Chiang had never before disagreed on such fundamentals. Meanwhile, the Cairo Conference did not help reduce the distance between the two with regard to the form and extent of outside assistance in postwar Indochina. By the time of the Cairo Conference, neither Roosevelt nor Chiang had substantiated their Indochina solutions with concrete policy measures. Their disagreement between "international trusteeship" and "Chinese big brother" therefore did not go beyond a conceptual polemic. The disagreement was nevertheless profound. Both leaders anticipated the end of the colonial system in Asia after the war. In its place Roosevelt wanted to install an enlightened Western governance of Asia peoples, or an internationalized Philippine system. The system would theoretically be able to placate Asian nationalism and to keep former Asian colonies integrated with the West. Chiang's program was not intended to isolate the oriental world again from the West, but after the Western powers' uninvited domination of Asian affairs was broken by Japan, Asia's reorganization and reconstruction must assume Asian characteristics. In the Chinese leader's mind, this naturally meant restoration of China's centrality in Asian affairs.

At Cairo, so far as Indochina was concerned, Roosevelt and Chiang were both successful in conducting negative diplomacy. Neither allowed himself to be maneuvered by the other side into assuming a follower's position. Both failed to advance their respective policy objectives regarding Vietnam. The diplomatic stalemate between the Chinese and the American governments would eventually prove unfortunate to the Indochinese countries and beneficial to France. Suffice it to say, relative to inter-Allied politics, the Cairo Conference may have been the sole opportunity for the Allied governments to articulate a decolonization principle regarding the French colony.[23] But the chance was missed.

Options

The Roosevelt–Chiang failure at Cairo to formalize a decolonization policy for Indochina stalled their governments' foreign policy planning. The U.S. State Department had always been aware of the president's opinion on Indochina.[24] The policy planning staff in the State Department however consistently maintained that the U.S. government had a "categorical commitment" to releasing the French Empire, including Indochina, from the Axis' yoke. According to a post-Cairo planning document of the State Department, "this *Government* is pledged to the restoration of the French Empire," but "the *President* has suggested placing Indochina . . . under an international trusteeship [emphasis added]."[25] Such behavior certainly exceeded the State Department's role of offering advice to the Chief Executive and was little short of insubordination.

The policy favored by the planning staff of the State Department called for "restoration of Indochina to France subject to some measure of international accountability," which was also Secretary of State Cordell Hull's own preference.[26] State Department officials agreed with Roosevelt that the French colonial record in Indochina was poor. But they did not believe that America's own record in the Philippines was good enough to allow the U.S. government to hold a moral edge over other colonial powers. Nor did they share the president's view that after the war France should relinquish its great power status. On the contrary, in the postwar years U.S. foreign policy would need a strong, independent, and friendly France as a "bulwark against the spread of anti-democratic movements" in Europe.[27] America's postwar interests in Southeast Asia also mattered. In the State Department's view, the strategic importance of the region to U.S. security had been accentuated by the war in the Pacific. Economically, America would continue to need raw materials from the area and, more importantly, would need to enlarge its trade and investments in countries there. Politically, in addition to its lingering obligations in the Philippines, the United States would not be able to evade a responsibility for preserving stability and promoting progress throughout Southeast Asia. While forecasting an overextension of America's commitments in "an area where, except for the Philippines, it has been relatively little concerned in the past," the planning staff of the State Department did not believe that the United States would be able to pull the things off in Southeast Asia without other Western powers regaining their influence there.[28] As summarized by the Department's Security Technical Committee, U.S. foreign policy in postwar Far East would have to begin either with a "blank sheet" or with a "restored *status quo ante*." The "blank sheet" approach, which projected a Southeast Asia minus European colonial empires, was not the State Department's choice.[29]

Viewing European colonial powers as America's potential allies in postwar Southeast Asia, the State Department regarded the Chinese government as posing an unnecessary hindrance. During 1943, when President Roosevelt was still actively soliciting Chongqing's partnership in his Indochina enterprise, some planning officers in the State Department already considered China as a postwar nuisance. At Security Technical Committee meetings, it was suggested that "containment of China" be envisaged for placating "a fear of Chinese domination" among Asian nations.[30] On the eve of the Cairo Conference, members of the Subcommittee on Territorial Problems reached a consensus that "in Southeast Asia the expansionist designs of China were feared as much as were those of the European powers." In 1944, the same committee conceded that the Chinese government had hitherto made no territorial claims in Southeast Asia. It nevertheless concluded that the seven and a half million Chinese nationals living in the region constituted a convenient instrument for China to pursue a disguised colonial policy.[31]

There is no evidence that the Chinese government was aware of the State Department–White House divergence over Indochina. In any event, it would be difficult for Chiang and his aides to imagine that President Roosevelt might have less control over the State Department than Chiang did over the Waijiaobu. To Chinese officials, the president *was* the U.S. government. Therefore, they took the Chiang–Roosevelt impasse over Indochina at Cairo seriously. A pre-Cairo consensus among KMT officials was that the Chinese government should take advantage of its diplomatic status enhanced by the war to resuscitate China's leadership in Asian affairs. In 1944 this was replaced by with recognizable trends of thought among KMT policy makers. One called for continuation of the pre-Cairo policy aimed at achieving Chongqing's maximal objectives in Indochina, with or without Washington's endorsement. At the other end of the spectrum was a recommendation that China temporarily shelve its decolonization objective regarding Indochina and switch to a policy of improving Chinese interests in the area through negotiations with the French. A third position was to restrain Chongqing's own ambitions about Vietnam and search for an accommodation of Chinese interests to President Roosevelt's trusteeship formula.

Supporters of the first option were officials involved in foreign policy planning operations in the Waijiaobu and the Supreme Council of National Defense. They were responsible for translating the ideas of Chiang's *China's Destiny* into policy measures, rarely concerning themselves with the daily realities of Chongqing's wartime diplomacy. In 1944 the KMT government's participation in the Dumbarton Oaks Conference provided an occasion for these policy planners to undertake flamboyant memorandum writing. Mistaking the forthcoming inter-Allied meeting for a preliminary peace conference, Chongqing's foreign policy strategists devoted much of their energy to the question as to what kind of international management of postwar Asian affairs would serve China best.[32] They strongly favored a regional body for East Asia. Without such an organization, a Waijiaobu memorandum asserted, "various problems relating to peace in the Far East would likely be overlooked by the powers, and China would be hurt most." These officials regarded America's Monroe Doctrine in the Western Hemisphere as an ideal model for China. Corresponding to America's leading position in a pan-American system, "in the future, China's importance and leadership in a Far Eastern regional organization should also be understood and recognized by the other countries."[33]

According to KMT planners' opinion, the China-centered regional body should be entrusted with enormous decision-making authority over states and areas in East Asia. It should have the authority to decide long-term policies of the United Nations toward Japan,

Korea, and Siam. It should assume responsibilities for helping Southeast Asian colonies achieve independence. It should also be put in charge of all "mandated islands" in the Pacific. In these operations, "China's special relations" with "Annam, Burma, Malaya, and Dutch Indies, . . . should be respected by other governments." These officials did not define the "special relations" merely in cultural terms. For instance, in the case of the Dutch Indies, a long-term scheme for Chinese control was contemplated. It was proposed that the Chinese government foster the existing Chinese communities in the Dutch colony into "embryonic states of Chinese nationals," and then "grant open support to these at a proper time in order to use them as China's periphery and buffer zone."[34]

The policy design for Vietnam was outrightly overbearing. A position paper produced by the Waijiaobu is worth a complete translation here:

> "Policy Measures regarding Vietnam"
>
> (1) Use armed forces to control *Beiqi* [Chinese term for the Tonkin area of Vietnam] and the Laos, which will not only consolidate [China's] national defense in the southwest, but will also enable [China] to whip on [*qüce*] Vietnam, and thus to dominate *Zhongnan Bandao* [Mid-South Peninsula, or the Indochinese Peninsula] and keep Siam and Burma under surveillance.
>
> (2) Apply diplomatic stratagem to consolidate the position of Chinese nationals [in Vietnam]: (a) strive for a most-favored nation status in order to lay the basis for [China's] counter-weighing the French with economic strength; (b) negotiate with the French-Indochina regime for releasing Chinese nationals from various tyrannical laws and regulations; (c) promote education among Chinese nationals and enhance their level of literacy; and (d) open new consulates in *Shunhua* [Chinese name for Thanh Hoa] and Cambodia to extend protection for Chinese nationals and to facilitate trade.
>
> (3) Employ political means to induce the Vietnamese nationality to lean inward [*neixiang*]: (a) support Vietnamese youth and strengthen their national confidence; (b) link up the Chinese and the Vietnamese cultures and restore the traditional spirit of mutual assistance and mutual trust between China and Vietnam; (c) try to sit Vietnamese representatives in the postwar international peace conference and to eliminate the French suzerainty in Vietnam; (d) increase the number of permanent diplomatic envoys in Vietnam so as to enhance Chinese-Vietnamese relations and Vietnam's international status; and (e) propagate widely the spirit of the Atlantic Charter on national self-determination and President Roosevelt's statement to the Pacific War Council that "after the war Vietnam should not be returned to France but be assisted by the Allies to achieve self-government ability, and that a so-called trusteeship should be applied there to help the Vietnamese people gain independence," so as to instigate the Vietnamese people to achieve national self-determination.[35]

The document listed military, diplomatic, and political means for achieving Chongqing's policy objectives as if they were mutually supplementary. Yet it can be easily recognized that these were designed for different contingencies. Option one, based on military prowess, was aimed at resuscitating China's ancient controlling position vis- à -vis Vietnam and the rest of the continental Southeast Asia.[36] In 1944, however, the problem for such a policy was that crippled militarily by its war with Japan, Chongqing was in no position to project its postwar military posture and strength in any realistic manner.

The second, diplomatic, orientation anticipated France's return to Indochina after the war. By that time, KMT planners expected, France would have been badly weakened by the war and thus would be in no position to resist China's diplomatic offensive. The Chinese government, buttressed either by its military strength in South China or by international support, would be able to extract significant concessions from the French through negotiations. In contrast to option one that relied on hard, or military, force, the diplomatic approach sought to strengthen China's "soft" presence in Vietnam consisting of cultural, economic, and ethnic elements. The objective of China's coercive diplomacy with France was to displace the remnant of French influence in Indochina gradually. As a matter of fact, wartime conditions had already proven favorable to China's coercive approach to deal with the French.[37]

The third and political option was the closest to Chiang's big-brother stratagem. It was derived from an assumption that at the war's end a strong Vietnamese nationalist movement would emerge to Chongqing's advantages. At the time, the strongest Vietnamese nationalist movement, Viet Minh, was based in its own homeland and was beyond Chongqing's manipulation. Meanwhile a number of Vietnamese political groups sought refuge in China during the war but were ineffective due to internal quarrels.[38] Therefore, although KMT planners could stretch their imagination to anticipate that the Vietnamese "periphery" would rally to the Chinese "center," in the war years the Chinese government did not possess a suitable instrument to induce such result. Also interesting about the political strategy is how it molded President Roosevelt's trusteeship formula to suit Chinese purpose, viewing the formula largely as a useful piece of propaganda for inciting pro-Chinese feelings among the Vietnamese.

Except for the idea about an East Asian regional organization, the schemes above were part of Chongqing's hidden agenda not intended for inter-Allied diplomacy. The Waijiaobu actually recommended to Chiang Kai-shek that unless the other governments at the Dumbarton Oaks Conference brought up the colonial question of Asia, the Chinese delegation should avoid discussing it. Chiang concurred but went even further. He instructed the Chinese delegation not to "insist on anything."[39]

Chongqing's self-restraint spared its delegation embarrassment at Dumbarton Oaks. During the conference, the other governments were interested mainly in setting general rules for a world peace organization but not in any particular regional issue. The Chinese delegation was certainly not in position to change the conference agenda decided by the Big Three. Chongqing had other reasons to conduct a low-profile diplomacy. During 1944, Chongqing's military position was moving from bad to worse. In the year Japan's *Ichigo* (Operation No. 1) offensive, though failing to have any strategic impact, succeeded in sending Chongqing's military reputation to the abyss. Under such circumstances, any Chinese attempt at Dumbarton Oaks to broach Chongqing's assertive foreign policy would have been a laughing stock among the other Allies.

Furthermore, in the summer and fall of 1944, the relationship between Roosevelt and Chiang deteriorated radically. The so-called Stilwell affair, in which Chiang resisted President Roosevelt's pressure for placing all Chinese forces under General Joseph Stilwell's command, actually induced the two leaders to conduct their communications via quasi-ultimatums. Aside from his resentment against foreigners' interference in the KMT political-military establishment, Chiang feared that the implication of Stilwell's command might turn American aid in the direction of the Chinese Communists. Although President Roosevelt finally decided to recall Stilwell, the affair put Chongqing on the defensive in its relations with Washington.[40]

At Dumbarton Oaks, consequently, the Chinese delegation made merely a ceremonial contribution to the Allied discussions regarding the organization of a United Nations. At the conference, the predicament of Chongqing's search for a new role in international affairs was captured in a Chinese diplomat's observation: "We stand in the position of a great power but entertain the anxiety of a small state."[41]

Strains in the Chongqing–Washington relationship afforded opportunities for the French. By the summer of 1944, after breaking with the Vichy regime, Chongqing had maintained an ambassadorial relationship with the French Committee for National Liberation (FCNL). Zinovi Pechkoff, Charles de Gaulle's ambassador to Chongqing, was convinced that Chongqing's general attitude toward France would eventually be influenced by Washington.[42] But leaders of the FCNL believed that concrete issues between France and China had to be settled through direct negotiations. At the time, an on-going talk between the Chinese and the Dutch governments on Chinese interests in the Dutch Indies indicated that Chongqing was willing to hold bilateral discussions on Southeast Asian colonies.[43]

The French were anxious to show Chongqing that compared with the Dutch they were far more enlightened on colonial issues and more sensitive to Chinese concerns. In late August, representatives of the FCNL approached the Chinese Embassy in London and conveyed de Gaulle's desire to conclude an agreement with China on Indochina. Ambassador Koo received the French overture favorably. In his report to Chiang, aside from noting the marked difference between French and Dutch attitudes, Koo pointed out that after the war France would again become a potent force in international affairs. Therefore, the ambassador recommended, the Chinese government should seize the opportunity and actively foster contacts with the FCNL.[44]

Koo's recommendation arrived in Chongqing at a time when Chiang Kai-shek was under a dual pressure of Japan's military offensive and President Roosevelt's diplomatic demarche regarding the Stilwell affair. On October 10, 1944, Chiang sent a message to Roosevelt rejecting a compromise offered by the president some time earlier over the Stilwell affair.[45] On the same day, Chiang talked to Pechkoff with extraordinary cordiality. In the conversation, Chiang went out of his way to please the French ambassador, saying that the Chinese always felt closer to the French than to the Anglo-Saxon and desired to have France's assistance in China's national development. Renouncing any Chinese designs on Indochina, Chiang asked the ambassador to convey to General de Gaulle that "we are very willing to help your government to re-establish a French administration in that colony." With some foresight, Chiang promised that French colonial troops in Indochina would receive "brotherly treatment" in China should they be forced out by the Japanese.[46]

Two weeks later, Chongqing recognized de Gaulle's Provisional Government of France based in Algeria. The rapport between Chongqing and the FCNL continued to gain momentum in 1945. In January, a Sino–French Committee of Scientific Cooperation was established in Chongqing, and cultural-exchange activities followed. In March, the two governments conducted communications about future negotiations for settling the pending questions between China and France.[47]

During the remainder of the war, however, the affable atmosphere between the Chinese and the French was substantiated by any diplomatic breakthrough. Had Chiang not been disheartened by his feud with Roosevelt, he might not have been so anxious to talk to the French in the first place. In Chongqing some officials indeed endorsed Ambassador Koo's positive approach toward France, but there were also those who cautioned Chiang about the timing for talks with the French. Before the Chiang–Pechkoff conversation took place, a memorandum from the Supreme Council of National Defense advised Chiang that timing for starting negotiations with the French should hinge upon the likelihood of Chongqing's military entry into Indochina. If the government had a definite plan and the ability for carrying through a military occupation in Indochina, then talks with France should be postponed until the Chinese occupation forces became ready. But, if conditions should presage the impracticability of such an operation, Chongqing ought to initiate negotiations with the French before the latter could ascertain China's military intentions toward Indochina.[48]

Throughout the war Chiang could not commit to a military operation in Vietnam. General Zhang Fakui, commander of the Fourth War Zone of China, and his staff actively engaged in making plans for an offensive strategy against Japanese forces in North Vietnam, believing it part of their tasks. From time to time, the thought of an invasion also surfaced in Chongqing's military agenda, but a defensive posture was always preferred to an offensive one along the Chinese–Indochinese border. In the spring of 1945, when the Chinese government adopted an counter-offensive strategy, embodied in two plans coded as "Ice Man" and "White Tower," preparations for an invasion of Indochina was at last underway. But, according to these plans, Chinese forces were not to attack Japanese troops in Indochina unless the latter attempted to move northward blocking KMT Army's main thrust toward China's east coast.[49]

While opting for a conservative military posture, Chiang Kai-shek guarded arduously his commanding authority over Indochina. After a Southeast Asian Command (SEAC) was formed under the British Vice Admiral Lord Louis Mountbatten in August 1943, Mountbatten endeavored to persuade Chiang to yield Indochina and Thailand to his new command. Chiang stubbornly resisted the proposition until the last moment of the war. The British attributed Chiang's intransigence to saving "face."[50] Even General Albert C. Wedemeyer, Stilwell's successor in China, believed that it would be "militarily sound" to integrate Thailand and Indochina into the SEAC because Chiang's China Command "has no military capabilities or plans for either."[51]

But Chiang was thinking politically. In fact, he was willing to concede that the divide between his and Mountbatten's *military* authorities in Thailand and Indochina should be decided by the progress of Allied offensive in these areas. Meanwhile he was insistent that any *political* issue arising in these countries be decided by an American–British–Chinese committee under his direction.[52] In other words, to Chiang, the crux of the controversy was neither about the prestige of the commanding authority over Indochina and Thailand nor about the responsibility for fighting the Japanese in these countries. The real issue involved postwar political control in Southeast Asia. Given the known Anglo-French common interests in the region, Chiang's resistance against the British in the command dispute indicated the limits of his diplomatic overture with the French.

Therefore, when an assertive policy in Indochina was blocked by Chongqing's military weakness and talks with the French were deemed premature, the only remaining option for the KMT regime was to seek cooperation with the U.S. government. As a matter of fact, after the Cairo Conference exposed the divergence between Chongqing's and Washington's thinking about postwar Asia, some senior officials in Chongqing began to worry about the future of the Chinese–American alliance. In their opinion, more important than Chongqing's particular stance on postwar issues in Asia, such as Korea and Vietnam, was the general understanding reached by the Chinese and American leaders at Cairo about their cooperation during and after the war.[53] These officials called for modification of Chongqing's original foreign policy objectives in order to remove some causes for mutual misgivings between Chongqing and Washington.

T. V. Soong was the most prominent proponent of this orientation, once telling American officials that he endeavored consistently to keep other KMT leaders' "hands off Indochina."[54] In late 1943 and early 1944, the FCNL and French Governor-General of Indochina, Jean Decoux, made separate statements promising new rights to the peoples of Indochina after the war. Responding to Chiang Kai-shek's directives on studying these documents, Soong, on behalf of the Waijiaobu, made a strong argument against negotiation with the French. According to Soong, President Roosevelt's trusteeship solution for Indochina had caused "deep apprehension" among the French. To preempt the Roosevelt policy, the French now tried a scheme of "taking away the firewood from under the cauldron [*fu di chou xin*], that is, to negotiate with China before the Allied victory." Soong believed that Chongqing must not fall into this trap but should seek a thorough solution of the Indochina problem in complete concert with Roosevelt's policy.[55]

In July, authorized by Chiang, Soong approached U.S. Ambassador Clarence Gauss with a proposition that a new American–British–Chinese conference be held in Washington to determine these governments' responsibilities for administering "liberated areas" in Asia after the war. Promising China's complete cooperation with President Roosevelt's leadership, Soong especially requested Washington to offer "some exposition" of its policies toward Indochina, Dutch East Indies, and Thailand. He made it clear that although the Chinese government was willing to discuss with the Netherlands government the future of the Dutch East Indies, it did not want to include the French in any discussions regarding Indochina.[56]

Soong's overture did not pass muster in the State Department and the Joint Chiefs of Staff. When consulting with the JCS, the State Department was opposed to the conference proposal on the ground that such a meeting could compromise the secrecy of Allied military strategies and also hold implications for the general peace settlement. Meanwhile, the State Department was willing to indulge Soong's request for "exposition" by informally outlining U.S. policy regarding military administration of liberated areas in Asia. The JCS was even opposed to such an informal communication with Chongqing, arguing that any such communication should only cover "broad over-all policy" but not specifics.[57] When Soong finally got a response from the State Department in mid-September, he was told that so far as Indochina was concerned, the American government had not yet made a decision. He was especially disappointed and puzzled by the State–JCS rejection of his conference proposal. By this time, Chiang had already decided to cut himself loose from Soong's abortive initiative, telling Gauss that he had never authorized Soong to seek another conference with American and British leaders.[58]

In contrast to the active personal diplomacy between Roosevelt and Chiang in 1942 and 1943, this episode underscored how low the general relationship between Chongqing and Washington had fallen since the Cairo Conference. So far as the Chinese government's search for an Indochina policy was concerned, it was blocked in every direction that Chongqing's strategists tried to turn.

Drifting

T. V. Soong's request for an "exposition" by Washington of its Indochina policy indicated that in 1944 even the most enthusiastic supporters of the American alliance in Chongqing began to wonder about U.S. government's intentions in Southeast Asia. In that year dissension at the State Department against President Roosevelt's trusteeship formula rose perceptibly. The Office of European Affairs took the lead in articulating an alternative policy for returning the French to Indochina, arguing, among other things, that the president's anti-French policy would not be supported by other major powers "except possibly China."[59]

In his communications with the department during the year, Roosevelt did not retreat from his view that Indochina should be denied to France. But he hesitated to make a final decision. While the British and the French were increasing their pressure on the president with regard to France's restoration in postwar Indochina, the matter was further complicated by the prospect of French resistance groups' participation in the Allied military effort in the territory.[60] In mid-March, just a few weeks before his death, Roosevelt discussed Indochina with his adviser Charles Taussig. In the conversation the president kept the trusteeship idea intact. But now he was willing to allow France to serve as the sole trustee for Indochina "with the proviso that independence was the ultimate goal."[61] Scholarly interpretations vary greatly of this seemingly about-face in Roosevelt's attitude toward France.[62] But, because President Roosevelt's last discourse on Indochina consisted of a concession (French return to Indochina) and a condition (Indochina's ultimate independence), history as it has happened cannot reveal how, had Roosevelt lived longer, the U.S.–French relationship over Indochina would have evolved.

History does reveal another change in Roosevelt's Indochina policy that occurred long before the president's death. That was the removal of China as America's principal partner in postwar Indochina. After the Cairo Conference, any meaningful communication about Indochina between Chongqing and Washington stopped. During the rest of the war, believing that at Cairo he "never could break through to" "this fellow Chiang," Roosevelt ceased searching for a personal working relationship with the Chinese leader with regard to postwar Asia.[63] Together with the Chinese government's military setbacks and the Stilwell controversy in 1944, Chiang's difficult attitude at Cairo toward political issues in postwar Asia helped persuade Roosevelt that after the war the KMT regime would not be a reliable partner in international affairs. Amidst the Stilwell controversy, Roosevelt told Ambassador Koo that the United States could not care less about Indochina and that it was free for China to take. At the time Koo did not know how to construe the president's "generosity." In retrospect, Roosevelt must have said these words with disgust about Chongqing's intentions toward Indochina and with disillusionment about the prospect of American–Chinese cooperation in the territory.[64] Later, although in his occasional discussions of Indochina Roosevelt continued to refer to China's cooperation, this was merely part of a fixed rhetoric. Shortly before his death, as the Taussig conversation indicated, China's role in Indochina disappeared even from the rhetoric. Ironically, during the final months of President Roosevelt's life, the Chinese government at last resigned to the idea that China act as a junior partner of the United States in Indochina.

Since late 1944 KMT leaders had been conscious that the stock of "great power China" was in rapid decline in U.S. foreign policy. But, not until the Yalta Conference did they realize how far President Roosevelt would go in reversing his Asian policy based on "great power China." At first they were dismayed by the Chinese government's exclusion from the Yalta Conference; then they were shocked after learning in a piecemeal manner the content of a secret accord on the Far East reached by the conferees. With the Cairo Conference as a precedent, Chinese officials simply could not believe that the U.S. government could conclude agreements with other Allies on East Asia behind China's back. The Yalta Conference suddenly reminded KMT leaders that the international status of their government might not be better than that of the Peking Government during the Paris Peace Conference of 1919. Yalta made a bitter reality crystal clear to Chongqing: China's nominal ranking as one of the Big Four had neither ended its diplomatic isolation nor enabled it to avoid victimization by big power politics. As a result of Yalta, KMT leaders were horrified by the prospect that they would soon have to face an intruding Soviet Red Army in Manchuria.[65]

To avert such a nightmare, Chiang and his senior advisors believed that they would first need a thorough understanding with the United States. Then, talks with Moscow would also be necessary for containing the Soviet military expansion in northeastern China. Under such circumstances, any attempt by Chongqing to assert its predominant position in postwar Indochina would not only be futile but would also hinder the urgent task of improving relations with Washington. Besides, an assertive Indochina policy might even become a precedent to weaken Chongqing's own effort to restrain the Soviet Red Army in Manchuria.[66] Therefore, in April, when the KMT government sent its delegation to the U.N. conference in San Francisco, Chiang Kai-shek was prepared to accept any American program concerning Indochina. He authorized T. V. Soong, head of the Chinese delegation to San Francisco, to support any of the following solutions likely favored by the U.S. government: (1) Indochina's return to France, (2) Indochina under a French trusteeship, and (3) Indochina under a multinational trusteeship. Indochina's independence was conspicuously absent in Chiang's list. The Waijiaobu justified this opportunistic policy by arguing that the most urgent issue for Chongqing was to gain Washington's sympathy through its own cooperative gestures, and that Chinese interests in Indochina could be enhanced under any of the above conditions as long as the Chinese and the American governments were on the same side.[67]

Thus, President Roosevelt's earlier assertion that he had Chiang's "whole-hearted" support to his Indochina policy was finally substantiated by Chongqing's unconditional capitulation to Washington's will. But it was too late for Roosevelt to administer the development. Between April and June, when visiting in the United States, Soong was greeted by the new president, Harry Truman. Their three meetings during these months did not help improve Chongqing's precarious diplomatic position wrought by the Yalta Conference.[68] And, during these meetings, Indochina was not even mentioned. Soon after Soong's arrival in Washington, American Ambassador Patrick Hurley cautioned Chiang that Truman might change his predecessor's Indochina policy. He advised the Chinese government not to bring up the subject with Washington at this moment lest it cause unnecessary misunderstanding.[69]

Historians will likely continue to disagree on the question whether Truman or Roosevelt was to blame for the retreat of Washington's Indochina policy from anticolonialism.[70] It can only be speculated that had Roosevelt lived longer, he might have used the now willing Chinese ally to reinforce his resistance against the British–French pressure in Indochina. Clearly, the Truman presidency guaranteed that there would be no renewal of an American–Chinese partnership on Indochina. During the initial months of the Truman Administration, by comparison with his serious concerns about Moscow's intentions in Europe, President Truman only had a marginal interest in Southeast Asian affairs.[71] And he depended on the State Department's advice in this regard. In his second week in the White House, Truman read and concurred with a State Department memorandum saying that "as a further basis for peace and stability, we favor the establishment by China of close and friendly relations with Korea, Burma, Thailand, Indochina and other neighboring areas, without Chinese domination over such areas." The State Department meant a *French* Indochina.[72]

When the White House was adjusting its attitude toward France and Indochina, a policy gap occurred between Washington and its leading officers in China. In March Japanese troops in Indochina launched a coup to establish Japan's direct control of the area. The five-year collaboration between Japan and the French colonial authorities was thus terminated. As a result, more than five thousand French colonial troops fled into China. In May the FCNL sent General Gabriel Sabattier, commander of the French troops in China, to Chongqing to discuss with Chiang Kai-shek how the "New France" could cooperate with China militarily.[73] No time to wait for a result from T. V. Soong's mission in the United States, Chiang solicited advice from General Wedemeyer and Ambassador Hurley. Wedemeyer advised Chiang not to support the French unless it became absolutely certain that they would use Chinese assistance purely for anti-Japanese operations and that they would operate under Chiang's command. Hurley concurred with Wedemeyer. He informed Chiang of a recent request he sent to Washington for clarification of U.S. Indochina policy, urging Chiang to wait for Washington's response.[74]

In early June a message from the State Department to Hurley resolved the puzzlement in Chongqing about Washington's current policy toward Indochina. While denying any basic change in policy, Hurley was informed that, as accepted by the governments at the Yalta Conference, a voluntary principle would guide the general application of the trusteeship formula for dependent areas. Since a French consent on trusteeship in Indochina "seems unlikely," the message continued, President Truman intended to ask the French government to promise that the Indochina peoples' liberties and self-government be enlarged. Hurley was also instructed that the French offer of assistance in the war against Japan be considered "on their military merits."[75]

Now that Washington's attitude was clarified, the KMT government began to readjust its own policy accordingly. The first public sign of Chongqing's new policy appeared in an editorial of the *Zhongyang Ribao* in late July. Although reiterating Chongqing's intention to "liberate [*jiefang*]" all Japan's insular possessions in the central and northern Pacific, the editorial articulated a new attitude that all territories in Southeast Asia and the southern Pacific should "be restored to their original status [*huifu yuanzhuang*]."[76] By supporting the restoration of the prewar status quo in Southeast Asia, the KMT leadership rescinded its wartime anti-colonialism. Unable to consult Washington directly over Indochina, Chongqing could just pledge its allegiance to American leadership in this manner. But if at the time KMT leaders still harbored a hope to use concessions in Indochina in exchange for Washington's support in Manchuria, the ploy had no effect whatsoever on the American policy during the concurrent Sino–Soviet negotiations in Moscow. Eventually, only by making a number of major concessions at Moscow was Chongqing able to conclude a treaty with the Soviet government.

At war's end, there existed no international agreement on Indochina's postwar status. For the purpose of receiving Japanese surrender, the territory was divided into two occupation zones by an Anglo-American agreement at the Potsdam Conference. British and Chinese troops would occupy separately the southern and northern zones divided by the 16th parallel. Although the Potsdam decision significantly modified Chiang Kai-shek's military authority in Indochina, its assignment of the northern zone to Chongqing reflected an ironic reality: although the Chinese government had fought the Japanese poorly during the war, at war's end the Chinese forces held the strongest military position among the Allies in respect to continental Southeast Asia.[77]

But by this time Chiang was no longer craving for his government to act alone as a "big brother" in supporting Vietnamese independence. The best scenario he could imagine now was Chinese–American cooperation in North Vietnam to counterbalance the British–French combination in the south. At the time, his wife Song Mailing was in the United States to sound out President Truman's intention. On August 29, the same day when Ho Chi Minh declared the establishment of his provisional government in Vietnam, Madam Chiang talked with Truman and queried him about Indochina. Truman responded by expressing his satisfaction with France's willingness to work toward Indochina independence. Madam Chiang then reminded Truman that President Roosevelt had advocated trusteeship for the territory. To this Truman answered bluntly that "as far as he was concerned," the American government had never discussed trusteeship for Indochina.[78]

As a result, in postwar Vietnam the Americans had no responsibilities other than a small military mission for assisting the repatriation of recovered Allied prisoners and observing the Chinese operation of disarming the Japanese. Politically, the U.S. government tried to sit on the fence between Asian nationalism and European colonialism. As defined by a State Department memorandum, the problem for the U.S. government in East Asia was "to harmonize . . . its policies in regard to the two objectives: increased political freedom for the peoples of the Far East and the maintenance of the unity of the leading United Nations."[79] The U.S. government was soon to learn that this position was untenable.

Chongqing could not turn away from Vietnam as easily. Now the Chinese government had to consider under what conditions China would want to live with a restored French colony at its southern frontier. Having seen that Washington jettisoned Roosevelt's trusteeship formula and taken a spectator's position in Indochina, KMT leaders realized that their government alone would have to face the British and the French in the area. At the time, Chongqing's principal asset in dealing with the French was Chinese troops in North Vietnam. In mid-September, however, Chiang began to worry about China's political opportunity in Vietnam when he received a report from Qian Tai, Chongqing's ambassador to the FCNL in Algiers. According to Qian, the French government was planning to despatch 40,000 troops to Vietnam within two months. At the time the Chinese government already installed in North Vietnam a formidable force under General Lu Han. But among these only 38,000 troops were intended for occupation purpose. The rest was destined for transportation to northern China, where a new round of civil war between the KMT regime and the Chinese Communists just began to unfold.[80]

Fearing that he would be unable to maintain China's military superiority in Indochina, Chiang tried for the last time to enlist American support in Indochina. On September 19, Chiang instructed Wang Shijie, who was attending the five-power conference of foreign ministers in London, to revive the trusteeship idea with the Americans and the Russians. Acting upon Chiang's directive, Wang talked to Secretary of State James F. Byrnes, suggesting that either Indochina be put under an international trusteeship or France pledge publicly to grant the territory independence within ten years. Byrnes would abet neither. Wang was not surprised. Later he told Ambassador Koo that he had made the proposals to Byrnes just for "testing him out." Wang's recommendation to Chiang was that negotiations with the French should proceed promptly.[81] By this time even T. V. Soong had given up hope for Sino–American collaboration over Indochina. When Chiang was charging Wang Shijie to make the last ditch effort to pursue the ghost of a Chinese–American partnership in Indochina, Soong vouched to Charles de Gaulle in Paris that the Chinese government would welcome France as its Asian neighbor again and would not in any manner hinder France's rights in Indochina.[82]

In late August 1945, the Chinese occupation of North Vietnam commenced under a fourteen-point program, which directed the Chinese military authorities in Vietnam to consult only with their French counterparts with regard to occupation operations. General Lu Han was at first troubled by the obvious contradiction between the program and China's Indochina policy at the time of the Cairo Conference. He was soon made *au courant* by Chiang himself with regard to Chongqing's current stand.[83] In March 1946, after a few months of bargaining, a series of agreements on Vietnam was concluded between the Chinese and the French governments as part of a general readjustment of their bilateral relationship. Chinese troops in Vietnam proved a useful leverage for winning concessions from the French. But, as of this time, these matters became marginal to the KMT government, for its power to rule China was being decided by its struggle with the Chinese Communists in Manchuria.[84]

* * *

By the end of the Pacific war, it became clear that the wartime American–Chinese diplomacy for recasting Southeast Asia's international order had been a futile exercise. The two governments' efforts to forge a partnership for decolonizing Indochina failed not because their policies lacked new visions or their alliance had no tangible strength to prevent the return of the French colonial rule. In view of the postwar Indochina wars, either Roosevelt's trusteeship formula or Chiang's big-brother device would have changed the political dynamics in Indochina and would likely have averted the first Indochina war between Vietnamese nationalists and French colonialists. Both leaders understood that the Chinese government, with Washington's diplomatic endorsement and financial support, would have to provide the bulk of the occupation forces in postwar Indochina. At war's end, Chinese troops were indeed available for any possible American–Chinese scheme in Indochina.

Other reasons for the failure have to be considered. Both Washington and Chongqing had their particular security needs in the postwar world. President Roosevelt failed to bring the State Department around in respect to Indochina partially because he himself did not totally disagree with the department's argument that the United States would have vital foreign policy needs in postwar Europe. When Truman took over, the contest with the Soviets in Europe further became a fixation in U.S. foreign policy. Washington's Europe-first orientation thus resulted in its correlative deference to European allies' intentions more than to Asian peoples' aspirations in Asia. As for Chiang Kai-shek, his obsession with the Chinese Communists in North China was compounded by Soviet threat from Northeast Asia. Yet, although Chongqing's anti-Soviet foreign policy in the north eventually prompted its compromise with the French in the south, the policy itself was not necessarily a snag to a U.S.–Chinese partnership in Indochina.

The most interesting phenomenon in the American–Chinese diplomacy over Indochina, though, is that their partnership was wrecked by a fundamental disagreement even when both American and Chinese leaders were enthusiastic about a partnership between them. From the very beginning Roosevelt and Chiang had rather different approaches to the Indochina question. In the final analysis, their disagreement was not so much about Indochina's status as about China's new international role. President Roosevelt's pre-Cairo invitation to Chiang for a joint American–Chinese enterprise in Indochina was part and parcel of his paternalistic approach of "making China a great power." His trusteeship formula was intended not only to keep Indochina within the Western orbit but also to retain China as an American client. KMT leaders, some of them vehemently nationalistic, regarded the Pacific war and the ensuing American support to China as favorable conditions for redressing the wrongs that foreign imperialism had inflicted on China during the past century. They wanted to reestablish Chinese influence in former "dependencies" like Korea and Vietnam as but the first step to restore China's centrality in Asian affairs. To these leaders, therefore, the Rooseveltian trusteeship became a refined Western device to limit China's potential. President Roosevelt's fancy about a super client in China and Chinese leaders' dream of a glorious, predominant Chinese state posed a question about what kind of power modern China should become. World War II was the right historical juncture to raise this question, though the question separated the two wartime allies apart and led American officials to consider the need to contain a rising China even before "containment" became a trademark for America's postwar foreign policy in dealing with the Soviet Union. The KMT regime's desperate search for mending its partnership with Washington in the final months of the war did not invalidate the question. Neither did American officials forsake the notion of containment against China, nationalist or communist.

Notes

1. King C. Chen, *Vietnam and China, 1938–1954* (Princeton: Princeton University Press, 1969), 97–98; Stein Tønnesson, *The Vietnamese Revolution of 1945: Roosevelt, Ho Chi Minh and de Gaulle in a World at War* (London: Sage, 1991), 57. In China's wartime foreign policy planning, terms like "Indochina," "Vietnam," and "Annam" were used interchangeably. What Chinese officials really meant was Vietnam, one of the three Indochina countries. This practice will be followed in this chapter.
2. Subcommittee to Investigate the Administration of the Internal Security Act and Other Internal Security Laws of the Committee on the Judiciary, United States Senate, *Morgenthau Diary (China)* (Washington, D.C.: 1st Session of the 89th Congress, 1965), 1: 887.
3. Sun Yat-sen, *San Min Chu I: The Three Principles of the People* (Chungqing: Ministry of Information of the Republic of China, 1943), 7, 34–35.
4. Robert E. Sherwood, *Roosevelt and Hopkins: An Intimate History* (New York: Harper, 1948), 572–573.
5. Zhang Fuochen to Ni Guanghua, January 4, 1944, T. V. Soong papers, box 4. This telegram cites the contents of two despatches that Soong sent to Chiang on his conversations with President Roosevelt in 1942.
6. U.S. Department of State, *Foreign Relations of the United States, 1942* (Washington, D.C.: G.P.O., 1960), 3: 578–581 (hereafter cited as *FRUS* with year or subtitle). Wm. Roger Louis, *Imperialism at Bay: The United States and the Decolonization of the British Empire, 1941–1945* (New York: Oxford University Press, 1978), 155–157, rightfully questions Roosevelt's assertion about Chiang's authorship of the trusteeship idea, calling the president's act "embellishment."
7. Memorandum on Chiang-Currie conversation, August 3, 1942, Currie papers, box 4.
8. *Zhonghua Minguo Zhongyao Shiliao Chubian–Dui Ri Kangzhan Shiqi* (Preliminary compilation of important historical documents of the Republic of China: The period of the war of resistance against Japan), 7 vols, Historical Commission of the Central

Committee of the Kuomintang, comp. (Taipei: Zhongguo Guomindang Zhongyang Weiyuanhui Dangshi Weiyuanhui, 1981), vol. 3, book 1, pp. 700, 703, 715 (hereafter cited as *ZZSC*, volume (book): pages); memorandum, "Excerpt from minutes on my conference with Chiang Kai-shek on August 6, 1942," Lauchlin Currie Papers (Hoover Institution), box 4.

9. Memorandum on Chiang-Currie conversation, August 3, 1942, Currie Papers, box 4. Ibid.
10. *Xian Zongtong Jiang Gong Sixiang Yanlun Zongji* (Complete works of the late President Chiang [Kai-shek]), 40 vols, Historical Commission of the Central Committee of the Kuomintang, comp. (Taipei: Zhongguo Guomindang Zhongyang Weiyuanhui Dangshi Weiyuanhui, 1984. Hereafter cited as *Zongji*), 19: 347, 35: 202–205; *FRUS: China, 1942*, 174.
11. Memorandum, "Re: Chinese post-war aims," December 4, 1942, Currie Papers, box 5.
12. For the issue of Korea, see Chapter 3.
13. *ZZSC*, 3 (2): 773–778; *FRUS, 1942: China*, 749–752, 754–755, 760; *FRUS, 1943: China*, 882–883.
14. *ZZSC*, 3 (3): 97.
15. *ZZSC*, 3 (1): 746–748; *FRUS: China, 1942*, 185–187.
16. "Record of Conversation with the President and Mr. Hopkins," July 16, 1943, T. V. Soong Papers, box 32.
17. Chiang Kai-shek, *China's Destiny* (New York: Roy Publishers, 1947), 58; "Reminiscences of Wellington Koo," (Chinese Oral History Project of the East Asian Institute of Columbia University, New York) 5 (B): 370 (hereafter cited as *RWK*); Waijiaobu memorandum, "The president's [Chiang's] instructions on diplomatic problems," n.d. (1943), and Waijiaobu memorandum, "The status of this department's work for implementing the president's instructions," n.d. (1943), Victor Hoo (Hu Shize) Papers, box 3.
18. *Zhongyang Ribao*, August 7, 1943.
19. *FRUS, Conferences at Cairo and Teheran, 1943*, 325.
20. Jiang Yongjing, *Hu Zhiming Zai Zhongguo: Yige Yuenan Minzuzhuyi Weizhuangzhe* (Ho Chi Minh in China: a feigned Vietnamese nationalist) (Taipei: Zhuanji Wenxue Chubanshe, 1972), 183, 205 n. 22.
21. Cordell Hull, *The Memoirs of Cordell Hull* (New York: MacMillan Company, 1948), 2: 1597; Roosevelt to Hull, January 24, 1944, Roosevelt papers, President's Secretary File (PSF), box 74.
22. Samuel I. Roseman, comp., *The Public Papers and Addresses of Franklin D. Roosevelt; 1944–45 Volume: Victory and the Threshold of Peace* (New York: Random House, 1950), 562–563; memorandum by Chester Hammond on the 33rd meeting of the Pacific War Council, July 21, 1943, Roosevelt Papers, MRF, box 168.
23. There is, of course, the British policy at Cairo to consider. Important studies of the American–British diplomacy over Indochina include Walter La Feber, "Roosevelt, Churchill, and Indochina, 1942–1945," *The American Historical Review*, 80 (1975): 1277–1295, Christopher Thorne, "Indochina and Anglo-American Relations, 1942–1945," *Pacific Historical Review*, 45 (1976): 73–96, and Donald C. Watt, "Britain, America and Indo-China, 1942–1945," in his *Succeeding John Bull: America in Britain's Place, 1900–1975* (Cambridge: Cambridge University Press, 1984), 194–219. These studies agree that before and after the Cairo Conference, the British consistently opposed President Roosevelt's anti-French policy in Indochina.

24. "Indication of Contact with the President on Postwar Matters," n.d., Records of Harley A. Notter (Postwar Planning) (RG 59), box 54 (hereafter cited as Notter records).
25. P-241a, September 30, 1943, Notter records, box 8; T-398, November 2, 1943, Notter records, box 65; T-404, November 9, 1943, ibid.; CAC-66a, February 5, 1944, Notter records, box 109.ST minutes 21, July 2, 1943, Notter records, box 79; P-251a, March 1, 1944, Notter records, box 58.
26. CAC-66a, February 5, 1944, Notter records, box 109; Hull, 2: 1598–1599.
27. PWC-176, May 30, 1944, Stanley K. Hornbeck papers, box 124; CAC-239 preliminary, July 1, 1944, Notter records, 112.
28. CDA-147, April 17, 1944, Notter records, box 123.
29. CDA-147, April 17, 1944, Notter records, box 123; ST minutes 16, May 7, 1943, Notter records, box 79.
30. ST minutes 16, May 7, 1943, Notter records, box 79; ST minutes 21, July 2, 1943, ibid.
31. T minutes 56, November 11, 1943, Records of the Undersecretary of State (Dean Acheson) (RG 59), box 9; T-504 preliminary, July 3, 1944, Notter records, box 67.
32. Waijiaobu program for Dumbarton Oaks, June 7, 1944, Hoo papers, box 3; Waijiaobu memorandum, "Postwar international peace organization and other related issues," n.d. (1944), Hoo Papers, box 7; memorandum by the Supreme Council of National Defense, "Draft program on conditions for Japan to accept when it surrenders unconditionally," n.d. (1944), Hoo Papers, box 8.
33. Waijiaobu memorandum on the Dumbarton Oaks Conference, June 7, 1944, Hoo Papers, box 3; Waijiaobu memorandum, "Postwar international peace organization and other related issues," n.d. (1944), Hoo Papers, box 7.
34. Ibid.; Waijiaobu memorandum, "(D) The Colonial problems in the Pacific and general security problems: policies toward the Dutch Indies that ought to be adopted by our government," June 7, 1944, Hoo papers, box 3.
35. Waijiaobu memorandum, "(D) The colonial problems in the Pacific and general security problems: [a] policy measures regarding Vietnam," June 7, 1944, Hoo Papers, box 3.
36. The latest Chinese occupation of the Tonkin area had taken place between 1420 and 1428, when the Ming emperor of China tried abortively to deny Vietnam independence. The best study of the traditional Vietnamese–Chinese relationship is Keith W. Taylor, *The Birth of Vietnam* (Berkeley: University of California Press, 1983).
37. For instance, in late summer 1943, after breaking diplomatic relations with the Vichy government, the Chinese authorities took unilateral action to assume control of the Chinese section of the Indochina–Yunnan railway, which France had owned according to its treaties with China. The French Committee of National Liberation under Charles de Gaulle asked the U.S. government for help but with no result. See *FRUS, 1943: China*, 889–891.
38. See King C. Chen, 33–99, for an original discussion of Chongqing's wartime relations with Vietnamese partisans.
39. T. V. Soong to Wei Daoming, July 29, 1944, Wellington Koo (Gu Weijun) Papers, box 70; Chiang Kai-shek to Kong Xiangxi, August 19, 1944, ibid.; T. V. Soong to Wei Daoming, September 13, 1944, ibid.; Koo to Chiang Kai-shek, n.d. (1944), Koo Papers, box 68.
40. Michael Schaller, *The U.S. Crusade in China, 1938–1945* (New York: Columbia University Press, 1979), 147–175.
41. Minutes of the meeting of the Chinese delegation, September 9, 1944, Koo Papers, box 75.

42. Jin Wensi, *Waijiao Gongzuo De Huiyi* (Reminiscences on diplomatic missions) (Taipei: Zhuanji Wenxue Chubanshe, 1968), 93; Zhonghua Minguo Waijiaobu, *Zhongguo Zhuwai Ge Dai Gong Shiguan Liren Guanzhang Xianming Nianbiao* (A chart of titles for the heads of China's missions to foreign countries) (Taipei: Shangwu Yinshuguan, 1969), 73; Tønnesson, 55.
43. Jin Wensi, 136–146; Jin Wensi to Waijiaobu, "Report on the settlement of the Dutch Indies problems," March 30, 1944, and "Report on the negotiations for a new Chinese-Dutch treaty," June 22, 1945, Wunsz King (Jin Wensi) Papers, box 1.
44. Koo to Waijiaobu, August 25, 1944, Koo Papers, box 68.
45. Schaller, 173.
46. Ling Qihan, *Zai Henei Jieshou Riben Touxiang Neimu* (Inside story of the receiving of Japanese surrender in Hanoi) (Beijing: Shijie Zhishi Chubanshe, 1984), 32.
47. Chinese Ministry of Information, *China Handbook, 1937–1945* (New York: The MacMillan Company, 1947), 174–175.
48. Wu Nanru to the Supreme Council of National Defense, "Our government's stand on the French Indochina," n.d. (between May and August 1944), file 287, Quanzong Hao (general archival number) 43 (Supreme Council of National Defense Files), Zhongguo Di Er Lishi Dang'anguan (The Second Historical Archives of China), Nanjing.
49. *FRUS, 1942: China*, 749–760; *FRUS, 1943: China*, 882–888; *ZZSC*, 2 (5): 201–206, 213; ibid., 3 (3): 74, 565–566, 606; ibid., 2 (6): 597–602; "Chang Fa-k'uei [Zhang Fakui] Diaries," entry on September 24, 1943, and entry on June 4, 1945, Chang Fa-k'uei (Zhang Fakui) Papers, reel 3, flash no. 2, part 2; Zhang Fakui, "Reminiscences of the war of resistance against Japan," *Wenshi Ziliao Xuanji*, 15 (July 1988), 174, 176, 203; Liu Qi et al., ed., *Yuanzheng Yin Mian Kangzhan* (The crusade in India and Burma to resist Japan) (Beijing: Zhongguo Wenshi Chubanshe, 1990), 1–2, 52–54, 107–110, 151–163; Liang Jingtong, *Shidiwei Shijian* (The Stilwell affair) (Beijing: Shangwu Yinshuguan, 1973), 92–93.
50. Louis, 278; *FRUS, Conferences at Cairo and Teheran*, 887–888; John J. Sbrega, *Anglo-American Relations and Colonialism in East Asia, 1941–1945* (New York: Garland, 1983), 115–157.
51. Grace P. Hayes, *The History of the Joint Chiefs of Staff in World War II: The War Against Japan* (Annapolis: Naval Institute Press, 1982), 627; Wedemeyer to Marshall, July 10, 1945, Wedemeyer Papers, box 1539.
52. *ZZSC*, 3 (3): 270–271; Thorne, 301.
53. Zhongyang Yenjiuyuan Jindaishi Yenjiusuo, *Guomin Zhengfu Yu Hanguo Duli Yundong Shiliao* (Historical materials on the nationalist government and Korea independence movement) (Taipei: Zhongyang Yenjiuyuan Jindaishi Yenjiusuo, 1988), 617–622.
54. "Note on conversation with Cordell Hull and with Stanley Hornbeck on September 22, 1943," Soong Papers, box 30.
55. Soong to Chiang, January 4, 1944, Soong papers, box 4. For backgrounds of the French statements in question, see Evelyn Colbert, *Southeast Asia in International Politics, 1941–1956* (Ithaca: Cornell University Press, 1977), 38–39, and Tønnesson, 135–136.
56. *FRUS, 1944: China*, 1165.
57. State Department memorandum for the Joint Chiefs of Staff, August 12, 1944, Records of the Office of Chinese Affairs (RG 59), box 11; *FRUS, 1944: China*, 1167–1169.
58. *FRUS, 1944: China*, 1166, 1169.

59. Memo by the Office of European Affairs, "American Policy with regard to Indochina," June 30, 1944, Acheson records, box 9.
60. *FRUS, 1944*, 3: 769–784; La Feber, "Roosevelt, Churchill, and Indochina: 1942–1945," 1290–1291.
61. *FRUS, 1945*, 1: 124.
62. See, for instance, Louis, *Imperialism at Bay*, 28; Watt, *Succeeding John Bull*, 216; La Feber, "Roosevelt, Churchill, and Indochina," 1295; and Kimball, *Juggler*, 153.
63. Edgar Snow, *Random Notes on Red China, 1936–1945* (Cambridge: Harvard University Press, 1974), 127.
64. Gu Weijun (Wellington Koo), *Gu Weijun Huiyilu* (Memoirs of Gu Weijun) (Beijing, Zhonghua Shuju, 1987), 5: 577–578.
65. RWK, 5 (E): 841, 864–866, 869–872; *ZZSC*, 3 (2): 542–543.
66. This latter point was not missed by the U.S. State Department's planning staff. In a planning document, CAC-66a, February 5, 1944, Notter records, box 109, the French fear of Chongqing's designs in Tonkin and the Chinese fear of Moscow's designs in Manchuria were both discussed.
67. Chiang to Soong, April 3, 1945, Koo papers, box 81; Waijiaobu to Chiang Kai-shek, "Report for approval with regard to the programs that are intended for discussion with the American, British, and Soviet governments outside the San Francisco Conference," March 25, 1945, ibid.
68. RWK, 5(E): 836; Harry Truman, *Memoirs by Harry S. Truman: Year of Decisions* (New York: Doubleday, 1955), 1: 81, 90–91, 296–298; *ZZSC*, 3 (2): 548–549.
69. *ZZSC*, 3 (1): 210–217.
70. For two different arguments, see Gary R. Hess, "Franklin Roosevelt and Indochina," *The Journal of American History*, 59 (September 1972): 353–368; La Feber, "Roosevelt, Churchill, and Indochina, 1942–1945."
71. Melvyn P. Leffler, *A Preponderance of Power: National Security, the Truman Administration, and the Cold War* (Stanford: Stanford University Press, 1992), 92; George C. Herring, "The Truman Administration and the Restoration of French Sovereignty in Indochina," *Diplomatic History*, 1 (Spring 1977): 97–117.
72. Truman, 1: 121.
73. Jiang Yongjing, 210–212; Archimedes L. A. Patti, *Why Viet Nam? Prelude to America's Albatross* (Berkeley: University of California Press, 1980), 88, 94–95.
74. "Minutes of Meeting No. 58 with the Generalissimo [Chiang Kai-shek], 28 May 1945," Wedemeyer papers, box 1550; Patti, 106.
75. Grew to Hurley, June 7, 1945, Top Secret General Records of Chungking Embassy, China, 1945, box 1.
76. *Zhongyang Ribao*, July 24, 1945.
77. When the British occupation in South Vietnam began in mid-September, General Douglas D. Gracy had under his command only one battalion of his 20th Indian Division plus a reconstituted French company. Unprepared for the difficult task, later Gracy had to rely on the surrendered Japanese troops to maintain order under the 16th parallel. See, Patti, 298, 307, 562 notes 4 and 5; Ellen J. Hammer, *The Struggle for Indochina, 1940–1955: Viet Nam and the French Experience* (Stanford: Stanford University Press, 1966), 113.
78. *FRUS, 1945*, 7: 540–542.

79. Ronald H. Spector, *Advice and Support: The Early Years of the U.S. Army in Vietnam, 1941–1960* (New York: Free Press, 1985), 53–54; PR-18 Preliminary-a, August 31, 1945, Notter records, box 119.
80. Actually, the postwar military balance of power in Indochina would remain in favor of China till the end of the Chinese occupation. In March 1946, when Chongqing signed agreements with the French government to settle the Indochina question and other bilateral issues between them, there were about 185,000 Chinese troops in North Vietnam. The French troops in the south only numbered 15,000. See Spector, 52, and Hammer, 152.
81. Chiang to Wang Shijie, September 19, 1945, Koo papers, box 57; Wang to Chiang, September 22, 1945, ibid.; RWK, 5 (E): 887.
82. Ling Qihan, 5.
83. Ibid., 5–7, 13–15, 130–131.
84. For the relationship between the KMT government's Indochina policy and the Chinese Civil War of 1945–1949, see Ling Qihan, *Zai Henei Jieshou Riben Touxiang Neimu*, and King C. Chen, *Vietnam and China, 1938–1954*, chs. 3 and 4.

CHAPTER FIVE

Reassert Chinese Authority in a Frontier

Among those "dependencies" of the Chinese Empire that in the process of China's territoriality transformation became either externalized or internalized to the Chinese national state, Mongolia stood out as a unique case. Although during the Qing Dynasty the Mongols constituted one of the ethnic constituencies of the empire, the Manchu statecraft maintained distinctions between Inner Mongolia and Outer Mongolia. The two parts went in different directions in their relations with the Chinese state in the twentieth century. When World War II ended in Asia, the Outer Mongols' three-decade long struggle for independence saw a decisive result. In the meantime, the Inner Mongols stayed in the Chinese side of the border and strived for materializing their political aspirations within the frame of the Chinese state. Modern politics separated issues like Mongolia and those like Korea and Vietnam into "domestic" and "foreign" affair categories. During World War II the former hardly made to the glamorous stage of international diplomacy. In the postwar years, however, it was such "domestic" problems that became critical to both the shape of China's "geo-body" and the color of China's political system.

In August 1945, a Sino–Soviet treaty was concluded, which, among other things, led to the KMT government's recognition of the independence of the Mongolian People's Republic (MPR), which had existed in practice in the past two decades. The MPR thus became one of the first countries to gain full-fledged independence in the wake of World War II. Yet, the fact that this development was part of a momentous trend of national self-determination in the world soon became obscured in the Cold War nimbus. In the postwar years the MPR was denigrated by Western powers as the Soviet Union's oldest satellite (in comparison to the other lesser "Eastern bloc" countries). The KMT government also cried foul play on the part of Moscow in separating the MPR from China. In 1953, four years after being ousted to Taiwan by the Chinese Communist Party (CCP), in an exercise of blaming foreign causes for its failure in China, the KMT government nullified all the agreements that it had concluded with the Russians in 1945, including that concerning the MPR.[1]

The 1953 about-face of the KMT's Mongolia policy was a public demonstration that the KMT never accepted the MPR independence as a fulfillment of the Mongolian people's right of self-determination. But, in the late 1940s, the "Mongolian question" went far beyond the Chinese central authorities' attitude toward the status of a "peripheral" people; the question was tied closely to the KMT regime's own fate. In the first place, the KMT regime's 1945 agreement on MPR independence was offered as a quid pro quo for Moscow's promise not to assist the KMT's cardinal domestic enemy, the CCP. Then, after conceding a hard border between China and the MPR for a wrong reason (the CCP), the KMT regime embarked on a road to ruin by hopelessly upholding a set of rigid, conservative policies about the "soft boundaries" between the Chinese and the Inner Mongols in the years to come.[2] In other words, by intransigently refusing to deal with the "Mongolian question" as a matter of Mongolian national self-determination, the KMT regime cost itself dearly in a triangular contest with the CCP and Inner Mongols in North and Northeast China.

Manchuria and Inner Mongolia in postwar China., enlarged part of “Zhonghua Minguo Wai Menggu.”

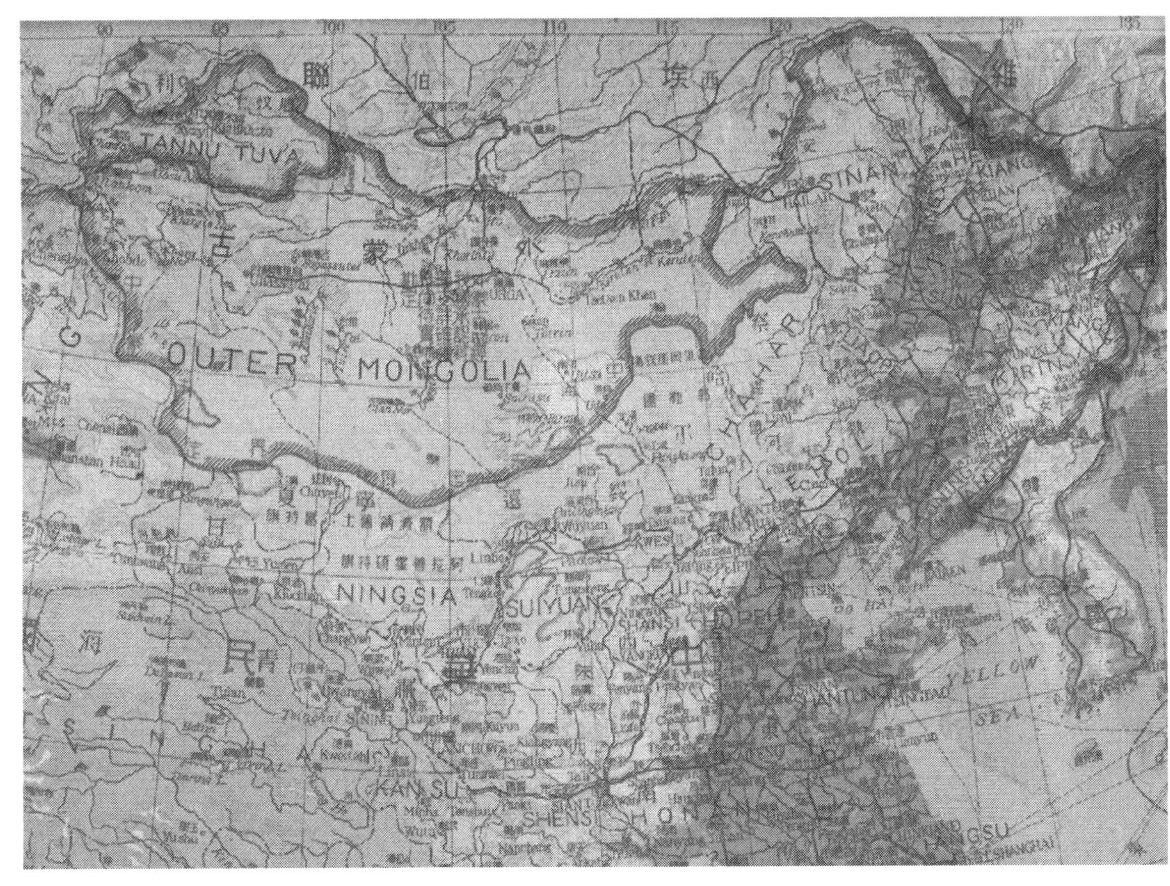

Source: http://commons.wikimedia.org/wiki/file:1947_zhonghua_minguo_quantu.png#filehistory. The original publisher cannot be verified

"Mongolian Question"

The birth of the Republic of China in the early twentieth century was greeted by events that once more threatened to redefine the very conception of "China." Among these were developments that resulted in Outer Mongolia's practical separation from China.[3] Never declaring Outer Mongolia a "lost territory," Chinese officials nevertheless admitted that the eventual solution of the "Mongolian question," meaning the "recovery" of Outer Mongolia, would have to involve diplomacy with the government in Moscow. Meanwhile, successive Chinese governments in the republic period, either in the hands of warlords or KMT partisans, took steps to erase the "inner" part of the question, that is, Inner Mongolia, from China's political landscape. The orientation resulted in complete disappearance of Inner Mongolia's name from China's political map after 1928 and the area's severe sinicization in both cultural and demographic terms. So, at the end of World War II, for the KMT government, the question of Inner Mongolia did not even exist. Yet, like any other ethnic questions of the modern times, although the question of Inner Mongolia could be renamed, painted in different colors, or wrapped up in various forms, it could not be entirely obliterated.

The development of Inner Mongolian nationalism prior to World War II was best described and reported to the outside world by Owen Lattimore, a prolific and acute American observer of China's Inner Asian frontier. The Inner Mongols' prewar drive for autonomy developed around Prince Demchugdongrub (Prince De), *zasag* of the West Sunid Banner. In the 1930s, when China was struggling alone against Japanese encroachment, KMT leaders became briefly willing to use the "way of controlling the remote through mollification" (*rou yuan zhi dao*) to appease frontier regimes and ethnic groups. In September 1933, one and a half years after Japan created its puppet Manchukuo, the KMT government reluctantly permitted Prince De to set up a powerless "Mongolian Autonomous Political Council." Such a meager allowance did not satisfy the Mongolian prince and, two years later, he began to collaborate openly with the Japanese. In September 1939, under Japan's protection, Prince De became the head of a "Coalition Autonomous Government of the Mongolian Frontier."[4] About the melodrama between the KMT and Prince De, Lattimore wrote: "He [Prince De] has not 'gone over' to Japan; he has been tied hand and foot and thrown to the Japanese [by the KMT regime]."[5]

The KMT regime viewed the threat from Japan as a reason to double its effort to extinguish non-Han peoples' ethnopolitical aspirations, which, like the continual challenge from the CCP, were deemed detrimental to the already weak Chinese state. During the 1930s and 1940s, the Chinese–Japanese conflict constituted a powerful stimulus to Chinese, or Han, nationalism. By the time when the undeclared Sino–Japanese war began in the summer of 1937, the KMT's presentation of Chinese nationalism, as its official ideology, had already gone through a few versions. The time had been long passed since the KMT supported "five-race republic" (*wu zu gonghe*) in China and the non-Han peoples' right of national self-determination.[6] Under Chiang Kai-shek, the KMT had become largely a partisan sheath for a military driving toward political centralization. China's war with Japan provided the KMT with one more justification to pursue its "one nation, one state" doctrine.[7] In the war years, Chiang personally set the tone for the party's official rhetoric that denied China's multinational character. His racial-nationalist theory was spelled out in the notorious book, *China's Destiny*, issued in 1943, in which China was depicted as a one-nation country that in history had absorbed many "clans" (*zongzu*, or *zongzhi*).[8]

Under this assumption, those undeniable interethnic tensions in China became mere "frontier problems" involving some peculiar, undefined groups. To KMT officials, the Inner Mongols' demand for autonomy was no more than some Mongolian aristocrats' self-promoting scheme. Thus, officially, the KMT government did not have a policy about ethnic issues as such, but just one concerning the administration of frontier regions. In the war years, KMT documents categorized the borderlands as either "remote frontiers" (*yuan bian*) or "near frontiers" (*jin bian*). The distinction between the two types was made not in any geographical sense, but only according to the degrees of their political, economic, and cultural proximity to China. For instance, Inner Mongolia was viewed as one of the "near frontiers," even though it was geographically more remote to Chongqing, the KMT's wartime capital in southwest China, than was Tibet, which by definition was a "remote frontier."[9]

During World War II, the KMT regime supported the principle of national self-determination in the international scene in order to promote Chinese prestige among Asian nations vis-à-vis Western colonial powers. Meanwhile, the KMT regime denied any relevance of the principle with regard to China's "frontier affairs." From their experience in the past, KMT officials were convinced that the government's concessions to "frontier" groups would only invite more troubles. A case often cited was the KMT government's prewar effort to "mollify" Prince De, which ultimately seemed to prove the folly of the conciliatory approach. The government's obvious double standard on the issue of national self-determination eventually caused a sense of embarrassment among Chinese diplomats. Late in World War II, officials of the foreign ministry suggested to restrain China's criticism of Western countries' colonial problems and opposed inclusion of the principle of national self-determination in the U.N. charter. They feared that China's aggressiveness in these matters could invite other governments' meddling in China's alienated frontiers like Mongolia, Xinjiang, and Tibet.[10]

Yet, in Owen Lattimore's view, the KMT regime did not have to be caught in such a self-wrought predicament. In the summer of 1941, in an attempt to facilitate American assistance to China's war effort, President Franklin D. Roosevelt recommended Lattimore to Chiang Kai-shek as a personal advisor. During his one-and-half-year tenure in Chongqing, Lattimore engaged KMT leaders in discussions of China's frontier questions and even presented a few memoranda on relevant topics to Chiang himself.[11] These documents criticized the Chinese government's policy of sinicization in the past and urged the Chinese officialdom to pay close attention to the importance of ethnic minorities. Sensitive to the KMT regime's drive for national unity and political centralization, Lattimore suggested that a change of the government's orientation toward the frontier peoples might as well serve its own purposes. The key was to attract the peoples of Mongolia and Xinjiang with right policies, but not to alienate them further by use of coercive means. Among Lattimore's concrete policy suggestions, the measures to foster non-Han peoples' cultural autonomy stood out. He recommended that the KMT learn from the Soviet model, citing Moscow's method of dealing with minority nationalities as "one of the most successful Soviet policies." At the beginning of a memo on Inner Mongolia, Lattimore wrote: "Settlement of all Inner Mongolian problems is inseparably connected with the full recovery of the Northeast."[12] These words would prove prescient for the postwar KMT–CCP contest in these areas.

Lattimore, however, had little impact on the KMT thinking about the frontier question. After reading Lattimore's memoranda, Wang Chonghui, secretary-general of the Supreme Council of National Defense (SCND), commented that while making some good points, Lattimore underestimated the Soviet factor in the Xinjiang and (Outer) Mongolian situations, which, in Wang's opinion, was the "cause of the particularization" (*teshuhua*) of these regions.[13] Wang was in charge of the KMT government's wartime policy planning. His opinion about "foreign factors" in China's "frontier affairs" was well shared among KMT officials. Thus, in the war years, as Japan occupied a great portion of Inner Mongolia, KMT officials easily treated Inner Mongols' continuous aspiration for autonomy in such a way as if it was a new "Mongolian question" fostered by the Japanese. Indeed, as a CCP document of the time observes, Japan's policies among the Inner Mongols were effective because they simply reversed the KMT's prewar measures.[14] But, when contemplating postwar policies toward the Mongolian populace, the KMT government did not begin with a reevaluation of its earlier orientations. Instead, its policy planning focused on how to accomplish the task of overcoming the Japanese legacy, meaning Japanese-organized political and cultural institutions and Japanese-affected anti-Chinese social psychology in Inner Mongolia.

In the KMT regime's wartime planning documents, the official terminology used for the government's postwar goal in Inner Mongolia, "restoration of the Mongolian banners" (*mengqi fuyuan*), precluded any consideration of meaningful reforms of the government's frontier policies. The whole issue was reduced to a small part of China's postwar demobilization. Toward the war's end, when a disagreement did emerge among KMT officials concerning the definition of "restoration," it was between those who wanted a complete return to the prewar (pre-Japanese) conditions and those who favored a selective preservation of Japanese establishments for the sake of a more effective governmental control over the Mongolian banners. Of course, neither of these went beyond the ideological realm set by Chiang's *China's Destiny*.[15]

Between late 1944 and early1945, the Mongolian and Tibetan Affairs Commission (MTAC) of the Chinese government, in pursuance of the fundamentals set forth in Chiang's book, produced a few "principles" to guide the government's postwar policy toward the frontier regions. The policy was to hold the "interest of national defense as the standard, national equality as the basis, and formation of all racial groups into one state-nation [*guo zu*] as the ultimate goal." Under this formula, any autonomous sentiment in the frontiers would be antithetic to the KMT's nation-building objectives. As for Outer Mongolia and Tibet, the two regions where the Chinese authorities lost control, the MTAC suggested that "high-degree self-government" be offered to them to lure them back to the Chinese orbit. But the Inner Mongols and other non-Han frontier peoples, since they were already under the authorities of various Chinese provinces, should only seek "local autonomy" in the same manner as the local Han communities. Mindful of the proposition, made by Lattimore as well as some liberal elements in the KMT, that the Soviet federation of republics and the British Commonwealth could serve as models for China's readjustment of internal ethnic relations, the MTAC contended that only its own formula was suitable to China's particular conditions and needs.[16]

Throughout the war, the KMT government's general attitude toward non-Han peoples' autonomy was summarily expressed in a question posed by Zhu Jiahuan, head of the party's organizational department in the early 1940s: "With the skin gone, where can the hair adhere to?" The "skin" was the supposedly solid Chinese interior, and the "hair" the vacillating ethnic frontiers.[17] To the KMT officials' dismay, when World War II concluded in Asia, their government did not hold a "skin" position to attract the "hair." So far as the "Mongolian question" was concerned, the KMT government found in its hand a situation far more intricate than a mere "Japanese legacy."

"International Conspiracy"

At war's end, released from the straitjacket of the Sino–Japanese war, Inner Mongolian nationalism got a new breath of life. Several Inner Mongolian groups of different political persuasions took action in seeking a new future for their people. By far the most popular autonomous movement emerged in eastern Inner Mongolia. Led by a group of assorted individuals, including secret partisans having Soviet connections and former officials of the Japanese-supported Manchukuo regime, the movement posed a challenge both to the hard international border between China and the MPR and the soft inter-ethnic fault line between the Han and the Inner Mongols within China.[18]

The KMT regime did not learn about these developments immediately. During the initial months of peace, the KMT government lacked information about the conditions in North and Northeast China. Its intelligence network only began to catch up in early 1946. The initial reports pointed to an international conspiracy involving the Russians, the Outer Mongols, and the CCP. According to a KMT "top secret" report dated March 1, 1946, Soviet leaders, including Stalin himself, discussed the issue of Inner Mongolia early in the year. They allegedly decided that "no matter how our [KMT] government would evolve, the Soviet Union will continue its decided orientation toward Inner Mongolia, that is, to lure Inner Mongolia into independent autonomy (*duli zizhi*)." The same report also included Moscow's "directive" to a "puppet eastern Mongolian autonomous republic and communist league." Moscow allegedly ordered these organizations to control as large as possible the territory of Manchuria. If in the process they encountered difficulties with KMT troops, the "directive" advised, the Mongols could count on the assistance of the Soviet Red Army. Another piece of intelligence reported Moscow's instruction to MPR leaders on giving military assistance to the CCP and a "Comintern army" in Inner Mongolia and Manchuria in the event that the KMT government failed to produce "proper solutions" in these areas. It was also reported that the eastern Inner Mongols received from the Russians 150 thousand Japanese rifles, three thousand Soviet automatic rifles, and other light weapons.[19]

Reports like these seemed credible to KMT leaders but were in fact misleading or erroneous. For instance, by 1946, the Comintern had been dissolved for three years. There was neither an autonomous republic nor a communist league nor a Comintern army in eastern Inner Mongolia. In January 1946, the eastern Mongolian autonomous government declared its "high-degree self-government" (*gaodu zizhi*) but still named the Chinese republic as its "suzerain state" (*zongzhu guo*). It never identified itself as a "republic."[20] The alleged Soviet policies on Inner Mongolia's independence and on the MPR's involvement in the KMT–CCP civil war were out of cadence with Moscow's China policy of the time, which was to maintain a "correct" stand in the Chinese turmoil. As for Soviet military assistance for the eastern Inner Mongols, it occurred only on a small scale during the Soviet occupation of Manchuria. Otherwise, in October 1945, the eastern Inner Mongols' small security garrison recovered on its own an unknown number of weapons abandoned by the Japanese near Solon, site of the Solon Banner then under the Soviet control. KMT agents seem to have blown up that event into a story about Soviet aid to eastern Mongolia.[21] As for the many alleged meetings between CCP, Soviet, and MPR officials, the KMT simply did not possess reliable sources for such sensitive information.

By nature, any intelligence is probably not completely free of misinformation or misconstruction of facts; yet the KMT intelligence about Inner Mongolia was exceptionally biased. According to the recollection of a member of the KMT's intelligence establishment, except for some secret contact with Prince De's regime in western Inner Mongolia, in the war years the KMT intelligence organizations' knowledge about eastern Inner Mongolia and the vast pastoral area in between was "almost a blank." After the war, the KMT government was anxious to find out Soviet and MPR intentions in Inner Mongolia. In the process it adopted a predetermined syllogism: the Soviet Union wanted to dominate Mongolia and Manchuria; there was no difference between the Russians, the Outer Mongols, and the CCP; and the Soviet bloc was bound to come to conflict with China and the United States. The intelligence network's task was to verify these assumptions. Consequently, intelligence operatives in the field concerned themselves mainly with answering uniform questionnaires from their superiors sitting in the capital, Exaggeration, distortion, and fabrication of "facts" became necessary practices for them to provide recipes catering to their superiors' particular tastes.[22] Such so-called intelligence was therefore more reflective of KMT policy makers' own mind-set than of the actual developments in Inner Mongolia and the Northeast.

This is not to say that there was no international involvement in the ethnopolitics of China's northern frontier. After Japan surrendered, the brief Soviet–MPR occupation in North China and Manchuria created opportunities for MPR personnel to actively agitate among Inner Mongols for a unified Mongolia.[23] The problem was that KMT leaders were too anxious in blaming international irregularities to see the intraethnic nature of the MPR agitation. In other words, the "Outer" and "Inner" Mongols were ethnically identical in that they had been similarly alienated in the past by the policies and practices of the Chinese authorities. In addition, the KMT's constant accusation about international conspiracies did not accord with the actual international conditions in Inner Mongolia, which were constantly changing. Toward the end of 1945, according to a piece of information obtained by the KMT's Northeast Field Headquarters, the Soviet military authorities in Manchuria had informed eastern Mongolian leaders that the Soviet government, because of a concern about international criticism, would be unable to provide assistance to Inner Mongolia's "independence movement."[24] This information was accurate, but it did not alter the KMT authorities' overall estimate of the Soviet intention in Inner Mongolia.

With or without the Soviets' direct involvement, KMT leaders were convinced of the existence of an international conspiracy. For one thing, after recognizing MPR independence, the KMT saw Outer Mongolia change from a thorny "internal problem" into a constant source of international troubles. For another, as long as the CCP (which was always regarded by Chiang Kai-shek and his associates as a mere instrument of Moscow) had a hand in Inner Mongolia, the international conspiracy was a present and real danger to China's integrity. From the point of view of the KMT officials, there was no lack of evidence to incriminate the CCP for agitating among the "ignorant and poor Mongolian masses." The KMT reporting on CCP–Inner Mongolian relations, however, often contained massive misrepresentation of CCP intentions and stubbornly refused to admit that the Inner Mongols were capable of spontaneous nationalist aspirations. Yet again, accuracy was unimportant as long as the intelligence seemed to bear out the KMT leadership's convictions.[25]

The KMT leadership's obsession with international conspiracies should be understood in historical context. After all, the Chinese government had just signed Outer Mongolia away under Soviet pressure during the Moscow negotiations, and foreign influence continued to loom large over the KMT regime's relations with Tibet and Xinjiang. In addition, during the initial postwar months, the government's "takeover" operations in North China and the Northeast ran into serious difficulties because of the CCP competition and Soviet entanglement. But, it should be pointed out that these frustrations could also have led to a different reaction.

Actually, different opinions existed even within the KMT itself. Between the summer of 1945 and the spring of 1946, a so-called reform group became quite active during the KMT's sixth national congress and the following second plenary session. Some high-ranking KMT officials regarded the development as serious "deterioration of the party discipline."[26] On these occasions, the "reformers," appalled by the deteriorating conditions of the northern frontier, demanded democracy within the party, advocated overturn of the recent Sino–Soviet treaty, and urged Chiang to dismiss the apparently ineffective Xiong Shihui, commander of the Northeast Field Headquarters, from his post. Notably, they also favored a renovation of the party's frontier policies. Chiang had to reason with these people but at times felt it necessary to use intimidation to keep them in line. In the end, the "reformers" proved ineffectual in most of their demands. But, in respect to frontier policies, their dissension did bring about some results on paper.[27] The sixth congress acknowledged the party's lack of effort in the past to help "frontier peoples" (*bianjiang ge zu*) and agreed to add "realization of a high-degree self-government by the Mongols and Tibetans" to the party's current interpretation of the Three People's Principles. Then, in early 1946, the second plenum adopted a more detailed resolution on frontier issues that included a promise to restore the prewar Mongolian political council.[28]

In such an atmosphere, Chiang was compelled to defend his foreign policy in front of the Chinese public and also to make some tantalizing gestures toward the non-Han peoples of China. In modern China, perhaps nothing else could be more shameful to China's collective memory than "unequal treaties" and "lost territories." Understandably, the Sino–Soviet treaty of August 1945 with Outer Mongolia on the price tag was not well received by the members of the KMT and the Chinese public. With the KMT's turbulent national congress in the background, Chiang was anxious to polish the public image of his foreign policy. In late August 1945, he delivered a speech at the Supreme Council of National Defense. Concealing from his audience the fact that KMT negotiators in Moscow had treated Outer Mongolia as a bargaining chip in exchange for the Soviets' cooperation in the CCP question, Chiang described the Moscow diplomacy as a logical step to implement the KMT's promise to support weaker nations' right to autonomy. To make himself sound more convincing, Chiang promised to "ensure equality for all the nationalities (*minzu*) within the country" and to give a sympathetic hearing to demands for self-government or independence made by "frontier nationalities situated in regions outside the provinces."[29] For a moment, "high-degree self-government" seemed perhaps not utterly impossible for frontier peoples.

The Inner Mongols were responsive to the gesture. In January 1946, in its inaugural manifesto, the eastern Mongolian autonomous government cited Chiang's speech in justifying its legality. The eastern Mongols actually expressed gratitude to the KMT leader.[30] Soon, an eastern Mongolian delegation was dispatched from Wangiin Sume (Wangyemiao in Chinese, today's Ulanhot) to Chongqing with a petition for recognition. Seeing what was coming, the KMT government held an interdepartmental meeting and decided to receive the delegation in the capital. But Xiong Shihui, then squatting in Peiping (today's Beijing) and fuming over the Soviets' uncooperativeness in Manchuria, intercepted the mission and then turned it back. He did not believe that the government would be able to accomplish anything in receiving the delegation.[31] Thus, a chance for the KMT to develop a political strategy regarding eastern Mongolia was lost.

The occasion, however, was in fact never much of a chance for the eastern Inner Mongols. The delegation would not have been able to accomplish its mission even if it had reached Chongqing, which was to get the KMT government's recognition of the eastern Mongolian government. First, Chiang Kai-shek's speech, a major reason for the eastern Mongolian mission, was a propaganda piece that did not break any new ground for the KMT's ethnic policy. Indeed, the speech's terminology sounded fresh. Unlike Chiang's *China's Destiny*, which used the term *minzu* (nation or nationality) only to denote the state-nation (as in *zhonghua minzu)* and used the term *zongzu* (clan) to refer to non-Han peoples in China, Chiang's speech used *minzu* throughout to refer to non-Han peoples. This seemed a good sign to the Chinese-reading eastern Mongolian leaders. Yet, the new usage did not change the KMT government's policy of denying a nationality status to the Inner Mongols or any other non-Han people. As a matter of fact, when Chiang's speech was issued in English, its official translators carefully converted all the references of non-Han peoples as *minzu* into "racial groups" but not "nations" or "nationalities." The speech also treated these "racial groups" differently. Its special reference to peoples in "regions outside the provinces" effectively excluded Inner Mongols and the Moslem peoples of Xinjiang, both of which were "within the provinces," from the benefit of the so-called new policy.[32] In other words, the "new policy" was designed to dupe Tibet, the only territory remaining outside the Chinese provinces after the MPR's independence, into rescinding its de facto separation from China; it promised no autonomy to non-Han peoples in areas that were administered as provinces. Chiang's speech therefore continued the old policy of differentiating between the "remote" and "near" frontiers.

Secondly, even if the central government, for various reasons, had been willing to make a change of policy regarding frontier peoples' autonomy, it would have encountered a strong resistance from its regional apparatuses. At the time, KMT officials in Manchuria and Inner Mongolia urged the central government not to tolerate eastern Inner Mongolia's "peculiar autonomy" (*teshu zizhi*), lest it undermine the government's anti-CCP operations. Wu Huanzhang, the designated governor of the Xing'an province who never reached his post, argued that in Manchuria, the Mongols and the Han people had long become economically and culturally interdependent, and that political difficulties in the region could be reduced if the Mongolian league system, in his opinion the last barrier between the Han and the Mongols, was completely abrogated. The KMT authorities in the Rehe province agreed, contending that the real problem in the area was the obsolete Mongolian banner system. Allegedly the system blocked the government's anti-Communist pacification campaigns.[33] A report from Suiyuan repudiated the notion that in the area the Han–Mongolian relationship was one between the ruler and the ruled or the oppressor and the oppressed. Instead, the report contended that it was the Mongols who were privileged in many aspects, and, without the incitement from a small group of ambitious elements, they would have lived together with the Han "harmoniously like brothers." The authors of the report warned against any encouragement by the KMT central government to the Inner Mongols' autonomous tendency, asserting "the beneficiary will learn to appreciate the bounties from his patron only after the patron's power is established."[34]

KMT officials, however, did have some inkling of the difference between the postwar popular movement in Inner Mongolia and the prewar movement under Prince De. A theory afloat was that autonomous aspirations were high in certain Mongolian areas not because the Inner Mongols longed for autonomy but because the "fainthearted Mongolian youth" had fallen for the "CCP's temptation," thus identifying the youth, not the traditional elites, as the core of the postwar movement. In the case of the CCP, the knowledge of the popular character of the Inner Mongolian autonomous movement resulted in the party's diligent effort to channel the mass movement into its own orbit. For the KMT, ironically, this knowledge only fostered a complacent attitude among responsible officials. Fu Zuoyi was the commanding officer of the KMT's "takeover" operations in Suiyuan and Chahar. He did not believe that Inner Mongolia's autonomous movement deserved too much attention because, as he once guaranteed to Chiang Kai-shek, "there is absolutely no problem among princes of the Suiyuan Mongols." In the Northeast, Xiong Shihui was of the same mind and was strongly opposed to a proposition that the KMT government change its reliance on Mongolian princes in managing Inner Mongolian affairs. He advised Chiang that "the gravity of the Mongolian society still rests on its honest members," meaning the upper echelon of the Inner Mongolian society.[35]

In sum, despite its resolutions and public statements on frontier matters around the end of war, the KMT government did not for a moment give up its invariable drive for forging a "Great Chinese Nation" (*da zhonghua minzu*) through assimilating non-Han peoples. Except for Outer Mongolia and Tibet, "self-government" for frontier non-Han peoples was qualified as "local," which in the KMT official terminology meant merely autonomy for communities, Han and non-Han, below the county level. Under this definition, the Mongolian political council promised by the KMT's second plenum, if ever established, would have been a mere titular body.[36] As a matter of fact, in early September 1945, just ten days after Chiang's well-publicized speech, the Ministry of Interior quietly modified the wording of its internal planning documents. The controversial phrase "high-degree self-government" was replaced with the conventional "local autonomy." The original use of the ethnic-territorial term "Inner Mongolia" was also replaced with the Chinese-centric term "frontier." Soon, the Executive Yuan (Council) instructed its branches that the term "Inner Mongolia" should be avoided altogether in government documents because it had been used by the Japanese to promote Inner Mongols' separation from China.[37] Thus, under the KMT's postwar statist drive, in the name of "restoration," even this originally China-centric term became politically incorrect.

"Restoration"

"Restoration" (*fuyuan* or *huifu*) was a term widely used in postwar China. Yet, to different groups of people, its meaning varied tremendously. To most Inner Mongols, "restoration" meant a rollback of Chinese provinces in Inner Mongolia and reestablishment of the ethnic territory according to its "original" geographic features. To Chinese officials at the local levels the term meant resumption of their prewar duties. But to the central authorities of the KMT government, "restoration" of the Mongolian banners actually meant expansion of its control to areas that it had never been able to reach before the war. In this sense, the KMT government's Inner Mongolia policy became less about Inner Mongolian nationalism than about Chinese nationalism. In other words, the KMT government's takeover operations in the northern frontier renewed the Chinese nationalist Northern Expedition that had started in the mid-1920s but fallen short of reaching its goal. A problem for the KMT regime, however, was that the CCP, a collaborator in the Northern Expedition, also revived its northward effort after Japan's surrender. This time, the CCP was the KMT's deadly competitor.

Pursuing a long-standing dream of national unification and battling along the way an "international communist fifth column," the KMT leadership found the theme of Chinese nationalism vitally important. Chiang Kai-shek attached such importance to the theme that in March 1948, a difficult moment in his war against the CCP, he used his small air force to carry out an airborne propaganda campaign, seeking to use "cardinal principles of righteousness" and "nationalist conscience" to censure the CCP and to expose how the CCP was merely a tool of Moscow. Later in the year, Chiang told his generals that "nationalist conscience can overcome the fifth column that relies on foreign influence," and therefore the government troops must "strengthen their nationalist conscience and use the spirit of resistance against Japan to annihilate the bandits [the CCP]."[38] Many years later, a former KMT official would recall the rigid and unimaginative policies of the KMT government of this period, saying that by sticking to Chinese nationalism, the KMT government tramped into a "dead-end street" and "could not strike out in new directions."[39] This diagnosis is certainly applicable to the KMT regime's postwar policy toward the Inner Mongols.

Typical of its propensity to rely on the military approach in solving complicated social-political questions, the KMT regime's initial operations for "restoring" Mongolian banners were part of its military thrust. Xiong Shihui, commanding officer of the Northeast Field Headquarters (responsible for the Northeast and Rehe) and Fu Zuoyi, commander of the 12th War Zone (responsible for Suiyuan and Chahar), were supreme authorities in their respective regions. Chiang vested these two with tremendous power in both civil and military affairs. Shortly after Japan's surrender, the KMT government abolished the "Manchukuo" administrative structure and divided Manchuria, now called the Northeast, into nine provinces (three prior to Japan's occupation). At Xiong's headquarters, a "Northeast Committee on the Recovery of Mongolian Banners" was set up. In September 1945, the government adopted "Urgent Measures and Solutions in Recovered Areas," under which "missions of propaganda and consolation" (*xuan wei tuan*) and "missions of propaganda and direction" (*xuan dao tuan*) were sent to Mongolian banners in Suiyuan, Chahar, Rehe, and the Northeast. These missions were charged to convey to the local populace the "center's benevolent intentions," to issue emergency relief, to escort former league and banner officials back to their posts, to investigate Mongolian officials' wartime behaviors, and to help the government's chief officials in the regions deal with puppet organizations and restore local order.[40]

All these steps were taken under an assumption that the so-called Mongolian problem was just a short-term effect of the wartime politics. Presumably, when the government's political and military takeover was completed, the problem would vanish or become marginal. These steps were hurriedly put into place in order to create the image, if not reality, of the KMT authority and to prevent the Russians and the CCP from fishing in the troubled water. These measures, however, were bound to fail exactly because their precondition, the KMT's solid military control of the areas concerned, had not been established. At war's end, not yet out of its seclusion in China's southwestern corner, the KMT government was unable to establish its influence with the Inner Mongols simply by sending propaganda teams. Because of the uncertain military situation between the KMT and the CCP, many KMT appointees never reached their posts, and some Mongolian notables simply declined to accept KMT appointment. In a more fundamental sense, however, these measures would not have been able to produce lasting results under any circumstances: they failed to address directly the Inner Mongols' autonomous demands, and these could not be easily appeased by the KMT center's stated "benevolent intentions" and usually stalled relief operations.

After a few months into the postwar peace, it became clear that the Mongolian question was not closer to a solution and that the Soviets could not be directly blamed for it. The issue maintained its magnitude and momentum among KMT officials because the CCP seemed to have taken full advantage of the Inner Mongols' discontent. Therefore, in early 1946, the MTAC proposed a stopgap measure to tackle the problem from its ethnic roots. It was suggested that the administrative authorities of the Chinese counties and Mongolian banners be clearly defined and separated. The assumption was that the separation would reduce Han–Mongol frictions and consequently deprive the CCP of a favorable condition for conducting anti-KMT agitation among the Mongols.[41] But the MTAC massively underestimated the difficulties involved in such a segregation operation: by that time, many counties and banners became intricately intertwined, and, in some cases, counties and banners were just different names for the same areas. Therefore, in practice, a segregation program would only intensify, not alleviate, the county-banner conflict.

In mid-March 1946, the "Mongolian question," especially the situation in eastern Mongolia, became troublesome enough to cause the KMT government to hold an interdepartmental meeting. Blaming the eastern Inner Mongols for dividing the country, the participants nevertheless admitted that a decision about Mongolian autonomy should not be delayed any longer. But the issue was so sensitive and controversial in the KMT government that, aside from urging the Northeast Field Headquarters to speed up its takeover operations in Manchuria and to prevent the eastern Mongolian autonomous movement from spreading to the west, the meeting did not produce any new policy. Seeing no clear way out, Chiang concluded that a decision on the Mongolian question had to be postponed.[42]

But the issue was not put on the backburner for long. In the spring of 1946, the Soviet troops left the Northeast and consequently, the only international restriction on the KMT–CCP conflict in the region was removed. In the two parties' ensuing military scramble for the Northeast, the KMT at first achieved an upper hand. In the summer of that year, after occupying all the major cities in the southern part of the region, KMT forces pushed northward and at one point forced the CCP to abandon Harbin and Qiqihar, two major cities in northern Manchuria. The KMT forces also made progress in Rehe, Chahar, and Suiyuan. By mid-October, Fu Zuoyi's troops entered Zhangjiakou, which since Japan's surrender had been the center of the CCP's Jin-Cha-Ji (Shanxi, Chahar, and Hebei) military district and the site of a CCP-sponsored "Inner Mongolian Autonomous Movement Association." By the time, a full-scale civil war between the KMT and the CCP was well under way, even though America's mediation effort under General George Marshall would linger for a short while. On November 15, over the objection of the CCP and some lesser parties, the KMT government confidently called into session a national congress to adopt a new constitution. Amidst these seemingly encouraging developments, the time seemed to have arrived for the KMT authorities to make a decision on the Mongolian question.[43]

In July 1946, Chen Cheng, chief of staff of the Defense Ministry, proposed to Chiang that reorganization of the government's frontier establishment was necessary for the moment and vitally important for the future. He proposed that the matter be considered immediately. Sharing Chen's sense of urgency, Chiang gave the task to the Supreme Council of National Defense (SCND). He instructed the SCND to call a meeting of relevant ministries and departments to study the question of Mongolian autonomy and find a solution within ten days. The SCND passed the ten-day deadline without proposing any solutions.[44] In late August, another push for a decision came from within the KMT. On the recommendation of the party's "supervisory committee on the implementation of the resolutions of the second plenum," the Standing Committee of the KMT Central Committee adopted a decision to overhaul the government's frontier establishment. The decision was again handed to the SCND for consideration. In September, Chiang gave the SCND and the ministries concerned a week to complete their deliberation. Once again, the second deadline was passed without any result.[45]

The KMT government's tardiness in reaching a decision was due to an insurmountable internal disagreement on whether and how much concession should be made to the Inner Mongols. Officials from the agencies directly involved in Mongolian policy planning, such as the MTAC, the Ministry of Interior, the Executive Yuan, and the Organizational Department of the KMT, were willing to make at least some nominal concessions to the Inner Mongols. These agencies either had Mongolian members in their staff or shouldered the burden of reducing the distance between the KMT's public statements and actual policies. The concessions under consideration included elevation of the Mongolian leagues to the same level with the provincial governments, establishment of a Mongolian political council as a coordinating body for the Mongolian areas, appointment of more Mongolian figures at the provincial and national levels of the government, and change of the MTAC into a full-fledged ministry. These, clearly, remained tremendously distant from the kind of ethnic reforms demanded by the Inner Mongols, who wanted first and foremost an autonomous territory under a Mongolian government.[46]

Even these minimal concessions, however, proved unacceptable to another group of KMT officials. In opposition stood a front of diehard "irreconcilables," including mainly officials of the Defense Ministry, the Department of Military Ordinance under the Military Council, and the officials responsible for executing the government's Mongolian policy on the spot, that is, Xiong Shihui in the Northeast and Fu Zuoyi in Suiyuan and Chahar. Rejecting as ever any true ethnic connotation of the Mongolian question, they had an especially strong objection to any concession to the Inner Mongols at the expenses of the existent provincial structure. Categorizing Mongolian leagues and banners as medieval and ineffective administrative systems, they accepted nothing less than enforcement of political homogenization and cultural assimilation whenever possible.[47]

Fu Zuoyi proved the single most effective local administrator and military commander in stopping the central government adopting what he deemed an unwise frontier policy. Ever outspoken in chastising "soft" Mongolian policies that originated from central government agencies, he could in practice invalidate the central government's policy decisions simply by procrastination. In the summer of 1946, Fu delayed the center's deliberation of a plan for Mongolian local autonomy by not responding to the Executive Yuan's request for his comments on the document. Then, in early 1947, the Executive Yuan adopted a piece of legislation on the same issue. Fu Zuoyi was again asked to second the document. Yet, again, Fu used his old tactic to interrupt the legislative procedure.[48]

Fu Zuoyi's ability to counteract the central government's Mongolian policy reveals much about the KMT's power structure as well as its frontier policy. Originally a renowned general in Yan Xishan's "Jin-Sui" (Shanxi and Suiyuan) clique, Fu did not rally to Chiang Kai-shek's side until the late 1930s. Before the Japanese–American war began in the Pacific in 1941, Fu's troops won several battles against the Japanese-backed puppet army in Suiyuan and, during the rest of the war, he became Chiang's indispensable commander to keep the Japanese at bay. In his postwar contest with the CCP, Chiang needed Fu more than ever to "restore" the central government's authority in Suiyuan, Chahar, and Rehe. Like any other strong local figure in the KMT power structure, Fu's strength was in his regionalism, not his connection with the KMT center. The Mongolian question was not the first occasion in which Fu went his own way. Fu's actual veto power on the Mongolian question illustrated the fact that he and the center both knew any decision on the matter could not be implemented without his cooperation. Fu's notorious record against ethnic reforms in Inner Mongolia made him one of the "frontier mandarins" most hated by the Inner Mongols. In the view of the Inner Mongols, the KMT central government's reluctance to overrule Fu made it an accomplice to the Mongol-phobic general.[49]

More sensitive than any other top KMT leaders to maintaining the delicate balance between the center and the local forces, Chiang pushed the government to find a solution to the Mongolian question but would not sacrifice the local balance of power for it. The center-local balance was especially vital during the war against the CCP. Thus, in early November 1946, after his own deadline was ignored for the second time, Chiang readily approved a measure that the SCND promised would be a better alternative than the policies preferred by the two opposing groups discussed above. Granting that both groups had good intentions either to placate the "Mongolian situation" (*meng qing*) or to preserve the state's integrity, the SCND felt that neither offered a suitable remedy to the current Mongolian problem. A proper solution had to pass two tests: it needed to promote Mongolian autonomy, and at the same time it needed to preserve the existent administrative structure at the provincial level. The SCND offered a seven-point formula to meet these criteria. The primary ingredient in the formula was to use a political accommodation scheme to dissuade Mongolian activists from pursuing their particular, separatist agendas. Accordingly, the Chinese authorities at different levels were to accommodate more Mongolian personalities and "certain concrete authority" was to be vested in these appointments. In lieu of the Mongolian political council sought by some Mongolian petitioners, a "Mongolian local autonomy promotion committee" would be established to propagate the KMT doctrines and help implement local Mongolian autonomy within provinces. Having satisfied leading Inner Mongols' desire for power, the SCND suggested, the proposed stratagem would be able to induce the Inner Mongols to "lean inward and not fall into the temptation of the Soviet Union, Outer Mongolia, and CCP."[50] Chiang found the formula "feasible" and wanted it to be implemented. But, even with Chiang's support, the SCND did not get a chance to test its political-bribery scheme. Bai Chongxi, the KMT's defense minister, effectively stopped the policy by contending that the Inner Mongols and, especially, of the provincial governments concerned should be consulted first.[51]

Not surprisingly, the provincial authorities' opinions were that in late 1946 and 1947 the government had even fewer reasons to worry about the Mongolian question than in the early postwar months. In a March 1947 report on work regarding Mongolian banners, the Northeast Field Headquarters listed many "achievements." Reportedly, in the past year or so the headquarters had implemented military, political, cultural, and economic measures in the Mongolian banners of the Northeast without much difficulty. By the time of the report, "a great number of people from the puppet [meaning eastern Mongolian] and the bandit [meaning CCP] troops have rallied to the government, Mongolian compatriots' (*mengbao*) determination to lean inward has become increasingly firm, and the puppet eastern Mongolian organization in Wangyemiao [a.k.a Wangiin Sume] is on the verge of collapse." The only remaining problem was Ulanfu's group in western Mongolia, and it was "obviously incited and controlled by Outer Mongolia."[52]

The reality was that, having entered into a partnership with the CCP in the spring of 1946, eastern Mongolian leaders pushed the CCP leadership into agreeing on the establishment of a unified Inner Mongolian autonomous government. Such a government was set up in May 1947, and the event marked Inner Mongols' "revolutionary independence" from the KMT government on the CCP model. The Inner Mongols finally obtained a unified government poised to reclaim Inner Mongolia's "original territory." But, the development was also a victory earnestly sought by the CCP: by playing the autonomy card right, the CCP consolidated its relationship with the eastern Mongols and thus secured a number of much needed base areas in western Manchuria and Rehe.[53]

The MTAC estimated the situation more honestly than Xiong Shihui's headquarters. In its yearly report for 1947, the commission pointed out that because of the intense struggle with the CCP, the government had to stop pushing certain measures devised to establish its authority among Inner Mongols. One of these was the government's "reform" attempt to collect old seals from Mongolian local officials that had been issued to them by the bygone Manchu court. Despite the fact that the traditional Mongolian elites were largely swept aside by the turbulent events of recent years, the KMT government and the traditional Mongolian ruling class still took the matter of seals seriously. Symbolic as the matter might look, the KMT regime deemed it necessary to use new seals to show to the Inner Mongols that the long overdue authority of the central government had arrived. But the old Mongolian elites were deeply suspicious and wanted to keep the old seals as proof of their own power and status. The government also had plans for further assimilation through measures such as organized migration, readjustment of the relationship between Mongolian banners and Han counties, and promotion of economic development in Mongolian areas. All these measures were ethnically provocative in the first place, but it was the uncertainty created by the KMT–CCP military conflict that effectively prevented their implementation.[54]

Between the summer of 1947 and the spring of 1948, the CCP successfully conducted a series of military operations in the Northeast. As a result, the KMT's military influence in the region declined significantly. Then, between September 1948 and January 1949, the CCP launched three campaigns (the Liao-Shen, Huai-Hai, and Ping-Jin Campaigns) that effectively ended KMT power in North and Northeast China. As components of the KMT's military policy in these areas, the KMT government's Mongolian measures had no chance of survival after the regime's military defeat. The MTAC's reports in early 1948 already saw the writing on the wall. One of these pointed out that after the KMT government had achieved "restoration" in forty-seven banners at one point or another, most of them now returned to "chaos," meaning that they "betrayed the state" again and attached themselves to the CCP. According to the MTAC's estimate, three-tenths of the Inner Mongolian population, or approximately 600,000 people, had become refugees of war.[55] In March 1948, seeing the inescapable bankruptcy of the government's "restoration" measures with Mongolian banners, Chen Lifu, head of the KMT's organization department, wrote a letter to Chiang urging him to make an "early decision" on Mongolian autonomy "in order to pacify the Mongolian people."[56] But it was already too late for any "early decision," either on Inner Mongolian autonomy or on the KMT's own fate in China.

Nevertheless, during the last two years of KMT power in the mainland, the KMT government continued to fumble in vain for guiding principles to solve its Mongolian imbroglio. Even after the KMT government fled to Taiwan in late 1949 and thus lost any practical contact with Inner Mongolia, the MTAC would not become delinquent of its charge. For instance, in 1951, the commission drafted a "plan for temporary measures of frontier administration in case of a counteroffensive in the mainland." The plan proposed no counterpart to the CCP's Inner Mongolian Autonomous Region but promised the Inner Mongols six league governments under a temporary "Mongolian political council in the battlefield."[57]

* * *

Between 1945 and 1949, the KMT regime's ethnopolitics with regard to the Inner Mongols were counterproductive to its own principal postwar objective, which was to establish once and for all the central government's authority throughout China as it was defined by the KMT. The KMT's loss of the Inner Mongols' support in a critical strategic region bridging North China and the Northeast created opportunities for its deadly enemy, the CCP. The connection between the KMT's failure in the ethnopolitical arena and on the battlefield should be clear. As history has shown, after being ousted from North China and the Northeast, the KMT government's days in China were numbered. A conclusion can be drawn from this episode: even to a Han-centric government like the KMT regime, "peripheral" problems were actually central in importance and "gray" areas were not obscure, but dangerously obtrusive. This was so in spite of the regime's diligent effort to eradicate the issue of non-Han peoples' nationalism from China's social and political life.

In the final analysis, the "peripheral" questions in the "gray" frontier regions were always at the very hub of the Chinese nationalist ideology and played a defining role in the formation of China's self-image. This was true for both the KMT and the CCP. While by and large sharing a conception about China so far as its hard borders were concerned, the two parties' different approaches toward the "soft boundaries" between the Han and non-Han peoples proved consequential to their competing claims to China's political power. Now let's examine some pieces of the puzzle on the CCP side.

Notes

1. Xiaoyuan Liu, *A Partnership for Disorder: China, the United States, and Their Policies for the Postwar Disposition of the Japanese Empire, 1941–1945* (New York: Cambridge University Press, 1996), 258–286; Peter S. H. Tang, *Russian and Soviet Policy in Manchuria and Mongolia, 1911–1931* (Durham: Duke University Press, 1959); *Zhonghua Minguo Zhongyao Shiliao Chubian; Dui Ri Kangzhan Shiqi* (Preliminary compilation of important documents of the Republic of China; the period of the war of resistance against Japan), 7 vols, Historical Council of the Kuomintang Central Committee, comp. (Taipei: Zhongguo Guomindang Zhongyang Weiyuanhui Dangshi Weiyuanhui, 1981. Hereafter cited as *ZZSC*), 7 (1): 946–999.
2. Prasenjit Duara, *Rescuing History from the Nation: Questioning Narratives of Modern China* (Chicago: University of Chicago Press, 1995), 65, defines "soft boundaries" as the "cultural practices . . . identify a group but do not prevent the group from sharing and even adopting, self-consciously or not, the practices of another."
3. "Outer Mongolia" and the "Mongolian People's Republic" carry different ethnopolitical connotations, and the former is clearly China-centric. In this study "Outer Mongolia" is used to reflect the perception of the KMT government. As a matter of fact, until today, "Outer Mongolia" is still marked as part of China's political map in Taiwan.
4. *Demuchukedonglupu Zishu* (Autobiography of Demchugdongrub), *Neimonggu Wenshi Ziliao* (Historical and literary materials of Inner Mongolia. Hereafter cited as, NWZ), 13: 6–17, 88–95.
5. Owen Lattimore, "The Eclipse of Inner Mongolian Nationalism," in his *Studies in Frontier History: Collected Papers 1929–58* (London: Oxford University Press, 1962). This is a piece originally published in 1936.
6. Minority "nationalities' right of self-determination" was included in the "proclamation of the first national congress of the KMT, 23 January 1924," *Minzu Wenti Wenxian Huibian* (Collected documents on the nationality question), United Front Department of the Chinese Communist Party Central Committee, comp. (Beijing: Zhonggong Zhongyang Dangxiao Chubanshe, 1991. Hereafter cited as, MWWH), 28.
7. For the racial discourse of Chinese nationalism, see Kauko Laitinen, *Chinese Nationalism in the Late Qing Dynasty: Zhang Binglin as an Anti-Manchu Propagandist*

(London: Curzon Press, 1990), and Frank Dikotter, *The Discourse of Race in Modern China* (Stanford: Stanford University Press, 1992). John Fitzgerald's *Awakening China: Politics, Culture, and Class in the Nationalist Revolution* (Stanford: Stanford University Press, 1996) offers a nuanced analysis of Chinese nationalism in the first half of the twentieth century.

8. Chiang Kai-shek, *China's Destiny* (New York: Roy Publishers, 1947), 29–43.
9. "Outline of the plan for postwar construction of frontier political establishments," n.d. (later than 1943), 141/112, Meng Zang Weiyuanhui, Zhongguo Di'er Lishi Dang'anguan (archives of the MTAC, the Second Historical Archives of China. Hereafter, MZW, ZDLD).
10. Gu Weijun, *Gu Weijun Huiyilu* (Memoirs of Gu Weijun) (13 volumes. Beijing: Zhonghua Shuju, 1982–1994), 5: 532; Ministry of Foreign Affairs, "Organization for postwar international peace and other related questions," 1944, Victor Hoo (Hu Shize) Papers, box 7; Xu Shuxi to T. V. Soong, January 20, 1945, T. V. Soong Papers, box 30.
11. Lattimore to Lauchlin Curry, July 27, 1941, Owen Lattimore Papers, box 27; "Chungking, 7 November 1941: Chu Chia-hua, Head of the Organizational Board of the Kuomintang," ibid. ; "Chungking, 14 November 1941: Dined with Generalissimo [Chiang Kai-shek]," ibid.; "Chungking (Huangshan), 5 December 1941: Generalissimo," ibid.; "Chungking, 2 November 1942: Weng Wen-hao," ibid.; Owen Lattimore, *China Memoirs: Chiang Kai-shek and the War against Japan* (compiled by Fujiko Isono. Tokyo: University of Tokyo Press, 1990), 105–106, 110–111.
12. Lattimore, "Memorandum on Outer Mongolia," September 1941, 35: 55–61, Kang Zhan Shiqi, GW, JZD (the period of the war of resistance, revolutionary documents, archives of President Chiang Kai-shek. Hereafter, KZ/GW/JZD); Lattimore, "Memorandum on Sinkiang Province," (before September 1941) Lattimore Papers, box 28; Lattimore, "Memorandum on Inner Mongolia," n.d., ibid.
13. Wang Chonghui, "Supplementary comments on the Xinjiang question," September 1, 1941, 3: 53–54, KZ/GW/JZD.
14. Committee on frontier general mobilization for the national revolutionary war in the second war zone, "How the anti-Japanese guerrilla base in the Daqing Mountains was created," July 1939, *Daqingshan Kangri Youji Genjudi Ziliao Xuanbian* (Selected materials on the anti-Japanese base in the Daqing Mountains) (Huhhot: Neimenggu Renmin Chubanshe, 1987), 2: 63.
15. Office of the commissioner to Chahar Mongolian banners, "Military and political conditions of the puppet Mongolia," 1940, *ZZSC*, 6 (2): 422–472; MTAC, "Draft plan for the recovery in [Mongolian] leagues and banners," August 1944, 141/3663, MZW, ZDLD; memorandum by the Counselors' Office of the Military Council, December 1944, 761/171, Junshi Weiyuanhui, ZDLD (archives of the Military Council. Hereafter, JW, ZDLD).
16. Wu Zhongxin to Chiang Kai-shek, "Plan for recovering the lost Mongolian banners and for postwar political establishment in Mongolia and Tibet," August 27, 1944, 055/1631, ZTF, GSG; Wu Zhongxin and Luo Liangjian to Chiang Kai-shek, May 26, 1945, 055/0501, ibid; KMT political conference, "Principles on Mongolian local autonomy," March 28, 1934, vol. 051, Zhengzhi, Tejiao Dang'an, JZD (Political affairs, specially submitted archives, archives of President Chiang Kai-shek. Hereafter, ZZ/TD/JZD); Chen Bulei to Chiang Kai-shek, March 13, 1937, vol. 002, Jiaofei, TD, JZD (bandits suppression, specially submitted archives, archives of President Chiang Kai-shek. Hereafter, JF/TD/JZD); Sun Fu to Chiang Kai-shek, August 7, 1938, *ZZSC*, 3 (2): 408–409.

17. Zhu Jiahua, "Frontier problems and frontier works," October 21, 1942, 510/3, Guofang Zuigao Weiyuanhui Dang'an, Kuomintang Dangshi Weiyuanhui (archives of the Supreme Council of National Defense, at the Historical Council of the Kuomintang Central Committee, Taipei. Hereafter, GZWD, KDW).
18. On August 18, 1945, an "Inner Mongolian people's revolutionary party" issued a "declaration of Inner Mongolian people's liberalization," and on January 16, 1946, the same group launched an "eastern Mongolian people's autonomous government." There were other developments. On September 9, 1945, a "provisional government of Inner Mongolian people's republic" was set up by some Mongolian youths and former officials of Prince De's wartime regime; on October 8, 1945, an autonomous government of Hulunbuir was established in Hailar; on November 26, 1945, an "alliance of Inner Mongolian autonomous movement" was organized under the CCP's aegis in Zhangjiakou.
19. The party-administration-army joint office, "Research report on current conditions in the Northeast and Inner Mongolia, 1 March 1946," "Weekly report on current conditions in the Northeast and Inner Mongolia, 17–23 March 1946," and "Special report on current conditions in the Northeast and Inner Mongolia, 16–30 March 1946," 197/1, Yaxisi, Waijiaobu, Waijiaobu Dang'an Zixunchu (archives of the Western Asian Division of the Ministry of Foreign Affairs, at the Office of Archival Information, the Ministry of Foreign Affairs, Taipei. Hereafter, YXS/WJB, WDZ). The term "national autonomy" was never used in KMT documents. They sometimes used "independent autonomy" in contrast to "local autonomy," an ethnic-blind program promoted by the KMT authorities.
20. "Manifesto on the establishment of eastern Mongolian people's autonomous government," 4/1/5, Dongmeng Zhengfu (files of eastern Mongolian government), Inner Mongolian Archives, Huhhot (hereafter, DZ); "Administrative program of the eastern Mongolian people's autonomous government," 4/1/2, DZ; "Eastern Mongolian people's autonomous constitution," ibid.
21. Dugurjav, "Memories about the days and nights of the Inner Mongolian first cavalry division," *Xing'an Dangshi Wenji* (Essays on the party history of Xing'an) (Ulanhot: Office of the Party History of the CCP Committee of the Xing'an League, 1993), 2: 210.
22. Shen Zhongyu, "The Chiang Kai-shek clique and Demchugdongrub's reactionary force of Inner Mongolia," *Neimenggu Wenshi Ziliao* (Literary and historical materials of Inner Mongolia. Hereafter, NWZ), 15: 136–137.
23. Fu Zuoyi to Chiang Kai-shek, March 15, 1946, doc. 35022506/vol. 6, Erdi Yingmou, Tejiao Wendian, Jiang Zhongzheng Zongtong Dang'an (the part on Russian imperialist conspiracies, specially submitted telegrams, archives of President Chiang Kai-shek. Academia Historica, Taipei. Hereafter, EY/TW/JZD); Fu Zuoyi to Chiang Kai-shek, March 25, 1946, doc. 35023332/vol. 6, ibid.
24. Xiong Shihui to Wang Shijie, December 25, 1945, 18/1094, Waijiaobu, Zhongguo Di'er Lishi Dang'anguan (archives of the Ministry of Foreign Affairs, at the Second Historical Archives of China, Nanjing. Hereafter, WJB, ZDLD). "Independence movement" (*duli yundong*) was the term used in Xiong's report. At the time, eastern Inner Mongols sought unification with the MPR but not an independent state of their own.
25. Memorandum by Sun Fushen, July 19, 1947, 112/93, YXS/WJB, WDZ; Executive Yuan to Ministry of Foreign Affair, July 6, 1947, 106/4, WJB, ZDLD; KMT department of organization to the Supreme Council of National Defense, August 9, 1946, 004/114.2, GZWD, KDW; Bai Chongxi and Wang Shijie to Chiang Kai-shek, December 31, 1946, 39: 411–413, Kanluan Shiqi, Geming Wenxian, Jiang Zhongzheng Zongtong Dang'an

(the period of rebellion suppression, revolutionary documents, archives of President Chiang Kai-shek. Hereafter, KL/GW/JZD); Secret Bureau to Chiang Kai-shek, May 4, 1947, ibid., 39: 419; Chen Cheng to Chiang Kai-shek, November 1946, ibid., 8: 439.

26. *Wang Shijie Riji*, March 1–17, 1946 entries, 5: 279–287.
27. Ministry of Interior to the MTAC, August 3, 1945, 141/3178, MZW, ZDLD; *Zai Chiang Kai-shek Shenbian Ba Nian–Shicongshi Gaoji MuliaoTang Zong Riji* (With Chiang Kai-shek for eight years: senior member of the aides office Tang Zong's diary), compiled by the Ministry of Public Security Archives (Beijing, Qunzhong Chubanshe, 1992), May 5–21, 1945 and March 1–17, 1946 entries, 507–512, 595–600.
28. Executive Yuan to the MTAC, August 24, 1945, 141/3179, MZW, ZDLD; Executive Yuan to MTAC, August 24, 1945, 141/3179, MZW, ZDLD; MTAC to the Executive Yuan, October 2, 1945, ibid.; "Resolution on the political report," passed by the KMT's sixth national congress, May 17, 1945, in Qin Xiaoyi et al., ed., *Geming Wenxian di qishiliu ji: Zhongguo Guomindang Lici Quanguo Daibiao Dahui Zhongyao Jueyi'an Huibian (shang)* (Revolutionary documents, volume 76: collected important resolutions of the KMT's national congresses, part one) (Taipei: Zhongyang Wenwu Gongyingshe, 1978), 410; "Resolution on the party's constitution and policies passed by the sixth national congress," May 18, 1945, in Xiao Jizong et al., ed., *Geming Wenxian, di qishi ji: Zhongguo Guomindang Dangzhang Zhenggang Ji* (Revolutionary documents, volume 70: collected party constitutions and platforms of the KMT) (Taipei: Zhongyang Wenwu Gongyingshe, 1976), 395; Bai Yunti et al. to Chiang Kai-shek, October 17, 1946, 055/1655, ZTF, GSG.
29. Contrary to his practice in *China's Destiny*, Jiang used *minzu* in his original Chinese text to refer to the non-Han peoples of China, which I translate here into "nationalities." But the official English version of the speech, "National independence and racial equality," August 24, 1945, *The Collected Wartime Messages of Generalissimo Chiang Kai-shek, 1937–1945*, compiled by Chinese Ministry of Information (New York: Kraus Reprint Co., 1969), 854–860, translated the term into "racial groups."
30. "Manifesto on the establishment of the eastern Mongolian people's autonomous government," January 19, 1946, 4/1/5, Dong Meng Zhengfu, Neimenggu Dang'anguan (archives of eastern Mongolian government, at the Archives of the Inner Mongolian Autonomous Region, Huhhot. Hereafter, DMZ, NMD).
31. "Autobiography of Demchugdongrub," NWZ, 13: 144; "Historical materials on the puppet Mongol army," NWZ, 38: 92–94; Chiang Kai-shek to the Committee on Mongolian-Tibetan Affairs, April 10, 1946, 141/3626 (record group/file number), MZW, ZDLD; MTAC to the Executive Yuan, March 20, 1946, 141/1060, ibid.
32. The Chinese version of the speech can be found in *Xian Zongtong Jianggong Sixiang Yanlun Zongji* (General collection of the late president Jiang's thoughts and words) (40 volumes. Taipei: Guomindang Dangshi Weiyuanhui, 1984), 21: 170–175.
33. Chiang Kai-shek to Wang Chonghui, March 30, 1946, 004/144.1, GZWD, KDW; Executive Yuan to the civil officers division of the National Government, March 20, 1947, 213/1212, GZ, ZDLD; Executive Yuan to Supreme Council of National Defense, April 16, 1947, 004/144.3, GZWD, KDW.
34. Congress of Suiyuan to Chiang Kai-shek, March 11, 1946, 055/1657, ZTF, GSG.
35. "Society to promote restoration of Mongolian banners in the Northeast" to the KMT central committee and Chiang Kai-shek, March 18, 1947, 128/0233, Guomin Zhengfu, ZDLD (archives of the National Government. Hereafter, GZ, ZDLD); Fu Zuoyi to Chiang

Kai-shek, July 11, 1946, doc. 35010309/vol. 6, EY/TW/JZD; Xiong Shihui to Chiang Kai-shek, August 12, 1946, 055/1635, ZTF, GSG.

36. *Zhonghua Minguo Shi Neizheng Zhi (Chugao)* (History of the Republic of China: a chronicle of domestic administration), compiled by Sinica Historica (Taipei: Guoshiguan, 1992), 32–44.
37. Ministry of Interior to the MTAC, September 4, 1945, 141/3178, MZW, ZDLD; Executive Yuan to the Ministry of Foreign Affairs, March 27, 1946, 197.1, YXS/WJB, WDZ.
38. Zheng Wenyi to Chiang Kai-shek, March 7, 1948, vol. 13, 324, KL/GW/JZD; Chiang Kai-shek's speech at a military conference, August 2, 1948, vol. 13, 391–394, ibid.
39. "Reminiscences of Chen Kuang-fu," oral history project of Columbia University (1961), 89.
40. Jiang Kefu, *Minguo Junshi Shiluegao* (Brief military history of the Republic of China) (4 volumes. Beijing: Zhonghua Shuju, 1987), 4 (1): 7–8; Chiang Kai-shek to Chen Bulei, August 5, 1945, 003/3350, GZWD, KDW; National Government's appointment of Xiong Shihui as director of the Northeast Field Headquarters, September 1, 1945, *ZZSC*, 7 (1): 34; National Government's appointment of governors of nine Northeast provinces and two mayors, September 4, 1945, ibid., 36–37; "Urgent measures and solutions in recovered areas," September 1945, *ZZSC*, 7(4): 401.
41. Wang Shijie and Xiong Shihui to Chiang Kai-shek, November 1945, 019.48, Yataisi, WJB, WDZ (archives of the Asian-Pacific Division of the Ministry of Foreign Affairs, at the Office of Archival Information, the Ministry of Foreign Affairs. Hereafter, YTS/WJB, WDZ); MTAC to the administrative bureau (of the Executive Yuan?), February 28, 1946, 141/1080, MZW, ZDLD.
42. Luo Liangjian to Chiang Kai-shek, August 12, 1945, 055/1653, ZTF, GSG; Zhang Zhongwei to Luo Liangjian, March 15, 1946, and MTAC to the Executive Yuan, March 20, 1946, 141/1060, MZW, ZDLD; Chiang Kai-shek to Wang Chonghui, April 22, 1946, 004/144.1, GZWD, KDW. The conference involved MTAC, ministries of interior and foreign affairs, military administrative and military ordinance departments, and KMT propaganda and organizational departments.
43. Jiang Kefu, *Minguo Junshi Shilue Gao*, 4 (1): 87–88, 105, 111,180–186, 230–231; Zhou Enlai's press release on the KMT's opening of the national congress, November 16, 1946, in *Zhou Enlai Yijiusiliu Nian Tanpan Wenxuan* (Selected documents on Zhou Enlai's negotiations in 1946), compiled by the Documentary Research Office of the CCP Central Committee and the CCP Committee of Nanjing (Beijing: Zhongyang Wenxian Chubanshe, 1996), 689–691.
44. Chiang Kai-shek to Wang Chonghui, July 27, 1946, 004/144.1, GZWD, KDW.
45. Organizational Department of the KMT to the Supreme Council of National Defense, August 28, 1946, 004/144.2, GZWD, KDW; Chiang Kai-shek to Wang Chonghui, September 23, 1946, 004/144.1, ibid.
46. Organizational Department of the KMT to the Supreme Council of National Defense, August 28, 1946, 004/144.2, ibid.; Chiang Kai-shek to Wang Chonghui, September 23, 1946, 004/144.1, GZWD, KDW; Secretariat of the Executive Yuan to the MTAC, November 22, 1946, 141/1085, MZW, ZDLD.
47. Department of Military Ordinance to Wang Chonghui, March 30, 1946, 004/144.1, GZWD, KDW; Fu Zuoyi to Song Ziwen, February 5, 1946, ibid.; Wang Wenhao to Wang Chonghui, April 19, 1946, ibid.

48. Fu Zuoyi to the National Government, September 24, 1946, 055/1632, ZTF, GSG; *Wang Shijie Riji*, December 1, 1946 entry, 5:436–437; MTAC report on important works in 1947, 141/3243, MZW, ZDLD; MTAC, "Plan for important central work during the first half of 1948," January 27, 1948, 141/3200, ibid.
49. Jiang Shuchen, *Fu Zuoyi Zhuanlue* (Biography of Fu Zuoyi) (Beijing: Zhongguo Qingnian Chubanshe, 1990), 65–72, 75–101, 104–105, 113–119, 123–124; Secret Bureau to Chiang Kai-shek, August 1, 1947, 39: 437, KL/GW/JZD; Investigation and Statistics Bureau of the KMT Central Committee to Chiang Kai-shek, February 11, 1947, 055/1657, ZTF, GSG; "A brief narrative of the 19 September [1949] peaceful uprising in Suiyuan," in *Suiyuan "Jiu Yi Jiu" Heping Qiyi Dang'an Shiliao Xuanbian* (Selected archival and historical materials on the September 19 peaceful uprising in Suiyuan), compiled by Inner Mongolian Archives (Huhhot: Neimenggu Renmin Chubanshe, 1986), 1–14.
50. Wang Chonghui to Chiang Kai-shek, November 7, 1946, and Chiang Kai-shek to the Supreme Council of National Defense, November 19, 1946, 004/144.2, GZWD, KDW.
51. Wang Chonghui to Chiang Kai-shek, April 13, 1947, 004/144.3, ibid.; Xu Shiying memorandum on principles for Mongolian local autonomy, June 7, 1947, 055/1632, ZTF, GSG.
52. "Report on takeover in Northeast Mongolian banners," from the report by the chairman of the National Government (Chiang Kai-shek)on the works of the Northeast Field Headquarters, March 1947, *ZZSC*, 7(1): 88–93.
53. Prioritizing its national-wide political maneuvering with the KMT, until November 1946 the CCP resisted Inner Mongols' demand for organizing a unified Inner Mongolian government, for the move would overturn the existing administrative system in China and also throw away any legal pretense of the CCP–Inner Mongolian cooperation. But, by early winter of 1946, a full-scale war between the CCP and the KMT had started to close the door for a negotiated settlement. Meanwhile, KMT troops were advancing in North China and Manchuria. On one hand, these conditions freed the CCP from its earlier "legalistic" consideration and, on the other, created the CCP's urgent need for solid rural bases in Rehe and western Manchuria. Interestingly, the Inner Mongolian autonomous government of 1947 recognized Inner Mongolia as part of the Chinese republic but did not recognize the KMT government as the legitimate central government. Therefore, this was a "revolutionary independence" from the KMT authorities but not a "state independence" from Chinese sovereignty.
54. MTAC, "Report on important works of the MTAC in the thirty-sixth year [1947]," n.d., 141/3243, MZW, ZDLD; Central Planning Bureau, "National defense construction," December 21, 1943, Hsiung Shihui (Xiong Shihui) Collections, box 1. During the first few month of peace, the KMT government considered seriously a plan to move a few million Han people to fill in the "population blanks" in the vast northeastern and northwestern border regions. In late 1945, acting upon Chiang Kai-shek's directive, the Executive Yuan proposed to move immediately 100,000 discharged troops to the northern border areas. It was also proposed that 20,000 households be moved to the northwest in the next five years.
55. Chu Minshan, "Report on works of the committee on restoration in Northeast Mongolian banners," March 4, 1948; 055/1633, ZTF, GSG; MTAC (Xu Shiying) to the Executive Yuan (Zhang Qun), January 27, 1948, 141/3200, MZW, ZDLD; MTAC report on its works in the past year, April 14, 1948, 141/131, MZW, ZDLD. The figures are from the document by Xu Shiying. It is not clear whether they meant only the Mongols or the

entire population also including the Han. The KMT government had not vital statistics on the Mongolian population, and different estimates ranged between 1.5 to 2 million. But, according to a recent authoritative publication in China, *Dangdai Zhongguo de Neimenggu* (Inner Mongolia of contemporary China) (Beijing: Dangdai Zhongguo Chubanshe, 1992), 564, the Mongolian population in 1947 was 0.832 million. Its source is not clear.

56. Chen Lifu to Chiang Kai-shek, March 3, 1948, 055/0500, ZTF, GSG.
57. MTAC, "Plan for temporary measures of frontier administration in case of a counter-offensive in the mainland," December 1951, 019/48, YXS/WJB, GSG.

PART III

Chinese Communist Ethnopolitics

CHAPTER SIX

"National Question" with Chinese Characteristics

Since the disintegration of the Soviet Union and Yugoslavia, ethnic conflicts between some former members of these by-gone multinational systems have proved that the Communist solution of the "national question," when still in place, succeeded only temporarily in sealing the craters of these volcanic bodies. Today, China is the sole "multinational" system in the world that continues to operate within the Marxist ideological matrix.[1] The most intriguing question, then, appears to be how long the Chinese system will be able to last. After the two Marxist models in East Europe failed to stamp out pugnacious ethnic emotions and when the Marxist ideology is in general retreat in today's China, what can be the reason or reasons for a Communist conglomeration of nationalities to continue in China? But, we may be asking a wrong question. If the historical Chinese Communist movement can be viewed as a site that incorporated various and even conflicting convictions and propensities, then a one-dimensional gaze focusing on "Communism" would result in a serious distortion of the phenomenon. As Benjamin I. Schwartz pointed out, in the Chinese Communist movement at least three sets of ideologies "supplemented and complicated" one another. These are Confucianism, nation-state outlook, and Communism.[2] From such a perspective, the conventional paradigm in the field becomes inadequate, which tends to analyze the Chinese Communist Party's (CCP) ethnopolitics in the framework of the Marxist–Leninist–Stalinist theories on the "national question."[3] This chapter makes an effort to understand the CCP's ethnopolitical practices in a dynamic process involving interactions among the party's Communist dogmas, nationalist convictions, and ethnicist tendencies.[4] None of these dominated the party's thinking all the time. Their relative positions in the CCP's policy making were often determined by circumstances beyond the party's control. The period for investigation is from 1921 to 1945, a time span that saw the CCP's tentative approaches to the "national question" and its gradual adoption of a relatively stable stance during China's war against Japan, the heyday of Chinese nationalism. The meaning of this historical period is not understood merely in its own right but, more importantly, in the long historical process of transformation of Chinese territoriality.

Bolshevism in China

In the early decades of the twentieth century, Chinese radicals easily fell for Communism at least for two reasons. First, frustrated by China's experience at the Paris Peace Conference of 1919, participants of the May Fourth Movement angrily rejected China's traditionalism and challenged the warlord-controlled state. The most iconoclastic of these young intellectuals, a group that produced the early members of the CCP, bid farewell with "ordinary" nationalism. In other words, instead of promoting national spirit through glorifying China's past, they were attracted to the future-oriented Marxism that repudiated the existent Western world system and promised a new society. Secondly, at the time Chinese revolutionaries were not only

An ethnopolitical perspective of the Red Army's Long March, based on a CIA map on the ethnolinguistic groups of China made in 1967.

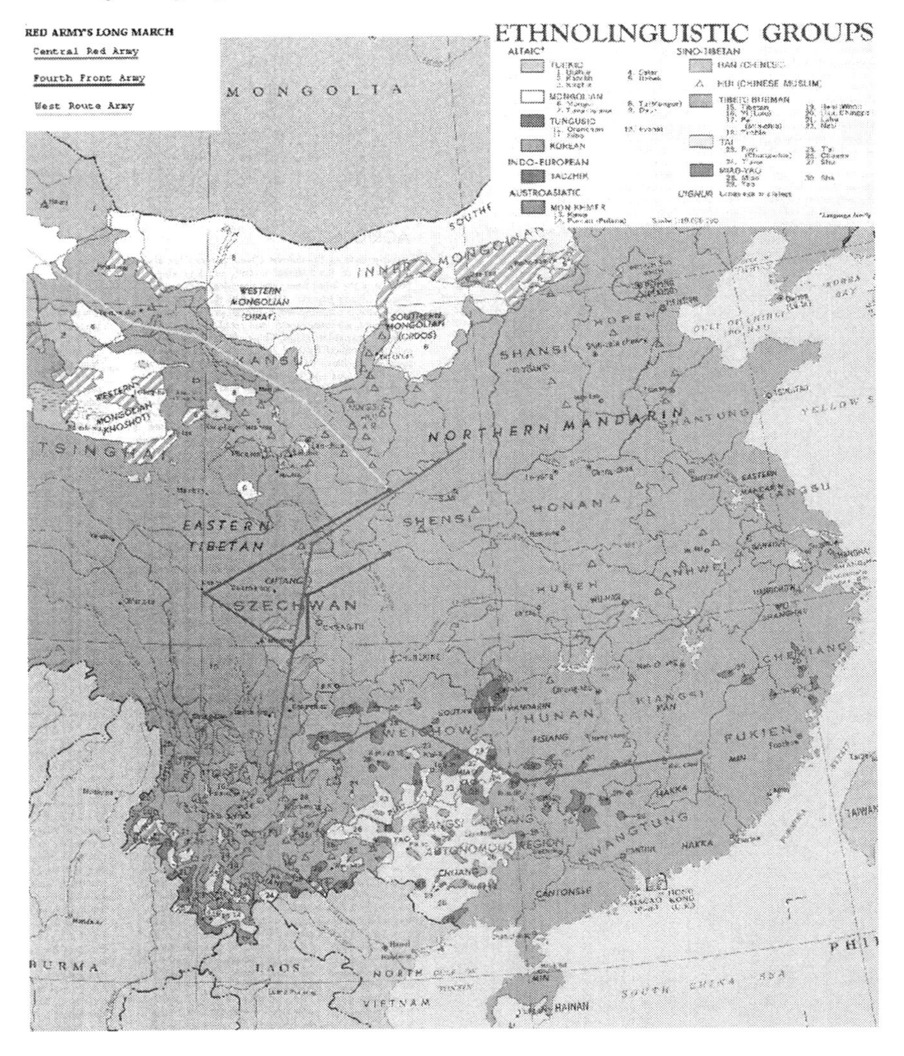

Source: Perry-Castaneda Library Map Collection, the University of Texas at Austin, http://www.lib.utexas.edu/maps/china.html.

flowing with the torrents of new thoughts; most of all, they were searching for an organization for action and a source of support. The arrival of the Bolshevik version of Communism in China was therefore politically logical: only Soviet Russia and its international extension, the Comintern, were willing and able to provide the Chinese revolutionaries with much-needed assistance and organizational guide.[5]

At the onset, the burgeoning CCP received the Bolshevik package of dogmas and political strategies with a simple mind. To founders of the CCP, the proletarian class struggles stood out as the winning formula of the Bolshevik model. The Bolshevik strategy on the "national question," despite its tremendous importance to Lenin and associates, hardly aroused Chinese Communists' attention. Indeed, if left to its own device, the CCP would have ignored China's "national question" for a long time. China's demographic character and political geography decided that the party's early membership was consisted overwhelmingly of Han intellectuals from southeastern China. Unlike Sun Yat-sen and associates who initially based their revolution on an anti-Manchu ethnic nationalism, the early CCP members had neither substantive knowledge about China's ethnic affairs nor pressing reasons to attach any political importance to China's non-Han peoples. The first CCP resolution, adopted in the summer of 1921, demonstrated a sole concern with urban working classes.[6] At a time when the young CCP overlooked the peasants, the vast majority of the Chinese population, it could not possibly be interested in the non-Han peoples of China, who were habitually viewed as residents of remote borderlands. This "oversight," however, was soon "corrected" by a wind from Moscow.

In January 1922, the Comintern sponsored the first "Congress of the Toilers of the Far East" in Moscow. The CCP, the KMT, and some other political groups sent a joint delegation. In Moscow, the Chinese delegates were unexpectedly subject to a barrage of criticisms from the Comintern leadership and the Mongolian delegation. The issue was China's traditional policies toward Mongolia. Expectedly, the CCP delegates indicated conformity with the Comintern leadership. The Moscow conference also became the first occasion for the CCP to learn systematically about the Comintern's general stand on the "national question." Afterwards, the gist of the Comintern policy was taken back to China, and the CCP's "Bolshevism" was upgraded accordingly.[7] In July, at its second national congress, the CCP adopted a resolution on "International Imperialism and China and the Chinese Communist Party." Attesting to Moscow its ideological orthodoxy, in this and other related documents the party strove to meet the Comintern's requirements for those member parties whose own countries possessed colonies. Thus, the CCP "denounced sternly" China's own imperialist and "tyrannous suppression of the colonies" and support the colonial peoples' national liberation movements.[8]

This meant the CCP's unequivocal support of the "liberation" of the non-Han peoples in China's frontier regions. It proclaimed that these peoples should first establish their own democratic, self-governing states (*minzhu zizhibang*), and, then, only on the basis of a "free federation principle," they should join a democratic Chinese republic in forming a Chinese federation of republics.[9] The exercise, however, did not afford to the CCP much new insight about the conditions of China's ethnopolitics. In this matter, indeed, "the cliches of Bolshevism substituted for independent analysis."[10] What is more interesting is that the cliché borrowing was executed through a Chinese, or, more accurately, Han, frame of mind. When applying the standard Marxist political-economic analysis to China's interethnic situation, the CCP made a stark contrast between the "burgeoning capitalist" China proper (*benbu*) and the "nomadic, primitive" non-Han frontiers (*jiangbu*). In identifying the peoples of

Tibet, Mongolia, and the "Muslim territories" (*Hui jiang*, meaning Xinjiang, Nianxia, and Qinghai) as the "alien races" (*yizhong minzu*), the party betrayed its perplexity about the ethnic and cultural barriers between these "border peoples" and the Han as well as its total nescience of the other non-Han groups who resided among the Han in China proper.[11] The alleged political-economic differences between the *jiangbu* and the *benbu*, compounded by the recurring warlord warfare of the time, led the CCP to conclude that, for now, unification between the borderlands and China proper was not only infeasible but also undesirable.[12] In the meantime, the CCP did not substantiate its support to the borderlands' separation with any program for action.

Clearly, the CCP's initial stand on the "national question" resembled Leninism only in appearance. During the Bolsheviks' struggle against Russia's old regime, Lenin regarded the "national question" as the "yeast for the revolution" and believed that political mobilization of the non-Russian groups in the Tsarist empire could speed up the collapse of the old state system.[13] The CCP was in practice oblivious to such a value of China's non-Han groups. This was for a good reason. To the Bolsheviks, the "national question" involved a strategic relationship between the Russian proletariat and the proletarians of the other national groups, or between the Bolshevik party and the "social democrats of the various frontier regions" of Russia.[14] To the CCP, as indicated in the aforementioned documents, the "nomadic, primitive" "alien races" of China's borderlands were not up to such a strategic partnership with Chinese working classes. The CCP was yet to grasp the practical significance of the "national question" to its revolutionary strategy.

Ironically, in the early 1920s the CCP's enfeebled Leninism was quite suitable to the purpose of the Soviet–Comintern cartel. In organizing its management of Asia's revolutionary movements, Moscow compartmentalized the continent. Mongolia and Tibet were not included in the Chinese sector. Identifying the "bourgeois" KMT as the main revolutionary force of China, leaders in Moscow urged the KMT not to rush into any organizational contact with the frontier peoples but to concentrate on the political and propaganda work in China.[15] Working with the KMT within a Moscow-directed "united front," the CCP inevitably operated under the same restriction. In view of the Soviet government's manifest interests in Outer Mongolia (Mongolian People's Republic, or MPR, after 1924) and Xinjiang, the true motives behind Moscow's advice to Chinese revolutionaries were not difficult to fathom. Among the CCP principals, at least Mao Zedong voiced some suspicion that "national self-determination" in the frontiers would actually create opportunities to foreign powers.[16] Yet, as a whole, the CCP was not in position to contradict Moscow. In the early 1920s, throughout the Chinese–Soviet diplomacy concerning Outer Mongolia, the CCP remained a loyal supporter of Moscow's policy.[17]

The logic of the Soviet strategy in East Asia was geopolitical, not national. Its goal in Outer Mongolia, now the Mongolian People's Republic (MPR), was to create a buffer against any hostile, Chinese or foreign, forces based in China. Thus, after double-crossing their Chinese nationalist beneficiary by working for the detachment of Outer Mongolia from China, leaders in Moscow double-crossed their Mongolian protégés by separating "Outer" and "Inner" Mongolias in their game plan. Around the mid-1920s, Moscow allocated the revolutionary responsibility for *Inner* Mongolia back to the Chinese.[18] Neither the KMT nor the MPR, however, accepted the division of Mongolia. While relying on Moscow's support in their respective military or diplomatic efforts against the warlord regime in Beijing, the KMT and the MPR worked for the reunification of Mongolia in different senses. It was in this extremely complicated "friendly" competition that the CCP had its first and brief flirtation with China's ethnopolitics.

In the summer and fall of 1925, the CCP's northern branch under Li Dazhao became involved in organizing an Inner Mongolian People's Revolutionary Party (IMPRP) in Zhangjiakou (a.k.a. Kalgan). Li, assisted by several Inner Mongolian members of the CCP, intended to develop in Inner Mongolia a supra-ethnic "peasants–workers–soldiers" movement as a flank support to the KMT–CCP Northern Expedition against Beijing. The idea did not fly. On the one hand, the CCP cautiously played out the "united front" strategy, avoiding usurping the KMT's leading position in Inner Mongolian politics. Li and associates made efforts in the name of the KMT and thus produced hardly any independent CCP influence among the Inner Mongols. On the other, since the CCP's purpose in Inner Mongolia was not to agitate a national liberation movement for the Inner Mongols, the party leadership decided to defer to the Comintern and the MPR in matters related to the ethnic aspect of the Inner Mongolian affairs. This orientation actually released the CCP from any organizational and political responsibilities for the IMPRP.[19] In sum, the CCP's early involvement in Inner Mongolian politics neither resulted in its achievement of a decisive influence over the Inner Mongols, nor did the episode change the CCP's tendency of marginalizing the "national question" in its overall strategy.

Revolutionary Independence

Mao Zedong's doubt about the usability of the self-determination doctrine in the frontier regions indicated that, in its formative years, CCP members were not totally oblivious to these regions' intricate conditions since the collapse of the Qing. But, since the CCP's task of political mobilization in China proper was already overwhelming and the party's influence in the borderlands was next to nil, the CCP welcomed the Comintern's responsibility for these areas. By contrast, the KMT, also assisted by Soviet Russia in the mid-1920s and for a short while also condemning China's internal imperialism in the past, never accepted the Comintern's admonition on postponing its activities in the frontier regions.[20] As articulated by Sun Yat-sen, the KMT's goal was to "unify the territories of the Han, Manchus, Mongols, Hui, and Tibetans into one state, that is, to combine the Han, Manchu, Mongol, Hui, and Tibetan races into one people."[21] Between the Comintern (as the international ideological regulator) and the KMT (as the domestic political partner), the CCP managed to maintain ideological "correctness" and political discretion, criticizing the KMT's statist tendency without at the same time replacing the KMT's political agenda with one of its own.

In April 1927, Chiang Kai-shek split with the CCP and the Soviets and massacred CCP members and supporters in Shanghai. The KMT began its decisive turn to the right. The Comintern's advisory position and the CCP's free-riding stratagem within the KMT came to a sudden end. Chiang's action opened many doors for the KMT to reach compromises with the established foreign and domestic conservative forces in China. Then, in 1928, the KMT formally installed itself in Nanjing as the ruling party of China's new "central government." Meanwhile, the CCP's principal concern was to find a way to keep its movement alive. Some of the more innovative CCP members, Mao Zedong among them, found the value of the peasant movement in the countryside. As far as the "national question" was concerned, however, for a while it disappeared almost completely from the CCP's daily agenda.

In the summer of 1928, when the CCP held its sixth congress in Moscow, the party did reaffirm its Bolshevik stance on the "national question" with a brief resolution. But the real significance of the resolution was to postpone the party's deliberation of this allegedly "enormously significant" issue to the next party congress.[22] Under these circumstances, the party's already anaemic Inner Mongolian venture went into a coma. Seventeen months after the KMT coup, a neglected CCP organization in Inner Mongolia complained, "Since the KMT–CCP split, . . . has [the party leadership] ever found a moment to look after Inner Mongolia?"[23] In the next few years, only the party's polemic literature occasionally made a reference to the "national question." For instance, in 1931, Wang Ming, a Comintern protégé, attacked the CCP's "opportunistic" tendency under the leadership of Li Lisan, another Soviet returnee. Wang named "great Hanism" (*da hanzu zhuyi*) as one of the crimes of the "Lisan line," thus introducing the issue of ethnicity and alleged wrong doings into the CCP's brutal internal frictions. Wang Ming was on target in accusing the so-called Lisan line for lacking a Bolshevik attention to the "nationality question," though he himself did not specify any practical significance of the question to the CCP's political strategy either.[24]

In these years, the CCP's survival crisis was compounded by China's national plight caused by Japan's aggression in North China. The Mukden incident of September 1931 announced the beginning of Japan's open colonization of Manchuria. The Japanese military soon engineered a series of intrigues to expand its sphere of influence into Inner Mongolia and North China. In the process Japanese conspirators found Inner Mongolian nationalism moldable to serve their own purpose. Thus, before the CCP could learn how to use the "national question" as the "yeast for the revolution," Japanese intruders began to turn it into a virus for spreading the imperialist disease. But, to the CCP, its partisan crisis was severer than the national one: its archenemy Chiang Kai-shek was determined to annihilate Chinese Communism before dealing with the Japanese. In this deadly CCP–KMT struggle, Mao Zedong emerged as the most important figure in the CCP movement, using guerrilla bases in the countryside of southern China to keep the CCP alive. Maoist strategies soon led to a change of context for the CCP's "national question."

In noticing Stalin's theoretical contribution to the "national question," Lenin once praised him as the "marvelous Georgian."[25] Because in Tsarist Russia the ethnic Russians constituted only a small majority of the population, the Bolsheviks had to give the "national question" a prominent position in their overall strategy. This helped Stalin the Georgian, an ethnic minority, emerge as their chief theoretician in this regard. If the Russian case is relevant at all in proving the difficulty for people of the dominant ethnic group to achieve cross-ethnic insights, the CCP leadership of the Han background did not have much chance to foster a theorist or strategist of its own in the field of ethnicity. In charge of the CCP's northern apparatus, Li Dazhao was the party's only founding member who paid some personal attention to the "national question" concerning Mongolia. After Li was executed by the warlord regime in Beijing in 1927, the CCP would never find another top-ranking leader who could potentially be a "marvelous Georgian."[26]

Certainly, nothing in Mao Zedong's background could make him such a candidate. Mao started his revolutionary career as Li Dazhao's protégé. But, unlike his mentor, until the mid-1930s, Mao's activities were limited to southern China. Hunan, Mao's home province, was the home of the Miao, Yao, and Tong peoples. Mao's early writings did not make any reference to these groups. His first known encounter with non-Han peoples took place in the summer of 1926, when Li Dazhao sent some Inner Mongols to the Peasants Movement Training Institute in Guangzhou (Canton). At the time Mao was one of the instructors at the institute. He had enough interest to ask these Inner Mongolian trainees about the social and political conditions of their home areas.[27] A few months later, peasants of Hunan held their first conference of representatives. They invited Mao to provide some advice on the peasant movement. One of the conference's final documents was actually on the liberation of the Miao and Yao peoples in Hunan, contending that these groups must participate in the peasant movement on an equal footing with the Han.[28] Mao's connection with the document, however, is unclear.

These occasions suggest that even when Mao was exposed to matters concerning non-Han peoples, he kept his credentials as an expert on the peasant movement. After the CCP–KMT split, for a few years Mao led a peasant army to the countryside. His headquarters did issue some public statements that mentioned the non-Han peoples' rights. These were brief repetitions of the CCP's established rhetoric on the matter, such as the "Manchus, Mongols, Hui, and Tibetans decide their own rules." These propaganda pieces were devoid of the usual party jargons for the sake of their rural audience. The problem is, while Mao's troops lived off the overwhelmingly Han, rural areas of Jiangxi, this kind of propaganda on the frontier peoples made little sense to the local peasants.[29] Mao's unorthodox guerrilla warfare in the countryside was not matched by any independent-minded deliberation of his own on the "national question." Nevertheless, the guerrilla warfare helped create the Chinese soviet movement in the countryside, which significantly changed the premise of the CCP's discourse on ethnicity.

The Chinese soviet movement of the early 1930s reflected a strange combination between a dogmatism originated in the Comintern and a pragmatism rooted in China. Now that the KMT–CCP conflict became a reality, the Comintern wanted the CCP to launch an urban-centered soviet movement as the party's vehicle to political power. Under this orientation, in May 1930, Shanghai was chosen as the location of the "first congress of the soviet regions."[30] It soon became clear that the CCP could survive only in poor and arduous rural areas where the KMT influence was minimal. In November 1931, the CCP had to launch a "Chinese soviet republic" in Ruijin, a rural town of Jiangxi. Mao Zedong, creator of the base, was elected to head the "temporary soviet central government."[31]

This was the beginning of the CCP's "incipient state."[32] The party's rhetoric in respect to the "national question" was affected accordingly. At the inaugurating assembly of the Chinese soviet, Wang Jiaxiang, a returnee from Moscow, made a report on the "minority nationalities" question. Afterwards, the assembly adopted relevant resolutions. In these documents, the party reaffirmed its "absolute and unconditional" support of the minorities' right to national self-determination. The right however meant one of three choices presented to the non-Han peoples: they could choose to join the Chinese soviet in a federation, or to organize autonomous regions within the Chinese soviet territories, or to establish their own independent states. One more qualification was that in concert with the class-struggle dogma, the choice had to be made only by the "laboring masses" of the minorities. The CCP left no doubt about which of the three options was preferred by itself: the goal of the Chinese soviet government was not to organize states along national lines but to "establish a country without national barriers." Currently, the soviet government would grant complete legal and political equality to all groups within its territories regardless of gender, race, and religion, help "backward nationalities" to increase their economic productivity, and promote national languages and cultures. Inevitably, the CCP used the occasion to chastise its adversary, asserting that the KMT's "bourgeois policies" since Sun Yat-sen had failed to bring any improvement to China's minority nationalities.[33] Obviously, as part of the Chinese soviet's inaugurating manifestation, the criticism was intended less for censuring the KMT government than for establishing the credentials of the CCP's own new state.

As a rebellious force restrained to a small rural region, the Chinese soviet assumed more symbolic than substantive significance. Despite the "constitutionalization" of the issue of ethnicity by the Chinese soviet government, in the next few years the CCP was more insulated from China's ethnopolitics than in any other period of its history. The main force and leading core of the CCP were forced out of cities and confined to southern China's countryside where non-Han groups were either nonexistent or invisible. Five of the CCP's ten bases, including the "central soviet region," were in Jiangxi. The only non-Han population of the province, the She people, would not be identified as a distinct "nationality" until after 1949. The same is true of the Tujia group in Hunan and Hubei, where the CCP bases also existed.[34] Only in two remote and isolated soviet regions in Shaanxi and Guangxi, the Mongols and the Hui in the former and the Yao in the latter constituted a significant policy issue for local CCP organizations. Meanwhile, CCP apparatuses scattered in areas controlled by the KMT, or the Japanese, or regional warlords, such as Yunnan, Sichuan, Gansu, Manchuria, and Inner Mongolia, had to deal with non-Han peoples of their regions on a daily basis. Only indirectly, the CCP center in Jiangxi learned about the interethnic problems facing these struggling local organizations. These organizations were hard pressed to find any solution for their problems in the Chinese "soviet constitution."[35]

Neither did the Chinese soviet's minorities programs demonstrate a better comprehension of China's ethnic affairs than the CCP's earlier cliché-borrowing from the Russian Bolsheviks. Typically, the Chinese soviet was launched on November 7 of 1931, an anniversary of the Bolshevik revolution, to manifest its adherence to the model of Soviet Russia. Its three-option formula on the minorities' right to self-determination constituted another borrowing from Moscow. The formula was adapted, probably by Wang Jiaxiang, from Stalin's discussion of the issue in 1913.[36] In the aforementioned soviet documents, the CCP leadership made a conceptual adjustment in substituting the term of "alien races" with a more manageable one, "minority nationalities." The list of non-Han groups was expanded accordingly. The inclusion of the Miao and the Li reflected the party's southern environment. But, the addition of the Taiwanese, Koreans, and Annamese (Vietnamese) to the list indicated the party's continued confusion about the scope of *China's* ethnic affairs. In sum, the importance of the Chinese soviet's programs on the "national question" should not be overestimated: they neither provided a practical guidance to the party's action in the field nor made any breakthrough in the party's understanding of China's ethnopolitics.[37]

A real departure was made, though. It is not the content of the Chinese soviet's new minorities programs but the way in which they were proclaimed. Along with other "government programs," they helped unveil for the first time the CCP alternative, the "soviet state," to the official Chinese state under the KMT, the Republic of China. The real mission of the "soviet republic" was not state building but state destruction. It posed an open challenge to the "legitimate" official state with a rebellious mechanism. Such a contender's scheme had many precedents in Chinese history. In this context, the red Jiangxi regime's "nationality policies" were designed less for attracting the non-Han peoples toward the "soviet state," which would require much effort to overcome too many barriers in terms of space and time, than for encouraging these peoples' alienation from the official Chinese state. Earlier, in the mid-1920s, while still cooperating with the KMT, the CCP had struggled against the warlord regime in Beijing but not the Republic of China. The party's attitude toward the frontier "alien races" at the time indicated a passive acceptance of China's divisive conditions

(China's unity seen as "infeasible" and "undesirable"). In the 1930s, now that the KMT monopolized the Republic of China as its own party-state and was poised to unify entire China, the CCP leadership began to appreciate, though still in theory, the Leninist maxim that the "national question" was a revolutionary "yeast." Borderland peoples' alienation from the Republic of China, though not necessarily the abstract "China," was therefore positively encouraged.

The result of the Chinese soviet's experiment with the Leninist strategy was disappointing. Early in 1934, when reporting to the Chinese soviet's second national assembly, Mao could mention only one achievement of the CCP's "nationality policy" in the soviet regions, that was, these regions' serving as asylums for expatriate revolutionaries from Korea, Taiwan, and Vietnam. Mao pointed out that "the starting point of the soviet's nationality policy should be to rally all suppressed minority nationalities around itself and to increase the anti-imperialist and anti-KMT revolutionary forces."[38] While these Korean, Taiwanese, and Vietnamese revolutionaries' "rallying" to the CCP bases reflected a function of the Comintern's international network, China's non-Han peoples' not rallying indicated the extremely limited outreach of the Chinese "soviet republic." Mao's contention also reflected an assumption generally held within the CCP leadership. It was a conviction that when the old China lost its luster to attract the non-Han and the remote to rally to the Middle Kingdom, the CCP's revolutionary alternative could enlist these peoples' support like a magnet.

Soon after Mao's speech, the CCP made a breakthrough to reach the non-Han peoples in the borderlands and thus got a chance to test the hypothesis on the natural alliance between the CCP and the minorities. Ironically, the "breakthrough" and the "chance" came only after Chiang Kai-shek's deadly "annihilation campaigns" deprived the CCP of its own "soviet state" in southeastern China, the supposed rallying center for the minorities. As a result, the ethnogeographic relationship between the CCP and the non-Han peoples changed drastically: before the party could draw the "minority nationalities" toward itself, it was forced to embark on a strenuous migration toward the northwestern frontiers and to seek a sanctuary in areas where "minority nationalities" constituted a significant portion of the local population.

Interethnic Contact

Until embarking on its Long March in 1934, the CCP dealt with the "national question" largely in abstract and had little to do with China's actual ethnopolitics. None of the top CCP leaders had any extensive experience in interethnic matters. The Long March relocated the CCP's leading core to China's northwest and decisively gave the "national question" a manifest position in the party's policy making. Moving from the hotbed of the Chinese culture in the Yangtze River valley to the fault lines between the Han and the non-Han societies in the northern frontiers, for the first time in its history the CCP was compelled to develop a functional "nationality policy." The ideological dimension of the "national question," which had been a paramount factor to the CCP's "stand taking" in relation to Moscow, now became secondary. The party's newly adopted habitat put pragmatism in command.

In the spring of 1934, the Long March began as a rout. It went through a tortuous course spanning areas in southwestern China inhabited by the Miao, Yao, Yi, Qiang, and Tibetan peoples and ending in northwestern China where the Hui and Mongols made up a significant portion of the population. Inevitably, the CCP's relationship with these peoples assumed unprecedented importance. In June 1935, when the marching Red Army entered Sichuan, its general political department demanded all high-level cadres to spare no effort to gain the non-Han peoples' support. Messages in the same vein were also conveyed to the foot-soldiers through the Red Army's official organ, *Hongxing Bao* (Red Star). The Red Army headquarters warned sternly against the "foolish bigotry of great-Han chauvinism" within the troops and demanded the troops to take advantage of the local peoples' hatred against the "Han rulers" and to enlist their support to the Red Army.[39] The tricky part, of course, was how to convince the frontier peoples that the Red Army was different from the "Han rulers."

The CCP leadership soon discovered that in the unfamiliar interethnic environment, the Red Army's usually effective means to create a self-image of the "people's army" were not enough. A major policy readjustment was in order. Until this time, ethnic distinctions had not made much sense to the CCP strategy; class analysis had been universally applied to all kinds of group antagonisms. If there were cases that clearly demonstrated "national antagonism," CCP operatives' task had been to convert it into "class antagonism" and to forge a common front among the "laboring masses" of the ethnic groups concerned. Until the beginning of the Long March, the "correct" party line had used a "rightist opportunism" label to repudiate any suggestion that the CCP cooperate with non-Han ruling elites.[40] During the Long March, however, the Red Army was compelled to work with the ruling elites of the frontier peoples in order to get the quickest possible assistance from the populace. In November 1934, shortly before the Central Red Army entered the Miao and Yao areas in northern Guangxi, its political department adopted a set of "working principles" that anticipated an interethnic encounter. The troops were required to "develop intimate relationship and forge various kinds of political and military alliances with upper-class representatives" of the local minorities communities. The rationale for the new orientation was that while the anti-Han hatred was prevalent locally, the "extreme backwardness" of the local economic and cultural conditions had not allowed class struggles to develop within the population. Therefore, the ruling elites or headmen were still the "sole representatives of the national interests" of their groups.[41]

The upper-class orientation achieved some results in facilitating the Red Army's advance. The most prominent case was the "blood alliance" between Liu Bocheng, commander of the advance column of the Central Red Army, and Xiao Ye Dan, headman of the Gu Ji clan of the Yi in western Sichuan. Liu took the step in May 1935 under an instruction from Mao Zedong. The alliance allowed the Central Red Army to prepare in the Yi area a daring operation to cross the Dadu River and thus escaped a deadly encirclement by Chiang's forces.[42] The upper-class approach, however, was useful to the Red Army only to a certain degree. Not all upper-class members of the minorities wanted to collaborate with the Red Army. In these occasions the Red Army was greeted either by resistance or by emptied villages. Furthermore, ethnic antagonism might be avoided when the Red Army was only passing through a minority region and behaved wisely; it would however be an entirely different matter if the Red Army attempted to create permanent bases in non-Han areas. In 1935, the issue of the Red Army's selection of a new base area was at the center of a dangerous policy disagreement within the CCP leadership.

During the first few months of the Long March, the CCP leadership was troubled by the question as to what area should be the Red Army's destination. Not until mid-June 1935 did the CCP Central Committee opt for the border region between Shaanxi and Gansu in the northwest as the Red Army's new home.[43] Yet, as it turned out, the decision was not accepted by the Red Army's Fourth Front Army under Zhang Guotao. The ensuing split between Zhang and the CCP center over the Red Army's strategic direction has been well studied.[44] But the historiography has overlooked how the "national question" featured in the controversy.

Zhang's preferred location for a new base was first indicated in his organizing, in May, a "Provisional Government of the Northwestern Federation" in northern Sichuan. The stated purpose of the government was to "recover Tibet and Xikang in the west, pacify Xinjiang and Qinghai in the north, and conquer Yunnan and Guizhou in the south in order to create one region including also the soviet bases in Shaanxi, Gansu, Sichuan, and Guizhou."[45] In late June, when the First and Fourth Front Armies joined forces in Songpan, it became clear that Zhang and the CCP center could not agree where the Red Army's next move should be heading, north or south.[46] In early August, the CCP center adopted a resolution to reaffirm its June decision on a northwestern strategy. The document criticized Zhang's class-struggle orientation toward the Qiang and Tibetan groups in western Sichuan and contended that his "northwestern soviet federation" was "premature."[47] In the ensuing controversy the two sides used similar arguments to defend the strategic and topographic advantages of their respective preferences. The one issue that separated Zhang and the CCP center was concerned with whether or not non-Han peoples were compatible with the Chinese Communist movement.

After the Red Army's initial encounter with the minorities, Mao and most of the CCP leaders were convinced that the Red Army must not be severed from its social and ethnic roots in China proper, and it must not become a wanderer in an unfamiliar and unfriendly non-Han terrain. In early September, when making a last effort to maintain the unity of the Red Army, the CCP center warned the troops of the Fourth Front Army that a southward move would lead the Red Army into minority nationalities' areas like Xikang and Tibet. In these areas, the center predicted ominously, the Fourth Front Army "would only suffer from starvation and cold weather and would sacrifice lives in vain; . . . the southward move was to embark on a road to ruin [*nanxia shi juelu*]."[48]

The warning went unheeded. In repudiating the CCP center's assertion that the Tibetan area was the "most backward" in China and therefore could not be conducive to the revolution, Zhang Guotao called the attention of the Fourth Front Army cadre to the example of the MPR in Outer Mongolia and to foreign imperialist interests in Tibet. He contended that the Tibetan area was by no means insignificant and the revolution could flourish here. Zhang asked the Fourth Front Army to view the Tibetans "as an important part of the Chinese soviet movement who will provide tremendous assistance to the movement."[49] When the First Front Army under the CCP center headed toward its final destination in northern Shaanxi, Zhang and the Fourth Front Army lurched into their southward venture.

Zhang's enterprise in the Tibetan areas of Xikang lasted from November 1935 to June 1936. During this period, the Red Army created six regimes among the Tibetan population whose language did not even have terms for "Communism" and "Red Army." Among these regimes, the most famous was a "Bod-pa People's Republic" in Ganzi that claimed a territory of sixteen counties. Zhang promoted these governments through his army command and his "northwestern federation government."[50] The record of the Red Army's relationship with the local people was mixed. Special disciplinary codes were issue to the troops for avoiding ethnic incidents with the Tibetan and other local peoples; the Red Army's option of using peaceful means to settle disputes with the local populace achieved cooperation from, or at least neutralization of, certain members of the ruling elites. But, basically, Zhang's policy was to push radical social reforms wherever possible. In these reforms, land and livestock were redistributed, lower-class individuals who were deemed "highly revolutionary" by the Red Army were put in charge of the new governments, and separation between government and religion was implemented.[51] These measures did not ignite a revolution of the Tibetans' own and would soon disappear after the Red Army left the region. But, Zhang's class-struggle orientation, though contrary to the CCP center's upper-class approach of the time, did harvest a long-term result in recruiting a few hundred lower-class Tibetans from the Tibetan communities in western Sichuan and Xikang. These were organized into a "Tibetan Independent Division." After 1949, the cream of this group would play an important role in the CCP's effort to incorporate Tibet into the People's Republic.[52]

Despite the revolutionary appearance of these measures and the sincerity among Red Army operatives in helping the local people, the immediate purpose of Zhang's policies was to create a home base for the Fourth Front Army itself. This was difficult to achieve. Among all the Red Army's operations, the most urgent involved food collection. These affected adversely all classes of the Tibetan communities. A fundamental fact is that the sudden arrival of the Red Army in the Tibetan region created an unbearable burden to the local economy. At the time the Fourth Front Army was forty-five thousand strong. Military emergencies did not allow the troops to collect food always through inoffensive means. The local people often felt confused by the Red Army's behavior. To them, the Red Army's friendly demeanor contrasted sharply with previous Han armies but its "extortion [of food] was worse than Liu Wenhui."[53] Under such circumstances, an intimate relationship between the Red Army and the populace could not grow. Zhang Guotao later recalled this experience, saying that "as if we lived in a foreign land."[54] He himself had a paranoid distrust of the Tibetans. In the summer of 1936, the Fourth Front Army, under the Comintern's interference, finally decided to give up the southern venture and to join the CCP center in the north. Before leaving, Zhang ordered the execution of the commander of the Tibetan division who to the point had loyally served the Red Army. The Tibetan division would soon be dissolved after the Fourth Front Army arrived in Kansu.[55]

The Fourth Front Army neither perished as the CCP center predicted nor flourished as Zhang expected. Both sides of the controversy, while accusing each other for perpetrating "great-Han chauvinism," proved to suffer from the same ignorance about the Tibetan society. In the summer of 1936, the Second Front Army under He Long and Ren Bishi became the last main force of the Red Army to pass the Tibetan region. The Second Front Army was not involved in the quarrel between the CCP center and Zhang; therefore, its leadership's opinion on the Tibetan region was not polemic. After crossing the region, commanders of this force reported frankly to the CCP center that their "nationality work" had gained "neither experience nor achievement . . . in the Fan [Tibetan] area." Instead, they listed in their report a series of difficulties and problems that the Second Front Army had encountered.[56] Clearly, all units of the Red Army shared the similar experience of frustrations in the Tibetan areas. The CCP center's avoidance strategy, Zhang's abortive enterprise for interethnic engagement, and the Second Front Army's bewilderment unveiled the same truth: the party's earlier indoctrination with the Bolshevik formula on the "national question" had yet to bear any fruit.

As the first extensive encounter between the CCP and the Tibetan populace in western China, the Long March presents an interesting case showing how "contact" may affect interethnic relationships. It has been suggested that "an increase of contact gives rise to various manifestations of an increasing conflict of interests as each group tries to vindicate and defend its own customs and values."[57] As a unique group of the Han, the CCP and the Red Army poised to engage in a new kind of contact with the Tibetans. Their considerable sensitivity toward the culture, customs, language, and religion of the Tibetans signified the novelty of the contact, but the conflict between the two sides over a tangible interest, food, could not be avoided. The Red Army's extortion of foodstuff was a "necessary mistake" openly admitted by the CCP leadership. This was also the Red Army's worst offense remembered by the Tibetans in the years to come.[58] In the mid-1930s, running for its own life, the CCP's predicament was that it was not in position to deliver "national liberation" to the "minority nationalities" as prescribed by its ideology but had the imperative reason to become an economic desperado as dictated by its need for survival.

Mao Zedong risked the split of the Red Army to avoid this kind of contact with the non-Han societies. But his northward orientation could not prevent the CCP's marginalization from the Chinese society. In November 1935, the CCP center became entrenched in northern Shaanxi. The new base area situated in the big bend of the Yellow River that embraced part of Shaanxi, Suiyuan (part of Inner Mongolia), and Shanxi. A "cradle of the Chinese civilization" in antiquity, the area's centrality to the Chinese life had long been lost. Another symbolic mark left by the Chinese history, the Great Wall, stood along the northern limit of the new CCP base. It served as a constant reminder to CCP leaders how peripheral their movement had become to the Chinese society in both political and cultural senses. Eventually, the CCP would manage to develop a "Yan'an way" of revolution along the fault lines of the Han and the non-Han cultures, which would pave its way to power.[59] But the CCP did not shed its dogmatic "Bolshevism" before making a last, disastrous effort to "break through to the Soviet Union."

Between the winter of 1936 and the spring of 1937, the CCP center organized a "west route army" to open a corridor between the CCP and the Chinese–Soviet Union border. The Fourth Front Army provided the better part of the expedition force. En route to its uncertain destination (Xinjiang and Outer Mongolia were considered at different times), the former Fourth Front Army had its second contact with a non-Han group, the Hui in Gansu and Qinghai. This time, it was almost annihilated by the forces of the Hui warlords in the region.[60] Thus, unable to find sanctuaries in non-Han frontiers and failing to get direct assistance from the Soviet Union, the CCP was compelled to work completely from its Chinese roots for resurrection. This became possible in the summer of 1937 when Chiang Kai-shek, having survived a hostage crisis in Xian and beset by the popular anti-Japanese emotions in China, agreed to suspend temporarily his anti-Communist campaigns for the sake of a national war of resistance against Japan.

Two Wings of Nationalism

One of the interpretations in the field suggests that during China's war against Japan, the CCP seized the national crisis to mobilize the Chinese peasants, and that the resultant "peasants' nationalism" would eventually enable the CCP to win the struggle for national power.[61] Although this insight helps explain the rapid expansion of the CCP's popular basis, it does not depict a complete picture of the CCP's national politics in the war years. If nationalism is to be viewed as a trend of opposition politics provoked by some particular social-political circumstances, during the anti-Japanese war the CCP's political strategy embarked on a vital phase that saw not only the party's enlisting of the peasants' "popular nationalism" but also its embracing of the KMT's "official" or "elite" nationalism. In other words, although China's war against Japan may have benefited the CCP's struggle for power in the long run, the war did not create a circumstance that let the CCP crash the KMT's official nationalism with a popular nationalism of its own. What the CCP accomplished in the war years was to blend the two together, a feat that the KMT never accomplished.[62]

If the first KMT–CCP united front in the mid-1920s was largely facilitated by the KMT's temporary radicalization of its nationalist ideology, the two parties' cooperation for the second time in the anti-Japanese war was marked by the moderation of the CCP's programs. The CCP's prewar revolutionary stratagem was characterized by a dogmatic overcoat imported from the Comintern, a rebellious thrust against the Chinese state under the KMT, and a separatist counsel to China's "minority nationalities." These were all put in abeyance during the war. Now the CCP explicitly brandished the banner of nationalism, committed itself to cooperation with the KMT in defending the territorial and sovereign integrity of the Chinese Republic, and urged the minorities to rally around China in a common struggle against Japan. When asked by a suspicious American journalist which came first between China and the Communist Party, Mao Zedong answered that the question was tantamount to ask who came first between a father and his child. Then, he remarked: "We Chinese have to use our own brains to think and decide what can grow from the soil of China."[63]

The CCP's most important wartime policy readjustment was suspension of class struggles. The rationale was that an independent country would have different class interests but could not have common national interests; since China was not such a country and was on the verge of "state subjugation and racial extinction" (*wangguo miezhong*), it must have an "identical interest of the whole nation" in order to survive.[64] Since the CCP's encouragement to the non-Han peoples' struggle against the Chinese state had hitherto been a corollary to its own "class struggle" against the KMT, the wartime suspension of the in-fighting in the Han's "self-group," paradoxically or logically, led the CCP to demand that all interethnic struggles in China be suspended. This entailed the party's reexamination of a whole set of conceptions concerning the Han–minority relationship. The old Bolshevik dogmas on the "national question" had to be replaced with conceptions that could better serve the CCP's current agenda.

In May, 1937, Zhang Wentian, a leading member of the CCP politburo, published an article that restored the CCP's subscription to the Three People's Principles as the basis of a new national united front. A leap of faith was made by Zhang in substituting the CCP's "soviet republic" with the Republic of China as the state to defend. Shortly after, in a report to the Comintern, the CCP center indicated that at present the agenda of Chinese nationalism included nonrecognition of Japan's territorial occupation in northern and northeastern China and Inner Mongolia, protection of China's territorial and sovereign integrity, support of the minority nationalities' rights to *equality and* self-determination, and organization of the Republic of China on the basis of a free union of all nationalities of China.[65] Although the wording of the report still followed the Bolshevik scriptures, the CCP was sliding out of the Soviet orbit. An issue to the point was the status of the Mongolian People's Republic. In the report the CCP center stopped short of explaining the inconsistency between its own traditional support of the MPR's independence and the official stand of the KMT government that Outer Mongolia was an inalienable part of China. Actually, some time before the report was filed, in a conversation with Edgar Snow, Mao Zedong had already redefined the party's attitude toward the MPR, contending that after China became a democratic republic itself, Outer Mongolia would rejoin a Chinese federation on its free will.[66]

After adopting the "official" or KMT definition of the territorial domain of the Chinese state, the CCP still needed to redefine the "Chinese nation" (*zhonghua minzu*), a conception interchangeable with the "Han people" in the party's earlier documents.[67] In the summer and fall of 1938, Yang Song, a Soviet-trained senior cadre, delivered a series of lectures on the subject.[68] These were to help senior party leaders sort out those confusing definitions. Unlike the CCP leadership in the 1920s that had largely had an abstract, dogmatic interest in the "national question," leaders of the Yan'an period earnestly needed a "way of saying" (*shuofa*), if not a theoretical framework, to justify their current political orientation. The stated purpose of the Yang Song lectures was to refute Japan's propaganda that China was not a nation and that Japan and China belonged to the same race and shared the same culture (*tongwen tongzhong*). A hidden script of these lectures, however, was to ease out the Comintern influence on the CCP's thinking, which, as mentioned before, did not treat frontier regions like Tibet and Mongolia as part of the Chinese revolution.

Given the CCP's general ideological affinity with Moscow, Yang Song performed a delicate revisionist task within the matrix of Stalin's definition of "modern nations." The room for Yang to maneuver was to qualify the "Chinese nation" as a "modern nation." Accordingly, *zhonghua minzu* was used as the name for the "modern Chinese nation," a dynamic entity that had allegedly occurred in history and then had been and still was in a ceaseless process of reconfiguration. Ethnically, the modern Chinese nation included the Han and those historically assimilated non-Han groups. The "minority nationalities" of China were categorized as peoples who were not yet members of the *zhonghua minzu* but could qualify as "nationalities" under the Stalinist territorial-linguistic-cultural-economic test. Thus, China had a single modern nation (the "Chinese nation") but was a multinationality state. In this conglomeration of nationalities, the "Chinese nation" was indisputably the leading core at home and the sole representative of China abroad. In the current national crisis, all nationalities of China were compatriots commonly victimized by Japan's aggression. Under the circumstances, although the principle of national self-determination should continue to be understood as the minorities' right to national separation and independence (Yang stressed that the right must not be corrupted to mean merely "cultural or local autonomy"), under current circumstances the right should not be exercised by China's minority nationalities lest they fall into the Japanese embrace.[69] Thus, continuing to pay homage to the "marvelous Georgian," Yang managed to include into the Chinese cause all the ethnic groups in the territories claimed by the Republic of China.

Mao Zedong, however, was not satisfied. He once confessed that Stalin's writings, especially those concerning the Chinese revolution, were not among his favorite readings.[70] To Mao, Yang Song's attention to the theoretical subtleties of the Stalinist formula seemed travail. He preferred a big-stroke approach to the question of the "Chinese nation." In mid-October 1938, when talking to an enlarged conference of the CCP Central Committee, Mao declared that the "Chinese nation has indeed stood up!" Referring to the "minority nationalities," Mao deployed a plural conception of "various Chinese nationalities" (*zhonghua gezu*), contending that like all political parties and social classes, all nationalities of China should be included in the national united front. The minorities should be granted the right to administer their own affairs *provided* that they join the anti-Japanese struggle and align themselves with the Han in a unified state.[71] In another occasion, when further elaborating on the *zhonghua minzu* conception, Mao simply jettisoned Stalin's notion on the "modern nation" and treated the *zhonghua minzu* as an entity that seemed to have existed all along in history. As for the histories and cultures of the non-Han nationalities, Mao had nothing to say except noting that they had always been part of the *zhonghua minzu*. His notion of the history of the Chinese nation was therefore "mainly about the history of the Han."[72]

In a Comintern forum, Yang Song's definition of the "Chinese nation" would be more defendable than Mao's, but in China's wartime politics, Mao's was a more useful tenet for mass mobilization and collaboration with the KMT. Having turned to China's "glorious past" for an image of China's promising future, the CCP now promoted the traditional ideal of "grand unity" (*da yitong*) in order to inject national pride into the Han population. In the process, the party's interpretation of the minorities' "best interests" shifted ground. The about-face change of the CCP's relationship with the official Chinese state required the minorities to suppress their antagonism against the KMT regime as well. The logic seemed simple enough: no matter how bad China's internal imperialism might be, the Japanese imperialism was worse. Throughout the war years the CCP propagated interethnic harmony in China. Anti-Han nationalism of the minorities' was detrimental to China's war effort and therefore must be overcome.[73]

A scholarly opinion has suggested that the CCP's consistent promise of national self-determination to the minority peoples and the KMT's constant repressive policy against these peoples together gave life to a range of non-Han ethnonationalisms in China.[74] The argument overlooks the fact that in the war years the distance between the KMT's and the CCP's national politics was significantly reduced. Surely these parties were still competing against each other. But, as the CCP substituted its class-struggle orientation with an ethnocentric nationalism, the two Chinese parties were now competing on the same front and for the same leadership over the "Chinese nation." Like any other nationalism, Chinese nationalism was jealous against other nationalist competitors. In the war years it became the commanding ideology for the CCP to awaken the Han populace of China. In the meantime, the non-Han peoples' nationalisms had to be kept in dormancy.

Thus, the Leninist strategy of using the minorities' political aspirations as "revolutionary yeast" was reversed. The CCP lost "national self-determination" as the most powerful slogan in its rhetoric to attract the non-Han peoples.[75] In the war years, the CCP complained that the Hui and the Inner Mongols, the party's two closest neighbors, did not respond well to its call for a "national struggle" against Japan.[76] In view of the CCP's retreat from the principle of self-determination, these peoples' apathy toward the CCP's wartime propaganda did not come as a surprise. But the CCP managed to maintain an edge over the KMT in cultivating the minorities' good feelings. This was possible because the KMT's wartime policy toward the minorities became increasingly rigid and repressive.

In the war years, as a legal regime of the northwestern "Border Region," the CCP developed a set of cultural and socioeconomic programs for enlisting support from the Hui and Mongolian population within its domain. The KMT regime's high-handed policies, by contrast, provoked these peoples' antigovernment rebellions one after another.[77] After Chiang Kai-shek published *China's Destiny*, in 1943, the CCP seized the opportunity to stress the difference between it's and the KMT government's stand on the "nationality question." While Chiang argued that the ethnic groups in China were not distinctive nations but merely "the main and branch stocks [that] all belong to the same blood stream," the CCP defended these groups' "nationality" status.[78]

Clearly, the debate was not about who should be included in the "Chinese nation," but what should be the normative status of the member groups of the "Chinese nation." The tremendous importance of this debate, however, should not obscure a fundamental consensus between the CCP and the KMT reached in the war years. From a historical point of view, the consensus dwarfed the lingering differences. By the time of World War II, the two parties' presentations of the "Chinese nation" shared these features: the "Chinese nation," or *zhonghua minzu*, occurred in history long before the modern era; the Han was the magnetic nucleus of the "Chinese nation"; the formation of the "Chinese nation" involved other ethnic groups, named "clans" by the KMT but "nationalities" by the CCP, that had either assimilated into or amalgamated with the Han; the official boundaries of the Republic of China demarcated the territorial domain of the *zhonghua minzu*, which included all the borderlands inhabited by the non-Han groups; the *zhonghua minzu* was the common political identity for all members of the Republic of China; equality, not right to secession, should be the ultimate goal pursued by all ethnic groups in China.[79]

Until the time of China's war against Japan, the KMT and the CCP had used different terminology to present the Chinese nation; their designated member groups of the Chinese nation had also varied from time to time. Only a direst national crisis like Japan's invasion could bring the two parties to an agreement on the definition of the *zhonghua minzu*. In the war years the conception was absolutely necessary in two fronts: in the international scene, it justified China's right to survival as a nation-state; at home, it promoted a "national" war effort. In the long run, the wartime bipartisan consensus accomplished nothing less than the inventing of the "Chinese nation" for generations to come.[80]

Only in this general conceptual framework of the Chinese nation, should one understand the distinction between the KMT as a practitioner of nationalist politics of "coordination" and the CCP as one of communist politics of "mobilization."[81] Indeed, the distinction would eventually determine the two parties' fortune in their power struggle. So far as the non-Han groups were concerned, however, from the beginning of the Chinese–Japanese war, the CCP no longer followed the Leninist mobilization strategy that fermented the "yeast" of ethnonationalism. The CCP conducted a more subtle operation for channeling the non-Han peoples' political thrust into its own movement. Any non-Han ethnonationalist aspirations outside the party orbit would be viewed as "viruses" harmful to the body and soul of the "Chinese nation." The war years saw the burgeoning of the CCP's pragmatic ethnopolitical programs. In this period, the party launched its first systematic investigations of the Hui and the Inner Mongol societies, looking for ways to mobilize these peoples in the "correct direction." "Regional autonomy" by non-Han peoples was experimented in the CCP base areas as an alternative to "national self-determination." Training programs were conducted to prepare "minority nationality cadres" who would bring the party's various programs to the field. Wherever possible, the CCP cultivated working relationships with the local ruling elites of the Mongol and Hui communities.[82] For these endeavors, Mao Zedong set up a guideline that would remain valid in the years to come: the party's "nationality work" must fight a two-front battle against both the "great-Han chauvinism" among the party cadres and the "narrow nationalism" (*xia'ai minzu zhuyi*) of the non-Han groups.[83]

* * *

Although China's non-Han peoples have been named as "minority nationalities" and their affairs as "frontier," the "national question" is neither minor nor peripheral to the socio-political life of China. In the CCP's case, at different times and under changing circumstances, the question was successively a core issue in the party's international connection, a key element in the party's military and political strategies, and a defining matter in the party's view on what constituted the Chinese state. Chinese Communists never understood China's "national question" exactly in the same way as the Bolsheviks did in their European and Russian contexts. In the CCP's formative years, its leaders juggled Communist doctrines and their own Chinese-centric proclivity. In due course, China's and the CCP's own circumstances, not dogmas borrowed from Moscow, set the pivot for the party's approach to the "national question."

During China's war against Japan, the CCP made its first systematic effort to deal with the "national question." The result fell short of the party's expectations. By and large, according to the CCP standard, the Hui and the Inner Mongols remained aloof from the party and passive toward China's war against Japan.[84] Yet, the real significance of the CCP's theoretical exercises and practices during the war years was to mesh together the Bolshevik "national" stratagem and the Han-centric "Chinese nationalism." It has been contended that the key element in the Leninist strategy on the "national question" involved the Communist Party's promise of minorities' right to self-determination before it took power and cancellation of the right after the party took power.[85] The CCP followed a different course: circumstances forced it to forfeit the "promise" a decade earlier than the Leninist timetable. The Soviet system of nationalities was forged principally during a domestic revolution and at a time when Russia was not under serious external threat. By contrast, China's national crisis under Japan's invasion forced the CCP to substitute "prematurely" its supra-national rhetoric on minorities' right to self-determination with a program on "national equality" under the banner of Chinese nationalism. Among all the threads of the CCP's "indigenized Marxism-Leninism," this one would have the most lasting influence on the party's policy making in the years to come.

Notes

1. The official discourse in China uses *duo minzu guojia*, which can be translated literally into "multinational state," to refer to the multiethnic composition of the state. In the past decade or so, while the Chinese term has continued, a preferred English translation by the Chinese authorities is "multiethnic state."
2. Benjamin I. Schwartz, "The Maoist Image of World Order," in John C. Farrell and Asa P. Smith, ed., *Image and Reality in World Politics* (New York: Columbia University Press, 1967), 92, 98.
3. See June T. Dreyer, *China's Forty Millions: Minority Nationalities and National Integration in the People's Republic of China* (Cambridge: Harvard University Press, 1976), and Walker Conner, *The National Question in Marxist–Leninist Theory and Strategy* (Princeton: Princeton University Press, 1984).
4. Anthony Smith, *The Ethnic Origins of Nations* (Oxford: Blackwell Publishers, 1999), 55, defines "ethnicism" as a premodern predecessor to nationalism. It is an "*ethnie's*" "response to outside threats and divisions within" and "seeks a return to the *status quo ante*, to an idealized image of a primitive past." Since these qualities were overtaken by China's anti-imperialist nationalism of the twentieth century, this study borrows "ethnicism" to mean the Han-centric tendency in China's interethnic relations that has deep roots in China's long history.
5. Arif Dirlik, *The Origins of Chinese Communism* (New York: Oxford University Press, 1989), 13–14.
6. "The first resolution of the Chinese Communist Party," no date, *Zhonggong Zhongyang Wenjian Xuanji* (Selected documents of the Chinese Communist Party Central Committee), 18 vols, the Central Archives, comp. (Beijing: Zhonggong Zhongyang Dangxiao Chubanshe, 1992. Hereafter cited as, *ZZWX*), 1: 6–9.
7. Zhang Guotao, *Wo de Huiyi* (My memoirs) (Beijing: Xiandai Shiliao Congkan Chubanshe, 1980), 1: 138, 184, 196, 235–236; Department of the United Front Work of the CCP Center Committee, *Minzu Wenti Wenxian Huibian* (Collected documents on the nationality question) (Beijing: Zhongyang Dangxiao Chubanshe, 1991), 62 n. 2 (hereafter, *MWWH*); Zhou Wenqi and Chu Liangru, *Teshu er Fuza de Keti–Gongchan*

Guoji, Sulian he Zhongguo Gongchandang Guanxi Biannian Shi 1919–1991 (Unique and complex subject: a chronicle of the relationship among the Comintern, the Soviet Union, and the Chinese Communist Party, 1919–1991) (Wuhan: Hubei Renmin Chubanshe, 1993), 22–23, 33–34.

8. "Resolution on international imperialism and China and the Chinese Communist Party, July 1922," *MWWH*, 8; "Resolution of the CCP to join the Third Communist International, July 1922," *ZZWX*, 1: 67–72.
9. "Resolution on international imperialism and China and the Chinese Communist Party, July 1922," *MWWH*, 8; "Proclamation of the second national conference of the CCP, July 1922," *MWWH*, 17.
10. Dirlik, 270.
11. The CCP's ignorance about China's interethnic conditions would continue even after the party took power. This can be attested by a remark made by De Xiaoping in 1950: "With regard to the minority nationality question, not only we are yet to learn the rudiments; we haven't even got a clue." See Deng Xiaoping, *Deng Xiaoping Wenxuan* (Selected writings of Deng Xiaoping) (Beijing: Renmin Chubanshe, 1989), 1: 161.
12. "Proclamation of the second national conference of the CCP, July 1922," *MWWH*, 17.
13. Helene Carrere d'Encausse, *The Great Challenge: Nationalities and the Bolshevik State, 1917–1930* (New York: Holmes & Meier, 1992), 63.
14. Institute of Nationality Studies of the Chinese Academy of Social Sciences, *Sidalin Lun Minzu Wenti* (Stalin on the national question) (Beijing: Minzu Chubanshe, 1986), 6, 7, 25.
15. "Report to the Comintern Executive Committee on the organization and work of the Oriental Nations Department of the Siberian Bureau of the Russian Communist Party (Bolshevik), 21 December 1920," The First Research Section of the Party History Research Office of the CCP Central Committee, trans., *Liangong (Bu), Gongchan Guoji yu Zhongguo Guomin Geming Yundong, 1920–1925* (The Soviet Communist Party, the Comintern, and the Chinese nationalist revolutionary movement, 1920–1925) (Beijing: Beijing Tushuguan Chubanshe, 1997), 1: 51–52; "Resolution by the Presidium of the Comintern Executive Committee on the Chinese national liberation movement and the question of the Kuomintang, 28 November 1923," ibid., 342–343.
16. "Borodin's notes and reports, (later than) 16 February 1924," ibid., 469.
17. Chen Duxiu, "Our answer, 17 September 1924," *MWWH*, 60–61; Li Shouchang (Dazhao), "Mongol nation's liberation movement, 1925," ibid., 69–70; Qu Qiubai, "Lenin and Chinese people's revolution, 21 January 1926," ibid., 70–71; Chen Duxiu, "KMT's rightist conference, 23 April 1926," ibid., 73; "Resolution on national revolutionary movements adopted by the fourth national conference of the CCP, February 1925," *ZZWX*, 1: 329–341.
18. Christopher Atwood, "A.I. Oshirov (c. 1901–1931): A Buriat Agent in Inner Mongolia," in Edward Kaplan and Donald Whisenhunt, ed., *Opuscula Altaic: Essays Presented in Honor of Henrry Schwarz* (Bellingham: Center for East Asian Studies, Western Washington University, 1994), 56–57.
19. "Resolution on the Mongol Question by the first enlarged executive committee meeting of the fourth Central Committee of the CCP," October 1925, *MWWH*, 38–39; "Special meeting of the CCP Central Committee," February 21–24, 1926, ibid., 42; "Qijia's [code name for CCP Central Committee] opinion on the work with the Inner Mongolian KMT," December 1926, ibid., 50; "Comrade Liu Bojian's report from Kulun," September 8, 1926, ibid., 76–77.

20. "Proclamation of the first national congress of the Chinese Kuomintang, 23 January 1924," *MWWH*, 26–27.
21. Sun Yat-sen included these words in his "proclamation of the provisional president of the Republic of China," dated January 1, 1912. See the Second Historical Archives of China, *Zhonghua Minguoshi Dang'an Ziliao Huibian* (Collected archival materials on the history of the Republic of China), volume 2.
22. "Resolution on the nationality question, 9 July 1928," *ZZWX*, 4: 388.
23. "Zheng Peilie's report on the conditions of the Inner Mongolian work in the past, 5 September 1928," United Front Work Department of the Inner Mongolian Committee of the CCP and the Archives of the Inner Mongolian Autonomous Region, *Nei Menggu Tongzhanshi Dang'an Shiliao Xuanbian* (Selected archival materials on the history of the united front in Inner Mongolia) (no publisher, 1987. Internal circulation), 1: 41.
24. Chen Shaoyu, "To struggle for a more Bolshevized Chinese Communist Party, February 1931," *ZZWX*, 7: 630–631.
25. D'Encausse, 35.
26. In 1925 Li Dazhao wrote an article on "The Liberation Movement of the Mongolian Nation," *MWWH*, 69–70.
27. Office of Colleting Sources on Party History, the CCP Committee of Huhhot Municipality, "Report on the Investigation of the Conditions of the Suiyuan Peasant Movement during the Great Revolution Period," *Nei Monggu Dangshi Ziliao* (Historical Sources on the [Chinese Communist] Party of Inner Mongolia), 2: 256–259; *Mao Zedong Nianpu*, 1: 165–166; Jiyatai, "Early Revolutionary Activities in Inner Mongolia," *Neimengggu Tongzhanshi Dang'an Shiliao Xuanbian*, 1: 26; Jane L. Price, *Cadres, Commanders, and Commissars: The Training of the Chinese Communist Leadership, 1920–45* (Boulder: Westview Press, 1976), 80–81, 86 n. 17.
28. *Mao Zedong Nianpu*, 1: 173, 175; "Resolution on the liberation of the Miao and Yao by the first conference of the peasant representatives of Hunan, December 1926," *MWWH*, 52.
29. "Proclamation of the Chinese Communist Party by the Party Department of the Workers' and Peasants' Red Fourth Army, January 1929," *MWWH*, 96–97; "Public notice by the Headquarters of the Workers' and Peasants' Red Fourth Army, January 1929," ibid., 98–99.
30. *Mao Zedong Nianpu*, 1: 306; resolution on the question of the Chinese soviet, adopted by the Oriental Department of the Communist International, August 1930, *ZZWX*, 6: 616–621.
31. *Mao Zedong Nianpu*, 1: 358–360.
32. John Breuilly, *Nationalism and the State* (Chicago: The University of Chicago Press, 1993), 234 uses this term to define the CCP's effort in northwestern China after the Long March of 1934–1936. In this writer's opinion, the CCP's "state" began within the soviet experiment in southern China before the Long March.
33. Zhou Wenqi and Chu Liangru, *Teshu er Fuzai de Keti*, 223; "Outline constitution of the Chinese soviet republic, 7 November 1931," *MWWH*, 165–166; "Resolution on the question of minority nationalities in the Chinese territory by the first national assembly of the Chinese soviet, November 1931," ibid., 119–170.
34. Ren Yinong et al., *Minzu Zongjiao Zhishi Shouce* (Handbook of nationalities and religions) (Beijing: Zhonggong Zhongyang Dangxiao Chubanshe, 1994), 213, 219, 387–388; Jiang Ping, *Zhongguo Minzu Wenti*, 493–494.

35. "CCP Central Committee's letter to the CCP frontal committee of the Seventh Army, 16 June 1930," *MWWH*, 127; "CCP Central Committee's letter to the CCP Guangdong provincial committee, 4 January 1932," ibid., 176; "CCP Central Committee's letter to the CCP Sichuan provincial committee, 14 February 1932," ibid., 177–180; "CCP Central Committee's letter to the CCP Shaanxi provincial committee, 1 August 1932," ibid., 172; "CCP Central Committee's letter to all the CCP organizations and members in Manchuria, 26 January 1933," ibid., 193–195; Zhou Enlai, "Report on the Comintern resolutions, 24 September 1930," *ZZWX*, 6: 375–380; "Resolution on current situation and the party's tasks, 18 January 1934," ibid., 10: 43–46.
36. Stalin's definition of the right of self-determination is discussed in Connor, *National Question*, 33.
37. For different views, see Dreyer, 63–64 and Mackerras, 72.
38. Mao Zedong, "Report to the Second National Soviet Assembly [on behalf of] the Central Executive Committee and the People's Commissariat of the Chinese Soviet Republic, January 1934," *MWWH*, 210–211.
39. "Instruction on the winning over of minority nationalities, issued by the general political department of the Chinese Workers' and Peasants' Red Army, 19 June 1935," *MWWH*, 339–340; "Destroy the enemy in large numbers with offensive and create new Chuan-Shaan-Gan [Sichuan, Shaanxi, and Gansu] soviet regions, 10 July 1935," ibid., 296–297.
40. "CCP Central Committee's letter to the Sichuan provincial committee of the CCP, 19 February 1932," *MWWH*, 177–180; "Decision of the Sichuan provincial committee of the CCP on the acceptance of the outline of the thirteenth conference of the Comintern and the resolution of the CCP Central Committee's fifth plenum, 11 June 1934," ibid., 220–223.
41. "Instruction on the principles of the work within the Miao and Yao nationalities, issued by the political department of [the First Front Army of] the Chinese Workers' and Peasants' Red Army, 29 November 1934," *MWWH*, 244–246; *Mao Zedong Nianpu*, 1: 438–439.
42. *Mao Zedong Nianpu*, 1: 456–457; Jiang Ping, *Zhongguo Minzu Wenti*, 404.
43. *Mao Zedong Nianpu*, 1: 443–444, 448, 449, 454, 458.
44. For instance, Yang Kuisong, *Xi'an Shibian Xintan: Zhang Xueliang yu Zhonggong Guanxi zhi Yanjiu* (A new examination of the Xi'an incident: a study of the relationship between Zhang Xueliang and the CCP) (Taipei: Dongda Tushu Gongsi, 1995), and Benjamin Yang, *From Revolution to Politics: Chinese Communists on the Long March* (Boulder: Westview Press, 1990).
45. "Declaration on the establishment of the government of the northwestern federation of the Chinese soviet republic, 30 May 1935," *MWWH*, 268–270; "Congratulatory message from the CCP committee of the northwestern special region to the government of the northwestern federation of the Chinese soviet republic, 1935," ibid., 273–274.
46. Military Museum of China, *Mao Zedong Junshi Huodong Jishi* (Record of Mao Zedong's military activities) (Beijing: Jiefangjun Chubanshe, 1994), 158–159, 162; Jin Chongji, *Zhuo Enlai Zhuan*, 287–288.
47. Zhang Guotao, *Wo de Huiyi*, 256–261; "CCP Central Committee resolution on the political situation and tasks after the First and Fourth Front Armies joined forces, 5 August 1935," *MWWH*, 305–307.
48. Zhang Guotao, 3: 213–233; "Supplementary decision of the central politburo on current strategic orientation, 20 August 1935," *ZZWX*, 10: 545–546; "CCP Central Committee's

and the [Red Army] frontal command headquarter's instruction to the Left Route Army on changing its course and advancing northward, 8 September 1935," ibid., 10: 549–550; "CCP Central Committee's letter to all comrades on the execution of the policy of northward advance, 10 September 1935," ibid., 10: 553; "CCP Central Committee's decision on comrade Zhang Guotao's mistakes, 12 September 1935," ibid., 10: 557; *Mao Zedong Nianpu*, 1: 470–472.

49. "Zhang Guotao's report at the operatives' conference of the governmental organizations on the development and prospect of the Chinese soviet movement and our current tasks, 1 April 1936," *Zhongguo Gongnong Hongjun Disi Fangfianjun Zhanshi Ziliao Xuanbian, Changzheng Shiqi* (Selected documents on the battle history of the Fourth Front Army of the Chinese Workers and Peasants Red Army, the Long March period) (Beijing: Jiefangjun Chubanshe, 1991), 414–415, 419–420 (hereafter, *DFZZ*); "General political department of the Fourth Front Army's outline on the tactical orientation toward the Tibetan people, 29 May 1936," ibid., 490.
50. "Proclamation of the first national congress of the Bod-pa People's Republic, May 1936," *MWWH*, 495–496.
51. "Instruction on the minority nationality work from the Political Department of the Fourth Front Army, March 1936," *MWWH*, 358–361; "Outline on policies and tactics in dealing with the Tibetan people issued by the political department of the Fourth Front Army, 29 May 1936," ibid., 369–376.
52. Tianbao, "Red Army's Long March through the Tibetan area," Editorial Committee on the Documentary Series of the History of the Chinese People's Liberation Army, *Hongjun Changzheng Huiyi Shiliao* (Reminiscent materials on the Red Army's Long March) (Beijing: Jiefangjun Chubanshe, 1992), 2: 89–96.
53. Zhang Guotao, 3: 286–287. Liu Wenhui was the warlord who controlled Xikang.
54. Zhang Guotao, 3: 212–214, 276–278.
55. Liu Ruilong, "Unforgettable journey," *Hongjun Changzheng Huiyi Shiliao*, 2: 105–117; Guan Xianen, "For the victory of the Long March," ibid., 436–439; Ji Shibai, "Red Army's Tibetan Independent Division Remembered," ibid., 83–88; Li Zhongquan, "Unforgettable minority nationalities in Sichuan and Xikang," ibid., 434. In Red Army documents of the time, the Tibetans were named "Fanmin" or the Fan people. Liu Wenhui was the warlord in Xikang. The commander of the Tibetan division had a Chinese name, Ma Zun. His Tibetan name is not known to this writer.
56. "Conclusive report on the Second and Sixth Army Groups' political works during the Long March, by the political department of the Second Front Army of the Chinese Workers' and Peasants' Red Army, 19 December 1936," *MWWH*, 436–440.
57. H. D. Forbes, *Ethnic Conflict: Commerce, Culture, and the Contact Hypothesis* (New Haven: Yale University Press, 1997), 157.
58. This lesson was learned by the CCP. In 1950, when the CCP army was about to enter Tibet, Mao Zedong set up two principles. One was to support Tibetan autonomy, another was "*buchi difang*" or not to live off the local economy. See *Deng Xiaoping Wenxuan*, 1: 167.
59. For the subject, see Mark Selden, *The Yenan Way in Revolutionary China* (Cambridge: Harvard University Press, 1971).
60. "Chen Changhao's report on the failure of the west rout army, 30 September 1937," *DFZZ*, 976–991; Li Xiannian, "Clarification of a few questions in the history of the west route army, 25 February 1983," ibid., 997–1004.

61. Chalmers A. Johnson, *Peasant Nationalism and Communist Power* (Stanford: Stanford University Press, 1962).
62. Breuilly, 9–15, discusses nationalism as opposition politics, and Anderson, 113–116, 159–160 discusses a transitional relationship between popular and official nationalisms during the process of a revolution.
63. *Mao Zedong Nianpu*, 2: 528.
64. "Fundamental principles for the national united front, 20 November 1936," *MWWH*, 525–527.
65. Luo Fu, "Our opinion on the program for national unity, 11 May 1937," *MWWH*, 456–458; "Letter from the CCP Central Committee to the Comintern on a 'draft program for national unity,' 27 June 1937," ibid., 466–467.
66. Edgar Snow, *Red Star over China* (New York: Random House, 1938), 110.
67. One of the examples is "Resolution of the CCP Central Committee on the current political situation and the party's tasks, 25 December 1935," *ZZWX*, 10: 609–617.
68. In the mid-1930s, Yang Song, under the guidance of the Comintern but not the CCP center, was in change of the CCP apparatus in Manchuria. His position in the CCP in 1938 is not clear to this writer. But he participated in several meetings of the CCP politburo's standing committee in the year. See Zhang Peisen, *Zhang Wentian zai 1935–1938* (Zhang Wentian during 1935–1938) (Beijing: Zhonggong Dangshi Chubanshe, 1997), 314, 317, 331.
69. Yang Song, "On nation, 1 August 1938," *MWWH*, 763–768; idem, "On nationalist movements and the national question in the era of capitalism, 8 and 20 August 1938," ibid., 769–780; idem, "On national movements and the national question in the era of imperialism, August and October 1938," ibid., 781–801.
70. "Learn from historical lessons and oppose big-power chauvinism, September 1956" (this is Mao's conversation with a communist delegation from Yugoslavia), *Mao Zedong Waijiao Wenxuan* (Selected writings of Mao Zedong on diplomacy) (Beijing: Zhongyang Wenxian Chubanshe, 1994), 259.
71. Mao Zedong, "On the new phase, 12–14 October 1938," *ZZWX*, 11: 557–662.
72. Mao Zedong, "Chinese revolution and the Chinese Communist Party, December 1939," *MWWH*, 625–632.
73. Political department of the Eighth Route Army, "Political textbook for the anti-Japanese soldiers, December 1939," ibid., 807–808; Mao Zedong, "Question of independence and self-reliance in the united front, 5 November 1938," ibid., 607.
74. Connor, 67–92, argues that the CCP's self-determination strategy toward the minorities kept alive even when the party embraced the "Han ethnonationalism" during the war against Japan. Breuilly, 234–240, discusses the different effects of the KMT's "coordination politics" and the CCP's "mobilization politics" in China's "internal frontiers."
75. Liu Shaoqi, "Some fundamental questions in the anti-Japanese guerrilla warfare, 16 October 1937," *MWWH*, 561–565, and Kai Feng, "What is the disagreement between the party's central committee and the [Zhang] Guotao line? 22 February 1938," ibid., 760–761. These are two wartime documents favoring minority peoples' "independence." But both were written before Mao's "On the New Phase," which was delivered in October 1938. Not until July 1945, in "CCP Central Committee's slogans for the celebration of the eighth anniversary of the war of resistance" (*ZZWX*, 15: 175), would the minorities' "rights to self-government and self-determination" be restored to anticipate a new round of power struggle with the KMT.

76. "Outline on the question of the Hui nationality by the northwestern working committee of the CCP Central Committee, April 1940," *MWWH*, 648–656; "Outline on the question of the Mongolian nationality in the war of resistance by the northwestern working committee of the CCP Central Committee, July 1940," ibid., 657–667.
77. For instance, the Hai-Gu rebellions between 1938 and 1941 in Gansu, the Ikezhao incident of 1943 in western Suiyuan, and the Ily rebellion of 1944 in Xinjiang.
78. Chiang Kai-shek, *China's Destiny* (New York: Roy Publishers, 1947), 31; Zhou Enlai, "On China's new fascist authoritarianism, 16 August 1943," *MWWH*, 723–727; "KMT and nationalism, (editorial of the *Jiefang Ribao* [Liberation Daily]), 18 September 1943," *ZZWX*, 14: 566–576; Mao Zedong, "On coalition government, 24 April 1945," *MWWH*, 742–743; Chen Boda, "On *China's Destiny*, 21 July 1943," ibid., 945–949.
79. Actually, as an official policy, equality among China's various *zu* (racial or ethnic groups) was first started by Yuan Shikai in 1912. See Zhao Yuntian, *Zhongguo Bianjiang Minzu Guanli Jigou Yange Shi*, 425.
80. In Western literature, the use of terms like "Chinese nationalism" and "Chinese nation," for which there are no generally accepted Chinese counterparts, can easily miss the evolution of the terminology in China's nationalist discourse. In his illuminating study, *Muslim Chinese: Ethnic Nationalism in the People's Republic* (Cambridge: Harvard University, 1996), 81–93, Dru C. Gladney correctly points out an ill-informed practice in the field to use "Han" and "Chinese" as exchangeable conceptions. His discussion of the rise of a "Han nationalism" from Sun Yat-sen to Mao Zedong, however, overlooks Chinese politicians' attempt to project modern China as a multinationality or "multi-clan" "Chinese" (*zhonghua*) nation-state, not a uninational Han nation-state.
81. Breuilly, 237.
82. Wang Duo, *Wushi Chunqiu: Wo Zuo Minzu Gongzuo de Jingli* (Eventful fifty years: my experience in the nationality work) (Huhhot: Neimenggu Renming Chubanshe, 1992), 52–154.
83. Li Weihan, *Huiyi yu Yanjiu* (Reminiscence and study) (Beijing: Zhonggong Dangshi Ziliao Chubanshe, 1986), 1: 454–455.
84. For relevant CCP documents, see "Outline of the Northwestern Work Committee of the CCP Central Committee on the Question of the Hui Nationality, April 1940," *MWWH*, 648–656, and "Outline of the Northwestern Work Committee of the CCP Central Committee on the Question of the Mongol Nationality in the War of Resistance, July 1940," ibid., 657–667.
85. Conner, 38.

CHAPTER SEVEN

Solve Rubik's Cube in the Steppes

During the second half of the 1940s two landmark events happened to the Mongolian nation. On October 20, 1945, a plebiscite was held in the Mongolian People's Republic (MPR) that favored the MPR independence from China. Then, on April 29, 1947, an "Inner Mongolian Autonomous Government" was established in Wangyemiao of western Manchuria that marked the Chinese Communists' decisive control of the Inner Mongolian autonomous movement. Although these were significant developments in the Cold War and in the Chinese Civil War of the late 1940s, they were also part of two longer historical processes—the formation of the modern Mongolian nation and the development of China's "nationalizing" nationalism.[1] During China's long transformation from a traditional empire to a modern national state, an important development was the separation between China's "foreign" and "domestic" affairs. The process included redefinition of China's traditional frontier affairs according to commonly accepted norms in the international community. Resultantly China lost its ambiguous suzerainty over certain areas and established definitive sovereignty over some others. The case of Mongolia is unique because, due to certain historical conditions, a half of the Mongolian nation became "externalized" to China and became a separate state, and another half, by the establishment of the People's Republic of China (PRC), was solidly "internalized" and incorporated into Chinese sovereignty.

Following the Qing and the Republic of China, the PRC constitutes the third phase of China's nationalization. Its Communist founders were as devoted to "grand unity" (*dayitong*) of China as the Manchu monarchists, and to the "Chinese nation" as the Chinese Nationalists. This also means that the CCP's ethnopolitical stance was basically in agreement with its Nationalist predecessor. The cliché about the CCP's "creative" application of Marxism to China has to be balanced by an unstated premise: the CCP "creatively" continued China's ages-old practices in the name of Marxism. Contrary to supranational Marxism, the CCP's ethnopolitical enterprise, in its finalized form during China's war against Japan, was as nationalistic, state-oriented, and wary of foreign interference as the KMT's. As such, the evolution of the CCP's ethnopolitical stance between 1921 and 1945 was no longer a process in which the CCP gradually achieved a "mature" understanding of China's "national question"according to Marxist doctrines. Irrespective of the Communist jargons used by CCP leaders in their policy deliberations or statements, Marxism and Soviet precedents were far less influential on the CCP's ethnopolitical behaviors than usually presumed. In the meantime, traditional Han-centric ethnoculturalism, China's ethno-demographic and ethno-geographical conditions, foreign encroachments along China's ethnic frontiers, the anti-Japanese war, and the CCP's constant marginalization in China's political life all played significant roles in shaping the CCP's ethnopolitical stand.

After Japan surrendered in August 1945, the CCP and the KMT again openly stood on the opposite ends of China's political spectrum, waging respectively a "war of liberation" (*jiefang zhanzheng*) and a "suppression of rebellion" (*kanluan*) against each other. Although the Chinese Civil War between 1945 and 1949 appeared a struggle between Communism

CCP "liberated regions" and Inner Mongolian autonomous movements.

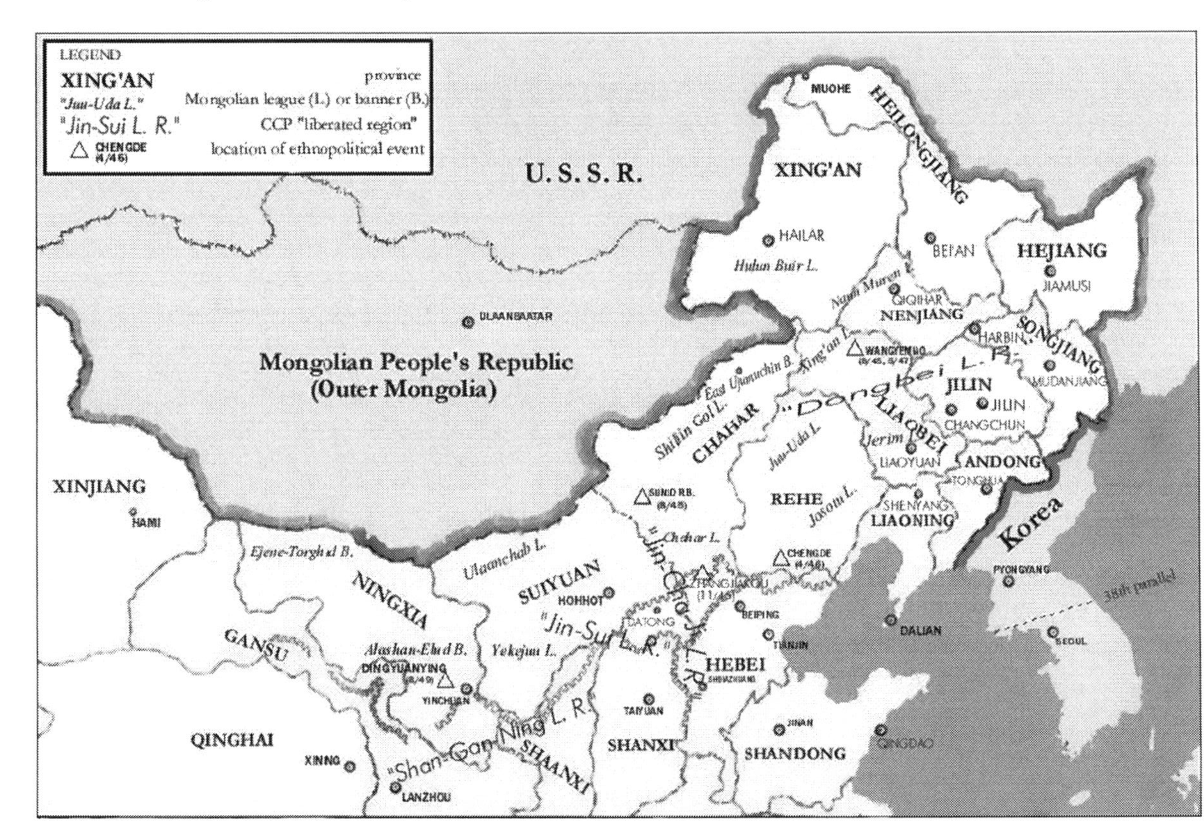

"Nei Menggu Meng Qi Weizhi Tu" (Map of the locations of Inner Mongolian leagues and banners). The map was first published in *Neimenggu Jianying* (Snapshots of Inner Mongolia) by the Inner Mongolian Autonomous Government in September 1947. The map claims a region for Inner Mongolian autonomy from western Manchuria in the east to Ningxia in the west. The two banners are the national banner of the Republic of China and that of the Inner Mongolian Autonomous Government, symbolizing that this was autonomy within the ROC.

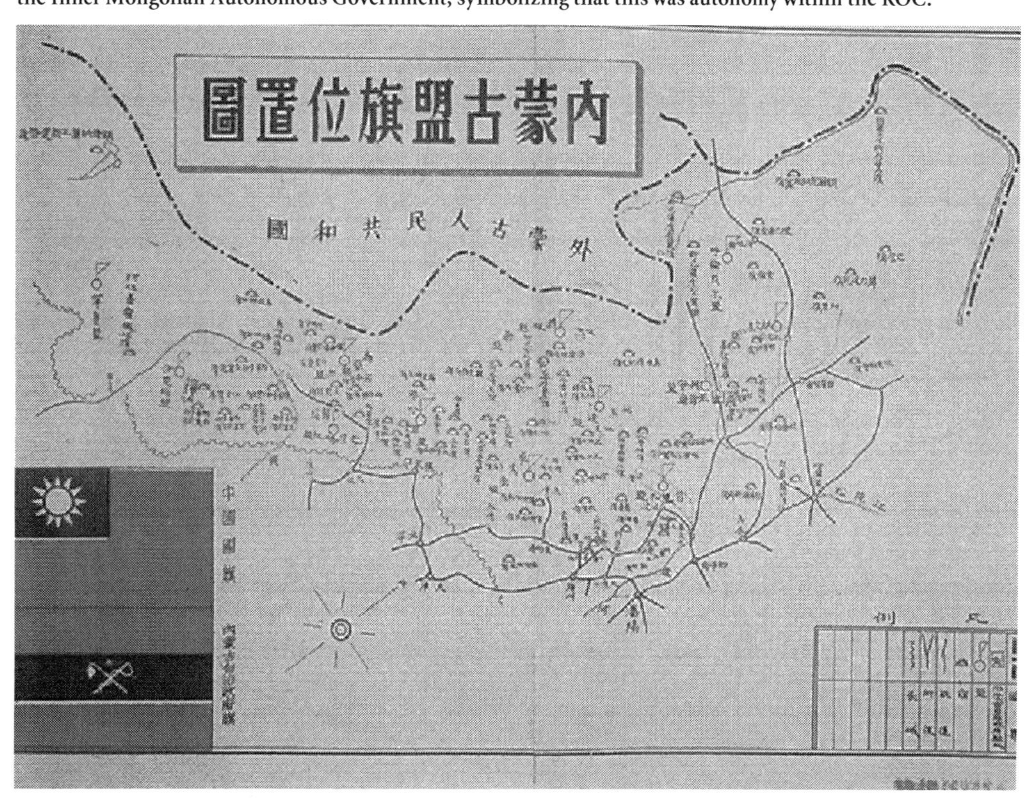

Source: www.als.gov.cn/main/tour/whals/tpxw/images.

and Nationalism, it was actually a military competition between China's two "nationalizing" agents. During the civil war the CCP did not change its coordinative nationality policy. Maintaining a political edge over the KMT by implementing social and economic reforms among the minorities, the CCP nevertheless insisted that all nationalities' "liberation" must be achieved as part of the Chinese revolution. The CCP's "internalization" of the Inner Mongolian autonomous movement was an example to the point.

Bloc, National, and Ethnic Politics

At the end of World War II the so-called Mongolian question entered decisive phase. During the first half of the twentieth century, the Mongolian question was one of the issues that reflected China's ongoing nationalizing process. The contest between separatist Mongolian nationalism and centralizing Chinese nationalism was the crux of the whole question. The bifurcation of Mongolia into an "outer" and an "inner" sector during the Qing continued to affect the evolvement of the Mongolian question in the republic period. After Mongolian nationalism was commandeered by the Soviets in Outer Mongolia and was suppressed by the Chinese authorities in Inner Mongolia in the prewar years, the fate of the Mongolian people became an "international domestic issue" without a clear destination. The Mongolian question was rekindled during World War II in the following senses: Japan's wartime socio-political policies and anti-Chinese agitations among the Mongols of Manchuria and Inner Mongolia prepared a new wave of Mongolian autonomous movements in China, the on-going dispute over the status of Outer Mongolia between the Chinese and the Soviet governments became an item in the inter-allied diplomacy, and the Soviet–Mongolian forces' entry into the war against Japan through certain Mongolian areas in China in August, 1945 made the issue of Mongolian unification, or "Pan-Mongolism," more real than any time before.

While the Han-Chinese and the Mongols of all political persuasions had opposing dispositions respectively for internalizing or externalizing the Mongolian question, interested foreign powers calculated and decided their attitudes according to their strategic interests. Outer Mongolia's permanent externalization to China could not be avoided. Since its de facto separation from China in the 1920s, the "Mongolian People's Republic" (MPR) had fallen into the increasingly tightened grip of the Soviet Union. After treating Outer Mongolia as a renegade "special district" for two decades, in its treaty with the Soviet Union in August, 1945 the KMT regime finally agreed to give up its sovereignty claim over the territory in exchange for Moscow's promise not to support the CCP in Chinese politics.[2] As the KMT regime's principal ally in the war against Japan and a staunch supporter of a unified China after the war, the U.S. government nevertheless did not commit itself to the KMT agenda of regaining control in Outer Mongolia. Policy makers in Washington could accept a settlement of the Sino–Soviet dispute over Outer Mongolia one way or another as long as it was achieved peacefully. After Japan's defeat, from a Cold War perspective American policy makers classified the MPR as a region entrenched solidly in the Soviet bloc. In the words of an American diplomat in China, "as far as the United States and American interests are concerned, the Mongolian People's Republic, . . . is about as important and pertinent as Atlantis. To all intents and purposes it is a closed case."[3]

The "inner" half of the Mongolian question was far from a closed case. Several autonomous regimes emerged in Inner Mongolia and Manchuria after Japan's surrender; Inner Mongolian nationalism became an important factor in the renewed civil war between the KMT and the CCP. The KMT regime's official view was that all the political agitations among the Inner Mongols were of Soviet or Chinese Communist backgrounds. American officials' opinions on the Inner Mongolian situation varied. But there was a consensus, as phrased by U.S. Embassy in Moscow, that no matter whether the Inner Mongols were under the CCP influence, or to be absorbed into the MPR, or to form an autonomous government of their own, "the end result was likely to be the same—subservience to Moscow."[4]

Thus, the KMT from its partisan stand and the U.S. government from its "bloc politics" perspective readily assigned Inner Mongolian nationalism to the side of their adversaries. Although critical of the KMT's rigid and suppressive approach toward China's ethnic minorities, American officials never offered any direct advice to the Chinese government in this regard, which, in any case, was China's "internal" problem. More important, when Washington valued the KMT official nationalism as an anti-Soviet asset in the Cold War, the ethnopolitical aspect of this nationalism had to be tolerated as well. Once identifying the KMT regime with China, the U.S. government inevitably shared its view that Moscow, the CCP, and Inner Mongolian nationalists were similarly detrimental forces to China's national unity.

This "bloc" perception grossly underestimated the inter-national and interethnic factors and their effects within the opposing camp. In the case of Inner Mongolia, while the KMT and the U.S. policies were generally negative toward the Inner Mongolian autonomous movements and thus alienate the Inner Mongols from their own camp, the CCP performed the role of China's nationalizing agent and internalized the Inner Mongols.

After Japan's surrender, the CCP strategists immediately recognized the strategic importance of Inner Mongolia to their competition with the KMT for Manchuria. In the meantime the CCP leadership did not have a grasp of the political conditions in Inner Mongolia. From the CCP center to its local apparatus, the notion was that an autonomous movement needed to be started by the party not only for mobilizing the Inner Mongols but also for strengthening the CCP's rear area and its connection with the Soviet–Mongolian Army. Before adopting any concrete policy, the CCP leadership decided to wait for information about Outer Mongolia's attitude and about the Inner Mongols' social and political conditions.[5]

Like the KMT government, the CCP considered Inner Mongolia largely in connection with Outer Mongolia. But the CCP and the KMT took opposite stands on the matter: while the KMT feared the MPR's agitation among the Inner Mongols, the CCP wanted to create an Inner Mongolian movement to facilitate its own relationship with the MPR. Clearly, at least at the beginning, CCP leaders believed that the cross-border ethnic factor would be beneficial to its own connection with the Soviet bloc.

Also like the KMT, the CCP leadership failed completely to anticipate the Inner Mongols' political spontaneity at the end of war. In view that the CCP was so masterful in conducting mass movements and propagated so much about the KMT government's suppressive policies toward the non-Han peoples of China, this lack of foresight was especially astonishing. The scarcity of information about the Inner Mongols was just part of the reasons. A more important reason was the CCP leadership's fundamental underestimation of the Inner Mongols as a people. During World War II, frustrated by their abortive efforts to mobilize the Mongols to participate actively in China's war against Japan and viewing Inner Mongolia as a backward society in terms of Marxist historical materialism, CCP leaders formed a rather negative opinion about the Inner Mongols' political quality. One of the CCP's wartime document contended:

> Today apathy, decadence, and corruption are prevalent within the Mongolian nation; these phenomena have deprived the Mongolian people, upper and lower classes alike, of confidence in their own nation. Feeling powerless and seeing no way out, they become

> fully dispirited, weak, and dependent. These conditions indicate that the Mongolian nation's liberation must rely on assistance from outside revolutionary forces, and that the Mongolian nation's liberation movement can be successful only by combining itself with the Chinese revolution.[6]

Upon Japan's surrender, the CCP denounced Prince Demchugdongrub (Prince De), the best-known Inner Mongol collaborator with Japan, as a "Mongolian traitor" (*meng jian*). Aside from him, the CCP center could not see any other influential political force in Inner Mongolia. The CCP was poised to make another try to offer its assistance from the outside to Inner Mongols by starting an autonomous movement. During the initial postwar months "Mongolian autonomy" in the CCP policy was merely a slogan without concrete contents. In the next two years the CCP leadership would have to go through a winding course to decide how to respond to the Inner Mongols' own demands for autonomy.

In its renewed military struggle against the KMT government, the CCP took its first test in the issue of Inner Mongolia that would measure the party's ability to involve non-Han ethnic groups in its political and military operations. The CCP center wisely relied on Yun Ze as its principal ethno-strategist. A Tumed Mongol trained in Moscow during the 1920s, Yun Ze spent most of the war years in Yan'an, helping with the CCP's training programs for "minority cadres" and management of the border region's Mongolian affairs. These endeavors earned him the reputation as the party's expert in nationality affairs. During the CCP's seventh national congress in the early summer of 1945, Yun Ze was elected as an alternate member of the CCP Central Committee. When Japan surrendered, the CCP immediately sent Yun Ze back to Inner Mongolia in a manner typical of the CCPBKMT takeover competition at the time: he was appointed as governor of Suiyuan and mayor of Guisui (Hohhot). But these official titles soon became irrelevant as the KMT established control in Guisui ahead of the CCP. Yun Ze could only reach Zhangjiakuo (Kalgan), where he became affiliated with the CCP's Jin-Cha-Ji (Shanxi-Chahar-Hebei) Bureau.[7]

Soon Yun Ze demonstrated his ability as a deft party operative. In October 1945 the CCP center learned that a self-appointed Mongolian government appeared in Prince De's palace in the West Sunid Banner that was then occupied by units of the Soviet–Mongolian Army. Yun Ze was harried there to deal with the situation. In West Sunid he found out that the so-called government was but an empty name and involved only a small group of Mongolian youths and former members of Prince De's wartime collaborative regime. Yun Ze easily persuaded these people to give up their government. But he had to spend more time quarreling with the local Soviet commander who insisted on the government's continuation. The quarrel ended when the higher authorities on the Soviet side intervened and recalled the commander.

To Yun Ze and the CCP center, the West Sunid episode was a rude awakening. Three things became abundantly clear. First, in spite of the CCP's unflattering view of Inner Mongols as a politically impotent people, a strong autonomous tendency was obviously seething in Inner Mongolia. It became transparent that in the war years the CCP leadership misconstrued the Inner Mongols' reluctance to become involved in the war against Japan as evidence of political numbness. Secondly, now that the Inner Mongols' political activism was evident, it must be kept in the CCP's orbit lest it be manipulated by the KMT, create difficulties to CCP operations, or grow into an unstoppable separatist movement to harm China's territorial integrity. And, thirdly, the West Sunid incident educated the CCP leadership that an ethnic separatist movement might be encouraged by "friendly" foreign influence, even though in this particular case the Soviet and MPR authorities eventually cooperated with the CCP.[8]

Ironically, the West Sunid incident indicated how the Soviet–American rivalry in postwar China helped the CCP's effort to internalize Inner Mongolian nationalism. After the West Sunid regime appeared, the supreme command of the Soviet Army in Manchuria became extremely concerned with an allegation carried by the American press that the Soviet Union and the MPR wanted to foster an Inner Mongolian republic. Marshal I. Ra. Malinovskii instructed the Soviet unit in Zhangbei to investigate. At the same time the MPR sent an official to Zhangjiakuo to consult with the CCP. In Zhangjiakuo the three sides reached an agreement on letting the CCP conduct Inner Mongolian affairs as a Chinese problem. This, however, did not end the CCP's trouble with its comrades from the other side of the border. When the Soviet–Mongolian troops stayed in Inner Mongolia, according to the Jin-Cha-Ji Bureau's reports, they took away more than 60% of the Shili-yin Gool League's and most of the Chahar League's livestock. The heist, these reports observed, was an "unprecedented calamity in a long time." "Now people living in [the Mongolian] banners are in great panic and the society is in chaos." This man-made disaster put an extra burden on the CCP's operations in these Mongolian banners, which to a large extent involved relief efforts. On the other hand, in a negative way the situation facilitated the CCP's effort to start government-like organizations in these areas. In early October the *zasags* (banner rulers) of the Chahar League agreed to set up a joint office under the CCP's leadership. The office was soon escalated into the league government. The principal reason for the Chahar Mongols' cooperation with the CCP was the looting by Soviet–Mongolian troops. The banner officials were anxious to have a unified and effectual governing body to shield them from the foreign occupation.[9] This development seemed to repeat Chinese peasants' rally to the CCP in northern China in the war years for the purpose of saving themselves from the Japanese invader.

National and Frontier Priorities

Even though CCP operatives in Mongolian banners had to function as agents of the "Chinese authorities" in helping the local people fend off an obnoxious foreign occupation force, this was not their original mission. Their charge was to prepare the land and people for the CCP's power struggle against the actual Chinese central government of the time, the KMT regime. For this purpose, the Jin-Cha-Ji Bureau first organized a small "committee on the Mongolian people's liberation" as an intermediary to work among the Mongols. After the West Sunid incident, it became clear that the committee was too small to handle the rising autonomous sentiment in Inner Mongolia. Consequently, in early November, the Jin-Cha-Ji Bureau and Yun Ze proposed to the CCP center to establish an "Alliance of the Inner Mongolian Autonomous Movement" (*neimenggu zizhi yundong lianhehui*).[10]

The Alliance was designed to meet multiple purposes. As defined by a CCP participant, the Alliance functioned as a party, a government, a military establishment, and a mass organization all at once.[11] The CCP needed the amalgam as a leading body to coordinate its Mongolian work in different areas, as a united-front instrument to reach out to Inner Mongols of different backgrounds, and as a preparatory body for a full-fledged Inner Mongolian government in the future. According to Yun Ze, with the Alliance the CCP wanted to erect a banner of national liberation around which the Inner Mongols could rally. But, when the Alliance was launched, it was only a stopgap measure for the CCP: on the one hand, it was needed to win over the Inner Mongols whose autonomous and territorial aspirations had to be answered in certain manner; on the other, before a full-scale war with the KMT government began, the CCP must maintain its own "legal" façade. The Alliance, without claiming to be a government, would not appear an open challenge to the administrative structure of the Republic of China.[12]

On November 26, an assembly of 76 delegates formally launched the Alliance at Zhangjiakuo. Yun Ze was elected as the chairman of its executive committee. To demonstrate the Alliance as an organization for entire Inner Mongolia, these delegates represented thirty-seven banners scattered in six provinces from Ningxia in the west to Heilongjiang in the east. Some of the delegates indeed came from banners, but there were banners that could not send their delegates in time or were not aware of the assembly at all. In the latter cases, delegates were selected for these banners from people already working with the CCP in Zhangjiakuo. The charter of the Alliance subscribed to the "new democracy" crafted by Mao Zedong, targeted "reactionaries within the KMT" as its enemies, and set as its current goal the formation of "local, democratic and autonomous political power" that would grant equality to all nationalities and accommodate all classes. Right after the assembly, the Alliance sent a message of greeting to the CCP center and also announced its existence to the world through the New China News Agency and the Jin-Cha-Ji Bureau's propaganda organ.[13] Through the Alliance the CCP committed itself publicly to the idea of Inner Mongolian autonomy. The Alliance's stand in the CCPBKMT struggle was similarly unequivocal. What remained to be seen was where the Alliance stood in those concrete historical disputes between the Inner Mongols and the Han Chinese. This matter would directly affect the Alliance's ability to accomplish its mission of winning over the Mongolian populace to the CCP's side.

In ethnopolitics, symbolism is as important as tangible policies. As the CCP's leading operative in Inner Mongolia, Yun Ze understood this thoroughly. From the moment of the Alliance's existence, Yun Ze invoked Inner Mongols' historical memories by identifying the new organization with a long line of ethnic heroes from Genghis Khan to famous members of the Inner Mongolian People's Revolutionary Party of the 1920s.[14] The location of the Alliance's headquarters was also important. Zhangjiakuo was improper because of the city's Han character. At the time, Guisui (Hohhot) was deemed by many as the political center of Inner Mongolia. In history, however, the place twice became associated with Inner Mongols' submission to alien rule, to the Manchus in the 1630s and to the Japanese 300 years later. Known as the "door-lock to the [Chinese] capital" ever since the Qing Dynasty, Guisui was successively the site for the Suiyuan (meaning "pacification of the remote") General's headquarters of the Qing government, the capital of the Suiyuan Province of the Chinese Republic, and the home of Prince De's regime under the Japanese. As a matter of fact, Yun Ze's first postwar assignment was to assume the governorship in Guisui, which was blocked by the KMT occupation of the city ahead of the CCP.[15] Denied access to Guisui, the Alliance opted for another location, which, ironically, was Prince De's palace in West Sunid despite the fact that the CCP and the Alliance denounced Prince De as a "Mongol traitor" and a "devil prince." The move was not made because, soon after the Alliance was launched, Yun Ze and his associates went to the east to deal with the problem of another spontaneous autonomous movement in eastern Mongolia and western Manchuria.

In his effort to indoctrinate the Inner Mongols, Yun Ze did not expect that the communist dogmas could be readily comprehended even by educated Mongolian youths. Once he told the young trainees in the Alliance's military-political school that they should not try to grasp Marxism during the brief training period and that for now it was sufficient for them to have just "a taste of the CCP." By this Yun Ze meant that a sense about the fundamental differences between the CCP's and KMT's nationality policies should be adequate to attract the Inner Mongols to the CCP's side.[16] But, in the postwar years, the CCP and the KMT were not the only options that the Inner Mongols had to choose from. By committing itself to Inner Mongolian autonomy the CCP indeed achieved a tremendous edge over the KMT in the ethnopolitical arena, but the CCP did not have monopoly over the issue. To Inner Mongols, a powerful autonomous movement in eastern Mongolia provided a third alternative.

Before Yun Ze's Alliance relocated to eastern Mongolia, the CCP had already maneuvered with the eastern Mongolian autonomous movement for more than a year. In late December 1945, when CCP troops pushed into northern Jehol and western Manchuria, they encountered the question of eastern Mongolia. Due to the size of the Mongolian population in this area, which was reportedly two million (actually less), and the strategic position that they occupied, the CCP center immediately sensed the importance of the matter. During the next month the CCP center and its Northeast Bureau agonized over a policy to deal with the situation. Yun Ze's Alliance in western Mongolia was a precedent that the Northeastern Bureau might emulate, but conditions in eastern Mongolia were different. In the west, the Alliance was set up to start a CCP-led Mongolian movement and to preempt any Mongolian initiative outside the party's orbit, whereas in the east a well-organized popular movement had emerged ahead of the CCP's "nationality work." As viewed by CCP officials, the movement centered in Wangyemiao of the Xing'an League in western Manchuria had many "incorrect" features: it stressed the Mongolian–Han contradictions but ignored class struggles within the Mongolian society; it pursued "great Mongolism" (*da menggu zhuyi*) in insisting on Mongolian governance of territories where the Han population already constituted the majority; it had a neutralist tendency in the current KMTBCCP struggle and refused to allow CCP troops to enter certain areas; finally, it strived for *national* independence or accession to Outer Mongolia, which was incompatible with the CCP's formula of "national liberation" through a CCP-guided autonomy. Yet, these "mistakes" could not be corrected in haste by the CCP because, for one thing, the movement seemed to have the sympathy of Soviet and MPR officials in Manchuria, and, for another, it was feared that any abrasive move by the CCP might tip the delicate Mongolian–KMT–CCP triangle in favor of the KMT.[17]

To the CCP the ethnopolitical situation in eastern Mongolia was more complex than the politics in China proper involving the KMT, the CCP, and the "third force" of the Democratic League. In China proper, opposition to the KMT was everything. In cultivating cooperation with the Democratic League, the CCP craved the latter's head-on conflict with the KMT government. In ethnopolitics of the northern frontier, however, the CCP shared with the KMT a common ethnocultural root on which rested the official conception of Chinese sovereignty. The Soviet–Mongolian factor added to the complexity. In a word, in the question of eastern Mongolia the CCP was faced with a Rubik's Cube-like situation—the success of its operation was measured by its ability to achieve eventually perfect alignment on every facet of the question.

In late 1945 and throughout 1946 the CCP pursued a two-pronged strategy against the KMT, which included a military effort for controlling Manchuria and North China and a political, "legal" maneuvering with the KMT in the arena of public opinion. In mid-January 1946, the CCP submitted to the national political consultative council a "draft outline for peaceful state reconstruction," advocating a unified, democratic, and constitutional new China under the leadership of Chiang Kai-shek. Gauged with this frame, eastern Mongols' program for independence and self-determination appeared extreme to the CCP center.

Thus, in mid-February the center instructed the Jin-Cha-Ji and Northeast Bureaus that the party must not support eastern Mongols' programs lest itself be tarnished by KMT's "rumors."[18]

At this juncture, disagreements on a policy toward eastern Mongols emerged among responsible CCP cadres. In a report responding to the center's cautionary February directive, the Northeast Bureau made a plea for a positive approach toward the eastern Mongols. The bureau pointed out that when the eastern Mongols initially expressed their hope to access to Outer Mongolia, they did not have the benefit of knowing about the KMT–Soviet treaty of August 1945, which virtually sanctioned Outer Mongolia's independence and, by implication, Inner Mongolia's being part of China. In the past few months, however, Outer Mongolian leaders and CCP cadres had already brought the eastern Mongols around in this regard. Now the eastern Mongols adopted a pro-CCP stand and agreed to pursue autonomy under the Chinese central government. At an assembly on January 16 the eastern Mongols adopted "basically correct" programs. For instance, their program for autonomy "automatically recognized China as the suzerain state," which, according to the bureau, was good enough to repudiate the KMT's disinformation that the Inner Mongols were seeking independence. In a separate message, Peng Zhen, secretary of the Northeast Bureau, assured the CCP center that "now the eastern Mongolian people's autonomous movement is basically under our influence, and their principal armed force of two thousand strong is under the leadership of the youth league and may be subject to our command." Peng further suggested that "we must accept" the eastern Mongols' demand for incorporating into their administrative region certain territories in Jehol which had been part of Xing'an Province during Japan's occupation.[19]

To a significant degree, the Northeast Bureau's favorable impression of the eastern Mongolian movement was derived from CCP personnel's positive experiences in western Manchuria with pro-CCP figures such as Askhan, who was the commander of the eastern Mongolian armed force. In Jehol, however, CCP operatives encountered rather different personalities. In southern Jehol they had to deal with Bai Yunhang, whose brother Bai Yunti was one of the high-positioned Inner Mongols in the KMT government. CCP cadres viewed Bai as a nuisance because of his ambiguous attitude toward his KMT brother and his attempt to organize Mongolian armed forces and governments in areas where the CCP had already established itself. Another figure was He Zizhang, who was a strong influence in northern Jehol and wanted to close his region to the CCP. Both Bai and He acted in the name of the eastern Mongolian movement. Thus, the CCP reporting from the Jehol painted the eastern Mongolian movement as a de facto Mongolian state led by a group of "upper-class bureaucrats" and ex-collaborators with Japan. Allegedly this group did not care about ordinary people's welfare. Their party, the "Inner Mongolian People's Revolutionary Party," was "very leftist in programs but very rightist in action." The CCP's Ji-Re-Liao (Hebei-Jehol-Liaoning) Branch Bureau was especially opposed to accepting the eastern Mongols' demand for incorporating the former Xing'an territories within Jehol into their region, contending that the step would destroy the "integrity of Jehol" and would be against the will of the province's Han majority.[20]

The eastern Mongols sensed the difference between the Northeast Bureau and the Ji-Re-Liao Branch Bureau. Among them a word circulated that the "Eighth Route Army" in the east was better than that in the west. To the CCP center, however, the problems encountered by its regional operatives were less important than what the eastern Mongolian movement might mean to the CCP's general strategies at the national and international levels. A few days after receiving Peng Zhen's reports, the center decided to stick with its earlier decision that the movement in Wangyemiao should not be supported in its current form. Its directive, dated February 24, deserves a complete quotation:

> Northeast Bureau, West Manchuria Branch Bureau, and Jehol Branch Bureau:
>
> Having studied the programs and activities of the east Mongolian people's autonomous government, we believe that under current domestic and international circumstances, the establishment of such an autonomous, republic type of government is still *excessively leftist* and disadvantageous to the Mongolian nationality, the Chinese people, and the Soviet–Outer Mongolian diplomacy. It can only provide the reactionaries with an anti-Soviet and anti-communist excuse, and create *fear among the narrow nationalists among the Chinese people.* Today east Mongolia should pursue local autonomy in accordance with article six, section three of the "program for peaceful state reconstruction." This is to set up an autonomous region under the Liaobei and Jehol provincial governments, or *at most to request organization of a single province as an ordinary local government.* It should not form a relationship with China as one between a suzerain state and an autonomous republic, and there is no need for it to have a separate currency, a separate army, and even a separate national color (there is a rumor about this, please verify), etc. If they want to have an autonomous region below the provincial level, our liberated area can already guarantee its implementation; if they demand to establish a province, we can also help them to achieve the goal. These are realistic and feasible approaches, and can in essence satisfy their demands. Now they make a big fanfare by issuing declarations, despatching delegates, and filing petitions. This way, they cannot achieve anything in practice and will only run into stonewall. Please patiently persuade them to change orientation along this line, and, in addition, *they should be warned that if they insist on the current orientation, we will not be able to support them and, if necessary, will have to renounce in public any relationship with them.* PS. To our knowledge, the Soviet Union is not aware and not supportive of their actions. Please investigate and report *what on earth is the origin of their actions.*[21] (emphasis added)

The "internalizing" intention of the directive is self-explanatory. CCP leaders were seasoned revolutionaries. They calculated and executed carefully policies through the party system. In stressing the "mass line," they welcomed spontaneity of the masses only to the extent that it could be channeled into the party orbit. Still, it was remarkable that CCP leaders at the center could easily be concerned about a hypothetic "fear" among "narrow" Chinese nationalists but would not appreciate the Inner Mongols' genuine aspiration for autonomy. The terminology on the Mongols' "excessively leftist" tendency stressed the eastern Mongols' demands as adventurous tactics against the KMT regime but downplayed these demands' ethnopolitical essence against the *Han–Chinese* authorities. It indicated the CCP leaders' mindset focusing on their partisan competition with the KMT for power but averting from the Mongols' struggle for nationhood. The last sentence of the directive betrayed the CCP leadership's continued disbelief that the Mongols should be able to take political initiatives on their own.

At the time all the sides involving in the CCP policy discussion agreed that Yun Ze should go to the east to deal with the government in Wangyemiao.[22] On March 10, 1946, the center issued a directive to the regional bureaus concerned on Yun Ze's function as a coordinator for the party's policies in western and eastern Inner Mongolia. A general orientation toward the east Mongolian movement was laid out for Yun Ze. The CCP center wanted the eastern Mongolian government of high-degree self-government to be reduced in territory and modified in form. Ideally, the eastern Mongolian leaders should be persuaded to accept the principle of "regional autonomy" (*quyu zizhi*). In practice this meant that their government should be confined to administering only the Mongols residing in the new Liaobei and Xing'an provinces set up by the KMT government after the war (an area including the Xing'an, Kholon Buir, and part of Zhirim leagues), and should eventually be turned into a Mongolian–Han coalition government. But Yun Ze was cautioned not to act too hastily lest the eastern Mongols be pushed toward the KMT. Yun Ze's eastward mission, therefore, differed from his earlier trip to West Sunid—he was not to abolish but to coopt the Wangyemiao regime. Yet Yun Ze understood the similarity between his missions, which, defined by him afterwards, was to "overcome two independence movements."[23]

Yun Ze's trip to Wangyemiao however did not happen right away. This time the chosen location for his mission of suasion was Chengde of Jehol. A CCP participant recalled later that the choice was made partially for a protocol consideration: Chengde was a middle point between the two sides. Actually Chengde was much closer to Zhangjiakuo, where Yun Ze stationed, than to Wangyemiao. A more important reason was for the CCP to control the direction of negotiations between Yun Ze and eastern Mongolian leaders. The CCP's Ji-Re-Liao branch bureau was in Chengde and watched over the development of the negotiations closely.[24] When the negotiations ended, Yun Ze's success exceeded the CCP center's expectation. The final document of the Chengde meeting proclaimed:

> The orientation of Inner Mongolian national movement is autonomy for equality, not autonomy for independence; liberation [of the Mongolian people] can be achieved only under the CCP's leadership and assistance. The Alliance of Inner Mongolian Autonomous Movement is the unified leading body of Inner Mongolia's autonomous movement.

Under these principles the eastern Mongolian government was to be reorganized into a "general branch" of Yun Ze's Alliance, and it would be responsible only for the four Mongolian leagues in the east. Now that a branch of the Alliance, the eastern Mongols were also required to join the anti-KMT struggle.[25]

The CCP scored a major victory in the merger between the Alliance and the eastern Mongolian movement. Still playing the game of "political consultation" with the KMT, the CCP, by dissolving the eastern Mongolian government, pulled the rug from under the KMT propaganda that the CCP was selling Inner Mongolia out to the Russians. The merger also opened the territories of eastern Mongolia for CCP military operations, which would soon prove highly valuable to the CCP's military strategy against the KMT in western Manchuria. In addition, eastern Mongolia's submission to the Alliance provided substance to the latter. In the late 1940s the total Mongolian population in the area of Inner Mongolia was less than 1.5 millions. Of these 1.16 millions lived in the four eastern Mongolian leagues (Kholon Buir, Zhirim, Zuu Uda, and Zosotu).[26] The Alliance was no longer just a body-less head.

The eastern Mongolian leaders had not expected the result of the Chengde meeting. Having come to Chengde to achieve an autonomous government for entire Inner Mongolia, they instead got a nongovernmental body in the Alliance. The KMT government's rigid attitude did not give them any room to bargain with the CCP. In other words, the civil war between the two Chinese parties was not much of a chance for the Mongols to "use the Han to control the Han." Neither could they play a game of procrastination in Chengde.

To decide China's central political power, the Chinese civil war chose the Manchurian and Inner Mongolian frontiers as its first battleground. The eastern Mongolian territories were under constant pressure of the KMT military force, and leaders from Wangyemiao were anxious to end their isolation.

In addition, the political ideology of the eastern Mongolian leadership created opportunities to the CCP's line of arguments. Khafungga and Temurbagana, the two principal eastern Mongols, were leftist revolutionaries themselves and had Comintern connections before the war. Temurbagana was actually an old acquaintance of Yun Ze's when both were trainees in Moscow in the 1930s. During the negotiations, a key step Yun Ze took to overcome eastern Mongols' resistance, authorized by the Ji-Re-Liao branch bureau, was to induct these two into the CCP.[27] After they themselves being "internalized" by the CCP, these eastern Mongol leaders could no longer argue effectively with Yun Ze because he represented the party line on the "correct road" for the liberation of the Mongolian nation.

Autonomy as Rebellion

The CCP's victory at Chengde was incomplete. The popular character of the eastern Mongolian movement decided that its direction could not be easily altered by a few leading figures. Somehow Yun Ze sensed this. After the Chengde meeting, he returned to Zhangjiakou, suspecting that once returning to Wangyemiao the eastern Mongolian leaders would not carry out the Chengde decisions and would continue to maintain their independence.[28] Indeed, after these leaders returned, the eastern Mongolian congress voted to modify the Chengde decisions. Although the congress agreed to dissolve the "Eastern Mongolian People's Autonomous Government," it also decided to establish a new government. The CCP representative present in Wangyemiao did not see how this expression of popular will could be contradicted. Therefore a compromise was made: the new government would be organized but as the governing body of the Xing'an province. Thus the CCP's requirement for "legality" and the Mongols' desire to have their own government could both be met.[29] This formula nevertheless preserved an ethnopolitical stronghold from which the eastern Mongols could continue to bargain with the CCP.

Clearly, as long as the CCP continued its "constitutional struggle" with the KMT, it would not support the Inner Mongols' demands for a Mongolian government and for a unified Inner Mongolian territory. Until late 1946, the "regional autonomy" in the CCP policy differed significantly from the "autonomous region" practice in the People's Republic of China after 1949. From the CCP center to Yun Ze, the "regional autonomy" was understood to mean separate, low-level self-government by Inner Mongols in different provinces. The practice was therefore compatible with the KMT idea about "local autonomy" (*defang zizhi*).[30] Yet, in December 1946 the CCP center decided to end its balancing game between the KMT's official Chinese nationalism and Inner Mongolian nationalism and embraced the idea of an autonomous government for Inner Mongolia as a whole.

As early as in August, 1946, Yun Ze called the CCP center's attention to the matter of unified government for Inner Mongolia, pointing out that this was demanded strongly by the Mongolian people and should be used to advance the CCP's Inner Mongolia strategy. Yet the CCP leadership turned around on the matter only four months later. During these months the KMT government decided to hold a national congress unilaterally and thus excluded the CCP from the constitutional contest. The forthcoming KMT "national congress" also caused a concern within the CCP that the KMT regime might make some placating gestures toward the frontier ethnic groups. Meanwhile, the KMT's military offensive in Manchuria and Inner Mongolia put a tremendous stress on the newly forged collaboration between the CCP and the eastern Mongols. Certain elements in the eastern Mongolian movement began to question openly the wisdom of the collaboration. Under these circumstances, the CCP center became realized that its relationship with the Mongol populace must be upgraded. It was now opportune for the CCP to capitalize on the issue of Inner Mongolian autonomous government.[31]

It was also time for Yun Ze's group to relocate to eastern Mongolia. When the group returned from Chengde to Zhangjiakuo in the late spring of 1946, the CCP's military situation in Suiyuan and Chahar deteriorated rapidly. In late September, the Jin-Cha-Ji Bureau had to abandon Zhangjiakuo to the advancing KMT troops and retreated southward into Hebei.[32] To maintain the Alliance's "Mongolian" character, Yun Ze convinced the bureau that the Alliance should not retreat into Han areas in the south but should march northward into the grassland of Shili-yin Gool. Yun Ze's suggestion made sense ethnopolitically, but it was a poor idea strategically. Separated from the CCP's main force, in the grassland the Alliance was soon caught in a struggle for survival against superior KMT troops and local forces under anti-communist princes.

In the end the Alliance did not benefit even ethnopolitically from staying in Shili-yin Gool. Shili-yin Gool was then the least sinicized area in entire Inner Mongolia. The Mongol herdsmen there viewed members of the Alliance, most of whom did not speak the Mongolian language or spoke different dialects of the language, as *manzi* (southern savages) and outsiders. Still holding an undisputable authority over the local populace, princes and *zasags* in the area maintained an opportunist stand in the CCPBKMT struggle. These conditions frustrated Yun Ze's effort to make the region a reliable base for the Alliance. The CCP center and the Jin-Cha-Ji Bureau soon recognized the mistake and ordered Yun Ze to take his group to the area between eastern Mongolia and western Manchuria where the CCP's military influence could provide protection.[33]

The Alliance's eastward move in early 1947 proved vital to both the CCP and the Inner Mongols. The move marked the end of the CCP's complacent strategy to "start a movement" for the Inner Mongols and brought the CCP into direct competition with a truly spontaneous mass movement. As for the Alliance, the eastward move saved it from extinction. In following the CCP's precedent of strategic relocation in the mid-1930s, Yun Ze and his associates made their own "long march" from western to eastern Mongolia. What they did next was to commandeer the eastern Mongolian movement on behalf of the CCP.

In later April and early May, under the CCP center's specific directives and with the direct assistance of the Northeast Bureau, Yun Ze again accomplished his mission by installing himself as the head of the newly organized Inner Mongolian Autonomous Government based in Wangyemiao. In the CCP's official history, the event has been identified as the beginning of the Inner Mongolian Autonomous Region. When it was established, however, the autonomous government was just a political organization without a territory. The territorial autonomy of Inner Mongolia would not flesh out until the CCP won the civil war in 1949. The 1947 event, then, had two immediate meanings: it effectively abolished any spontaneity left in the eastern Mongolian autonomous movement by absorbing the movement into the CCP's political structure; it proclaimed the Inner Mongols' open rebellion against the KMT even though their autonomy was proclaimed within the Republic of China.

The CCP's commandeering of the eastern Mongolian movement effectively put the initially spontaneous third force under its control. The development however did not end the Mongolian question. Soon questions like the Inner Mongols' right to "self-determination" in accordance with the Leninist formula, restoration of Inner Mongolia as an administrative region, and "class struggles" in Mongolian areas would arise among Yun Ze's Inner Mongolian leadership, the CCP center, and CCP apparatuses responsible for Manchurian and northern China affairs. But now these became "internal" to the CCP's policy making. In other words, the CCP's incorporation of the eastern Mongolian movement in the spring of 1947 further "internalized" the Mongolia question. The settlement of these questions would be done according to the party line. As for the issue of national self-determination, at the beginning of the PRC, Zhou Enlai, the premier of the PRC, explained to members of the People's Political Consultative Council that although minority nationalities' right to self-determination (*zijue*) should be recognized, in the PRC these nationalities would exercise their right to self-government (*zizhi*) lest foreign imperialists use the issue to split China.[34] Initially, the plan for making Inner Mongolia an integral administrative region met Han–Chinese officials' stubborn resistance. The provinces of Chahar, Suiyuan, and Jehol were separately abolished in 1952, 1954, and 1955, and their areas were incorporated into Inner Mongolia. Yet as the political climate in the PRC changed in the years to come, the territory of the Inner Mongolian Autonomous Region would be modified and remodified continuously.[35] As for "class struggles," it would continue to plague the Inner Mongolian society until the end of the Mao Zedong era in the PRC. During the "Great Proletarian Cultural Revolution" of the 1960s and 1970s, tens of thousands of cadres and ordinary people in Inner Mongolia, including Yun Ze and his former eastern Mongolian counterparts, were labeled as "class enemies" of the People's Republic and became victims of the largest group persecution of that period.[36]

* * *

The CCP's Inner Mongolian experience in the late 1940s unfolded along the direction of China's territoriality transformation since the mid-nineteenth century. The apparent difference between the CCP's and the KMT's attitudes toward Inner Mongols' demand for autonomy did not put the two Chinese parties in opposing positions where China's territorial and administrative sovereignties were at stake. Their respectively positive and negative stances about Inner Mongolian autonomy were determined by the power struggle in China proper, not by the dynamics of the Mongolian frontier per se. In the meantime, both parties firmly opposed Inner Mongolia's accession to the Mongolian People's Republic. As a revolutionary force struggling for seizing power in China, the CCP did not find much usefulness in the Leninist formula about using frontier nationalities' separatist tendency as a revolutionary "yeast." On the contrary, from the very beginning of the Chinese civil war, the CCP wanted to appeal to the sentiment of Chinese nationalism and shed itself of any suspicion that it was conspiring with the Soviets at the expenses of China. Thus, even before taking power in China, the CCP already functioned as a centralizing agent in overcoming frontier separatism.

Not operating in a political vacuum, eastern Mongolian autonomists of the postwar years were leftist revolutionaries in their own right. In the existent hierarchy of the communist world, however, their leftist politics proved more useful to the CCP than to themselves. It is ironic that the supposedly supranational ideology, communism, served the CCP well in channeling an Inner Mongolian revolution into the Chinese revolution. Afterwards the Inner Mongols would have to go through all the upheavals of the Chinese revolution with the rest of China. The CCP's centralizing enterprise would not always be assisted by a homogenizing ideology. As the next chapter shows, in the Tibet question the CCP encountered a situation rather different from that of Inner Mongolia.

Notes

1. Rogers Brubaker, *Nationalism Reframed: Nationhood and the National Question in the New Europe* (Cambridge: Cambridge University Press, 1996), 85–86, defines "nationalizing" nationalism as a post-independence stance by a "core nation" that claims ownership of the polity and seeks means to promote its cultural, economic, linguistic, and demographic attributes and its political hegemony in its "own" state as compensations to its pre-independence sufferings. China never lost its independence, but its "semi-colonial" status fostered the "victim mentality" of its "core nation," the Han.
2. Shagdariin Sandag and Harry H. Kendall, *Poisoned Arrows: The Stalin–Choibalsan Mongolian Massacres, 1921–1941* (Boulder: Westview Press, 2000) presents a chilling chronicle of Moscow's control of the MPR through systematic purging of Mongolian revolutionary leaders who struggled for Outer Mongolia's independence and collaborated initially with the Soviets. For the KMT–Moscow diplomacy on Outer Mongolia at the end of World War II, see Xiaoyuan Liu, *A Partnership for Disorder: China, the United States, and Their Policies for the Postwar Disposition of the Japanese Empire, 1941–1945* (Cambridge: Cambridge University Press, 1996), 258–286.
3. Walton Butterworth to the Secretary of State, June 1947, John F. Melby papers, box 2.
4. U.S. Embassy, Moscow to the State Department, October 18, 1946, General Records of the Department of State Central Files: China: 893.00 Mongolia/10–1846.
5. "CCP center's directive to He Long and Lin Feng on organizing local Mongolian autonomous governments and armed forces, September 16, 1945," *MWWH*, 960; "Jin-Cha-Jin bureau's request for direction on policy toward 'Inner Mongolian liberation committee,' September 29, 1945," *ZZWX*, 15: 377–378; "Request to the center for direction by Nie Rongzhen et al., with regard to work orientation in Inner Mongolia, September 29, 1945," ibid., 378–379; "Center's directive to the Jin-Cha-Ji and Jin-Sui bureau on work orientation in Inner Mongolia, October 23, 1945," ibid., 375–377.
6. "Outline by the northwestern work committee of the CCP center with regard to the question of the Mongolian nation in the war of resistance, July 1940," *MWWH*, 659.
7. Hao Yufeng, *Wulanfu Zhuan* (Biography of Ulanfu) (Hohhot: Neimenggu Remin Chubanshe, 1990), 337–340, 342, 355–356, 359–360.
8. Wang Shusheng, "Great deeds recorded in history and valuable legacy to the coming generations," *Wulanfu Jinian Wenji*, 1: 375–376; "Jin-Cha-Ji central bureau's telegram to the center on the situation and policies in Chahar Mongol area, October 27, 1945," Inner Mongolian Autonomous Region Archives, *Neimenggu Zizhi Yundong Lianhehui–Dang'an Shiliao Xuanbian* (Alliance of Inner Mongolian autonomous movement: selected archival and historical materials) (Beijing: Dang'an Chubanshe, 1989), 3–5.
9. "Report for instruction with regard to the question of establishing the provisional government of the Inner Mongolian people's republic in the Chahar league, October 27,

1945," *MWWH*, 972–973; "Recent conditions in the leagues and banners of Chahar and the work in Chahar and Shili-yin Gool leagues, October 27, 1945," ibid., 966–971.

10. "Recent conditions in the banners of Chahar and works in the Chahar and Sili-yin Gool leagues, October 27, 1945," *MWWH*, 966–971; "CCP Ji-Cha-Ji cental bureau's report on the establishment of the alliance of the Inner Mongolian autonomous movement, November 8, 1945," ibid., 974; "CCP Jin-Cha-Ji central bureau's report to the center on the political power in the Chahar and Sui [sic] leagues, November 9, 1945," ibid., 975.
11. Wang Duo, *Wushi Chunqiu*, 198.
12. Wang Shusheng, "Great deeds recorded in history and valuable legacy to the coming generations," *Wulanfu Jinian Wenji*, 1: 375–376; "CCP center's telegram to the Jin-Cha-Ji bureau to approve the establishment of the alliance of the Inner Mongolian autonomous movement, November 10, 1945," *MWWH*, 976; "Important points in current policies toward Inner Mongolia, November 23, 1945," ibid., 981.
13. Wang Duo, *Wushi Chunqiu*, 197; "Name list of the delegates of the alliance of the Inner Mongolian autonomous movement, November 25, 1945," *Neimenggu Zizhi Yundong Lianhehui*, 14–17; "Charter of the alliance of the Inner Mongolian autonomous movement, November 27 , 1945," ibid., 27–31; "Proclamation of the inaugural assembly of the alliance of the Inner Mongolian autonomous movement, November 28, 1945," ibid., 32–34; "Message of greeting to chairman Mao and commander-in-general Zhu from the delegates to the inaugural assembly of the alliance of the Inner Mongolian autonomous movement, November 28, 1945," ibid., 34–35; "Bulletin of the inaugural assembly of the alliance of the Inner Mongolian autonomous movement, November 29, 1945," ibid., 41–43.
14. "Yun Ze's speech to the inaugural assembly of the alliance of the Inner Mongolian autonomous movement, November 26, 1945," *Neimenggu Zizhi Yundong Lianhehui*, 17–19.
15. Rene Grousset, *The Empire of the Steppes: A History of Central Asia* (New Brunswick, NJ: Rutgers University Press, 1970), 517; Zhou Qingshu, *Neimenggu Lishi Dili* (Historical geography of Inner Mongolia) (Hohhot: Neimenggu Daxue Chubanshe, 1993), 225, 227. In 1632, Abakhai (a.k.a. Huang Taiji), son of Nurhachi and founder of the Qing Dynasty, led an expedition against Lingdan, grand khan of the Chahar Mongols. Guihua (old city of Hohhot) was the west-most point Abakhai reached. The campaign forced Lingdan to flee into Tibet and thus removed the last obstacle for the Manchus to subjugate the Inner Mongols (at the time, eastern Mongols or Mongols south of the desert).
16. Zhao Zhenbei, "Glorious model and immortal achievements," *Wulanfu Jinian Wenjin*, 2: 96–97.
17. "Policy suggestion on Mongolian banners by the western military district of the north-eastern people's autonomous army, December 22, 1945," *MWWH*, 983; "Report by the CCP committee in western Liaoning on the discovery of the organization of Inner Mongolian people's revolutionary party, December 24, 1945," ibid., 1293; "CCP center's directive to Lin Biao et al., on policies toward the Mongolian nationality, December 25, 1945," ibid., 984; "Ji-Re-Liao branch bureau's report to the northeast bureau and the center on Mongolian and Han governments in northern Rehe, January 15, 1946," ibid., 989; "Ji-Re-Liao branch bureau's report on the Mongolian question in northern Rehe, January 26, 1946,"ibid., 995; "Report on conditions of Inner Mongolia from the seventh

division directly under the command of the northeastern anti-Japanese allied army to the northeast bureau, January 29, 1946," ibid., 996–997.

18. "Draft program for peaceful state construction, January 16, 1946," *MWWH*, 990–991; "CCP center's directive on a necessary cautious attitude toward the nationality question of Inner Mongolia, February 18, 1946," ibid., 1000.
19. "CCP northeast bureau's report to the center on the Mongolian question, February 20, 1946," *MWWH*, 1002–1003; "Request from Peng Zhen and Lü Zhengcao for the center's directive on the region of eastern Mongolia autonomy, February 20, 1946," ibid., 1004; "Order number 5 of the western Manchurian military district, February 1, 1946," *Neimenggu Dang'an* (Inner Mongolian Archives), 1991, no. 4: 35.
20. "Hu Xikui's materials and opinions about the eastern Mongolian question, March 3, 1946," *MWWH*, 1013–1014; "Huang Kecheng's report on conditions of eastern Mongolian autonomy, March 3, 1946," ibid., 1015–1016; "Ji-Cha-Re-Liao branch bureau's report on how to deal with the eastern Mongolian question, March 3, 1946," ibid., 1017; "Ji-Re-Liao branch bureau's report to the center on the question of the Mongolian work in Rehe, March 7, 1946," ibid., 1021.
21. "CCP center's directive to the northeast bureau on the impropriety of organizing the east Mongolian people's autonomous government, February 24, 1946," *MWWH*, 1011.
22. "Hu Xikui's materials and opinions on the east Mongolian question, March 3, 1946," *MWWH*, 1013–1014; "Huang Kecheng's report on the situation of east Mongolian autonomy, March 3, 1946," ibid., 1015–1016; "Ji-Cha-Re-Liao branch bureau's report on how to deal with the east Mongolian question, 3 March 1946," ibid., 1017; "Northeast bureau's telegram on east Mongolian work, 11 March 1946," ibid., 1024; "[Jin-Cha-Ji bureau's] telegram to the northeast bureau on the east Mongolian question, 13 March 1946," ibid., 1027.
23. The CCP Central Committee's directive on the question of eastern Mongolia, March 10 , 1946, *MWWH*, 1023; Yun Ze's report to the CCP Central Committee on the land and autonomy problems of Inner Mongolia, August 1, 1946, ibid., 1057–1058.
24. Ulijinaren, "In the torrent of Inner Mongolian national liberation movement," *NWZ*, 50: 202; Liu Chun, "Works in Inner Mongolia remembered," ibid., 45, 52. Actually, the Ji-Re-Liao branch bureau viewed Chifeng as the center of its Mongolian works. But the negotiation was so important that it had to be held outside the Mongolian area.
25. Yun Ze's speech at the April 3 conference, April 3, 1946, *Neimenggu Zizhi Yundong Lianhehui*, 49; the principal resolution of the conference on the unification of Inner Mongolian autonomous movement, April 3, 1946, ibid., 51–53.
26. Mongolian History Compiling Group, *Mengguzu Jianshi* (Brief history of the Mongolian nationality) (State Committee on Nationalities' series of brief histories of minority nationalities. Hohhot, Neimenggu Renmin Chubanshe, 1985), 402–403, 421.
27. Liu Chun, "Works in Inner Mongolia remembered," *NWZ*, 50: 52–59; *Wulanfu Nianpu*, 143–145; *Wulanfu Zhuan*, 401–410; Keligeng, "Recollections on the unification of Inner Mongolian autonomous movement," NWZ, 50: 154–155; Liu Jieyu, "The necessary path for the Inner Mongolian autonomous movement," ibid., 225–231. These sources disagree who between Khafungga and Temurbagana was first initiated into the CCP and whether or not Khafungga himself asked to be accepted by the party. Because both died during the "cultural revolution," they did not seem to leave behind recollective materials on the negotiations.

28. Yun Ze's report to the CCP Central Committee on the Chengde conference, April 5, 1946, *Neimenggu Zizhi Yundong Lianhehui*, 54–55. In the report Yun Ze viewed the Chengde resolution as an agreement on principles and called attention to "disagreements and variations" when the resolution was implemented in eastern Mongolia.
29. Dawa-Ochir, "What I witnessed and experienced," *NWZ*, 31: 168–169, 171–172; Khafungga's report to the Alliance on works in eastern Mongolia, July 25, 1946, *Neimenggu ZiZhi Yundong Lianhehui*, 87–88.
30. "Autonomous regions" in the PRC can be viewed as practices of "territorial autonomy" at least in name. But *quyu zizhi* in the CCP terminology of the 1940s meant autonomy below the provincial level. This meaning was quite clear in many CCP documents cited heretofore. After the autonomous alliance was established, Yun Ze especially explained to the CCP press that *quyu zizhi* was a necessary preparatory stage before autonomy for entire Inner Mongolia. It should be noted, however, that after 1949, *quyu zizhi* has also been used to describe the "autonomous region" practice by PRC publications as if the CCP has had a consistent policy in this regard. See, "Chairman of the Sui-Mongolian government Yun Ze discusses the question of Inner Mongolian autonomy," *Jin-Cha-Ji Ribao* (Jin-Cha-Ji daily), November 16, 1945, in *Neimenggu Zizhi Yundong Lianhehui*, 8–11, and Jiang Ping et al., ed., *Zhongguo Minzu Wenti de Lilun yu Shijian* (Theories and practices regarding China's nationality question) (Beijing: Zhonggong Zhongyang Dangxiao Chubanshe, 1994), 169–172.
31. "Yun Ze's report to the center on land and autonomous questions of Inner Mongolia, 1 August 1946," MWWH, 1057–1058; "CCP center's directive on the consideration of establishing an Inner Mongolian autonomous government, 26 November 1946," ibid., 1083. The KMT's national congress was held between November 15 to December 25, 1946. The long and futile KMT–CCP negotiations ended when Zhou Enlai, CCP's chief negotiator, returned to Yan'an on November 19. Earlier, in August, General George Marshall decided that his mission to mediate between the two parties had failed. He returned to the United States in January 1947. Many years later, as recorded in Liu Jieyu, "The necessary path for Inner Mongolian autonomous movement," *NWZ*, 50: 230, Ulanfu (Yun Ze) recalled that as long as the KMT and the CCP were still talking to each other, Inner Mongolia could have an autonomous movement but not an autonomous government.
32. "CCP Jin-Cha-Ji central bureau's report on the establishment of the alliance of the Inner Mongolian autonomous movement, 8 November 1945," *MWWH*, 974; "Yun Ze, chairman of the Sui-Meng government discusses the question of Inner Mongolia autonomy," from the November 16, 1945 issue of the *Jin Cha Ji Ribao* (Jin-Cha-Ji daily), *Neimenggu Zizhi Yundong Lianhehui*, 8–11; Wang Duo, *Wushi Chunqiu*, 210–212.
33. Hao Yufeng, *Wulanfu Zhuan*, 431–438; Wang Duo, *Wushi Chunqiu*, 213–236, 242–252; Yun Shiying and Chao Luomeng, "Recollections on work in the Shili-yin Gool league," *NWZ*, 50: 156–175.
34. Jiang Ping et al., ed., *Zhongguo Minzu Wenti de Lilun yu Shijian* (Beijing: Zhonggong Zhongyang Dangxiao Chubanshe, 1994), 170–172; *Mao Zedong Nianpu* (Chronicle of Mao Zedong's life), 3: 564–577; *Zhou Enlai Nianpu* (Chronicle of Zhou Enlai's life), 839–843.
35. Ministry of Civil Affairs, *Zhonghua Renmin Gongheguo Xianji Yishang Xingzheng Quhua Yange, 1949–1983* (Historical changes of the demarcation of administrative districts

above the county level in the People's Republic of China, 1949–1983) (Beijing: Cehui Chubanshe, 1986), 6–10.

36. For the persecution of Ulanfu and eastern Mongolian leaders during the 1960s, see Tumen and Zhu Dongli, *Kang Sheng yu Neirendang Yuan'an* (Kang Sheng and the unjust case of Inner Mongolian people's party) (Beijing: Zhonggong Zhongyang Dangxiao Chubanshe, 1995), and Hao Weimin et al., *Neimenggu Zizhiqu Shi* (History of the Inner Mongolian autonomous region) (Hohhot: Neimenggu Daxue Chubanshe, 1991), 293–339.

CHAPTER EIGHT

Break the Vicious Circle along the Himalayas

In contrast to the Chinese Communist-eastern Mongolian relationship in the initial years after World War II, there was no symbiotic element in the historical relationship between the Chinese Communist Party (CCP) that struggled for power in China and the Tibetan theocracy that eluded Chinese control for decades. Complete isolation of Tibet from Chinese politics between 1911 and 1949 meant that, unlike Mongolia and Xinjiang where the CCP managed to maintain direct or indirect contacts, Tibet was totally beyond the reach of the Chinese Communist movement. Then, in the early 1950s the CCP and the Tibetan establishment under the 14th Dalai Lama had their first direct encounter. What led the CCP in the direction of Tibet was an unfulfilled agenda from its revolutionary struggle in the past thirty years, but more importantly, a political inheritance from its Nationalist predecessors.

After enduring for thousands of years, China's dynastic tradition ended in 1911 when the Chinese state shed what was left of its imperial splendor and adopted a national form. Founders of the Republic of China (ROC) established many new precedents, one of which was that, unlike dynastic founders in the past who used armed forces to mark their imperial domains, builders of the ROC used legal proclamations to claim territorial inheritance from their imperial predecessor, the Qing Dynasty. The 1912 temporary constitution of the ROC declared that the area of China included China's twenty-two provinces plus Inner and Outer Mongolias, Tibet, and Qinghai. At the time, the central government in Beijing was yet to consolidate its control in several provinces in China proper, and Outer Mongolia and Tibet were breaking away from China.[1] Until the ROC perished in the mainland in 1949, none of its successive central governments could exercise de facto control in Outer Mongolia and Tibet. Nevertheless, the official definition of China's territorial sovereignty by ROC authorities achieved a permanent historical relevancy: as it delimited the arena in which the Chinese Communist Party (CCP) would imagine its revolution, the definition also demarcated the territory over which the CCP would claim sovereignty on behalf of the People's Republic of China (PRC).

Before the CCP took power, as Chapter 6 shows, Tibet was more of a political concept than a territorial reality to the CCP's operations. When collaborating with the Chinese Nationalists, or Kuomintang (KMT), the CCP recited Leninist principle of national self-determination and put Tibet together with other non-Chinese frontiers as territories where "Chinese imperialism" must be overthrown. After splitting with the KMT and setting up guerrilla bases in rural southern China, the CCP called all "minority nationalities" of China, including the Tibetans, to rebel against the official ROC and join its own "soviet republic." Not until the CCP headquarters and the Red Army embarked on their arduous Long March in the mid-1930s did the question of Tibet become substantive. In a dispute about the Red Army's destination between Zhang Guotao and the rest of the CCP leadership, for the first time the CCP had to consider practically the meaning of Tibet to the Chinese revolution. Mao Zedong's answer was that the direction of Tibet would mean extinction of the Red Army. This time, therefore, Tibet became important to the CCP only because the CCP must turn away

"Xizang Zizhiqu Zhengqu" (Political Districts of the Tibet Autonomous Region. English added).

Source: *Xizang Zizhiqu Ditu Ce* (Atlas of the Tibet Autonomous Region) (Beijing: Zhongguo Ditu Chubanshe, 2005).

In contesting the Chinese administrative structure of the Tibet Autonomous Region, this map issued by the Dalai Lama's government in exile suggests that Tibet consists of three parts and additional "autonomous prefectures" (AP) and "autonomous counties" (AC).

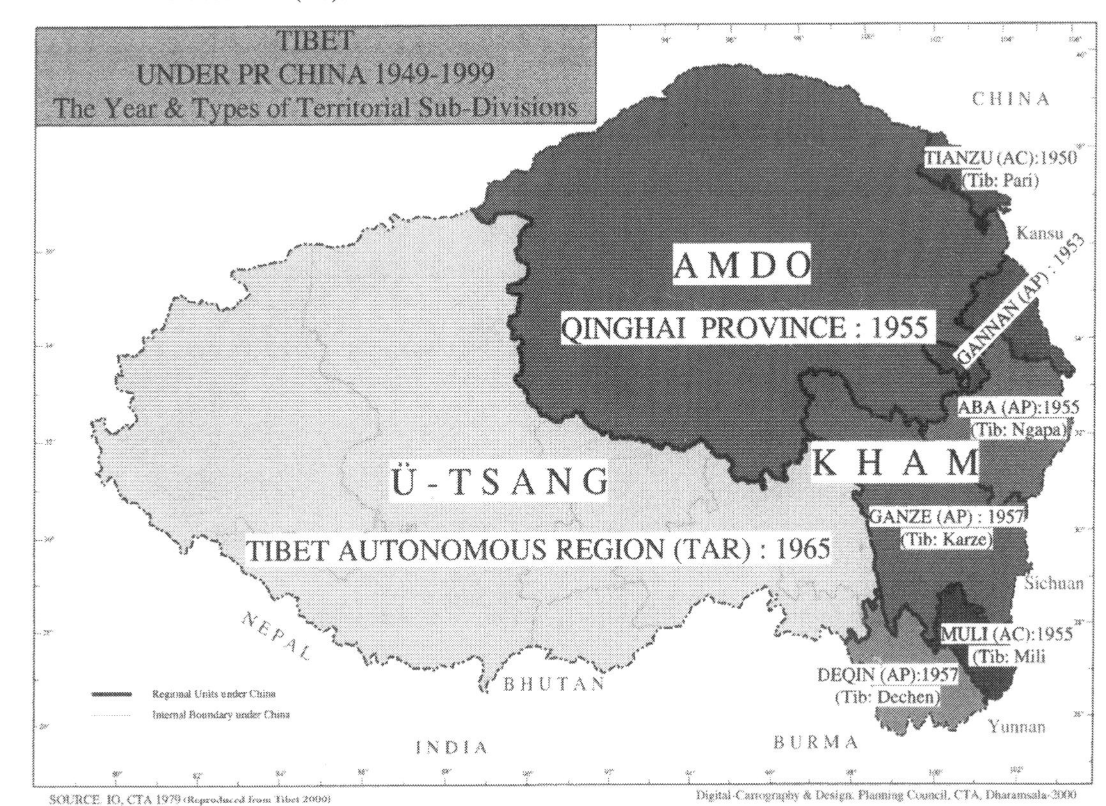

Source: http://www.tibet.net/en/index.php

from it. During China's eight-year war of resistance against Japan, the Chinese Nationalist Government found a haven in the neighborhood of Tibet, Sichuan, whereas the CCP based itself in northern Shaanxi and almost forgot about Tibet. When the CCP began its final round of power struggle with the KMT at the end of World War II, it started in Manchuria, the remotest possible location from Tibet in China. Consequently, the CCP's geo-path to power made Tibet the finish line for its "war of liberation" in the mainland.

Reverse a Verdict

The mid-twentieth century saw a rare synchronization of acts by the CCP and the Dalai Lama. In 1949, the CCP defeated the KMT and completed its transformation from a revolutionary movement to the ruling party of China. In the next year, the 14th Dalai Lama ended his years in waiting and assumed the reins of government in Tibet at the age of sixteen. In fact, it was the new Chinese government's military advance toward Tibet that forced the Dalai Lama to take over political responsibilities from Taktra, the old, panicky regent, two years earlier than scheduled. At the time, the CCP leadership welcomed the Dalai Lama's personal rule and viewed the development as potentially favorable to Beijing's démarche for a peaceful solution of the Tibetan question.

In the twentieth century, the so-called Tibetan question was a hot item on the plate for all the central governments from the late Qing to the PRC. It was part of the issue of homogenizing territories of the by-gone Chinese empire according to the nation-state norms. During the last few years of its rule, the Qing government tried from its deathbed but failed to turn Tibet into a province. Then, from 1911 to 1949, the central regimes of the ROC were bedeviled continuously by civil and foreign wars and managed merely to maintain a *de jure* claim of sovereignty over Tibet. In the mid-twentieth century, as the party presiding over the reunified Chinese state, the CCP was in a much stronger position than its imperial and nationalist predecessors to deal with the situation of Tibet. Yet, because of its social revolutionary programs and atheist ideology, the CCP was, by nature, the least likely to find a common ground with the Tibetan theocracy among the three types of central regimes in twentieth-century China. Having viewed the Dalai Lama establishment as a "parasite system" and Tibetan rulers as "running dogs" of British imperialism in the past, the CCP leadership now held the 14th Dalai Lama and his regime as the key to a peaceful solution of the Tibetan question.

A number of factors led the leaders in Beijing to prefer a "peaceful liberation" of Tibet to an outright military conquest. The unfamiliar and difficult terrain and the harsh weather conditions of Tibet gave CCP leaders pause for thought, and international reactions, especially concerns expressed by the newly independent India, could not be discounted either.[2] But the most important reason was one of ethnology with a unique Chinese Communist twist. As Mao Zedong pointed out, Tibet was a totally different ethnic region even in comparison with Xinjiang. Whereas there were hundreds of thousands of Han people in Xinjiang, there was almost none in Tibet.[3] Just as in the situation facing the Red Army in 1935, in advancing into Tibet in the early 1950s the People's Liberation Army (PLA) would no longer be operating with the Han–Chinese basis of the Chinese Communist revolution. Certainly in the 1950s Mao no longer saw the direction of Tibet as a road to ruin. Together with Taiwan, Tibet now assumed a symbolic significance to the CCP. "Liberation" of these two territories would mark the successful conclusion of the CCP's revolution against the old KMT regime, no matter how flimsy the connection had been between Tibet and the KMT. To the CCP, which had survived and thrived by operating along the "mass line" of class struggles, the vital question was how to establish its legitimacy among the Tibetan masses. The answer was a pragmatic yet expedient approach: get to the Tibetan people through the Dalai Lama. This was to turn the originally perceived vicious circle of the Dalai Lama-Tibetan mass relationship into a virtuous one.

This meant that the CCP had to rescind its past stance of identifying the Dalai Lama as the arch-criminal responsible for Tibet's alienation from China and all the social ills in Tibetan society. Decriminalization of the Dalai Lama became the first crucial step taken by Beijing in opening an era of cooperation between the two sides. In the summer of 1949 Mao Zedong began to consider a solution of the Tibetan question. At the time, a military advance from the northwest was contemplated, which could be implemented with a political cover of escorting the 10th Panchen Lama home from Qinghai, where the exiled 9th Panchen Lama died in 1937 and the 10th was enthroned in 1949. Although the direction of invasion was later changed to the southwest, to be conducted by the CCP Southwestern Bureau under Deng Xiaoping, the CCP leadership continued to deliberate this stratagem to the end of the year.[4] In February 1950, new thinking emerged in the Southwestern Bureau, which had been intensively investigating and deliberating over the Tibetan situation. It was suggested to Beijing that words be sent to Lhasa to persuade the "Dalai clique" to rid itself of British influence and achieve "national autonomy, unity, and mutual assistance" through negotiations with Beijing. The Southwestern Bureau made it clear that such an approach was to prevent the Dalai Lama from escaping into India, which would only make a resolution of the Tibetan issue more difficult. Beijing immediately approved this new orientation and instructed the Southwestern Bureau to use all possible means to start negotiations with Lhasa. The goal was to "keep the Dalai Lama in Tibet for reconciliation with us."[5] Thus, even before the 14th Dalai Lama assumed power in November of 1950, the CCP leadership already decided that he should be central to the solution of the Tibetan question.

The solution later became known as the "17-Point Agreement," which was concluded in May 1951 between the CCP government and an official delegation from Lhasa. The document would be constantly controversial in the years to come, but in 1951 the agreement offered the best possible *quid pro quo* formula for both Beijing and Lhasa. The agreement officially recorded Beijing's orientation of decriminalizing the Tibetan theocracy. In contrast to the CCP's practice in the past of using "patriotic" (*aiguo*) and "national-betrayal" (*maiguo*) to label the political stances of its allies and enemies, the document coined a peculiar term— "non-patriotic" (*fei aiguo*)— for criticizing only mildly Tibet's alienation from China before 1950. The agreement was a compromise between two asymmetric forces: unable to get any meaning international assistance, Lhasa recognized the futileness of its military resistance to the PLA after a military fiasco at Chamdo in October 1950; the CCP leadership admitted the hollowness of its political prowess within Tibetan society, learning from its Long March experience and recent investigations of the Tibetan situation.[6] Both sides therefore favored a negotiated political solution that could salvage or achieve the most basic goals held by each at the time. Beijing wanted Tibet "to return to the great motherland family of the People's Republic of China" so as to erase the last gap left in China's national defense contour in the mainland. Lhasa wanted to preserve the "current political systems" of Tibet and "the Dalai Lama's inherent power and position."[7] The 17-Point Agreement stipulated these points and formulated a type of Tibetan autonomy under Chinese sovereignty.

In 1959, after the Lhasa revolt and the Dalai Lama's exile into India, this compromise collapsed. The discrepancy between Beijing's "status quo" policy in Tibet proper and radical reforms pushed by CCP authorities in the so-called greater Tibetan areas in Sichuan and Qinghai had much to do with the collapse of the fragile power balance in Tibet. After all, Tibetan armed resistance began in Sichuan and Qinghai in the mid-1950s and then spilled over into Tibet proper, a development foreseen by CCP leadership years before. The pace of social transformation in Sichuan and Qinghai nonetheless accelerated along with the rest of China. It was only logical for CCP leaders to view these provinces as a pacesetter for Tibet, not the other way around. The 17-Point Agreement thus appears to have met its demise prematurely.[8]

Still, it should not be overlooked that Beijing never intended for the 17-Point Agreement to last. Even before the PLA began to march toward Tibet, Mao already decided that Tibet must be homogenized with the rest of China and "reformed into people's democratic Tibet."[9] For all intents and purposes, the 17-Point Agreement put the Tibetan system— defined by Beijing as a "feudal serfdom" with "theocratic dictatorship by the clergy and autocrats" on top—on death row with an unspecified date of execution.[10] When the agreement was concluded in 1951, a comfort zone was created for the Tibetan government in promising that changes in Tibet would not be implemented by Beijing from the outside but by the Tibetan government itself upon the Tibetan people's request. In the meantime Beijing would spare no effort to get a handle on the Tibetan people's will.

Convert the Dalai Lama

Beijing decided to include the Dalai Lama in its own Tibetan enterprise not because CCP leaders accepted his institutional positions (secular and religious) in Tibet, but because they assigned him an instrumental role to connect the party with the Tibetan masses. For the CCP–Dalai cooperation to last, Beijing must eventually be able to persuade the Dalai Lama to relinquish sooner or later his own "inherent power and position" in Tibet. While relegating reincarnation of Tibetan lamas to superstition, the CCP leadership was quite confident that the mindset of the two young Tibetan leaders, Dalai and Panchen, could be revolutionized in their current life time. In late 1949, when contemplating using the Panchen Lama to spearhead the CCP's political offensive in Tibet, Mao instructed CCP officials in the Northwest Bureau to carry out "proper political reform" of the young man and his entourage. Soon, the Dalai Lama replaced Panchen as the highest prize for the CCP's effort to win over and transform the leadership of Tibet. Beijing defined the effort as the "unshakable" priority in its Tibetan policy.[11]

Mao took the lead in converting the Dalai Lama to Beijing's cause. In conceding that the Dalai Lama and the Panchen Lama were the "Tibetan people's leaders," Mao held rather different estimates of the two. In his view Panchen already took the CCP's side, and the task in the future was not to let him slip into the camp of the Dalai clique. As for the Dalai Lama, Mao identified him as a "fence sitter" (*zhongjian pai*) between the "reactionary" and "patriotic" factions in Tibetan politics.[12] Thus, re-education of the Dalai Lama would be a difficult project for Beijing, and Mao took the task upon himself.

Based on information published in the PRC, we now know that from the conclusion of the 17-Point Agreement in 1951 to the Lhasa revolt in 1959, Mao sent eleven letters and telegrams to the Dalai Lama and eight to the Panchen Lama. During the same period Zhou Enlai sent four letters and telegrams to the Dalai Lama and two to the Panchen Lama, and Liu Shaoqi and Zhu De each wrote once to the Dalai Lama.[13] Such personal correspondence between the top CCP leaders and the Tibetan leaders indicated that after the 1951 settlement, Beijing did not treat Tibet as an ordinary administrative region. Neither did Mao treat the Tibetan leaders as ordinary provincial-level officials. Instead, Mao's personal attention created an aura reminiscent of the traditional relationship between emperors of China and rulers of China's dependencies. Occasionally, these letters were accompanied with gifts. For instance, an October 1953 letter from Mao to the Dalai Lama included a list of gifts: two amplifiers, four loudspeakers, an electric record player, twelve phonograph records, four bolts of yellow satin, ginseng from Changbai Mountain in the Northeast, and a mink coat. On the same day Mao also wrote a letter to the Panchen Lama and sent similar gifts to him. A careful difference was made to recognize the Dalai Lama's top position in Tibet—the Panchen Lama received only three bolts of yellow satin.[14] The choice was deliberate. Satin was among the traditional presents that Chinese emperors bestowed on rulers of "dependencies" or "tributary states," and yellow was the imperial color. It would stretch the point to suggest that the post-1951 Beijing–Lhasa relationship retained elements of the old tributary practices of the imperial period. Yet it is noteworthy that such gift exchanges did not exist between top CCP leaders and any other regional officials in the PRC.

For the purpose of winning over the Dalai Lama, ceremonial gestures were less significant than the personal intimacy represented by these letters. The main thrusts of Mao's letters included praise of the Dalai Lama's willingness to cooperate with Beijing and to work for a new Tibet, advice for patience with progress in Tibet, promise of unreserved assistance from the central government, and cautionary calls to guard against conspiracies of foreign imperialists and reactionary elements in Tibet. The last point reflected the central concern of the CCP work regarding the Dalai Lama and his associates. The work, characterized by the CCP Tibet Work Committee, was a united-front operation using anti-imperialism and patriotism as its principal weapons.[15]

After Mao and the Dalai Lama met each other during the Dalai Lama's visit to Beijing in 1954 and 1955, Mao's letters began to assume a warm personal touch. In one communication, the two leaders even exchanged flowers. Mao urged the Dalai Lama to write more often and more casually. In a letter Mao apologized for his cursive handwriting that might have made it more difficult for the Dalai Lama to understand the letter, obviously encouraging the Dalai Lama in a self-deprecating way to continue learning Chinese.[16] Evidently the face-to-face meetings between Mao and the Dalai Lama advanced the confidence-building between Beijing and Lhasa.

From September 1954 to March 1955 the Dalai Lama and the Panchen Lama visited several Chinese provinces and attended the National People's Congress in Beijing. CCP leaders in Beijing viewed their visit as evidence of Tibet's further leaning toward the central government and, therefore, an event of great significance.[17] Mao took full advantage of this rare opportunity to gain the young Dalai Lama's allegiance. When the Dalai Lama was in Beijing, Mao talked to him many times. So far the Chinese authorities have only released records of two of the conversations, while the Dalai Lama's memoir mentions four conversations. Melvyn Goldstein identifies in the second volume of his *History of Modern Tibet* five Mao–Dalai conversations, making his the most complete account of the Mao–Dalai encounter.[18] At these conversations Mao appeared affectionate, open-minded, considerate, and encouraging. The Dalai Lama appears to have been immensely attracted to Mao's leadership persona and ideas. During his visit in China's developing cities and industrial sites, the Dalai Lama was deeply impressed by CCP cadres' devotion to socialist construction and realized how backward Tibet was. At the end of his visit, the Dalai Lama told Mao that their conversations caused a tremendous change in his thinking. He promised that after he returned to Tibet, he would put Mao's ideas into practice, change his previously perfunctory relationship with CCP officials in Tibet, and start sincere cooperation with them. He was so taken by the idealism of the CCP leaders that he expressed to his CCP interlocutors a hope to become a party member. But he was persuaded to wait. To this day, the 14th Dalai Lama insists that he remains half Marxist and half Buddhist.[19]

There was however one bump in the generally smooth encounter between Mao and the Dalai Lama. At one of the conversations toward the end of the Dalai Lama's visit, Mao told the Tibetan leader that religion was poison. Mao's remark cannot be found anywhere in relevant publications in China. When recalling this incident on different occasions, the Dalai Lama has offered several versions of his reaction on the spot: he was "thoroughly startled" by Mao's "extraordinary remarks," "very afraid" in seeing Mao as "the destroyer of the *Dharma* after all," "a little scared" in realizing Mao as the "real enemy of the religion," and, most recently, sensing that "he [Mao] really trusted me, otherwise (there was) no reason to mention that."[20]

No matter what the Dalai Lama's dominant feeling was at the time, it did not seem to dampen his enthusiasm about Mao. After he returned to Tibet, the Dalai Lama offered Mao a dose of the "poison" in a long ode he composed to praise the Chinese leader. The ode compared "Chairman Mao" with "Brahma who created the world," and Mao's "campaign of peace" with "Mani's white umbrella that shields the heavens, the earth and the people with pleasant coolness." After eulogizing the Buddha—"Sakyamuni's religion of goodwill is like the clear and cool radiance of the infinite rays from the bright pearly moon,"—the ode continues: "Your [Mao's] will is like a mass of clouds and your call is like the sound of thunder. A sweet rain constantly emanates from them to unselfishly refresh the world." In the end, the Dalai Lama prayed: "May the benevolence of Buddha, the supernatural power of Dharmapala and the true words of God of Success make all my fine wishes come true!"[21]

It is likely that the Dalai Lama sent this piece along with his letter to Mao on July 6, 1955. Mao wrote back in November, expressing "great happiness" in receiving the letter and encouraging the Dalai Lama to "patiently" push progress in Tibet. These exchanges seem to display genuine affection rather than affectation. The Dalai Lama, thus, returned to Tibet with a mission. In Beijing, the Tibetan delegation and CCP officials agreed that Tibet would be made into a Tibetan Autonomous Region, and that a preparatory committee would be established under the Dalai Lama to help guide the early phases of this transition.[22]

The Dalai Lama's trip to Beijing resulted not only in his "change of mind" but also in a change of his political identity. In Beijing, he was elected as vice-chairman of the National People's Congress, and, upon returning to Tibet, he would become head of a new governing body. Both were important steps for the Dalai Lama to enter the political process of the PRC and for Beijing to integrate Tibet with rest of China. The transitional mechanism of the 17-Point Agreement was operating in high gear. These measures were not yet "democratic reforms" per se, but marked significant progress for Beijing's united-front stratagem of gaining political ground among the Tibetan ruling elites. In accepting these arrangements, as appraised by the CCP leadership, the Dalai Lama changed his political stance from the "middle" to the "left," the CCP's side. For a moment, an overriding concern in Beijing was that the young Dalai Lama should not become overzealous in making progress and resultantly isolate himself from the conservative majority of the Tibetan elites. That was why, in their 1955 and 1956 letters to the Tibetan leader, Mao and other CCP leaders urged the Dalai Lama to be patient and rally around himself as many people as possible.[23]

Reform Tibet, or Not

Mutual congeniality between Beijing and the Dalai Lama was short-lived, ending due to missteps in the CCP's push for "democratic reforms" in Tibet in 1956 and a trip to India that the Dalai Lama made in 1957.

Interestingly, in the mid-1950s the CCP leaders' new confidence about the Dalai Lama led to two courses of action that Beijing had initially perceived as mutually complementary but had turned out to be contradictory. That was, while cautioning the Dalai Lama not to act hastily lest he become out of touch with conservative Tibetan elites, leaders in Beijing seemed to feel that a push by the CCP could propel the reluctant Tibetan aristocrats and clergies to catch up with the Dalai Lama. In February 1956, in a conversation with a delegation of Tibetan officials, Mao indicated that the Tibetans should study the issue of "democratic reforms" after the Preparatory Committee for the Tibetan Autonomous Region (PCTAR) was established. In trying to put his guests at ease, Mao told them that reforms would actually improve Tibetan aristocrats' living conditions. Mao also stressed to those present that they must not misinterpret his words to mean immediate implementation of reforms, and that a preparatory period of one to three years would be necessary. He nevertheless had a clear message for the Dalai Lama and the Panchen Lama—"whenever feasible, action should be taken (to implement reforms)" (*ke xing ji xing*).[24]

The conversation took place at a juncture when both CCP enthusiasm for and Tibetan anxiety about reforms in Tibet had increased because of recent reforms in the Tibetan areas of western Sichuan, which had led to armed conflicts between local resisters and the PLA. Inevitably, the inaugural conference of the PCTAR, held in Lhasa in late April, became a sounding board for the reform tune, now gingerly played by Mao himself. To highlight the landmark significance of the event, Beijing sent a delegation of 800 plus members to Lhasa. At the conference, CCP officials including Chen Yi, Vice Premier of the PRC and head of the Beijing delegation, and Zhang Guohua, First Deputy Secretary of the CCP Tibet Work Committee (TWC) and Commander of the Tibetan Military District, hammered at two points in their speeches: first, reforms in Tibet were necessary and were already decided by the 17-Point Agreement; secondly, the timing for carrying out reforms would be decided by the Tibetans themselves.[25]

More telling, however, were speeches made by the two top Tibetan leaders. In heeding Mao's advice about moving ahead slowly, the Dalai Lama tried to dispel what he called a "malicious rumor and instigation" that reforms would follow the establishment of the preparatory committee. While recognizing socialism as the only path for Tibet to take eventually, the Dalai Lama asserted that Tibet still had a long way to go and that there was no point thinking too much about reforms at that time. In contrast, the Panchen Lama took a proactive stand on reforms. In reaffirming his belief that the central government in Beijing would not impose reforms on Tibet from the outside, the Panchen Lama demanded the Tibetan elites adopt a supportive attitude toward reforms. The Panchen Lama also stressed that the current Tibetan leadership was "duty-bound to lead all religious and secular people of Tibet" to support reforms. To substantiate his point, the Panchen Lama offered a concrete plan for first starting with some pilot reform projects in the area under his administration and then applying the experiences throughout Tibet.[26]

As a matter of fact, the Panchen Lama already took the initiative to coordinate the steps taken by the TWC for the sake of reforms. In January, the TWC began to move a great number of CCP cadres and Han personnel of various specialties into Tibet to meet the needs of the anticipated reforms. In March, the TWC dispatched teams to the Tibetan areas of Sichuan to learn about reform experiences that were to be applied to planned pilot projects in Shigatse, the Panchen Lama's turf.[27] In the context of historical grievances between the Dalai Lama and the Panchen Lama, the latter's assertion of his leading role in Tibetan affairs and coordination with CCP patrons must have been quite alarming to the Dalai Lama.

After the conference ended, what the Dalai Lama called a "malicious rumor" turned out to be true. The TWC somehow believed that the establishment of the PCTAR constituted an endorsement of its reform agenda for Tibet. In a July report to Beijing, the TWC contended that, ". . . currently the political situation of Tibet has already entered a new phase, and democratic reforms can and must be started." While continuing to move CCP cadres into Tibet to man many newly created agencies, the TWC launched the *Tibet Daily* in both the Chinese and the Tibetan languages and began to widely propagate the idea of reforms throughout Tibet. A step more menacing to the Tibetan authorities was that CCP officials in Tibet began to resort to the tactic of mass mobilization and organized a poor laborers' petition to the Dalai Lama for reforms. The TWC also began to implement its plan for inducting 50,000 to 80,000 Tibetans into the CCP and the Communist Youth League in the second half of the year. In the past, Beijing repeatedly instructed the TWC that every important decision about Tibetan affairs must be made by the central leadership of the CCP and that no steps could be taken in Tibet without Beijing's approval. It is therefore doubtful that in 1956 the TWC acted on its own without the nod from Beijing. These developments caused disturbances and, in some cases, open resistance. The three largest monasteries, Drepung, Ganden, and Sera, petitioned to the Dalai Lama and Beijing for postponing reforms in Tibet.[28]

According to the Dalai Lama's recollection, during the summer of 1956 and after a futile argument with Zhang Guohua over reforms and the resultant violence, he wrote three letters to Mao but did not receive any answer. In his autobiography, the Dalai Lama states that this was the first time he began to have doubt about Mao's intentions.[29] The contents of these letters remain classified in Chinese archives, but the Chinese government has published Mao's answer to the Dalai Lama, dated August 18, 1956. In his letter Mao was amicable as before, assuring the Dalai Lama that he had the CCP leadership's complete confidence. As for the initiation of reforms, Mao said that the time was not yet right but that mental preparations should be made now so that troubles could be avoided when reforms were implemented. The letter reflected the Dalai Lama's complaints about CCP officials in Tibet. Mao told the Tibetan leader that he was constantly worried about the Han officials' failure to gain the Tibetans' trust, and he asked the Dalai Lama to treat these officials as his own and educate them sternly when they made mistakes.[30]

It is hard to imagine how those seasoned CCP officials in Tibet could accept any "education" from the Dalai Lama. Leaders in Beijing nevertheless sensed that the reform gambit in Tibet already began to undermine the good rapport they had just built with the Dalai Lama during his recent visit. In a September directive to the TWC, the CCP Central Committee rejected the idea that reforms should be immediately implemented in Tibet. The directive stressed that hasty reforms in Tibet without the "genuine agreement" of the Tibetan leaders and Tibetan people could ruin the CCP's credibility. Nevertheless, the directive only went so far as to order the TWC to stop its pilot reform projects and cut back its propaganda for reforms. Not until March 1957, when the leading officials of the TWC were recalled to Beijing to discuss the Tibet work with the central leadership, was a firm decision made that reforms would not be carried out in Tibet for a minimum period of six years. Another decision was to abolish the preparatory measures already in place, which entailed the withdrawal of the

CCP cadres, troops, and Han workers that had recently moved into Tibet. The CCP leadership made a judgment that not only the Tibetan elites but also ordinary Tibetan people were against reforms.[31]

Whereas Beijing used about a year, from April 1956 to March 1957, to initiate and then suspend its reform stratagem in Tibet, it took just a half of that time for the Dalai Lama to jettison his newly gained Communist consciousness. When his Communist half was in chaos, the young Dalai Lama sought refuge in his Buddhist half. As he recalled years later, in 1956 he was caught between the CCP programs and the Tibetan opposition, and he felt unable to oppose "the people's violent instincts" without "helping the Chinese to [sic] destroy the people's trust in me." Therefore, the Dalai Lama sought a way out of the dilemma by withdrawing from his secular responsibilities in order to keep his religious authority intact. As he saw it, the only way to achieve this was to leave the country. An opportunity came when New Delhi invited him and the Panchen Lama to India to participate in the celebration of the 2,500th anniversary of the Buddha's nirvana.[32]

But Beijing did not see the trip merely as a religious affair. At first Beijing hesitated to grant permission for the Dalai Lama's trip abroad. In a July letter to the Dalai Lama, Zhou Enlai praised the Tibetan leader for declining recent invitations from India and Nepal, which the Dalai Lama had done reluctantly at the advice of CCP officials. Zhou pointed out that because he was needed in Tibet and American–British imperialists were quite active in India, the Dalai Lama should postpone the visit. In the letter Zhou also reassured the Dalai Lama that he had Beijing's "full trust." Then, in early November, Zhou sent another letter to the Dalai Lama and the Panchen Lama, now saying that the Indian and Nepalese governments recently sent invitations requesting the presence of the two Tibetan leaders at the Buddha's celebration, and that the two lamas could go if they wished.[33]

Three considerations were behind Beijing's change of mind. One was to forestall a petition for the Dalai Lama's India trip orchestrated by the three monasteries. Another was to use the trip to both appease and test the Dalai Lama who apparently was agitated by recent developments in and around Tibet. And the third was to use the Tibetan leaders' visit as part of Beijing's international united front strategy to consolidate the PRC's relationship with India, an international fence-sitter according to Beijing's analyses of the Cold War international politics.[34] In mid-November, a few days before the Dalai Lama's departure, Mao discussed briefly the Dalai Lama's forthcoming trip at a meeting of the CCP's Eighth National Congress. Remarkably, Mao only talked about the worst-case scenario: the Dalai Lama might not want to come back, curse the CCP everyday from abroad, and even declare Tibetan independence. From abroad he might call for an uprising by reactionary upper-class Tibetans to drive the CCP out of Tibet, but in the meantime evade any responsibility. Mao posed a rhetorical question: "Should I feel sad if one Dalai Lama runs away?" The answer: "I will not, even if nine more, ten in total, run away." About possible troubles in Tibet, Mao said, "I would be happy if such a bad situation emerges," for "we are never the first to launch offensive. We let them attack first, and then we can launch counter-offensive and ruthlessly destroy the attackers."[35]

Such talk by Mao presented a stark contrast to the party's positive assessment of the Dalai Lama just a year before. In view of Mao's position in the CCP, the talk would automatically lead to a sea change in the general attitude of CCP officials toward the Tibetan leader. Further research is needed to determine to what extent Mao was disappointed by the Dalai Lama's performance in relation to the year's abortive reform plan for Tibet. As far as his talk can reveal, Mao was bitter toward the Dalai Lama even before the latter made his trip to India.

The Dalai Lama refused to follow the travel arrangements suggested by Beijing, implying that he intended to visit Kalimpong, an Indian city where anti-Chinese Tibetans, KMT agents, and Western spies were active. In other words, the Dalai Lama might want to contact groups that were hostile toward the PRC. Interestingly, in his talk Mao used Zhang Guotao, the senior CCP leader who split with Mao over the destination of the Long March and then rallied to the KMT in the late 1930s, as the precedent for a runaway Dalai Lama. In this context, the Dalai Lama was no longer an "unpatriotic" Tibetan leader to be won over, but one of the CCP's own who showed a tendency of betrayal.

"Let Them Go"

Although in November 1956 Mao began to prepare the party for a new phase of work in Tibet without the Dalai Lama, the worst-case scenario he predicted did not materialize. In February 1957 the Dalai Lama returned to Lhasa. But in the eyes of the CCP leaders, he still failed the test. Whereas the Panchen Lama's return was never an issue to Beijing, the Dalai Lama hesitated and for a while considered staying abroad. To a large extent, his return was the result of Zhou Enlai's repeated conversations with him in India and Chinese diplomacy with the Indian government. Zhou told the Dalai Lama that reforms would not be carried out in Tibet for at least six years, and that neither India nor the United States would be able to provide any meaningful support to a Tibetan independence movement. This line of argument probably convinced the Dalai Lama and his entourage that it was in their best interest to return to Lhasa.[36] The Dalai Lama acted upon Zhou's advice and returned, but not before he visited Kalimpong against Zhou's repeated warnings. He also explicitly criticized CCP policies in Tibet in front of Chinese officials, and expressed a desire to establish a "unified greater Tibetan autonomous region" first and then transform it into a "Tibetan State" after the Soviet model of unionized republics.[37]

In the wake of these developments, some fence-mending measures were in order. Toward the end of his trip, the Dalai Lama criticized himself for wavering politically and expressed gratitude to the CCP leadership for continuing to trust him. In August 1957, Mao wrote to the Dalai Lama, praising him for rejecting bad advice from the Tibetans in exile during his India trip and admitting that the CCP policy had "defects" in prematurely pushing reforms in Tibet.[38] The Beijing–Dalai relationship was thereby patched up for the time being. But their 1955 partnership could never be restored.

Mao's August letter is his last known correspondence with the Dalai Lama. Since the 1990s, the Chinese government has released numerous documents regarding Tibet, but there is a curious gap for the year of 1958. In the year China was thrown into the hysteria of the Great Leap Forward. It seems that leaders in Beijing stopped writing to the Dalai Lama and the Panchen Lama, and the CCP Central Committee stopped its active search for a solution to the Tibetan situation. Indeed, under the "no reforms for the next six years" orientation, the TWC and the PLA troops in Tibet could not initiate any program except doing good deeds on a daily basis for gaining sympathy among ordinary Tibetans. As far as Beijing was concerned, a waiting game began. But judging from the few pieces of information available, Mao and his associates were not waiting for the Dalai Lama and the Tibetan elites to turn around and accept the necessity of reforms. They were waiting for an opportunity to apply a military solution to the Tibetan deadlock.

Quietly, in 1958 Beijing replaced its political maneuvering in Tibet with a military strategy. In June, Mao became convinced that preparations had to be made to deal with a general rebellion in Tibet. During the next few months, the CCP Central Committee advised the TWC:

> Now it appears that a military rebellion by a small number of reactionaries can consequently lead to relatively thorough liberation of the vast majority of the laboring people. Rebellion would be an inglorious bad thing for the Tibetan nation, but the [CCP] center's correct handling of the rebellion can turn the bad thing into a good thing for the Tibetan people.[39]

Militarily, Beijing's policy was not to use PLA troops to suppress scattered rebellions, but "let the poison out" for now and let "local rebellions develop into a general rebellion." As of January 1959, Mao's thinking about Tibet was firmly committed to war. Although not expecting a general military conflict in Tibet in the near future, Mao was certain that a "general decisive battle" would take place in a few years, and that the possibility of "using war to finally settle the [Tibetan] question" was a "good thing."[40]

Once the war solution ascended in Beijing's thinking about Tibet, whatever political value the Dalai Lama had left with the CCP leadership turned into liability. In a general military conflict over Tibet, the Dalai Lama could not possibly take Beijing's side. Yet in such a conflict Beijing still wanted to avoid being seen as the Dalai Lama's adversary, even though the war solution would inevitably surgically take out the Dalai establishment. The intended audience was the Tibetan people. When the Lhasa rebellion of March 1959 started the "general decisive battle" as he anticipated, Mao immediately decided that the Dalai Lama had co-conspired with others to start the rebellion. Yet he still suggested to the CCP Central Committee that if the Dalai Lama and followers tried to flee the country, "let them go." This became an order to the TWC and PLA troops in Tibet. Afterward, to placate ordinary Tibetans, Beijing put forth propaganda that the Dalai Lama had been abducted abroad by bad elements around him.[41]

When the last episode of the CCP–Dalai encounter in Tibet played out in 1959, it unfolded as if to fulfill Beijing's wishes. The Dalai barrier between the CCP and the Tibetan people finally disappeared. Yet what followed was a scenario that Beijing had tried to avoid since the beginning of the PRC—externally imposed changes in Tibet backed by force.

* * *

Since 1959 the CCP and the 14th Dalai Lama have made history together in producing the longest ever exile by a top Tibetan religious leader. During the Dalai Lama's 1956–1957 trip to India, Zhou Enlai pointed out to him that staying abroad, the Dalai Lama would lose both his political and religious status and turn himself into a refugee. Probably having an old Chinese saying, *pao de liao heshang, pao bu liao miao* (the monk can run away, but the temple cannot), in his mind, Zhou told the Dalai Lama: "You have a holy aspect. The holiness of a deity exists only in a holy temple and will disappear when the deity leaves the temple. Your temple is in Lhasa, not India, and it cannot be moved to India."[42] Interestingly, by the year of 1964 when the Tibetan Autonomous Region was officially established, Beijing had deprived the Dalai Lama of all his Tibetan and Chinese political titles but did not follow Qing emperors' precedents in deposing the 14th Dalai Lama religiously (in 1705 Kangxi deposed the 6th Dalai Lama, and in 1904 the Qing court briefly suspended the 13th Dalai Lama's title). This policy has remained to this date. Beijing may have believed that whatever lingering religious influence the Dalai Lama had within Tibet, it could not hinder Beijing's policies. The CCP leadership may also have wanted to keep religion as the sole basis for reconciliation with the Dalai Lama. As a matter of fact, in 1959, shortly after the Dalai Lama's exile, CCP leaders already began to talk about the Dalai Lama's return. Mao bet the Tibetan leader's return on a change of his world outlook, predicting that such a change would not occur in the near future but could happen after sixty years, after the whole world situation had changed.[43]

Ten more years are remaining to see how good of a prophet Mao was. In the past five decades the Dalai Lama has already changed, the world has changed, and China itself has changed beyond recognition. Yet these changes have continued to produce discord rather than consonance between the CCP and the Dalai Lama. Clearly, the so-called Tibetan question today is no longer the same as that facing CCP and Tibetan leaders in the 1950s. At mid-century the crux of the question was a contention over sovereignty between Beijing's centralizing nationalism, enfolded in revolutionary programs of Chinese Communism, and Lhasa's separatist tendency, obsessed with maintaining the sociopolitical status quo of Tibet. Today, although the two sides continue to box themselves into a dispute over sovereignty, the Tibetan question assumes a much larger significance in the context of China's re-rise and in the prospect of the globalizing twenty-first century. The Chinese leadership of Mao's generation tried to solve its Tibetan question with and without the Dalai Lama. It remains to be seen who holds or what is the key to the Tibetan question today.

Notes

1. "Temporary Constitution of the Republic of China, March 11, 1912," Zhang Yuxin and Zhang Shuangzhi, eds., *Minguo Zangshi Shiliao Huibian* (Collection of historical materials on the Tibetan affairs of the Republic of China) (Beijing: Xueyuan Chubanshe, 2005), 1: 42.
2. *Mao Zedong Xizang Gongzuo Wenxuan* (Selected writings of Mao Zedong on Tibetan work), Office of Document Research of the Central Committee of the Chinese Communist Party et al., comp. (Beijing: Zhongyang Wenxian Chubanshe and Zhongguo Zangxue Chubanshe, 2001), 9, 23; *Heping Jiefang Xizang* (Peaceful liberation of Tibet), Committee for Collecting Materials on Party History of the Tibetan Autonomous Region and Leading Group on Colleting Materials on Party History of the Tibetan Military District, comp. (Lhasa: Xizang Renmin Chubanshe, 1995), 64–66.
3. *Mao Zedong Xizang Gongzuo Wenxuan*, 61.
4. *Mao Zedong Xizang Gongzuo Wenxuan*, 1–4; *Heping Jiefang Xizang*, 47–66.
5. *Heping Jiefang Xizang*, 67–68.
6. The Tibetan government tried to block the PLA's advance toward Tibet at Chamdo of eastern Tibet, and the effort failed after the PLA occupied Chamdo in mid-October 1950.
7. *Heping Jiefang Xizang*, 125–128.
8. Wang Lixiong, *Tianzang: Xizang de Mingyun* (Sky burial: the destiny of Tibet) (Mirror Books, 1998), 171–174; Melvyn C. Goldstein, *The Snow Lion and the Dragon: China, Tibet, and the Dalai Lama* (Berkeley: University of California Press, 1997), 52–53; *Mao Zedong Xizang Gongzuo Wenxuan*, 59.
9. *Mao Zedong Xizang Gongzuo Wenxuan*, 6.
10. Committee for Colleting Party History Materials of the Tibetan Autonomous Region, *Zhonggong Xizang Dangshi Dashiji 1949–1994* (Chronicle of important events in the CCP history in Tibet) (Lhasa: Xizang Renmin Chubanshe, 1995), 50–51.

11. *Mao Zedong Xizang Gongzuo Wenxuan*, 4, 14; *Zhonggong Xizang Dangshi Dashij*, 46.
12. *Mao Zedong Xizang Gongzuo Wenxuan*, 50–51, 61–64, 69, 72–73.
13. *Mao Zedong Xizang Gongzuo Wenxuan*, 45–46, 56–58, 84–86, 90–91, 93–98, 106, 132–135, 150–151, 156–163; *Zhou Enlai yu Xizang* (Zhou Enlai and Tibet), Party History Office of the Tibetan Autonomous Region, comp. (Beijing: Zhongguo Zangxue Chubanshe, 1998), 26, 65–66, 75–78; *Xizang Gongzuo Wenxian Xuanbian (1949–2005)* (Selected documents on Tibetan work, 1949–2005), Office of Documentary Research of the Central Committee of the Chinese Communist Party and the Committee of the Chinese Communist Party of the Tibetan Autonomous Region, comp. (Beijing: Zhongyang Wenxian Chubanshe, 2005), 180–181.
14. *Mao Zedong Xizang Gongzuo Wenxuan*, 95–97.
15. *Zhonggong Dangshi Dashiji*, 43–44.
16. *Mao Zedong Xizang Gongzuo Wenxuan*, 132–133, 150–151. So far the Chinese authorities have only published Mao's letters to the Dalai Lama but not the latter's letters to Mao.
17. *Zhonggong Xizang Dangshi Dashiji*, 54.
18. *Mao Zedong Xizang Gongzuo Wenxuan*, 109–111, 113–117; Dalai Lama, *My Land and My People* (New York: Potala Corporation, 1962), 115–118; Melvyn Goldstein, *A History of Modern Tibet, Volume 2: The Calm before the Storm, 1951–1955* (Berkeley: University of California Press, 2007), 491–521.
19. *Mao Zedong Xizang Gongzuo Wenxuan*, 115–116; Goldstein, *A History of Modern Tibet, Volume 2*, 491–520.
20. The Dalai Lama, *My Land and My People* (1962), 118; the Dalai Lama, *Freedom in Exile: The Autobiography of the Dalai Lama* (New York: HarperCollins Publishers, 1990), 98–99; Goldstein, *A History of Modern Tibet, Volume Two*, 521 (based on the author's interview with the Dalai Lama in 1994); Thomas Laird, *The Story of Tibet: Conversations with the Dalai Lama* (New York: Grove Press, 2006), 326 (based on the author's conversations with the Dalai Lama between November 1997 and July 2000).
21. *Xizang Lishi Dang'an Huicui* (A collection of historical archives of Tibet), Archives of the Tibetan Autonomous Region, comp. (Beijing: Wenwu Chubanshe, 1995), 107: 1–7.
22. *Mao Zedong Xizang Gongzuo Wenxuan*, 132–133; *Zhou Enlai yu Xizang*, 40–42.
23. Goldstein, *A History of Modern Tibet, Volume Two*, 533–535; *Mao Zedong Xizang Gongzuo Wenxuan*, 132–133; *Zhou Enlai yu Xizang*, 65–67; *Xizang Gongzuo Wenxian Xuanbian*, 180–181; *Xizang Lishi Dang'an Huicui*, 106.
24. *Mao Zedong Xizang Gongzuo Wenxuan*, 136–139.
25. *Xizang de Minzhu Gaige* (Democratic reforms in Tibet), Committee on Collecting Party History Materials of the Tibetan Autonomous Region, comp. (Lhasa: Xizang Renmin Chubanshe, 1995), 47–48, 53–55.
26. *Xizang de Minzhu Gaige*, 49–52.
27. *Xizang de Minzhu Gaige*, 7–8.
28. *Xizang de Minzhu Gaige*, 8–9; *Mao Zedong Xizang Gongzuo Wenxuan*, 65, 83, 92; *Zhonggong Xizang Dangshi Dashiji*, 64–65.
29. The Dalai Lama, *Freedom in Exile*, 110–111. *Zhou Enlai yu Xizang*, 65–67, shows that in July Zhou Enlai answered a letter from the Dalai Lama dated May 28. *Mao Zedong Xizang Gongzuo Wenxuan*, 150–151, shows that in August Mao answered two letters from the Dalai Lama.
30. *Mao Zedong Xizang Gongzuo Wenxuan*, 150–151.
31. *Xizang de Minzhu Gaige*, 56–67.

32. The Dalai Lama, *My Land and My People*, 138.
33. *Zhou Enlai yu Xizang*, 65–67, 75–76.
34. *Zhou Enlai yu Xizang*, 315; *Pinxi Xizang Panluan* (Suppression of the Tibetan rebellion), Committee for Collecting Party History Materials of the Tibetan Autonomous Region and Leading Group on Colleting Party History Materials of the Tibetan Military District, comp. (Lhasa: Xizang Renmin Chubanshe, 1995), 120–121; Asian Department of the Ministry of Foreign Affairs, "Basic conditions and developments of India," 2/25/1956, Document No. 102–00055-01, Archives of the Foreign Ministry of the People's Republic of China; Central Investigation Department of the CCP Central Committee, "The reasons for and existing problems of the recent improvement of the Indian–American relations," *Diaocha Ziliao* (Investigation materials), No. 1 of 1957, 1/17/1957, Document No. 105–00837-03, Archive of the Foreign Ministry of the People's Republic of China.
35. *Mao Zedong Xizang Gongzuo Wenxuan*, 152–153.
36. *Zhou Enlai yu Xizang*, 142–155.
37. *Pingxi Xizang Panluan*, 116–119.
38. *Zhou Enlai yu Xizang*, 317; *Mao Zedong Xizang Gongzuo Wenxuan*, 162–163.
39. *Zhonggong Xizang Dangshi Dashiji*, 80; *Pingxi Xizang Panluan*, 64–69.
40. *Mao Zedong Xizang Gongzuo Wenxuan*, 164.
41. *Pinxi Xizang Panluan*, 81–82, 89.
42. *Zhou Enlai yu Xizang*, 330.
43. *Zhou Enlai yu Xizang*, 101; *Mao Zedong Xizang Gongzuo Wenxuan*, 180; *Xizang Gongzuo Wenxian Xuanbia*, 239.

PART IV

From World War to Cold War

CHAPTER NINE

The United States and Frontier China

When the Chinese Communist Party took power in China in 1949, the ideology-oriented Cold War international politics assigned a color code to China, which was red. Yet even kindergarteners know that a coloring book must have shapes for them to color. Two cartographic images of China could invoke strong emotions from the Chinese of the twentieth century: One was a begonia-leaf image, and the other was a rooster image. Whereas it is widely held that the Qing Dynasty bequeathed a geopolitical landscape to modern China, the years of World War II really saw the final shaping of the Chinese state as it is today. The cancellation of Japan's military empire in the Asia-Pacific region and the wartime inter-allied diplomacy were relevant events in this respect.[1] World War II in Asia not only reversed the destiny of several of China's "lost territories" and changed the status of some former "tributary states" to the bygone Qing Empire, it also had impact on China's ethnic frontiers that blended "domestic" and "foreign" affairs. The latter category deserves more attention. After all, "national" China took shape only after the "dependencies" (*fanshu*) of imperial China went separate ways in internalization and externalization. In World War II, American policy makers' strategic thinking about China's peripheries, because of the wartime alliance between the two countries, was consequential to both such internalization and externalization. As a power that approached China from the direction of the Pacific Ocean, before the war the United States was always concerned about its legal rights and commercial interests in China but exerted little influence on the territorial changes of China in modern times. World War II was a watershed in terms of American involvement in geopolitical decisions about Asian countries. Washington's wartime diplomacy not only had a hand in the bifurcated situation of postwar Korea and Vietnam but also in the altered shape of China's map image. Yet another precedent was the beginning of American policy makers' deliberations on China's ethnic frontiers.

European and Asian "Minorities"

During World War II, memory about the previous "Great War" and uncertainty about postwar stability caused a serious concern in the U.S. State Department's foreign policy planning, which was about the "minorities problem" in Europe. As defined in some lengthy studies by the State Department, a "minority" was a "group of people with a national consciousness distinct from that of the majority within a state, usually manifested by a difference of language and culture." In conceding that the minorities problem was "preliminarily an internal problem," the State Department nevertheless believed that the problem could not be solved without the "evolution of a genuine multinational or un-national state in which citizenship is as separate from 'nationality' as it is from religion." Yet what troubled State Department officials was not a remote timetable for the problem's solution, but the possible international ramifications of the problem in the immediate postwar years. If states of the world were in a constant fear that an aggressor state might use the problem as an excuse for war, there would be no international peace and stability. At the end of World War I, an international effort

This map for planning purpose by American strategists in World War II anticipated an initial military-political situation in postwar Asia. Note that whereas northern Vietnam was assigned to the Chinese government, Manchuria, Xinjiang, and Tibet, three frontier regions of China were not considered as under Chinese responsibility.

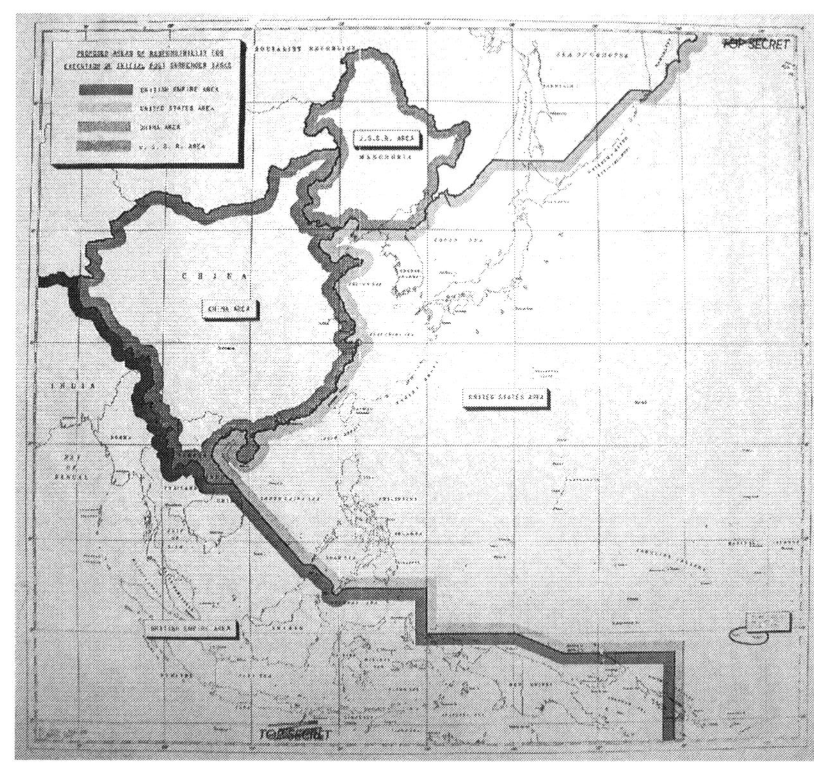

Source: Appendix "B" of Joint War Plans Committee 264/9, "Further Action as to Immediate Occupation of Japan and Japan-Held Areas," August 13, 1945, Records of the Joint Chiefs of Staff, National Archives II, College Park, MD.

An American view of the Soviet threat to China, 1948.

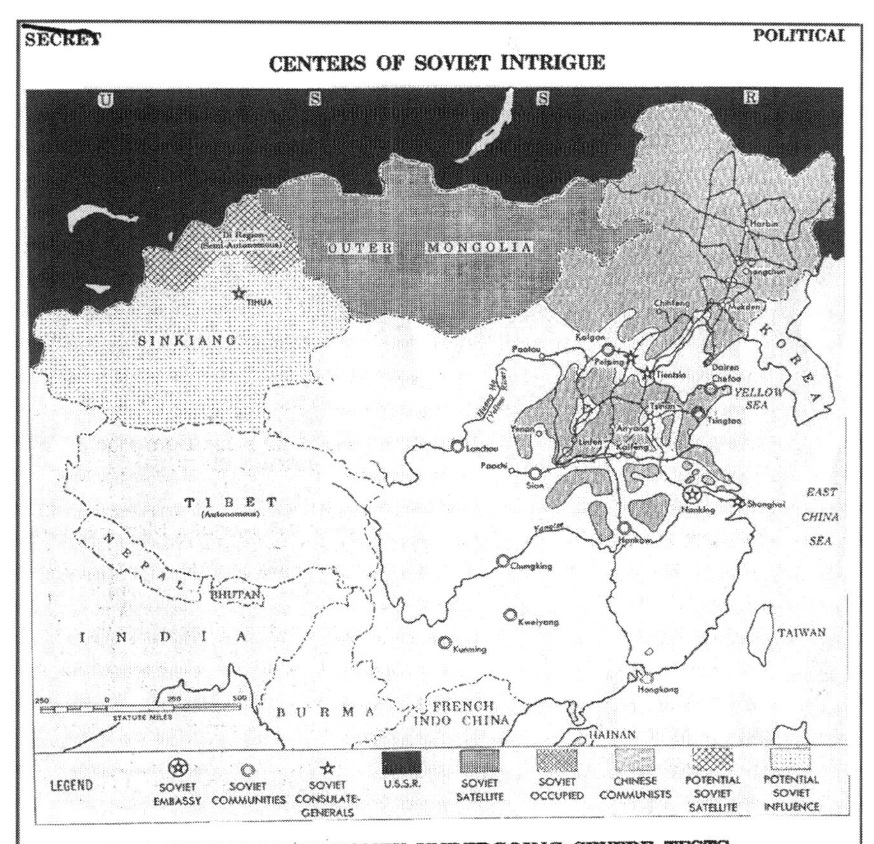

CHINA'S SOVEREIGNTY UNDERGOING SEVERE TESTS

Successful Communist military operations threaten the survival of the Chinese Government as an effective, national, political entity. Continued economic deterioration characterized by an unbalanced budget, spiraling inflation, lack of production, stagnation of commerce, and commodity shortages may culminate in financial collapse. Tribal rebellions in Sinkiang Province threaten China's ability to hold that area, and recognition of Outer Mongolia as an independent state has strengthened the autonomy movement of the Inner Mongolians. The Soviet position on the status of Dairen and Port Arthur has weakened Chinese authority in Manchuria by denying those ports to the government.

SECRET 7

Source: Duplicate of Intelligence Division, General Staff, U.S. Army, Department of the Army, "Strategic Intelligence Estimate of China," *Intelligence Review*, Supplement No. 3, August 1948, Truman Papers, PSF/Subject File, box 173.

occurred to solve the problem in Europe, which gave rise to a "Wilsonian moment" as many non-Western peoples seized the principle of "national self-determination" in trying to rid themselves of the colonial yoke.[2]

The beginning of World War II in Europe in 1939 indicated that the solution had failed miserably. Conscious that the United States was part of the failure, Washington's political strategists in World War II wanted to do a better job for the second time. These considerations led the State Department to conclude that after the war an international organization ought to assume a dual responsibility for, first, maintaining a peaceful international environment in order for European states to implement their policies toward minorities, and, secondly, redressing dangerous situations caused by any of these European states' improper policies toward minorities. The State Department believed that the United State must play a leading role in such an organization while watching closely European states' dealing with their respective minorities problems.[3] Thus, a policeman's role was prescribed for the United States in postwar European ethnopolitics.

By contrast, American policy makers never considered such an institutional approach for dealing with the problem of minorities in Asia. An arena for great-power rivalries, Asian politics seemed to have followed only one rule, which was power. China's "minorities problem" became an item in Western governments' contemplation of Asian security after Japan invaded Manchuria in 1931. After the Mukden Incident, American and British diplomats in China agreed that the event forced the Chinese government to change its attitude toward China's ethnic frontiers "from apathy to anxiety." A British diplomat noted: "The Mongols are always alive to the fact that they were once a great race and are eagerly awaiting the arrival of a new Genghis Khan to restore them to their former glory." The Chinese government therefore had better work out some arrangements with the Mongols to forestall any Japanese conspiracy. In the meantime, neither the American nor the British government felt that anything could be done about the deteriorating situation along China's northern frontiers. For even the Soviet Union, which had more crucial interests in the area than Western powers, did not seem able to curb the Japanese other than severing contacts between Inner and Outer Mongolia.[4] Thus, as far as the Western powers were concerned, during the 1930s Japan enjoyed freedom of action in China's northern peripheries. Before the United States engaged Japan in the Pacific war in late 1941, many Americans already accepted Japanese dominance in Manchuria and Inner Mongolia as an established status quo. Even well-informed individuals in America's official and academic circles could not see how China would be able to recover Manchuria and Inner Mongolia after its war with Japan was over. As they predicted, after the war Manchuria would probably remain under Japan's influence, and Inner Mongolia would become a buffer zone between China, Japan, and the Soviet Union.[5] In other words, the Republic of China would have to accept the Great Wall as its actual border in the north.

Pearl Harbor drastically altered the vision about postwar East Asia held by many in Washington's foreign policy community. In 1942, when the State Department started to organize its foreign policy planning operations, it drafted some questionnaires about postwar China. Inner and Outer Mongolia, Tibet, Xinjiang, and some other regions were listed in these questionnaires as the territorial problems that a liberated China would have to cope with. State Department officials expected that at the end of the war, difficulties regarding "several Chinese provinces comprising Inner Mongolia" would likely arise among China, Japan, the Soviet Union, *and* the "Mongols."[6] Thus, from the onset, the State Department's policy planning projected Inner Mongolia as an international question but not a domestic problem involving only the Chinese authorities and the Inner Mongols.

The State Department's reference to the "Mongols" was intentionally ambiguous because the implied entity, Outer Mongolia, was neither independent by international recognition nor subject to China's control. One definition of Outer Mongolia, given by the U.S. Office of Strategic Services (OSS), was that it was a "colonial experiment" of the Soviet Union.[7] To officials of the State Department, this problematic territory, along with Xinjiang, Tannu Tuva, and Manchuria, were contested areas between China and the Soviet Union. Before the war ended, the State Department adopted a stand that although the American government must oppose any arrangement detrimental to Chinese sovereignty in Manchuria, it could accept solutions about the other three territories as long as they were reached through peaceful means. Actually, a prevalent view in Washington in the war years was that China could not realistically hope to recover Outer Mongolia.[8]

Even in the case of Manchuria, for a while State Department officials entertained an idea radically different from the Chinese government's conception about its sovereignty there. It is remarkable that more than a year after the United States entered the war against Japan, a position paper by the Division of Far Eastern Affairs of the State Department proposed partition of Manchuria as a permanent solution of the Manchurian question. The paper argued that Manchuria had been a "cradle of conflict" in the past half century because none of the other four "races," Russians, Koreans, Japanese, and Mongols, had completely accepted China's sovereignty over Manchuria. If the Manchurian borders in the east, west, and north were redrawn according to "ethnological principles," future troubles could be avoided. Allegedly, China would benefit from such arrangements in not only retaining all the settled and most fertile lands and all of the 36 million Chinese nationals in Manchuria, but also regaining its rights in the Guandong (Kwantung) Leased Territories and nearly all foreign railroads and mining concessions. What would be the cost to China? In the east, China would have to cede some 110,000 square miles of land to Korea. Another 165,000 square miles of territories and their Mongolian residents in the north and the west would also secede from China.[9]

In the summer of 1943, a similar exercise was done by the British Foreign Office's Research Department. The resultant memorandum speculated that the Soviet Union would have two options in expanding its influence in postwar Northeast Asia. Moscow might either encourage the Chinese Communists to set up a soviet republic in Manchuria or use Mongolian nationalism to create a Soviet–Mongolian bloc. According to British officials, the latter option had the advantage of using the nationality principle and therefore appearing less disturbing to the Anglo-American opinion. In following the second option, the Soviets would encourage Japanese-trained Mongolian armed forces and political groups in Inner Mongolia and Manchuria to join with Outer Mongolia in a strong movement for unifying all Mongols in a single state, or a "Greater Mongolia." The memo noted that despite years of sinicization, Inner Mongolia had a larger Mongol population than Outer Mongolia. In northern Chahar and areas of western and northwestern Manchuria the Mongols were actually "ethnically preponderant" and could make territorial claims on "ethnographic grounds." Such a "Greater Mongolia" could push southward to the Great Wall and eastward to the Yellow Sea to separate Chinese Manchuria from the rest of China. In such a scenario the modern industry and the railway system in Manchuria would help the Mongolian nation achieve internal coherence. Because the scenario, if taking place, could drastically change the international landscape of Northeast Asia, the memo caused many questions in the Foreign Office as to whether or not the Soviet Union really entertained such an intention and whether or not the Chinese would in any circumstances allow this to happen.[10]

Interestingly, when American and British officials hypothesized postwar circumstances in Northeast Asia, they attached different significance to ethnicity. Whereas the State Department proposal for Manchurian partition intended, in a can-do spirit, to use the ethnic factor to macro-manage the troublesome Manchurian region, the Foreign Office's somber prediction feared that the issue of ethnicity in Inner Mongolia and Manchuria would only work to the Soviets' advantage. In the war years, however, policy designs for East Asia along an ethnological line thrived neither in Washington nor in London. The Western Allies', especially America's, wartime foreign policies were committed to promoting China as a strong and unitary power. Ethnopolitical scenarios concerning China, which by nature were divisive, must not be pursued and should be prevented.

"Chinese Unification"

At one of the State Department's policy planning meetings, this opinion was firmly expressed: "The question of Chinese unification is a key to the whole problem in considering security in the area [of East Asia]."[11] To American policy makers, the question of China's unity had three aspects. The first was internal political unification, meaning mainly the readjustment of the Kuomintang–Chinese Communist relationship. Although American officials could not agree whether or not their government should commit itself to the Kuomintang (KMT) regime in attaining the goal, such a commitment actually guided Washington's China policy during and after the war.[12] The second dimension of the question involved China's recovery of territories lost to Japan, including Taiwan and Manchuria. In November and December 1943, at the Cairo Conference, President Franklin D. Roosevelt officially committed the United States to assisting China to recover these territories. In making such a commitment, American policy makers had America's commercial and strategic interests in mind. It was expected that after recovering Taiwan, the Chinese government would grant the United States rights of using military bases on the island. Some officials in the State Department even suggested that a "nationality factor," or the ethnic similarity between the aborigines of eastern Taiwan and the mountain tribes of the Philippines, be used as a "lever" in negotiating with the Chinese.[13]

The third aspect of China's unity was more complicated. It was a gray category involving the vast areas of Mongolia, Xinjiang, and Tibet. These territories were "gray" because their settlement would overlap China's domestic and foreign affairs. In these territories Chinese sovereignty was either incomplete or merely nominal, and the Chinese government was in dispute not only with local ethnic groups but also with two members of the Grand Alliance, Great Britain and the Soviet Union. It was about these regions that the Chinese and the American governments could run into potential disagreements.

A divergence between the Chinese and the American understandings of these issues appeared during the first few months of the Pacific war. When contemplating how the Western allies could strengthen China's resistance against Japan through a psychological warfare, the U.S. Joint Chiefs of Staff suggested that the morale of the Chinese government could be enhanced if the U.S. government supported China to restore its territory not only to the status quo before 1937 but also to that before 1894.[14] The year of 1894 meant to indicate China's recovery of the rights and territories lost to Japan after the first Sino–Japanese war of 1894–1895. What American psychological warriors had in mind specifically were Taiwan and Manchuria. The Americans however did not seem to realize that to Chinese officials the territory of 1894 meant the entire domain of the Qing Empire at that time, including not only

Taiwan and Manchuria lost to Japan but also Mongolia and Tibet that became alienated from China after the Qing's overthrow in 1911.

In respect to these outlaying territories, the U.S. government at most adopted the attitude of an interested bystander. Officials in Washington had no particular preference about these territories' status as long as the Chinese, the British, and the Soviets could work out some mutually acceptable understanding. In the meantime, during the war China's disputes with the British and the Soviets respectively over Tibet and Mongolia must not in anyway hinder the common war effort of the Grand Alliance. In treating these regions as part of China's relationship with Britain and the Soviet Union, the State Department had nothing particular to offer on the Han–Tibetan and Han–Mongolian relationships per se. In other words, the Tibetan and Mongolian questions were not considered in the framework of "minorities problem." In addition, devoting much of their time and energy to contemplating postwar settlement of the "dependencies problem" in Asia, State Department officials never defined Tibet and Mongolia as such. In Asia, the State Department applied the "dependency" conception only to Western powers' and Japan's colonial possessions.[15]

Promoting China as one of the Big Four so that it could assist the United States in counterbalancing the British Empire and the Soviet Union in the postwar years, the Roosevelt administration usually showed a pro-China tilt in China's disputes with the other two great powers. In other words, Washington's wartime China policy tended to pamper China's "anti-imperialist" nationalism. Generally, Washington appeared more sensitive than London to Chinese nationalistic ego vis- à-vis foreign influence in China. The other side of this sensitivity was a calculated indifference toward the KMT regime's dealing with China's ethnic minorities. Washington never made it a focal point in its wartime China policy how China should recover or excise sovereignty in northern and western ethnic frontiers. In treating China as a sovereign national state and assisting the rise of China's power status, Washington worked for restoring and safeguarding China's territorial and administrative integrity mainly in the geopolitical frame of eastern China.[16]

Only occasionally was American liberalism visibly affronted by the KMT government's official nationalism. The State Department's reaction to Chiang Kai-shek's notorious book, *China's Destiny*, was an example to the point. After the book was released in 1943, State Department officials took it as evidence that "virus of nationalism" existed in China and was "capable of becoming a cancer." Their critique focused on the KMT regime's one-party authoritarianism against the CCP and liberal political forces in China and on its manifested ambition to become the leader of Asia. These tendencies convinced State Department officials that American policy must make an effort to direct Chinese nationalism into "healthy channels."[17] What was overlooked completely in this critique was the possible impact of Chiang's one-nation creed on China's ethnopolitical landscape, which treated ethnic groups in China as big or small "clan branches" of the "Chinese Nation" (*zhonghua minzu*).

A seasoned player in the "Great Game" for Inner Asia, the British government was more alert than Washington to the developments in China's ethnopolitical front. Chiang's book turned out to be more than a piece of propaganda. The KMT government actually directed its local apparatus in China's ethnic borderlands to follow Chiang's one-nation creed as a new policy guideline. The British consulate in Tihwa (Urumqi), Xinjiang, got wind of the directive. In February 1944, the British embassy in Chongqing transmitted the information to the Foreign Office along with its own comments. Interestingly, the embassy, then under Ambassador Sir Horace Seymour, chose to give a rather positive reading to Chongqing's new policy. The British embassy suggested that Chiang's creed "represents a considerable advance—if not a radical departure from—the views expressed by Dr. Sun Yat-sen on the subject of border races." According to the embassy, Chiang's assertion about the same origin of all the "races" in China was intended to "establish the racial unity and equality of all the peoples living within the borders of the Chinese Republic." Although Chiang's arguments might be "jejune and unconvincing," "they nevertheless offer an historical justification for the policy now pursued by the Chinese Government of conciliation towards the border races as peoples of equal status with the Chinese." The embassy however admitted that the same set of arguments could also be used to justify, "on the ground of family friendship and collaboration, a policy of economic and cultural penetration and political control which otherwise might have invited the stigma of imperialism."[18]

Officials at the Foreign Office did not share the embassy's sentiment. Annoyed by the Chinese government's wartime disposition of acting as a spokesman for Asian colonial peoples, Foreign Office officials believed that the KMT was hypocritical in denouncing European imperialism while "busy asserting imperial claims to dominate their non-Chinese neighbors, such as Mongolia and Tibet."[19] One of the Foreign Office commentaries on the embassy's dispatch ridiculed the ethnological arguments made in Chiang's book as "sheer nonsense" that "merely involve the whole issue of China's relations with these peoples in a cloud of humbug." Although under the new creed Chinese officials might behave better toward the non-Han groups, "on the other hand, the new theory disposes entirely of any possible claims of the Mongols or Tibetans to autonomy or separate national existence because it asserts them to be merely parts of the Chinese nation." To Foreign Office officials, this was as if the Nazis made a claim that all the Slavs were descendants of the German tribes and used it as a "better pretext" for conquering them.[20]

Whereas the British Empire in India might predispose British officials to favor "any possible claims of the Mongols or Tibetans to autonomy or separate national existence," Washington tended to frown upon separatist tendencies in China's borderlands lest they hinder America's search for a strong and stable Chinese partnership in East Asia. Moreover, the disagreement between the British embassy and the Foreign Office indicated the complexity of the matter. If taken out of the context of the KMT regime's usually repressive and assimilative policies toward the non-Han peoples in China, Chiang's one-nation creed might be interpreted as an effort to promote interethnic equality through minimizing ethnic differences in China. Such a policy intention could actually find sympathizers within the U.S. State Department. In considering the "minorities problem" in the European context, policy planners of the State Department believed that after the war any valid solution of the problem must work for the eventual elimination of the stigma of "minorities" as much as possible and place the problem on the "broader foundation of the protection of basic human rights."[21] The human rights idea, however, was not imparted to the Chinese government. Actually, throughout the war the KMT regime and the U.S. State Department never exchanged their views on China's or any other Asian country's "minorities problem." There was a war to be won in China's eastern provinces and the Pacific. China's "internal" ethnopolitical problems, which existed mainly in China's northern and western peripheries, were not even on the backburner of the wartime Sino–American partnership.

Therefore, when Owen Littimore made an effort to advise Chiang Kai-shek on China's ethnopolitics in the second half of 1941 and continued to do so in 1942, he was not acting in accordance with any official policy of the U.S. government, even though President Roosevelt himself recommended Lattimore to Chiang as a political adviser. Lattimore's advice to Chiang on China's ethnic frontier affairs was private in nature and was neither solicited by

Chiang nor encouraged by Washington.[22] More than three decades later, when recalling his service to Chiang in the early 1940s, Lattimore admitted that since he went to Chongqing as Chiang's personal adviser but not as "Roosevelt's man," he "must put loyalty to what I thought were the best interests of Chiang Kai-shek above everything else."[23] This situational loyalty to Chiang prevented Lattimore from being always forthright in offering his opinions to his Chinese employer. For instance, although urging Chiang to adopt a political program in Inner Mongolia for suspending the Chinese authorities' colonization policy and stopping provincial officials' tyrannical behaviors toward the Mongols, Lattimore was against an idea immensely popular among the Mongols that Inner Mongolia be organized into a single autonomous territory. His policy suggestion was intended to "make the Mongols actively patriotic toward China," whereas the autonomy idea, in his opinion, contradicted the KMT government's demand for "general increase of political unity" in China. Lattimore stressed to Chiang that the solution of the Inner Mongolia question must go hand in hand with general democratization of China. Democracy for the Inner Mongols, he contended, could also help the Chinese government attract Outer Mongolia back to China.[24]

After he returned to the United States and became director of the Pacific bureau of the Office of War Information in late 1942, Lattimore expressed a different set of thoughts to his largely official American audience. In a 1943 memorandum on Mongolia, prepared for the Council on Foreign Relations' confidential series of "Studies of American Interests in the War and the Peace," Lattimore observed that Mongolia had never belonged to China in history and the current Chinese government would have no chance to "recover" the "Mongolian People's Republic" by force. As for the political antagonisms in Inner Mongolia, Lattimore applied a sort of class analysis and suggested that the situation there was more complex than "racial antagonism" fostered purposefully by Mongolian elites, Chinese politicians, and Japanese intruders. Underneath the Mongolian elites' agitations, another level of antagonisms existed "at which the common people, both Mongol and Chinese, react in resentment against the princes, priests, generals, and magistrates whose pawns they are—but without knowing exactly what to do about it."[25] This socioeconomic insight was extremely important but its relevance to American foreign policy was unclear. In the postwar years the Chinese Communists would take advantage of these "lower-level" antagonisms in an effort to penetrate Inner Mongolian nationalism.

Lattimore's remarks to members of the Council on Foreign Relations would not have pleased the KMT leaders. In devoting a substantial portion of his *China's Destiny* to China's interethnic question, Chiang proved that he took the non-Han peoples and their territories seriously. Yet, despite Lattimore's confidence in Chiang's open-mindedness, KMT ethnopolitics continued heading toward a direction opposite to Lattimore's recommendations. As shown in Chiang's 1943 book, the KMT regime not only extolled China's traditional assimilation policy but also advocated a one-nation creed that threatened to drive the non-Han ethnic identities in China into oblivion.

China's "Three Corners"

When talking with Chiang, more than once Lattimore pointed out that China's century-old struggle against the "unequal treaty system" had been won already and now it was time for China to enter the next phase of taking care of its "three corners," namely the northeast, northwest, and southwest. He warned that if the minorities in these areas were pressed by

China, they would "recoil" toward Russian and British influence. Contending that China's traditional assimilation policy had failed to work, Lattimore especially cautioned Chiang that the Soviet Union's "outstanding success" with its own minority nationalities could be a lure to China's minorities as well.[26]

Lattimore was prescient about how an important, ethnic aspect of great-power politics in Asia would unfold. Yet his repeated call for attention to Inner Asian frontiers was a lonely voice in both China and the United States. In May 1942, while still being Chiang's advisor, Lattimore made a trip back to the United States. He wrote to Chiang and predicted that once Japan and the Soviet Union became involved in war with each other, China's interests in Manchuria, Mongolia, and Xinjiang would be significantly affected. Since Washington knew almost nothing about these Chinese interests, Lattimore explained, he could help China better if he stayed in Washington, using his expertise to prevent misunderstandings of Inner Asia on the part of the U.S. government.[27] Lattimore's opinion on the U.S. government's or, more precisely, the State Department's lack of knowledge about China's ethnic frontiers was on the mark. In 1942 he was however way ahead of the war's progress in suggesting that Inner Asian geopolitics be made a priority in Washington's China policy. To American policy makers, Moscow's intentions in northeastern and northwestern China were matters to be dealt with only when the war in the Pacific was won. Two years later, these issues were indeed on President Roosevelt's mind when he asked his vice-president Henry A. Wallace to visit China and to take Lattimore with him.

The Wallace mission to China in June 1944 was one of the riddles that gave FDR a reputation of Sphinx's temperament. American news media and the Chinese government were still trying to figure out the true purpose of the mission even after Wallace's party arrived in Chongqing.[28] There is no need to make one more speculation about the matter here. It is just relevant to point out that Roosevelt's insistence on Lattimore's inclusion in the mission, which would travel to China by way of the Soviet Far East and Inner Asia, was unequivocally based on the latter's expertise in these areas. He hoped that Lattimore could assist the vice-president in finding out a way to prevent Chinese–Soviet frictions along their borders in the future. On his first day in Chongqing, Wallace made a vague suggestion to his hosts that self-government be granted to those nationalities in the Far East that had so far not enjoyed the right. To the sensitive Chinese ears, their American guest implied the Mongols and the Muslim groups of Xinjiang.[29] Yet in China Wallace soon became immersed in more urgent issues such as the KMT regime's difficult military situation and its quarrels with the CCP. These would become the central concerns in his post-mission report to President Roosevelt. The report did make a point that after the war China could not realistically hope to resume sovereignty in Outer Mongolia because the region was under strong Soviet influence and might even attract the Inner Mongols. As for Lattimore's contribution to his mission, Wallace later would claim that Lattimore was mainly involved in handling "publicity matters in China" but offered to himself "no political advice at any time sufficiently significant to be recalled now."[30]

In a time when Washington focused on the prospect of great-power politics in postwar East Asia and contemplated the issue from America's strategic position in the Pacific, Lattimore's expertise in Inner Asian ethnopolitics had only marginal usefulness to the U.S. government. Only once, in August 1942, the State Department sought information from Lattimore about the Chinese government's view on postwar issues. He briefed the State Department on the KMT regime's intentions about postwar Japan, the colonial problem of Asia, the CCP, and China's industrialization. He also called for State Department officials' attention to China's "three corners," though with an overstatement that the "future area of China's industrial and economic development will probably be in a triangle based on Yunnan, Sinkiang [Xinjiang], and Mongolia, rather than along the coast."[31]

The State Department was indeed interested in China's "three corners," but what the State Department was really looking for was a knowledge that Lattimore could not provide—Moscow's intentions toward China's northern and northwestern frontiers, or whether these places would turn "red" or just stay "gray." So far the Soviet Union's non-belligerency in the Asian-Pacific war had allowed Moscow to conceal its policy objectives in this area even from its wartime allies. Washington's political strategists felt mystified about Soviet intentions in Asia in general and in northeastern Asia in particular. Before Moscow itself provided any clue to these questions, State Department officials went into different directions in hypothesizing the Soviet Union's Asia policy.

In August 1943, officials of the Far Eastern Division sought help from their colleagues in the European Division who supposedly had reliable information about Moscow's war aims in Europe. The resultant Far Eastern Division memorandum speculated that at war's end Moscow would have identical policies for the Far East and Europe and would act to create "sovietized governments among the peoples of Inner Mongolia, Manchuria, Korea," and other areas in the West Pacific.[32] Yet, two months later, when the State Department's planning staff considered the issue again, the Soviet factor in postwar Far East seemed to become less alarming. So far as the Mongolia question was concerned, the State Department did not expect any serious situation to rise. Presumably, although the Soviets would not abandon their position in Outer Mongolia, the Chinese government would be realistic and be satisfied with maintaining its "nominal sovereignty" there. State Department planners expected even less problems in the "inner" half of Mongolia. Since the areas of Inner Mongolia had been "increasingly assimilated to nearby Chinese provinces," a unified China should be able to control these areas effectively after the war.[33]

Although not expecting the ethnicity element in Sino–Soviet frontier relations to pose a serious challenge to U.S. foreign policy, the State Department was troubled by a different scenario: the Soviets might use the CCP as an instrument to exploit the prevalent anti-Western emotions in China and Asia. According to reports from the OSS, Soviet policy seemed to point to this direction. In early 1944, a similar concern led John Paton Davies, Jr. of the U.S. embassy in Chongqing to urge Washington to send a military observers group to Yanan before the Russians could enter the war against Japan and possibly turn North China into a Soviet satellite.[34] Officials of the State Department's Far Eastern Division agreed that in the event of Soviet entry into the Pacific war, the Western Allies would not be able to prevent the Soviet Red Army from occupying many areas of Northeast Asia. In early 1945, the State Department became convinced that the Soviets would scheme in Inner Mongolia, Manchuria, and Xinjiang. But, Moscow's behavior in these areas would be contingent on its general relationship with China—"The real question in Chinese-Russian relations is not so much 'territorial' as political; that is, the Russian attitude toward the Communist–Kuomintang problem."[35] The distinction made by American officials between a "territorial" and a "political" character of the difficulties between China and the Soviet Union was revealing. Although the United States could afford a bystander's position in respect to the "shape" of the Chinese state, it would not just stand by if the Soviet Union were found attempting to change the "color" of Chinese politics.

The KMT government apparently understood such American sentiment, and it continued to feed "intelligence" to American officials about the CCP's attempt to get access to Soviet assistance through inciting the Inner Mongols' secession.[36] Information of this kind about a "political" situation arising in China's northern borderlands and anticipation of Soviet entry into the Pacific war moved the State Department to contemplate actions by the United States. The State Department was especially troubled by possible negative reactions of the KMT government to Soviet entry into the Asian war through Inner Mongolia. In January, in making preparations for President Roosevelt's forthcoming summit with British and Soviet leaders at Yalta, the State Department drafted a series of position papers on the Far East. The first of these made reference to Inner Mongolia, pointing out that in the event of Soviet participation in the fight against Japan, Inner Mongolia's strategic location would make it a logical route of the Red Army's offensive. The KMT government, fearing that the Soviets would use the opportunity to establish contact with the CCP, had vowed to take some preemptive actions. In hoping to prevent forthcoming events in the Far East from leading to political and military "embarrassment and difficulties," the State Department recommended American interference. It was proposed that either a uniform command of the KMT and the CCP forces be established in China before Soviet entry, or, in case that the Chinese parties failed to work out an agreement, an "over-all American command of Chinese troops" be established. According to the State Department, the second course would be "highly advantageous" for it could prevent political difficulties between the Chinese and the Soviets in war and serve as a "stabilizing influence" in China in the immediate postwar years.[37]

Either of these arrangements would have ushered in a different beginning of China's postwar history, but neither materialized. When the State Department was drafting these policy memos, American mediation between the KMT and the CCP, performed by Patrick Hurley, was already underway. The effort in China would prove ineffectual. As for the proposed U.S. command of all Chinese forces, the Roosevelt administration could not broach the idea to the KMT regime *again* because it was already a failed formula in the scandalous Stilwell affair of 1944. Actually, the Stilwell episode of the wartime Sino–American relationship not only foreshadowed the futility of the State Department's recommendation about Inner Mongolia in early 1945 but also President Roosevelt's diplomacy at Yalta with regard to Outer Mongolia. The Stilwell affair marked the end of Washington's effort to turn Chiang Kai-shek's army into an effective tool to defeat Japan. Now Soviet assistance in the war had to be solicited with a price.[38]

The Roosevelt administration did not seem to understand the complexity of Outer Mongolia's international status until after Pearl Harbor. In early 1942, when contemplating a plan for launching air attacks against Japanese forces from Outer Mongolia, President Roosevelt learned from the War Department that the plan could not be feasibly implemented because the territory was beyond the KMT government's authority. It would have to be a Russian decision to open Outer Mongolia to the American Air Force. Obviously, Moscow's neutrality in the Asian war made such a decision unlikely. Later, aware of the stark contradiction between Moscow's determination to keep its Outer Mongolian buffer and the KMT regime's resolution to restore China's "original frontiers" and to extend its authority to "outlying provinces," the State Department and President Roosevelt shared a view that a Sino–Soviet conflict over Outer Mongolia must be averted. A border clash between Xinjiang and Outer Mongolia in the spring of 1944 indicated how such a conflict might break out any time. At first Roosevelt was so anxious about a crack in the Grand Alliance that he wanted to mediate between Moscow and Chongqing. Only a cautionary advice from the State Department persuaded him to adopt a more detached demarche in merely advising Chiang Kai-shek not to rush into any action that might endanger the Allied war effort.[39]

The Yalta Conference changed America's impartiality in the Sino–Soviet dispute over Outer Mongolia and put a Washington stamp on Moscow's ticket. At the summit, to induce Joseph Stalin to agree on Soviet entry into the fight against Japan, Roosevelt and Churchill accepted Stalin's price tag, which included a "status quo" clause on Outer Mongolia in a secret agreement. The agreement, in turn, became a precondition created by the Big Three for the Sino–Soviet negotiations in Moscow in the summer of 1945, which resulted in the Chinese government's concession on Outer Mongolia independence. This history is well known.[40] What should be emphasized here is that at Yalta, as Stalin used ambiguous "status quo" to cover Outer Mongolia's "red" politics and actual separation from China, President Roosevelt's endorsement of the Stalinian ambiguity had nothing to do with Mongolian ethnicity and everything to do with power politics. Although before and after the Yalta Conference Roosevelt consistently told Chinese officials that Stalin did not harbor any ambition about Outer Mongolia, the Yalta agreement endorsed the geopolitical reality on the Mongolian Plateau reflecting Soviet strategic interests. Befittingly, after the Yalta Conference, the State Department began to suggest that probably America's China policy should seek readjustment of China's territorial claims in Outer Mongolia and Tibet. Although promotion of "local autonomy" was one of the State Department's rationales, the principal motive of the proposition was to "accommodate British and Russian interests" in these territories.[41]

Not yet sliding into a Cold War mode in dealing with the Soviets, President Roosevelt nevertheless helped create the playground for forthcoming Cold Warriors in establishing geopolitical fault lines between Soviet and American influence. These lines were not all satisfactory to his successors. Before the war in the Asia–Pacific region ended, officials in Washington, irritated by Moscow's expansion in Central Europe, already began to question the wisdom of the Yalta concessions that put Outer Mongolia and various rights in Manchuria on the Russian side of the line.[42] A new era of postwar international politics was about to dawn in Asia.

Politics of "Color" and "Shape"

A significant phase in modern transformation of Chinese territoriality, the years of World War II were definitely about the "shape" of the Chinese state. Washington's wartime diplomacy helped China recover some of the "lost territories" and sustain the Chinese government's claim of sovereignty over much of the territorial domain bequeathed from the Qing Empire. Meanwhile, the same diplomacy also shared the responsibility for perpetuating Outer Mongolia's independence from China. It is therefore not far-fetched to suggest that the United States had a hand in changing the cartographic image of China from the shape of a begonia leaf to that of a rooster. Although America's wartime diplomacy was consequential to China's ethnic frontiers, ethnicity was a rare commodity in Washington's contemplation of its China policy. In those rare occasions when ethnicity did receive some attention, it was treated as an appendage to the constantly overriding theme of great-power relations. This pattern in America's China policy did not change in the postwar years even though China began to enter a period of intensified ethnopolitical contentions.

During the war, Stanley K. Hornbeck, chief of the State Department's Far Easter Division, observed in a State Department's internal communication that if the Western allies could enter a partnership for collective security with both Russia and China, then "we would bridge the chasm between Occident and Orient *and* the chasm of 'colors'."[43] After the war, however, Asia did not have a partnership that Hornbeck hoped for, neither were its affairs dominated by the cultural and racial chasms that he described. The unsynchronized conclusions of World War II in Europe and Asia greeted not only the arrival of peace but also a new kind of crises. Postwar international politics was indeed coded with colors, but the premise for such coding was ideological blocs, not cultures or races.

When the Cold War shadowed the world, policy makers in Washington and Moscow viewed China as one of the arenas whose "color" was yet to be determined. Yet postwar China was a crowded political stage, in which great powers, Chinese political parties, and non-Han ethnopolitical forces were all valid players. Whereas, backed by their respective international allies, the KMT and the CCP competed in China proper to decide China's color code, the Mongols, Tibetans, Uygurs and Kazaks intensified their own struggles in frontier China with an intention to alter China's shape. China's "Cold War" history would unfold with these underlying themes of "coloring" and "shaping."

Notes

1. Important studies are John W. Dower, *War Without Mercy: Race and Power in the Pacific War* (New York: Pantheon, 1986); John W. Garver, *Chinese–Soviet Relations, 1937–1945: The Diplomacy of Chinese Nationalism* (New York: Oxford University Press, 1988); Akira Iriye, *Power and Culture: The Japanese–American War, 1941–1945* (Cambridge: Harvard University Press, 1981); Xiaoyuan Liu, *A Partnership for Disorder: China, the United States, and Their Policies for the Postwar Disposition of the Japanese Empire, 1941–1945* (Cambridge: Cambridge University Press, 1996); W. Roger Louis, *Imperialism at Bay: The United States and the Decolonization of the British Empire* (New York: Oxford University Press, 1978); Michael Schaller, *The U.S. Crusade in China, 1938–1945* (New York: Columbia University Press, 1979); and Christopher Thorne, *Allies of a Kind: The United States, Britain, and the War against Japan, 1941–1945* (Oxford: Oxford University Press, 1978).
2. Erez Manela, *The Wilsonian Moment: Self-Determination and the International Origins of Anticolonial Nationalism* (Oxford: Oxford University Press, 2007).
3. CAC-250, "The Problem of Minorities in Europe," October 7, 1944, Harry N. Howard Papers, box 3; ISO-245, "The Problem of Minorities," March 26, 1945, ibid.
4. Despatch from the British Legation in Peking to the Foreign Office, No. 1390, October 23, 1933, L/P&S/12/2287; Ingram to Sir John Simon, January 17, 1934, and enclosures, ibid.; H. M. Military Attache of the Peking Legation to the Foreign Office, April 28, 1934, and enclosures, ibid.
5. "Draft Agenda for Meeting on Inquiry Part IV," March 23, 1939, and appendix, Philip C. Jessup Papers, box "122, folder AIPR Annexes No. 21–40"; Lattimore to Yarnell, April 29, 1941, Stanley K. Hornbeck Papers, box 449; Yarnell to Lattimore, April 29, 1941, ibid.
6. "China," n.d. (1942), Records of Harley A. Notter, box 11.
7. Hornbeck to William Langer, April 15, 1943, enclosure, "Summary of Outer Mongolia and Tannu Tuva Survey by Office of Strategic Services, February 23, 1943," Hornbeck Papers, box 300.
8. PG-34, "Sino-Russian Problems in the Post-War Settlement," October 4, 1943, Notter Records, box 119; "Summary Report of Vice President Wallace Visit in China," July 10, 1944, Franklin D. Roosevelt Papers/PSF, box 27.

9. Division of Far Eastern Affairs to Division of Political Studies, "Partition of Manchuria," March 13, 1943, General Records of the United States Department of State Central Files: China: 893.01 Manchuria/1673 (hereafter cited as *GRDS*).
10. "The U.S.S.R. and the Possibility of a 'Greater Mongolia'," August 3, 1943, FO371/35860.
11. ST Minutes 21, July 2, 1943, Notter Records, box 79.
12. Davies to Hopkins, December 31, 1943, Roosevelt Papers/PSF, box 27; Davies to Hopkins, November 16, 1944, ibid. In these letters John Davies, second secretary of U.S. embassy in China, made a point to Harry Hopkins that the Americans held a "congenial fiction" in identifying Chiang Kai-shek with China.
13. CAC-66a, "Military Government in the Far East," February 5, 1944, Notter Records, box 109; "Indications of Contact with President on Post-War Matters," n.d., Notter Records, box 54; ST Minutes 16, May 7, 1943, Notter Records, box 79.
14. JPWC3, "Joint Psychological Warfare Committee: Suggested China Plan," March 16, 1942, Records of Joint Chiefs of Staff, microfilm reel 13.
15. P-241a, "Official Policy and Views Affecting the Post-War Settlement in the Far East," September 30, 1943, Notter Records, box 58.
16. Memorandum for the President, "Unconditional Surrender of Japan and Policy toward Liberated Areas in the Far East in Relation to Unconditional Surrender," June 29, 1945, Harry L. Hopkins Papers, box 169–171: Big Three Conference Agenda (Potsdam) July, 1945.
17. Division of Far Eastern Affairs to Secretary of State, September 2, 1943, Hornbeck papers, box 70.
18. Seymour to Eden, February 5, 1944, and enclosures, FO371/41654.
19. Minutes on communication from Jones to Broad, April 28, 1942, FO371/31702.
20. Seymour to Eden, February 5, 1944, and enclosures, FO371/41654.
21. ISO-245, "The Problem of Minorities," March 26, 1945, Howard Papers, box 3.
22. For a detailed account of Lattimore's appointment and service to Chiang in 1941 and 1942, see Robert P. Newman, *Owen Lattimore and the "Loss" of China* (Berkeley: University of California Press, 1992), 55–96. Surprisingly, Newman's otherwise informative account leaves out completely Lattimore's ethnopolitical advice to Chiang.
23. Lattimore, "A Memorandum to Chiang Kei-shek," June 30, 1976, Lattimore Papers, box 28.
24. Lattimore, "Memorandum on Inner Mongolia," n.d. (August 1941), Lattimore Papers, box 28.
25. No. T-B 63, "Studies of American Interests in the War and the Peace: Territorial Series: Memorandum on Mongolia and the Peace Settlement, prepared by Owen Lattimore, 8 June 1943," Lattimore Papers, box 28.
26. Lattimore to Lauchlin Currie, July 27, 1941, Lattimore Papers, box 27; Lattimore's note on a conversation with Weng Wen-hao (Wong Wenhao), November 2, 1942, ibid.; Lattimore's note on a conversation with Chu Chia-hua (Zhu Jiahua), November 7, 1942, ibid.; minutes of the conversation between Jiang Jieshi and Owen Lattimore on July 31, 1941, ibid.; Lattimore's note on a conversation with Chiang Kai-shek, December 5, 1941, ibid.
27. Lattimore to Chiang, May 3, 1942, *Zhonghua Minguo Zhongyao Shiliao Chubian; Dui Ri Kangzhan Shiqi* (Preliminary compilation of important historical records of the Republic of China; the period of the war of resistance against Japan) (7 volumes. Taipei: Kuomintang Dangshi Weiyuanhui, 1981. Hereafter, *ZZSC*), 3:1: 744–745.

28. Liu Kai to the Ministry of Foreign Affairs, April 12 and 14, 1944, *ZZSC*, 3:1: 859–860; T. V. Soong to Chiang, May 13, 1944, ibid., 860–861; Wei Daoming to Chiang, May 15, 1944, ibid., 861; Newman, *Lattimore*, 115.
29. Newman, *Lattimore*, 108; Wang Shijie, *Wang Shijie Riji* (Diaries of Wang Shijie) (Taipei: Zhongyang Yanjiuyuan Jindaishi Yanjiusuo, 1990), 4: 338–339.
30. Wallace to Harry Truman, September 19, 1951, and enclosure, "Summary Report of Vice President Wallace's Visit in China," July 10, 1944, Roosevelt Papers/PSF, box 27.
31. T Document 44, "Principal Points of a Report by Owen Lattimore on China and Chinese Opinion on Postwar Problems," August 21, 1942, Notter Records, box 60.
32. FE memo, "U.S.S.R. Aims in the Far East," August 19, 1943, Hornbeck Papers, box 396.
33. PG-28, "Possible Soviet Attitudes towards Far Eastern Questions," October 2, 1943, Notter Records, box 119.
34. PG-28, "Possible Soviet Attitudes towards Far Eastern Questions," October 2, 1943, Notter Records, box 119; R & A No. 2211.1, "Russia and the Far Eastern Settlement," July 22, 1944, OSS Report, vol. 6 (microfilm reel 3); John Davies Jr. to Hopkins, January 23, 1944, enclosure, "Observers' Mission to North China," Hopkins Papers, box 334.
35. Hornbeck to Secretary of State, July 18, 1944, Hornbeck Papers, box 396; State Department to the Officer in charge of the American Mission, Chungking (Chongqing), February 12, 1945, Top Secret General Records of Chungking Embassy, China, 1943–45, box 1.
36. Edward Rice to the Secretary of State, May 21, 1945, GRDS: 893.00/5–2145.
37. Memorandum, "Far East: (1) China: (a) Political and Military Situation if U.S.S.R. Enters War in Far East," n.d., Hopkins Papers, box 169–171; State Department to the Officer in charge of the American Mission, Chungking, February 8, 1945, enclosure 5, "Memorandum for the President," January 9, 1945, Top Secret General Records of Chungking Embassy, China 1945, box 1.
38. Schaller, *The U.S. Crusade in China*, 147–176.
39. War Department to President Roosevelt, January 28, 1942, Roosevelt Papers/PSF, box 2; T-325; note by Harry Hopkins on a conversation with Winston Churchill, November 1943, Hopkins Papers, box 331; P-254a, "Chinese War and Peace Aims," March 1, 1944, Notter Records, box 10; CAC297, "Outer Mongolia," October 23, 1944, Notter Records, box 115; memorandum for the president, April 7, 1944, Roosevelt Papers/MRF, box 10; FDR to the Secretary of State, April 7, 1944, ibid.; The President to Generalissimo Chiang Kai-shek, April 8, 1944, ibid.
40. See Garver, *Chinese–Soviet Relations*, 209–228; Liu, *A Partnership for Disorder*, 242–286.
41. "Formosa," April 1943, Notter Records, box 63; PWC-195, May 15, 1944, Notter Records, box 110; Division of China Affairs memo, "Policy with respect to China," April 18, 1945, Records of Division of Chinese Affairs, box 10.
42. Grew to the Secretary of State, July 13, 1945, *Foreign Relations of the United States: Diplomatic Papers, 1945;VII* (Washington, D.C.: G.P.O., 1969. Hereafter *FRUS*), 934–938; Harriman to the Secretary of State, August 11, 1945, ibid., 152.
43. Hornbeck to Secretary of State, September 20, 1943, Hornbeck Papers, box 378.

CHAPTER TEN

Mongolia between Beijing and Moscow

In August 1945, China emerged a victor from its eight-year war with Japan. The triumph came with horrendous costs to millions of individual Chinese citizens. Collectively, in the last moment of the war, the Chinese people also had to accept a heavy price tag: Outer Mongolia's permanent separation from China as decided by the inter-allied diplomacy at Yalta and Moscow. Outer Mongolia's final, legal independence from China would forever be in the historical record of the Kuomintang (KMT, Nationalist Party), either as a credit or a blemish, depending on one's stand. In its 1945 treaty with the Soviet Union, the KMT regime also conceded to Moscow's demands for special privileges in Manchuria. To KMT leaders these concessions were part of a necessary trade-off to guarantee a favorable Soviet attitude toward their "party-state" in its postwar struggle against the Chinese Communist Party (CCP).

After Japan's defeat, the CCP did not return to its prewar, narrowly construed class-struggle orientation. Instead, while resorting to radical land programs in the countryside as a means to maintain Chinese peasants' support, the CCP did not abandon Chinese nationalism as a most effective ideology to woo anxious, patriotic groups in the cities. The momentum of China's arduous victory over Japan pushed China's political organizations and general public alike to strive more urgently for such goals as national unification, peaceful reconstruction, and achieving the country's deserved place in the international community. Although tailoring its public image to suit the national sentiment, the CCP nevertheless found the concessions in recent GMD diplomacy a partisan gain for itself. While the KMT regime's signing off of Outer Mongolia in its treaty with Moscow disgraced its foreign policy among patriotic Chinese and even embittered many KMT members, the CCP sought to capitalize on the postwar expansion of Soviet–Mongolian influence in northeastern China.

When bloc politics became increasingly dominant in the form of the Cold War in the postwar years, the "class brotherhood" of the CCP with the Mongolian People's Republic (MPR, or Outer Mongolia) took precedence over its nationalist considerations of Chinese sovereignty in Outer Mongolia. From the CCP's perspective in 1945, Moscow's success in annulling the KMT's hollow claim of sovereignty over the MPR could only strengthen the revolutionary bloc. In the long run, the development also would not contradict the CCP's goal of renewing China's national tie with Outer Mongolia after the KMT was defeated. Such trust in the Soviet ally would both sustain CCP leaders' confidence in their final victory and lead them to bitter disillusionment when they finally defeated the KMT in 1949. The simple fact was that its ascendance to power in 1949 transformed the CCP from a revolutionary movement into a national government. Meanwhile, its attempt to transform revolutionary ties with the MPR into a national bond was blocked. Thus, Outer Mongolia, not Inner Mongolia as predicted by some American officials in 1949, changed from a corridor connecting the CCP revolution and Moscow to one of the first "natural points of conflict" between the two communist giants.

From Party to State

From January to February 1949, Anastas I. Mikoyan, a member of the Politburo of the Soviet Communist Party, came to Xibaipo, northern Shaanxi, to meet with the CCP leadership. The Mikoyan mission was a stopgap for Mao's proposed trip to Moscow, which Mao had pressed in the past few months but was regarded as premature by Moscow.[1] In this first meeting between a senior Soviet official and the Mao-centered CCP leadership, the two sides had much to find out about each other and many views to exchange. This was also the first occasion when the CCP and Moscow found themselves on opposing sides over the Mongolia question. In 1960, as the Sino–Soviet polemics were flaring up, both sides agreed that the question of Outer Mongolia during Mikoyan's 1949 visit caused mutual misgivings.[2]

According to a report made by Mikoyan years later, during his three-day discussion with Mao, Mao raised three issues pertinent to Sino–Soviet relations.[3] The first concerned the continuation, after the CCP victory, of the Soviet military base in Lühun (Port Arthur), which had been obtained under the KMT–Soviet treaty of 1945. The second question was Soviet involvement with the separatist movement centered in Yili (Ili), Xinjiang. But the most troublesome was the third question, Outer Mongolia. The relevant paragraphs of the Mikoyan report are worth quoting here:

> On Mongolia. Mao Zedong himself raised the question of our attitude toward the unification of Outer and Inner Mongolia. I replied that we did not support such a unification since it would lead to the loss of considerable Chinese territory. Mao Zedong said that he was of the opinion that Outer and Inner Mongolia could unite and become part of the Chinese Republic. To this I replied that was impossible, since the Mongolian People's Republic had long since won independence. Following the victory over Japan, the Chinese state had also recognized the independence of Outer Mongolia. The MPR had its own army, its own culture, and was moving rapidly along the path of cultural and economic development. It had long since grown accustomed to the taste of freedom, and was unlikely ever to surrender that independence voluntarily. If it ever did unite with Inner Mongolia, then a united and independent Mongolia would no doubt form as a result. Ren Bishi, who was present during the conversation, replied to this that there were three million people in Inner Mongolia, and one million in Outer Mongolia. In connection with this information, Stalin sent me a telegram to give to Mao Zedong, which said:
>
> The leaders of Outer Mongolia support the unification of all the Mongolian regions of China with Outer Mongolia to form an independent and united Mongolian state. The Soviet government does not agree with this plan, since it means taking a number of regions from China, although this plan does not threaten the interests of the Soviet Union. We do not think that Outer Mongolia would agree to surrender its independence in favor of autonomy within the Chinese state, even if all the Mongolian regions are united in one autonomous entity. Clearly the final word on this issue belongs to Outer Mongolia itself.
>
> On hearing the contents of this telegram, Mao Zedong said that he would take note of it and that, of course, they did not defend the Great China chauvinist policy and would not raise the question of the unification of Mongolia.[4]

This exchange, if it indeed happened as Mikoyan alleged, is interesting for two reasons. First, it started the process through which the CCP–Moscow relationship would be transformed from an alliance between two revolutionary parties into dealings between two national governments. Yanan and Moscow however appeared in different gears in their relationship transition. This was best revealed by their different attitudes toward the KMT–Soviet treaty of 1945. In the spirit of camaraderie, Mao told Mikoyan that the CCP regarded the treaty as a "patriotic" one because it helped China in the war against Japan. This statement caused a telegram from Stalin the following day, saying: "When the Chinese Communists come to power, the situation will change radically. The Soviet government has decided to annul this unequal agreement. . . . "[5] This could be read optimistically by CCP leaders as a promise of a new, post-KMT, Sino–Soviet relationship. But, in the meantime, Stalin's readiness in confessing that the Soviet Union, just like any other imperial power, could impose inequality on China under the KMT also served a cautionary note to the CCP leaders. The question for Mao and his associates was whether or not they could count on Stalin not to do the same to their communist state.

Secondly, the Mikoyan mission not only dashed the CCP's hope for Outer Mongolia's "return" to China but also its illusion about Lenin's formula on socialist federation based on national groups' free will. The CCP's Mongolia complex was never a secret. However, now facing the Soviets in the Mongolia question, the CCP leadership seemed to lose its self-righteous confidence, which had hitherto been demonstrated in its criticism of the KMT's ethnopolitics. As reflected in the Soviet sources, the CCP leaders only used two meager arguments to defend their stand on Mongolia's reunion with China: (1) Inner Mongolia had more Mongolian population than Outer Mongolia, and (2) Mongolia's reunion could help the CCP win over the left wing of the KMT.[6]

Surprisingly, on this occasion the CCP leaders did not cite a word from Marxist dogmas in defending their position on Mongolia. By this time, the CCP leadership had already mustered enough knowledge about the Marxist–Leninist theoretic formula on the "national question" and should have been able to use it and even the Soviet model itself in defending a multinational Chinese federation. If, on the Mongolia question, the KMT regime had always felt frustrated by its weakness vis-à-vis Soviet power, power confrontation was not the question between the CCP and Moscow in 1949. At the time, in facing the Soviets, Mao probably suffered from a pupil's inadequacy in challenging the CCP's ideological mentor.

It should be noted that in 1945 Stalin used arguments about Soviet security interests to force the KMT to accept Mongolian independence. In contrast, in 1949 Mikoyan and Stalin persuaded Mao to back down with authoritative statements about the Mongols' right to self-determination, balanced by a seemingly magnanimous concern about China's territorial integrity. This tactic induced Mao to reaffirm the CCP's rejection of "great China chauvinism" and to continue the pretension that there was neither interest conflict nor ideological contradiction between the Soviet Union and the forthcoming Communist China over the issue of the MPR.

The Mikoyan mission decisively ended the CCP's earlier misconceptions about Moscow's intentions for Outer Mongolia. The CCP leaders were never so naive to believe that the Outer Mongols would voluntarily abolish their independence and rejoin China. They nevertheless never accepted the notion that the Mongolia question was purely about the Mongolian people's *self*-determination. In casting his questions to Mikoyan, Mao expected to get Moscow on the CCP's side with respect to inclusion of Mongolia in a Chinese federation, which the CCP had been advocating for the past three decades. The anticipated Soviet blessing did not come. Stalin's attitude not only shattered the CCP's desire for outdoing the KMT regime in recovering Outer Mongolia but also deprived the CCP of an opportunity to restore China's "grand unity." Although CCP leaders did not engage Stalin in a debate about China's or Mongolia's territoriality, the Soviet contention on the Mongols' exclusive right to determine their own status did not sound convincing and entirely sincere to the CCP leaders. That was why Mao repeatedly returned to the subject in talking with the members of the Mikoyan mission in 1949.[7] But the CCP leaders would not openly express their misgivings until Stalin's death. In April 1956, when talking with Mikoyan, Zhou wanted the new Soviet leadership to admit that during the Mikoyan mission Stalin made a mistake in handling the Mongolia question in an "evasive" way not befitting "party principles" and the "conversation between communists."[8]

At the time, the real reasons behind Moscow's unwillingness to see the emergence of a greater communist China were either too hard for CCP leaders to fathom or too dark for them to believe. Several years later, Zhou made an effort to understand Stalin's hesitation about the CCP during the Chinese Civil War. In recalling the Mikoyan mission with some senior CCP officials, Zhou asserted that at the time Stalin wanted the CCP to stop its southward offensive and preferred to have China divided along the Yangtze River in order to preserve the Soviet–American understanding at Yalta about their spheres of influence in China. Zhou reasoned that Stalin probably feared a third world war with the United States.[9] There is, however, no evidence that the CCP leadership applied the same analysis to Stalin's prevention of the CCP from moving northward into Outer Mongolia, which might have been motivated by a fear of Communist China itself.

Such fear was once expressed by N. V. Roshchin, the Soviet ambassador to the KMT government before the CCP takeover. At the end of 1948, in a conversation with Peng Zhaoxian, the interior minister in the KMT government, Roshchin admitted that Moscow suspected a Titoist tendency in the CCP. Therefore, he explained, it would be ideal to end the Chinese Civil War with foreign mediation because, if a big communist country emerged along the Soviet Union's eastern border, it would create serious problems for the Soviet government.[10]

Mutual suspicions and misunderstandings between the CCP and Moscow would neither slow down the CCP's sweeping triumph in China nor hinder the formation of a formal PRC–Soviet alliance. The Mongolia question, however, continued to bedevil the emerging partnership between the two communist powers. Although the Mikoyan mission dashed the CCP leaders' hope for incorporating the MPR into the PRC, it did not solve the question as to how Mongolian independence arranged by Moscow and the CCP's domestic enemy, the KMT regime, should be inherited by the incoming CCP government. After the CCP took power, the fate of the 1945 KMT–Soviet treaty had to be reconsidered, and Mongolia would be affected.

In June and July 1949, a secret CCP mission to Moscow headed by Liu Shaoqi had several meetings with Stalin. In a "report" hurriedly prepared in Moscow, the CCP envoys presented to Stalin a series of issues that they wished to discuss.[11] Conspicuously, despite Stalin's known qualification of the 1945 treaty as an "unequal" one, the Chinese still informed Stalin that the CCP was "completely willing to inherit the treaty" because it had helped the Chinese people in the past and would continue to do so in the future. The "report" also proposed some alternative "procedures" to deal with some technical aspects of the treaty for it to continue.

Interestingly, the "report" raised the Mongolia question not in relation to the 1945 treaty but as one of the grievances against the Soviet Union among some allegedly misinformed Chinese people ("democratic parties, students, and workers"):

> As for the question of the Mongolian People's Republic, our explanation is that the Mongolian people wanted independence, and we should recognize Mongolian independence according

to the principle of national self-determination. But if the MPR is willing to join China, we of course welcome it. This matter should be decided solely by the Mongolian people.

The Chinese wanted to know "whether or not these explanations are correct" in Stalin's opinion.[12]

To Stalin, the CCP's reiteration of its willingness to continue the 1945 treaty must have been both perplexing and satisfying. In considering the matter in conjunction with a statement made by the "report" that the CCP would obey decisions made by the Soviet Communist Party, Stalin could only take these as evidence that the CCP leadership lacked national consciousness. When making his response to the "report," Stalin repeated his view to the CCP envoys that the 1945 treaty was "unequal" but it had to be so at the time because the Soviet government was dealing with the KMT regime. He was quite willing to settle the treaty question with Mao, who was scheduled to come to Moscow in December. Sincerely or not, Stalin also rejected the notion that the CCP should obey Moscow's decisions, asserting that "both parties have to be accountable to their own people." This subject led him to lecture the CCP envoys: "One must protect his own state and national interests. You do not understand this because during a century of colonial and semicolonial conditions [Chinese] people's interests were violated by others wantonly."[13] While appearing generous and accommodating in general, Stalin remained adamant in dealing with the Mongolia question raised circuitously in the CCP "report." He told Liu in effect that as far as the Soviet government was concerned, the question of Outer Mongolia was settled, and that the Chinese and Mongolian comrades would have to talk to each other directly if any change should be made.[14]

Liu's mission was another bizarre episode in the CCP's inter-party diplomacy with Moscow on the eve of its transformation into China's government. If Liu and his co-envoys appeared overly respectful to Stalin, it was partially because of Stalin's stature in the minds of CCP leaders and partially because of CCP leaders' anxiety to dispel any suspicion in Moscow about its reliability. The "report" was an exemplary document that mixed Chinese Communists' explicit homage to Moscow's revolutionary hegemony with incoming PRC leaders' implicit exploration of Soviet foreign policy parameters. Liu overdid the first part. After learning of the envoys' suggestion about CCP obedience to Moscow, Mao thought such a notion was inappropriate even for internal discussions in the CCP. He immediately cabled Liu and asked him to get Stalin's agreement to delete the content from the "report."[15]

Old and New "Kitchen"

In the end of 1949, having learned from the Mikoyan and Liu missions about the Soviet government's view that the 1945 treaty was an "unequal" one, Mao made his trip to Moscow fully prepared to negotiate a new treaty with Stalin. Yet there is evidence that after the Mikoyan and Liu encounters, the Soviet side became less certain. In November, the Chinese side twice indicated to the Soviets that for the purpose of concluding a new treaty, Zhou Enlai would travel with Mao and participate in treaty negotiations. Moscow's reaction to the proposal was ambiguous.[16] Still, Mao was dumbfounded at his first meeting with Stalin on December 16. Completely departing from his earlier rhetoric about how the CCP victory would recast the Sino–Soviet relationship, at the meeting Stalin told Mao that because the 1945 treaty had been concluded "with the consent of America and England," the Soviet government "decided not to modify any of the points of this treaty for now," lest any change give the Western powers an excuse to raise other questions, such as Southern Sakhalin and the Kurils. Stalin offered instead to adjust certain aspects of the treaty "in reality" while maintaining all the old treaty provisions "in form." Then, during the next month, the treaty question was suspended in the air while the two sides only had exchanges of secondary significance. Mao, between his good and bad moods, used the time to visit several places in his host country.[17]

When Mao and Stalin met again on January 22, 1950, however, Stalin appeared a different person. Now he suggested that all the existing agreements between China and the Soviet Union, including the 1945 treaty, should be changed. He explained to Mao that in 1945 the war against Japan was "at the very heart of the treaty," but since Japan's defeat the treaty had become an "anachronism." When Mao reminded Stalin that changing the old treaty would contradict the Yalta decisions, Stalin said:

> True, it does, and to hell with it! Once we have taken up the position that the treaties must be changed, we must go all the way. It is true that for us this entails certain inconveniences, and we will have to struggle against the Americans. But we are already reconciled to that.[18]

Stalin's concession was vitally important to the CCP. Ascending to power in China, the CCP was making conscientious efforts to start China's interstate relations anew. On different occasions in the spring and summer of 1949, including those conversations with Mikoyan in Xibaipo, Mao defined a two-pronged foreign policy orientation with his characteristic lingo: "set up a new kitchen," meaning nonrecognition of treaties and diplomatic arrangements made by the KMT regime in the past and replacement of these with the PRC's own; and "cleaning the house before inviting guests in," meaning the postponement of establishing diplomatic relationship with "imperialist" countries until the new CCP government had purged China of vestiges of internal hostile forces and foreign imperialist influence.[19]

In practice, these processes involved not only a series of complex policy decisions regarding individual foreign countries but also a strenuous and slow grooming of the CCP's own diplomatic personnel that could carry out these policies. Although Mao chose to single out "imperialist" countries as the targets of the orientation, the policy had a general impact on China's foreign relations, and even the Soviet Union was not completely exempted.[20] Though never admitted by the CCP's official history, a new treaty with the Soviet Union at the beginning of the PRC would be the most important building block for the "new kitchen." Yet, after Mao's arrival in Moscow, Stalin appeared tenaciously nostalgic about the old Chinese "kitchen" until January 22.

With respect to Stalin's shifting preference of "kitchens," a couple of questions remain untouched by previous studies. One is why Stalin, not once but twice, changed his mind on the treaty question between the Mikoyan mission in February 1949 and his talk with Mao on January 22, 1950. Another is what policy readjustment or change of attitude happened on the Chinese side during the same period that may have affected Stalin's stand on the treaty question. An attempt to answer these questions is made here, in what has to be a hypothetical analysis waiting for further information from Chinese, Mongolian, and Russian archives. This analysis goes beyond the Cold War paradigm and finds that Stalin's vacillation had more to do with the Mongolian buffer between China and Russia than with the Cold War contest between the Eastern and Western blocs.

In the East Asian international politics of the late 1940s and early 1950s, a fundamental question was what force challenged the postwar status quo. In this period, despite their global competition dubbed the Cold War, both the Soviet Union and the United States followed the rules in a power-balancing game and were interested in maintaining their power relationship based on the military realities and diplomatic dealings wrought during World War II. In Asia, the Soviet stake in the balance was mainly reflected in the geopolitical consequences of the Yalta diplomacy and the Sino–Soviet negotiations in Moscow in the summer of 1945. It was the CCP, already a quasi-state force at the end of World War II, that posed the most serious challenge to the Yalta–Moscow system. This was so not only because the CCP was not a party of that system but also because the specter of the CCP victory in China threatened to insert a reunified China as a third force into East Asian affairs, which had hitherto been dominated by the two superpowers.

As of 1949, much of the American share of the Yalta–Moscow system had been demolished when the CCP drove the KMT regime onto the island of Taiwan. The development was not interpreted in the Kremlin as a pure gain for the Soviet Union because now the Soviet share of the system became problematic as well. Because a significant portion of the Yalta–Moscow spoils was underwritten by the 1945 treaty, in dealing with the CCP challenge, the Soviet leaders had to find out what was the CCP attitude toward the treaty. They also had to decide what should be the premise for the relationship between the Soviet Union and a Communist China. Hence the trial balloons during the Mikoyan and Liu missions. As shown above, on both occasions the Soviet strategy was to signal to the CCP that a new beginning of the Sino–Soviet relationship would be initiated upon the CCP victory in China. The Soviets hoped to discover the extent to which the CCP would want to cancel or modify the legacies of the KMT policy toward the Soviet Union. To Soviet leaders' surprise, although operating amidst the postwar upsurge of Chinese nationalism, CCP leaders appeared quite satisfied with the "friendly" existence of Soviet influence in Manchuria. Before Mao's visit in Moscow, therefore, it was the Soviet side that repeatedly made negative references to the "unequal treaty" of 1945, while the CCP appeared flexible with regard to this "patriotic" instrument.

Over only one concrete issue with the 1945 treaty, MPR independence, did the two sides completely lack such mutual accommodations. The CCP's Mongolian complex was sustained by CCP leaders' commitment to the traditional Chinese ideal of "grand unity," an ideological adaptation of the Soviet federal state model, and a political urge to outdo the KMT in defending the integrity of China's "national territory." To Stalin and his associates, the Mongolian buffer was not just a result of the 1945 treaty but also the culmination of more than three decades' Soviet security policy. After two rounds of encounters with the CCP leaders in 1949, Moscow was compelled to make two strategic readjustments in dealing with the CCP challenge. One was to shelve the notion that the CCP victory in China should be treated as an overriding factor in the next stage of the Sino–Soviet relationship. Especially, the CCP should be discouraged from believing so. Another was to stop posing the 1945 treaty as an open-ended question to the CCP. The Soviet government now wanted to uphold all the legal and political grounds provided by the treaty to fend off the CCP's overture on Mongolia.

In other words, although Moscow's postwar strategic focus in Asia was on the United States, this did not blunt the Soviet leaders' sense about the geopolitical challenge posed by the rise of Communist China. Actually, during the months between the CCP victory in China and the beginning of the Korean War, Communist China was the only geopolitical challenge to Moscow's security arrangements along its southeastern borders. To the Soviet leaders, in 1949 as in 1945, their advance position in Manchuria was negotiable, but the Mongolian buffer was untouchable.

This was the main reason that Stalin surprised Mao at their December 16 meeting. Although the name of Mongolia was not uttered even once during the meeting, the issue must have loomed large in Stalin's mind. In contending that *every* point of the 1945 treaty should be maintained, Stalin of course included the 1945 decision on Mongolia. To preempt Mao's possible contention about treaty revision based on the CCP victory, Stalin now used the Yalta system, or the superpower relationship, as his premise for discussing the 1945 treaty. This tactic clearly indicated that insofar as Soviet treaty rights were concerned, Stalin would deal with Mao in the same manner as he had dealt with KMT diplomats in 1945. Power relations, not revolutionary camaraderie, would underline the Stalin–Mao negotiations.

At the meeting, in a seemingly pliable response, Mao said that the CCP leadership had not considered the American–British angle. But CCP leaders certainly understood that their alliance with Moscow would affect the American–British angle. Mao's statement just disguised his surprise that Stalin should use the Western powers to delimit the new Sino–Soviet relationship. His words might also be a circuitous way to tell Stalin that the CCP regarded the treaty issue as a bilateral one between the PRC and the USSR, in which both sides' interests mattered equally. In countering Stalin's argument, Mao resorted to the public opinion of China, which allegedly believed that "as the old treaty was signed by the KMT, it has lost its standing with the KMT's downfall." This was in effect what Stalin had told the CCP leadership via Mikoyan. After listening to Mao, Stalin conceded that the old treaty should be revised, but this had to wait for two more years.[21]

In retrospect, Stalin's tactic erred in unnecessarily alienating Mao, who in the years to come would repeatedly grumble about Stalin's initial reluctance to sign a new treaty with him. Based on available evidence, it can be concluded that in coming to Moscow, Mao was already convinced of Soviet leaders' intransigence in maintaining Mongolian independence and was therefore ready to comply. The problem was that Stalin was just as convinced of the CCP leaders' determination to reincorporate the MPR into China.

In this regard, the first few diplomatic steps made by the new Beijing government in 1949 did not mollify Moscow's concern. On October 3, 1949, the Soviet Union became the first country to establish diplomatic relations with the PRC. In the next four days, seven other communist bloc countries, including the MPR, extended diplomatic recognition to the PRC and offered to establish diplomatic relations with Beijing. Each of these governments, except the MPR, received a positive reply from Zhou Enlai on the same day when its own request was sent to Beijing. Choibalsan alone had to wait for ten embarrassing days before hearing from Zhou.[22] This was a time when no event in Beijing's relationship with other communist bloc countries, especially with Ulaanbaatar, could escape the Kremlin's scrutiny. Beijing's positive response to Choibalsan was a good sign to Moscow, but the hesitant delay was suspicious enough to give Stalin pause for thought about the sincerity of the CCP leaders' diplomatic gesture toward the MPR.

Stalin did not wait idly for the CCP's next move, and he took an unusual step in preparing the MPR leadership for fending off Beijing's possible overture. In August 1949, Choibalsan visited Moscow for a medical examination. At the time, some MPR leaders wished to discuss with Moscow the MPR's entry into the Soviet Union. What featured in Stalin's conversation with Choibalsan in late September was, however, the issue of unification between Inner and Outer Mongolia. Stalin informed Choibalsan of a recent exchange with Mao on the subject and of Mao's favorable attitude. Choibalsan agreed that that would be "the right thing to do" while insisting that Inner Mongolia join the MPR and an independent Mongolia not become part of China. Then Stalin made these comments:

> So you are in favor of independence rather than autonomous privileges? I feel the same way. This is something you must decide for yourselves. But there is probably no need to hurry and decide under what conditions unification will take place. You need to adopt a clever policy that is not going to cause any dispute with China. Since Mao Zedong and his government are directing all their attention right now toward capturing Guangdong and completely liberating their own nation, they do not have time to consider domestic nationalities, nor do they have the experience. However, after the occupation of Guangdong, they will probably be willing to discuss this matter. There is something else you should also take into consideration. If you propose to Mao Zedong that Inner Mongolia should be unified with Outer Mongolia, he will probably object; he has his own problems. When Chiang Kai-shek took power he broke his nation into pieces and gave them to foreign imperialists. He even accepted the independence of Outer Mongolia. Mao Zedong, however, intends to put together what the Kuomintang dismembered, and make the country unified. Therefore, for Mao Zedong, it would be even more difficult to allow Inner Mongolia to unite with another nation. After the October Revolution, nations such as Finland and Poland separated from Russia and made into independent states. Only Lenin was able to do this. Mao Zedong is not Lenin, and cannot do this.

At that point, Choibalsan asked whether or not a unified Mongolia could become part of the USSR. Stalin responded:

> You would not need to become a part of the Soviet Union. In supporting the unification of Outer and Inner Mongolia, we wish for it to be a unified, independent state that does not fall under the jurisdiction of Russia or China. In the same mind-set, we have always stood for the unification of a single Bolshevik nation, and accordingly, have united Western Ukraine with Western Belarus, for example.[23]

In the light of Stalin's rejection of Mao's overture over Outer Mongolia during the Mikoyan mission, this conversation was typical of the satellite relationship between Moscow and Ulaanbaatar, which was less equal but closer than the CCP–Soviet partnership. Surely Stalin did not need to sound out Mongolian leaders' thinking for the sake of getting back to the Chinese, which he had already done in accord with Moscow's established two-Mongolia policy. The session took place only because Stalin wanted to prepare Choibalsan mentally for a new round of Sino–Soviet diplomacy that might affect the MPR. To Choibalsan, it was crystal clear that in greeting the ascending CCP power in China, the only "clever policy" for him to follow was to obey Stalin's order: to resist any possible CCP demarche for abolishing Outer Mongolian independence but not to scheme in Inner Mongolia, lest it disturb the Sino–Soviet alliance in the making. In making the distinction between Lenin and Mao, Stalin demonstrated his grasp of the nationalist, unifying drive of the emerging Communist China. Although still belittling the CCP's experience in dealing with "domestic nationalities," Stalin did not underestimate the CCP's determination to reverse the disintegrating process of the Chinese state. He was fully prepared for a maneuvering with the CCP leadership premised on an "international," not "internationalist," basis.

Yet Stalin over-prepared himself with regard to Mongolia. Arriving in Moscow, Mao was ready to put the Mongolia question aside for now and concentrate on another goal as the inaugural feat of the new China's diplomacy. This was a new treaty of alliance with the Soviet Union, a goal for which the Soviets had so far appeared more willing to cooperate. In Moscow, Mao told Ivan Kovalev, Stalin's personal envoy to the CCP who accompanied Mao on his trip, that "relying on agreements with the Soviet Union, we would be able to immediately revise and annul the unequal treaties concluded by the Chiang Kai-shek government with imperialist countries."[24] To the CCP leadership, a new treaty with the Soviet Union would not just accomplish its revolutionary goal of bringing China into the socialist camp headed by the Soviet Union but would also, just as important, facilitate its nationalist aspiration of equalizing China's standing with the international community in general.

On January 2, 1950, Mao's intention of discussing the 1945 treaty with the Soviet government was publicized by the Soviet press in the form of Mao's press interview. On the same day, Stalin sent Molotov and Mikoyan to Mao to probe his thinking about how the summit should proceed next. Mao took the opportunity to propose three options for dealing with the treaty question. Options two and three would not lead to a new treaty, and clearly option one was what Mao preferred:

> (A) To conclude a new Sino-Soviet treaty of friendship and alliance. This approach will bring about immense benefit. If the Sino-Soviet relationship is solidified on the basis of a new treaty, China's workers, peasants, intellectuals and the left wing of the national bourgeoisie will be thrilled, and the right wing of the national bourgeoisie will be isolated; in the international scene, we will be able to augment enormously our political capital to deal with imperialist countries, and to reexamine all the treaties concluded between China and these countries in the past.[25]

By "new treaty," Mao did not mean that *every point* of the 1945 treaty had to be scuttled. The next day, he sent a telegram to his colleagues in Beijing spelling out the connections between the prospective new treaty and the old one:

> In comparison to the old treaty, [the new treaty] may perhaps make some changes regarding the question of Lushun and Dalian, but the concrete content is yet to be negotiated. Meanwhile the objective of defense against possible aggressions from Japan and allies and recognition of Outer Mongolia's independence will remain the fundamental spirit of the new treaty.[26]

Thus a negotiation strategy of quid pro quos emerged from the CCP side: Communist China would join the Soviet camp and recognize MPR independence, and in return Moscow would agree to conclude a new treaty and modify its old treaty privileges in Manchuria.

The tricky part of this strategy was that Mao had no intention of using the Mongolia question as an explicit bargaining chip for other concrete issues. Mao might have two reasons for not doing so. For one thing, given Mao's reluctance in acquiescing in MPR independence, it would go against his nature to profess the CCP's concession on Mongolia before Stalin unequivocally supported a new treaty with China. For another, the GMD regime's disgraced diplomatic formula of 1945 was still fresh in the collective memory of the Chinese people, which had used Mongolia as a bargaining chip with the Soviet government. Mao certainly did not want to create even a slim impression that he was following Chiang Kai-shek's footsteps.

He would rather leave the credit for "losing" Mongolia entirely to his nationalist predecessor. Yet Mao understood his task perfectly: To wrest a new treaty from Stalin, he must firmly side with the Soviet Union against Japan *and allies*, meaning the United States, and he must leave Outer Mongolia alone.

Thus, the contemporary issue of the Cold War and the historical question of Mongolia became intertwined in the making of a new Sino–Soviet alliance. This signified the duality of an emerging, post-Yalta geopolitical status quo in East Asia: A Sino–Soviet bloc was being forged to counterbalance the United States in East Asia, but this bloc would be sustained by an internal balance of power between the two communist giants in Inner Asia, with Mongolia and China's other northern regions serving as buffer zones. This structure would become even clearer after the new treaty was signed.

To Stalin and his associates, Mao's vigorous push since his arrival for a new treaty and his perfect silence on the Mongolia question constituted a sharp contrast to CCP leaders' mindset on these matters during the Mikoyan and the Liu missions. For a while, they did not know how to proceed. Only after Mao sent impatient signals to the Kremlin through "cursing and complaining" did Soviet leaders realize that a new approach for dealing with Mao had to be adopted soon to avoid a disastrous failure of the first PRC–SSR summit.[27] Hence the Molotov–Mikoyan visit to Mao was staged on January 2 before Stalin himself could formalize a new demarche. On that day, Mao's continued silence on Mongolia must have been reassuring to the Soviets. As a matter of fact, when conversing with Mao on January 2, Molotov agreed on the spot, necessarily on behalf of Stalin, that Zhou should come to Moscow to participate in the negotiations for a new treaty. To Mao, the prospect of his visit in Moscow immediately brightened.

American Wedge

Yet Soviet leaders still could not completely trust Mao—the clever "Chinese Pugachev," in Molotov's words.[28] Nor did Mao take the treaty issue for granted after reaching his understanding with Molotov. On January 6, in a meeting with Soviet foreign minister, Andrei Vyshinsky, Mao applied further pressure in adopting a persuasive tone that he was "increasingly coming to the conclusion" about the necessity of concluding a new treaty between the PRC and the USSR. Vyshinsky, despite Molotov's concurrence with Mao four days before, repeated Stalin's December 16 argument that a new treaty or even "reviewing of the existing treaty" might provide the Americans and the British with an excuse to alter existing treaty arrangements and "cause damage to Soviet and Chinese interests." The Molotov–Vyshinsky contradiction necessarily reflected Stalin's own hesitation.[29] To the Soviets, a further test of Mao had to be administered. Here U.S. secretary of state Dean Acheson entered the picture.

On January 12, in a speech to the National Press Club in Washington, Acheson accused the Soviet Union for turning Chinese northern territories, including Outer Mongolia, into Soviet colonies. The Acheson speech was seen in the Kremlin as part of a malicious American wedge strategy against the Sino–Soviet alliance in the making. Yet, conversely, Acheson provided the Soviets with an opportunity to test Mao on two key issues in their emerging partnership: Communist China's side taking in the Cold War, and its acceptance of the Yalta–Moscow endorsement of the Soviet sphere in northeastern Asia. On January 17, Molotov and Vyshinsky visited Mao and invited him to act in coordination with the Soviet government in refuting Acheson.

According to Molotov's diary, on that day he and Mao understood each other perfectly on how the two governments should respond to the Acheson speech. In referring to the speech, Molotov called Mao's attention to Washington's "clear slander against the Soviet Union" and pointed out that Acheson's accusation of alleged Soviet inroads in China's northern territories was an "example of the extent of Acheson's fabrications." Mao appeared more sarcastic than angry. He said jokingly that "the Americans are making progress" as their secretary of state adopted the "kinds of scoundrels" usually made only by American journalists. Mao had a different concern about the Acheson speech, however. He asked Molotov whether or not the speech might be a "smoke screen" for an American occupation of Taiwan. Molotov did not deny the possibility, but he emphatically suggested that the Chinese government issue a statement to refute Acheson's fabrications, because they also insulted China by implying that the Chinese people had no control over their territories.

Mao agreed to do so but asked whether or not a statement by the Xinhua New Agency would be better. Molotov again stressed that a matter of this magnitude should be handled by the Ministry of Foreign Affairs of the PRC. According to Molotov's record, Mao agreed to take steps as suggested, but he pointed out that the statement would be issued by the deputy minister of foreign affairs because Foreign Minister Zhou Enlai was then on his way to Moscow. Then Mao launched himself into a presentation on how lately the Americans used different channels to test the ground for negotiations with the PRC and how, "to win time to put the country in order," the CCP devised tactics to "postpone the hour of recognition by the USA."[30]

Mao treated the matter of refuting the Acheson speech seriously. He personally prepared a statement and sent it back to Liu Shaoqi in Beijing on January 19. But instead of publicizing the statement through the Ministry of Foreign Affairs as he had promised Molotov, Mao ordered its publication under the name of Hu Qiaomu, chief of the PRC news agency. When the statement appeared in the *People's Daily* of January 21, it was decorated with a cartoon by the caricaturist Hua Junwu. Thus, the form of the publication made the statement more like a piece of sarcastic polemic than a solemn government protestation.[31]

Furthermore, the content of Mao's refutation of Acheson diverged remarkably from the Soviet government's statement issued under the name of Soviet foreign minister Vyshinsky on January 21. The Soviet piece targeted Acheson's remark on Outer Mongolia directly, stating that Mongolia had been an independent country for more than thirty years and that this fact had been accepted by both the Yalta Conference and the Chinese government in 1945. It also pointed out that a "normal diplomatic relationship" now existed between the MPR and the PRC.[32] In contrast, Mao's rejoinder not only did not utter a word to justify MPR independence but also avoided any reference to the MPR as a separate state. After accusing Acheson of making the "most shameless lie" in suggesting Soviet aggressions in "*China's* four northern areas [Outer Mongolia, Inner Mongolia, Xinjiang, and Manchuria; emphasis added]," Mao just pointed out that in the past two years the American government had made a series of self-contradictory statements about the relationship between the CCP and the Soviet Union.[33]

This peculiar difference between Mao's and Moscow's statements puzzled a Chinese participant in the Moscow negotiations for five decades. Shi Zhe was Mao's interpreter during the Moscow negotiations. When his memoir was first published in 1991, he did not or could not say anything about the Mao/Soviet divergence in refuting Acheson. But, in a more personal recollection told to his daughter, which was completed in April 1998, four months before his death, Shi could not resist adding one pregnant comment to his story: "How did Mao think about Acheson's lies? It cannot be known." On Mao's side in Moscow, Shi felt mystified by a certain attitude of Mao's that was at least incompatible with his open statement on the Acheson speech.[34]

Now it is no longer a mystery how Mao and other CCP leaders thought about the Soviet responsibility for separating Outer Mongolia from China. In a conversation with some Japanese socialists in July 1964, Mao blamed the Yalta diplomacy for allowing Moscow to place Outer Mongolia under its domination "under the pretext of assuring the independence of Mongolia." Obviously, Mao wanted to treat the matter as a case of China's victimization by deals among great powers rather than a result of the 1945 KMT–Moscow agreement on MPR independence.[35] A recent memoir by Wang Dongxing, another Chinese participant in the Moscow negotiations, reveals that in his last few years, Mao still fumed over Stalin's Yalta diplomacy along the same line: "They wanted to divide the world, to cut away China's Mongolia, to incorporate Xinjiang and the Northeast into the Soviet sphere of influence where no other countries would be allowed, and to include Japan in America? sphere of influence." The most recent accusation by a top CCP leader of the Soviet Union for separating Outer Mongolia from China was made by Deng Xiaoping during his 1989 conversation with Mikhail Gorbachev.[36]

Several previous studies have suggested that in the Acheson episode Mao coordinated with the Soviets well. Despite his misstep in the *form* of the Chinese statement, Mao took Moscow's side in attacking the Americans and thus satisfied Stalin's prerequisites for a new treaty with the PRC. Such interpretations discount the significance of an unpleasant encounter between Stalin and Mao after the publication of the Chinese statement.[37] As a matter of fact, if Mao's refutation was puzzling to Shi Zhe, it was outright alarming to the Soviets in turning on the red light on Mongolia. Although Mao's rebuttal did not directly raise the Mongolia question for the Sino–Soviet talks, its ambiguous reference to Mongolia along with other three regions as "China's" and lack of a clear justification of MPR independence did seem to confirm the Soviets' suspicion about Mao's continued ambition toward Mongolia.

Now they wanted to talk this over with Mao. Shi Zhe's memoir offers the only information available about the resultant encounter between Stalin and Mao. According to Shi, on a late January day, Stalin and Molotov had a brief meeting with Mao and Zhou in which Shi served as interpreter. In the conversation, Stalin and Molotov took turns castigating Mao for breaching his earlier promise to issue an "official" rebuttal of the Acheson speech. Stalin referred to the Chinese statement as a "worthless" remark issued under an individual's name, and Molotov accused Mao of "violating our agreement" and preventing the two sides' actions from "achieving our expected effect." Molotov's vehement language is understandable, because Mao's willfulness made him appear incompetent in Stalin's eyes. To Stalin, as long as he knew that the statement represented Mao's view, its form, in his words, "is no big deal." He nevertheless admonished Mao that "because we did not act as originally planned and fell out of steps with each other, a crack may have been created for the enemy to exploit."[38] If the *form* was no big deal, the only matter worth this condescending censuring, which was apparently out of sync with the two sides' generally equal dialogues in Moscow, was the *content* of Mao's statement. But, because in Moscow Mao did not explicitly make the northern territories an issue between Beijing and Moscow, understandably Stalin could only resort to ambiguity as well.

A question should be asked as to when and for what reason Stalin wanted to stage such an encounter with Mao. It seems unlikely that the meeting took place before January 25. On that day, Mao sent an upbeat telegram to Liu Shaoqi informing him of progress in the negotiations since Zhou's arrival on January 20. By now, the two sides had basically agreed on a draft treaty and, on the Chinese side, the preparations for other agreements had also advanced nicely. In Mao's words, "in general the work has proceeded rather smoothly."[39]

The smoothness, however, was interrupted by the Americans. The U.S. State Department did a follow-up on Acheson's accusation of Soviet territorial expansion in northern China by providing "proofs" to the press. These "proofs" were published by American newspapers on January 26. Therefore, only as a reaction to this new American offensive can Soviet leaders' abrasive behavior in their meeting with Mao and Zhou be understood. With the American action as evidence, the Soviets now had serious questions about the meaning and effect of Mao's rebuttal of Acheson. They felt it necessary to tell Mao face to face how he had ruined the "original plan" and "expected effect."

What was the Kremlin's original plan? If the plan was to frustrate Washington's wedge strategy against the Sino–Soviet alliance and silence official American propaganda on Soviet expansion at China's expenses, these goals could be achieved only if Mao openly and unequivocally committed himself to the Soviet position on the MPR and defended Soviet policies toward other northern Chinese territories as well. As a matter of fact, for the Soviets, in this case the means was really the goal. The Soviet leaders were so irritated by Washington's propaganda only because they were not sure whether or not the Chinese might actually agree with what the Americans were saying. In the Acheson episode, therefore, the PRC–USSR unity vis-à-vis the United States was just part of the issue. Another crucial aspect was the internal balance between the two communist powers.

Having decided to forgo the formality if not the substance of the Yalta–Moscow system, Stalin was anxious to know how far Mao would want to go in rolling back the Soviet Union's geostrategic position in Northeast Asia endorsed by Yalta. In Moscow, Mao said a lot but constantly refrained from supporting Mongolian independence in a positive way. Thus, Stalin, just like Shi Zhe, could not fathom Mao's real thinking about Soviet expansion in Northeast Asia even after reading Mao's rebuttal of the Acheson speech. If the Acheson episode was intended by the Soviet leaders as a test for Mao, then it appeared that Mao the examinee outsmarted the examiners—Stalin and Molotov— and cheated on the test with skill and style.

According to Shi, during the (later than January 26?) meeting, Mao appeared to be controlling his anger as Molotov and Stalin took turns reproving him, "not saying a word and keeping an emotionless face." Mao's indignation may, however, have been feigned. A few years later, when Mao recalled the occasion to a Polish Communist delegation, he said that "I just laughed in my nose and did not defend myself a bit."[40] Mao had a good reason to laugh because his handiwork neither budged on the Mongolia question nor gave the Soviets a reason to question his revolutionary spirit against the United States. Hence, Stalin and Molotov could ventilate their displeasure about Mao's mischief only by pounding on a secondary issue—the *form* of his statement.

Mongolian Crack

It is rather revealing that the Acheson episode, which could have been a good opportunity for Beijing and Moscow to show their solidarity to the world, caused such strong mutual grievances between the two sides. In qualifying his unpleasant meeting with Mao as an "exchange of opinions within a small group," Stalin obviously had no intention of creating new difficulties for the first communist summit, though the session inevitably became an occasion that sowed new seeds of distrust between Beijing and Moscow. The situation occurred mainly because Mao continued to hold his Mongolia card under the table and because the patience of his Soviet hosts was running thin. Mao was nevertheless determined that the Chinese side should decide when and how to lay the Mongolia card on the table.

On January 25, the Chinese delegation, under Zhou's direction, completed its draft agreement on the issues of the Lushun and Dalian ports and the Chinese Changchun Railroad. The draft agreement was presented to the Soviets as a one-package counteroffer to their earlier separate proposals on these matters. The Chinese draft agreement basically wanted to cancel all Soviet treaty privileges related to these establishments and thus make Moscow's intention of using a new treaty to preserve the old gains unattainable.[41] After listening to Zhou's report on the Chinese draft agreement, Mao expressed his opinion on how the Soviets should be rewarded, provided that they agreed to give up their rights and interests in Manchuria:

> We need to make one more statement. When the People's Republic of China was established, we declared nullification of all international agreements and treaties concluded between the old China and foreign countries. But Outer Mongolia was an exception. Although the independence of Outer Mongolia was processed by the KMT government, we respect the 1945 plebiscite by the Mongolian people in which they unanimously supported independence. Now, through negotiations the two governments [of the PRC and the USSR] should confirm the independent status of the Mongolian People's Republic. The Soviet Union ought to support China's stand on this matter and in the meantime to hope that Mongolia will respond by making a statement as well.

Zhou understood Mao's intention perfectly and said that "such an approach would be better."[42]

By now, Mao had laid out his stratagem for playing the Mongolia card: (1) Because the PRC had renounced all China's foreign treaties concluded by the KMT regime, *legally* the PRC had not accepted the independence of the MPR; (2) but the Chinese delegation could make an *additional* statement to *reconfirm* MPR independence only *after* the Soviets made concessions on other matters in the 1945 treaty; and therefore (3) MPR independence would appear to have been settled *through negotiations* just like other issues, though in reality there were no negotiations about the MPR at all.

Thus, after the interparty Mikoyan/Liu diplomacies in 1949 made it clear to the CCP leadership that the issue of Mongolia was nonnegotiable with Moscow, Mao finally found a way to insert the issue into the interstate diplomacy between himself and Stalin. The cleverness of Mao's tactic was twofold. First, in the actual negotiations in Moscow, the Chinese side would use the Mongolia question as a silent inducement for the Soviets to concede on other issues. In this regard, the Acheson episode proved an unsolicited help to Mao: It highlighted the suspense between Beijing and Moscow with respect to China's northern territories and gave Mao an opportunity to show his calculated ambiguity about Mongolia. Secondly, once Moscow agreed to a deal on other issues to the CCP's satisfaction, MPR independence would be declared as part of the package to impress the world and the Chinese public back home that the CCP had made an effort about Outer Mongolia but had to endorse its independence as a matter of principle and in exchange for Soviet concessions in Manchuria. This way, even though the CCP could not redress the KMT loss of Mongolia, its diplomacy in Moscow would still appear superior to the KMT's in recovering other rights in Manchuria.

Consistent with Mao's effort in Moscow of building up the Mongolia suspense, Zhou did not raise the topic at all during his negotiations with the Soviets. The silence on the Chinese side thus rendered the Soviet preparations for defending the 1945 arrangements about Mongolia a futile exercise.[43] Mao's tactic seemed to have worked. According to Shen Zhihua, who has examined Soviet archival materials on the Moscow negotiations,

Stalin's irritation was evident in his marginal notes in a copy of the Chinese counterproposal about Soviet interests in Manchuria. Yet somehow the Soviets managed to suppress their anger and accepted the essence of the Chinese document on January 28.[44] Although Stalin's need for a successful summit with Mao was overwhelming, his desire for Mao's acceptance of the Mongolian buffer also underlay his bitter concessions in Manchuria.

Consequently, only after reaching a basic agreement with the Soviets on the content of the new treaty did Zhou, at a meeting before January 31, inform Stalin of Mao's notion about issuing a statement on the MPR. Having endured the Mongolia suspense administered by Mao during the past two months, Stalin did not foresee this sudden end. His initial r eaction was defensive:

> Was not the Mongolia question settled long time ago? If there is no problem at all, why is a statement needed? Besides, since the Mongolian comrades are not here, for what purpose should we discuss the Mongolia question? What right do we have to discuss other peoples' fate?[45]

It has been suggested that on the occasion Stalin was "at his demagogical best," as if he had not interfered with other peoples' fate before.[46] This may be so, but the Chinese initiative did make Stalin nervous. The worst scenario for Stalin was that Mao would raise the Mongolia question *after* the Soviet government agreed to sign a new treaty with the PRC *and* to retreat from its privileged position in Manchuria. Zhou immediately put Stalin at ease, explaining to him what the Chinese side intended to do. Stalin relaxed and supported the idea. Hence came the end of the underplayed Mongolia drama in Moscow.

The PRC–USSR Treaty of Friendship, Alliance, and Mutual Assistance was signed on February 14. A Chinese–Soviet joint communiqué of the same date clarified the relationship between the new treaty and the 1945 treaty:

> In connection with the signing of the Treaty of Friendship, Alliance, and Mutual Assistance, and the Agreement on the Chinese Changchun Railroad, Lushun, and Dalian, Zhou Enlai, Premier and the Minister of Foreign Affairs, and A. Ia. Vyshinskii, Minister of Foreign Affairs, exchanged notes to the effect that the respective treaty and agreements concluded on August 14, 1945, between China and the Soviet Union are now null and void, and also that both governments affirm that the independent status of the Mongolian People's Republic is fully guaranteed as a result of the plebiscite of 1945 and the establishment with it of diplomatic relationship by the People's Republic of China.[47]

Also at Mao's insistence, the Agreement on the Chinese Changchun Railroad, Lushun, and Dalian explicitly stated that the old agreements on these issues were overturned because "since 1945 the situation in the Far East has changed fundamentally, e.g.: Imperialist Japan has been defeated, reactionary KMT government has been overthrown, and China has become a people's democratic republic and has established a new, people's government."[48] In this way, Stalin finally conceded to Mao's notion that the new treaty should not just be a negative instrument in dealing with the Western powers and Japan but should mainly be a positive response to the successful Chinese revolution.

Thus, as far as the Soviet Union was concerned, China's "old kitchen" was closed and the "new kitchen" was in business. Yet the CCP still had to invite the Soviets into China as privileged "guests." Although relinquishing their old treaty rights in Manchuria, the Soviets managed to get new rights from Mao, including joint-stock companies in Xinjiang, a monopoly over China's export of surplus industrial sources during the period of Soviet loans to China, and China's agreement to close Xinjiang and Manchuria to any third foreign interests. After Stalin's death, Mao would openly make many complaints about these arrangements, accusing Stalin of turning Xinjiang and Manchuria into Soviet "spheres of influence" or "semi-colonies." At last, Mao belatedly revealed his concurrence with Dean Acheson's 1950 incrimination of Moscow's design for colonizing northern Chinese territories.[49]

Clearly, the 1950 treaty inherited the 1945 treaty on the MPR. Surely, the shadow boxing between Mao and Stalin over Mongolia did not decide the success or failure of the entire realm of Sino–Soviet diplomacy between December 1949 and February 1950. Neither Stalin nor Mao could afford to fail in their first summit when their common strategy against the United States was at stake. This overall common concern was a powerful enough inducement to both sides and made the Moscow negotiations a "time when Mao's revolutionary ambitions and Stalin's power interests converged the most closely."[50] After the negotiations, a Eurasian communist monolith emerged in Western governments' eyes.

Nevertheless, during the better part of the Moscow negotiations, the Mongolia question hovered silently in the air; its settlement, or resettlement, was necessary for painting over, if not patching up, one of the major cracks in the PRC–USSR monolith. A question for Mao and Stalin to answer was that, after the CCP added China to the Soviet side of the global power equation, how should Moscow's geopolitical arrangements in Northeastern and Central Asia, which were first set up when China was still on the "other" side, be readjusted. In this question resided all the nationalistic poisons of a proclaimed internationalist brotherhood between Beijing and Moscow. The hypothesis presented here suggests that Mao's silent, suspenseful tactics induced Stalin to accept a Mongolia-for-Manchuria formula. The overall significance of this development was that a double-layered geopolitical balance of power finally materialized to replace the Yalta–Moscow system, which had only one fault line in Northeast Asia. In other words, whereas the Mongolian buffer and the 1950 formulas for Manchuria and Xinjiang served to stabilize the internal balance of the USSR–PRC bloc, the bloc was ready to counter America's security system Asia-wide.

Notes

1. Yang Kuisong, *Mao Zedong yu Mosike*, 258–270.
2. Wu Lengxi, *Shinian Lunzhan, 1956–1966: Zhongsu Guanxi Huiyilu* (Ten Years of Debates, 1956–1966: A Memoir of Sino-Soviet Relations) (Beijing: Zhongyang Wenxian Chubanshe, 1999), 1: 315–333.
3. The Chinese version of the report is published separately as A. M. Ledovsky, "Secret Negotiations between Mikoyan and Mao Zedong, January-February 1949, Part Two," trans. Li Yuzhen, *Dang de Wenxian* (Party Documents) 1 (1996): 90–96, and A. M. Ledovsky, *Sidalin yu Zhongguo* (Stalin and China), trans. Chen Chunhua, Liu Cunkuan et al. (Beijing: Xinhua Chubanshe, 2001), 58–72. For an English version, see Andrei Ledovsky, "Mikoyan's Secret Mission to China in January and February 1949," *Far Eastern Affairs* (hereafter *FEA*) 2 (1995): 78–94.
4. Andrei Ledovsky, "Mikoyan's Secret Mission to China in January and February 1949," *FEA* 2 (1995): 88–89.
5. Ledovsky, *Sidalin yu Zhongguo*, 141; Ledovsky, "Mikoyan's Secret Mission," 87.

6. Ledovsky, "Mikoyan's Secret Mission," 88–89; Goncharov, "Stalin-Mao Dialogue," 104–105.
7. Goncharov, "Stalin-Mao Dialogue," 107.
8. Information memorandum by I. Kalabukhov, first secretary of the Far Eastern Department of the USSR, "About the Claims of the Chinese Leaders With Regard to the Mongolian People's Republic," January 30, 1964, Cold War International History Project (CWIHP) Virtue Archive, http://wwics.si.edu.
9. Liu Xiao, *Chushi Sulian Banian* (Eight-Year Ambassadorship in the Soviet Union) (Beijing: Zhonggong Dangshi Ziliao Chubanshe, 1986), 4.
10. Zhou Qiliang and Chu Liangru, *Teshu er Fuza de Keti* (A Peculiar and Complex Subject) (Wuhan: Hubei Renmin Chubanshe, 1993), 456–457.
11. Xu Zehao, *Wang Jiaxiang Zhuan*, 456, 458–460.
12. "Report to the Soviet Communist Party Central Committee and Stalin on Behalf of the CCP Central Committee, 4 July 1949," Liu Shaoqi, *Jianguo yilai Liu Shaoqi Wengao* (Liu Shaoqi's Manuscripts after the Establishment of the State; hereafter *JYLW*) (Beijing: Zhongyang Wenxian Chubanshe, 1998), 1: 15–16.
13. Liu Shaoqi, Gao Gang, and Wang Jiaxiang to the CCP Center, July 18, 1949, *JYLW*, 1: 22–28 n. 16; Shi Zhe, *Wo de Yisheng: Shi Zhe Zishu* (My Life: In Shi Zhe's Own Words) (Beijing: Renmin Chubanshe, 2001), 306.
14. Andrei Ledovsky, "The Moscow Visit of a Delegation of the Communist Party of China in June to August 1949," *FEA* 4 (1996): 70, 83; Qiu Jing, "Meeting between the Two Red Giants," 211.
15. Mao Zedong to Liu Shaoqi, July 14, 1949, *JYLW*, 1: 21 n. 15.
16. Shen Zhihua, *Mao Zedong, Sidalin yu Chaoxian Zhanzheng* (Mao Zedong, Stalin and the Korean War) (Guangzhou: Guangdong Renmin Chubanshe, 2003), 132.
17. "Conversation between Stalin and Mao, Moscow, 16 December 1949," *CWIHP Bulletin*, issues 6–7 (Winter 1995–1996): 5; Pei Jianzhang, ed., *Zhonghua Renmin Gongheguo Waijiaoshi, 1949–1956* (Diplomatic History of the People's Republic of China, 1949–1956) (Beijing: Shijie Zhishi Chubanshe, 1994), 18–19.
18. "Conversation between Stalin and Mao, Moscow, 22 January 1950," *CWIHP Bulletin*, issues 6–7 (Winter 1995–1996): 7–8. For different views on Stalin's change of mind, see Shen Zhihua, "Clashes of Interests and Their Settlement during Negotiations on the Chinese-Soviet Treaty of 1950," *FEA* 3 (2002): 101–103; Pei Jianzhang, *Zhonghua Renmin Gongheguo Waijiaoshi*, 19–20; Yang Kuisong, *Zhonggong yu Mosike de Guanxi*, 617–618, and *Mao Zedong yu Mosike*, 297–298; Vladislav Zubok, " 'To Hell with Yalta!' Stalin Opts for a New Status Quo," *CWIHP Bulletin*, issues 6–7 (Winter 1995–1996): 24–27; Odd Arne Westad, "Unwrapping the Stalin-Mao Talks: Setting the Record Straight," ibid., 23–24, and "Fighting for Friendship: Mao, Stalin, and the Sino-Soviet Treaty of 1950," *CWIHP Bulletin*, issues 8–9 (Winter 1996–1997): 224–226; Heinzig, *The Soviet Union and Communist China*, 298.
19. Shi Zhe, *Zai Lishi Juren Shenbian*, 379; Pei Jianzhang, Zhonghua *Renmin Gongheguo Waijiao Shi*, 2–3.
20. Xiaodong Wang, "China Learning to Stand Up: Nationalism in the Formative Years of the People's Republic of China," in *Exploring Nationalisms of China: Themes and Conflicts*, ed. C. X. George Wei and Xiaoyuan Liu (Westport, Conn.: Greenwood Press, 2002), 77–100.
21. "Conversation between Stalin and Mao, Moscow, 16 December 1949," *CWIHP Bulletin*, issues 6–7 (Winter 1995–1996): 5. Mao's telegram is cited in Pei Jianzhang, *Zhonghua*

Renmin Gongheguo Waijiao Shi, 17–18, and for an English version see "Telegram, Mao Zedong to Liu Shaoqi, 18 December 1949," in *Chinese Communist Foreign Policy and the Cold War in Asia*, ed. Zhang and Chen, 128.

22. O. Chuluun, "The Two Phases in Mongolian-Chinese Relations, 1949–1972," *FEA* 1 (1974): 24; Ma Yong, comp., *Guoshi Quanshu* (Complete Manual of Country Affairs), 4 vols. (Beijing: Tuanjie Chubanshe, 1997), 3: 3077–3079. The other six countries were Bulgaria, Rumania, Hungary, North Korea, Czechoslovakia, and Poland.
23. Ookhnoin Batsaikhan, "Issues Concerning Mongolian Independence from the Soviet Union and China: The Attempt to Incorporate Mongolia within the USSR and the Positions of Soviet Leaders, Stalin, Molotov, and Mikoyan," 3–5, paper presented at the "International Workshop on Mongolia and the Cold War," Ulaanbaatar, March 19–20, 2004.
24. Goncharov, "Stalin-Mao Dialogue," 103–104.
25. "Telegrams to the CCPCC on Zhou Enlai's trip to the Soviet Union to Participate in the Negotiations" (1), January 2, 1950, in *Jianguo Yilai Mao Zedong Wengao*, by Mao Zedong (Mao Zedong's Manuscripts since the Foundation of the State) (Beijing: Zhongyang Wenxian Chubanshe, 1987), 1: 211 (hereafter cited as *JYMW*).
26. "Telegrams to the Center on Zhou Enlai's Trip to the Soviet Union to Participate in the Negotiations" (2), January 3, 1950, *JYMW*, 1: 213.
27. Wu Lengxi, *Shinian Lunzhan*, 1: 14, 146, quotes Mao's two speeches in 1956 and 1957 that include two slightly different versions of how Mao made his intention about a new treaty known to Stalin.
28. "Telegrams to the Center on Zhou Enlai's Trip to the Soviet Union to Participate in the Negotiations" (1), January 2, 1950, *JYMW*, 1: 211–212; Felix Chuev, *Molotov Remembers: Inside Kremlin Politics; Conversations with Felix Chuev* (Chicago: Ivan R. Dee, 1993), 81.
29. "From the Diary of A. Y. Vyshinsky: Memorandum of Conversation with the Chairman of the People's Central Government of the People's Republic of China, Mao Zedong, 6 January 1950," *CWIHP Bulletin*, issues 8–9 (Winter 1996–1997): 230–231.
30. "Document 17: Conversation, V. M. Molotov and A. V. Vyshinsky with Mao Zedong, Moscow, 17 January 1950," *CWIHP Bulletin*, issues 8–9 (Winter 1996–1997): 232–234.
31. "Telegram on the Publication of a Talk to Repudiate Rumors Made by Acheson, 19 January 1950," *JYMW*, 1: 245; "Central People's Government News Agency Director Hu Qiaomu Refutes the Shameless Rumor Made by U.S. Secretary of State Acheson," *Renmin Ribao*, February 21, 1950.
32. "Soviet Foreign Minister Vyshisky's Statement of Refuting Acheson's Absurd Accusations," *Renmin Ribao*, February 22, 1950; Shi Zhe, *Wo de Yisheng*, 349–350.
33. Mao Zedong, "Refutation of Acheson's Shameless Lies," in *Mao Zedong Waijiao Wenxuan* (Selected Works of Mao Zedong on Diplomacy) (Beijing: Zhongyang Wenxian Chubanshe and Shijie Zhishi Chubanshe, 1994), 126–128.
34. Shi Zhe's first memoir, *Zai Lishi Juren Shenbian*, which covers the years from 1924 to 1954, was published in two editions in 1991 and 1995. His second memoir, *Wo de Yisheng*, covers his life from 1904 to 1998. It was recorded by his daughter Shi Qiulang and was published in 2001. The quotation is from p. 349.
35. John Gittings, *Survey of the Sino-Soviet Dispute* (London: Oxford University Press, 1968), 166–167.
36. Wang Dongxing, *Wang Dongxing Huiyi Mao Zedong yu Lin Biao Fangeming Jiduan de Douzheng* (Mao Zedong's Struggle with the Lin Biao Counterrevolutionary Clique as

Remembered by Wang Dongxing) (Beijing: Dangdai Zhongguo Chubanshe, 2004), 141–142; "Information Note of Romanian Embassy from Beijing to Ministry of Foreign Affairs, 23 May 1989," CWIHP Virtual Archive, http://wwics.si.edu.

37. Goncharov, Lewis, and Xue, *Uncertain Partners*, 103, 104–105; Odd Arne Westad, "Fight for Friendship," *CWIHP Bulletin*, issues 8–9 (Winter 1996–1997): 225; Yang Kuisong, *Mao Zedong yu Mosike*, 300–301.
38. Shi Zhe, *Wo de Yisheng*, 351.
39. "Telegram to Liu Shaoqi on the Sino-Soviet Negotiations and the Status of Document Preparations, 25 January 1950," *JYMW*, 1: 251.
40. Shi Zhe, *Wo de Yisheng*, 351; Yang Kuisong, *Mao Zedong yu Mosike*, 301.
41. Shen Zhihua, "Clashes of Interests," 104.
42. Diary entry on January 25, 1950, in *Wang Dongxing Riji* (Wang Dongxing's Diaries) by Wang Dongxing (Beijing: Zhongguo Shehui Kexue Chubanshe, 1993), 195.
43. Zhou Enlai's telegram to Liu Shaoqi and the Central Politburo, February 8, 1950, cited in Jin Chongji, *Zhou Enlai Zhuan, 1949–1976* (Biography of Zhou Enlai, 1949–1976) (Beijing: Zhongyang Wenxian Chubanshe, 1998), 1: 35–39.
44. Shen Zhihua, "Clashes of Interests," 104.
45. Shi Zhe, *Wo de Yisheng*, 346–347.
46. Goncharov, Lewis, and Xue, *Uncertain Partners*, 120. These authors, relying on the recollections of Wu Xiuquan, a member of Zhou Enlai's negotiation team, mistakenly date the exchange on January 22. Because Zhou and his team arrived in Moscow just two days before, it was highly unlikely that he brought up this matter to Stalin at this date. The date also contradicts Wang Dongxing's diary entry on January 25 about the Mao-Zhou conversation on Mongolia (see note 42 above). Heinzig, *The Soviet Union and Communist China*, 362–363, proves that on January 31 Zhou handed the Chinese draft of exchange notes to Vyshinsky, the second point of which addressed MPR independence. Heinzig's source is Vyshinsky's letter to Stalin dated February 1, 1950, located in Archives of the President of the Russian Federation, Moscow. Therefore, most likely the Zhou-Stalin conversation on Mongolia took place between January 28 and 30.
47. "Chinese-Soviet Communiqué on the Conclusion of Treaty of Friendship, Alliance, and Mutual Assistance and Related Agreements, Moscow, 14 February 1950," in *Jianguo Yilai Zhongyao Wenxian Xuanbian* (Selection of Important Documents since the Establishment of the State), comp. Documentary Research Office of the CCP Central Committee (Beijing: Zhongyang Wenxian Chubanshe, 1992), 1: 118.
48. "PRC-USSR agreement on the Chinese Changchun Railroad, Lushun, and Dalian," *Jianguo Yilai Zhongyao Wenxian Xuanbian*, 1: 121; Zhou Enlai to Liu Shaoqi and the Central Politburo, February 8, 1950, cited in Jin Chongji, *Zhou Enlai Zhuan*, 1: 37.
49. "Mao's Conversation with Yudin, 31 March 1956," *CWIHP Bulletin*, issues 6–7 (Winter 1995–1996): 166; "First Conversation of N. S. Khrushchev with Mao Zedong, Hall of Huaizhentan [*Huairentang?*] [Beijing], 31 July 1958," *CWIHP Bulletin*, issues 12–13 (Fall/Winter 2001): 251.
50. Vojtech Mastny, *The Cold War and Soviet Insecurity: The Stalin Years* (New York: Oxford University Press, 1996), 88.

CHAPTER ELEVEN

Cold and Hot Wars along the Himalayas

China's ancient and recent histories have left much to decipher in respect to China's temperament in international occasions. One thing is certain, however: Since the 19th century, China's transformation from a traditional empire to a modern national state has never reversed. This historic change bridging two centuries has too often been overlooked. In the written history of China's modern times, it cannot be easily recognized that those periods of vastly different political significances are no more than a series of thresholds China stepped over when entering the international society. This chapter reveals how, in the thickness of the Cold War, China continued to follow the norms of international relations in its diplomatic performance and national-state building. Again Tibet is the subject, but it is considered in an international context. For the following reasons, the question of Tibet can typically illustrate the uninterrupted process of modernization of China's international personality. First, since the nineteenth- century China has transformed from a traditional East Asian empire of ambiguous central authority and assorted territories to a modern national state of definite sovereignty and rigorously administered boundaries. In the process the controversy over sovereignty in Tibet featured prominently. Secondly, the 1959 Tibetan uprising was an immediate cause for the deterioration of the Chinese–Indian relations. The development reflected a fact that the old imperial diplomacy along the Himalayas was replaced by a modern relationship between two national states. And, thirdly, the Tibetan affair served as a catalyst that changed the dynamics between and within the two Cold War international blocs. The episode showed how Cold War mentality and normative international behaviors became intertwined in the foreign policy making on both sides of the Cold War.

In 1959, an immediate historical result of the Lhasa uprising was that any lingering resemblance between the Chinese Communist Party's (CCP) Tibet policy and the Qing practices evaporated. From that moment, ethnopolitical or cultural differences no longer exercised much restraint on the authority of the central government in Beijing. The completion of China's domestic sovereignty also consummated the modernization of Chinese territoriality in the mainland. As China's normative identity as a national state became increasingly close to that of the Western countries, the relationship between the two sides remained hostile. Since it was the CCP that presided over China's historical transformation after 1949, a dual paradox occurred: the further Beijing advanced the anti-Western ideology and social system in China, the more complete the PRC's domestic sovereignty became and thus the closer the PRC was to the West in their normative relationship; then the more closely the PRC resembled the Western "nation-states" in international behaviors, the more were Beijing's foreign policies motivated by self-interests and viewed the Western bloc around the United States as enemies. In the end of the 19th century, Japan rose during the era of imperialism, and it logically joined the colonial competitions of the time as a new imperialist power. In the mid-twentieth century, the People's Republic of China (PRC) learned to stand on its feet in an era of the Cold War, and it could not exempt itself from the conventions of the age. After 1949, "leaning to one side" in the CCP's foreign policy was historically inevitable, but the leaning to the Soviet side was a choice of the moment by Beijing. In the early Cold War years, China's alliance with the Soviet

Disputed borders between China and India, a map produced by the CIA in 1988.

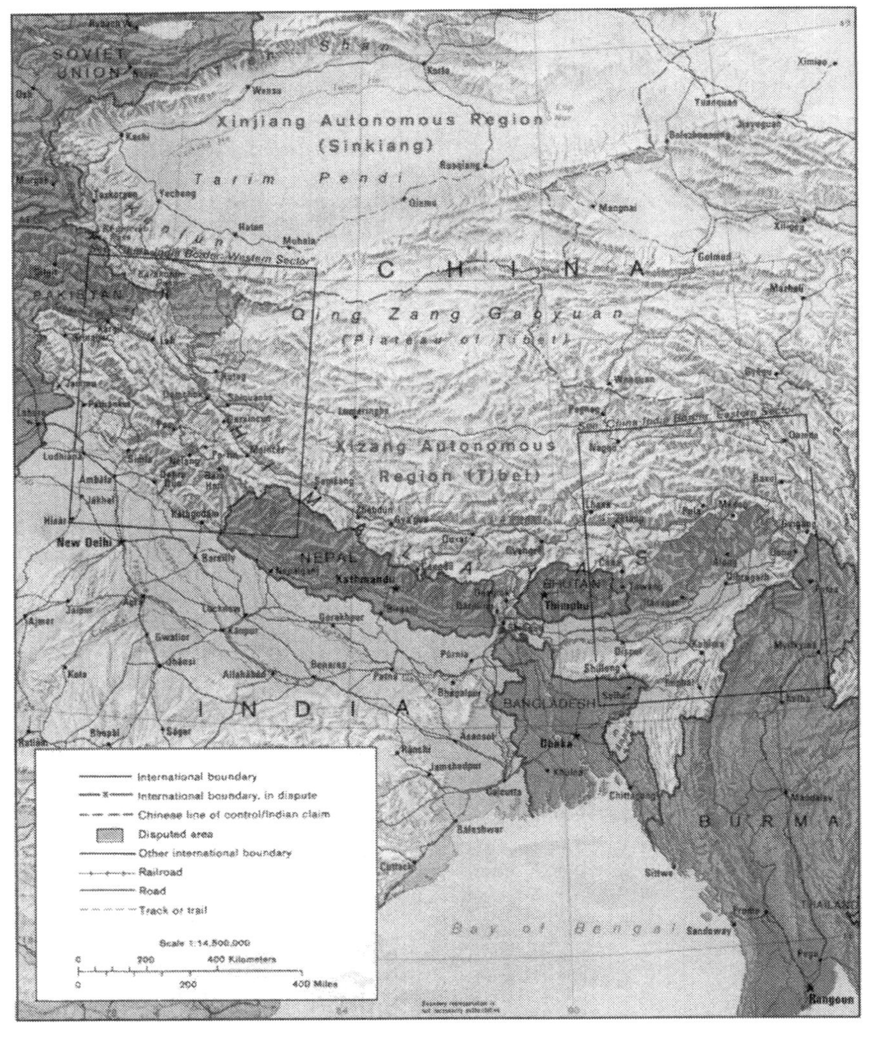

Source: Perry-Castaneda Library Map Collection, the University of Texas Austin, http://www.lib.utexas.edu/maps/china.html.

bloc was surely a challenge to the West. The alliance should however not be understood simply as China's rejection to the norms of international relations. The arrangements of international blocs during the initial years of the Cold War would not last, and the Tibetan uprising was among the catalysts that caused the collapse of these arrangements in Asia.

Second Cold War Front

The involvement of Tibet in the Cold War could probably be predicted in 1949. By the mid-1950s this was already a fact of life. The armed conflicts in Tibet after 1956 and Beijing's war for suppressing the Tibetan uprising in 1959 and 1960 not only fundamentally changed the political relationship between Beijing and Tibet but also set off a chain reaction of fallouts in China's foreign relations. In the wake of the Tibetan uprising, the Sino–Indian relations deteriorated rapidly, which led to a border war between the two countries in 1962. CIA analysts in the United States in those years and today's historians in China agree that the Sino-Indian war was one of the important reasons for the Sino–Soviet split in the 1960s.[1] Since the mid-1950s, the U.S. government also began to take advantage of the turmoil in Tibet and launched a secret war in the region to undermine Beijing's authority. When the Sino–Indian war broke out, Washington seized the opportunity to include India into its containment strategy against China. In view of these developments, Beijing's failure in achieving interethnic cooperation in Tibet toppled the first piece of dominos that sustained the great-power balance in Eurasia since the end of World War II. In a brief period of several years, China's long and tranquil borders from the northeast to the southwest became perilous again. Aside from facing the American threat from the direction of the Pacific, the PRC was now challenged from different directions along its inland frontiers. The Cold War to China became a two-front struggle.

The deterioration of the Sino–Indian relationship was a key event that caused drastic changes in China's immediate international environment. In May 1959, when talking to delegations from the Soviet Union and some East European countries, Zhou Enlai accused the Indian leadership for fearing reforms in Tibet and hoping to keep a backward Tibet as a buffer between China and India. Zhou asserted that this was the "crux of the Sino-Indian disputes." This line of argument would underlie China's official and scholarly analyses of the Sino–Indian conflicts ever since.[2] By contrast, China's opponents blamed Beijing for causing the conflicts. A 1962 CIA memorandum stated that at the beginning the Indian government cherished friendly feelings toward Communist China, but such feelings were seriously damaged by the PLA's invasion of Tibet in 1950, and that the "cartographic aggressions" conducted by the Chinese side in the next few years escalated the animosity between the two sides to open conflicts.[3]

In his *India's China War* published in 1970, Neville Maxwell analyzes the Sino–Indian conflicts in a longer time span and does not fall into the polemic about "responsibilities." He points out that in the 1950s, when the influence of the Chinese government reached the northern border of India, the impact on the Indian public was comparable to that of the Qing's New Administration policy in Tibet on the British public at the beginning of the century. What differentiated the two events was Indian independence:

> With independence, all that changed. The boundaries of India ceased to be the pawns of the British in their Great Games with their imperial rivals, and became the cell walls of a new national identity. No longer could boundaries be conceived or shifted by men whose concern was not territory but strategic advantages; henceforth they enclosed the sacred soil of the motherland, and politicians could tamper with them only at their peril.[4]

The India of the mid-twentieth century was certainly no longer a group of princely states or semi-independent provinces that saw the world from a religious perspective.[5] Similarly, when India, as a new national state, was claiming a geopolitical inheritance from the fallen British Empire, the PRC, with its revolutionary-state identity, also inherited the geopolitical claims of the by-gone Qing Empire. And the CCP leaders did not shy away from praising the Manchus' contributions to China's territorial expansion.[6] In other words, the historical background of the Sino–Indian conflicts was the two nations' respective modernization of territoriality. Between the two largest Asian countries was the highest international divide in the world. In the past two centuries, the divide served as a buffer between two colossal empires representing separately the Eastern and the Western "international relation cultures."[7] In the mid-twentieth century, however, the divide turned into a seam that stitched two national states together, both holding territorial sovereignty as sacred and inviolable and watching each other suspiciously. The ambiguous borderlines left by the old empires indeed created difficulties for the bilateral relationship between China and India. But more often border disputes between two states are symptoms but not causes of their mutual distrust. As for the Sino–Indian border war between the late 1950s and the early 1960s, it was a disastrous consequence of a difficult historical legacy that became "Cold Warrized."

On Beijing's side, the "Cold Warrization" began with its conception about establishing sovereignty in Tibet. Because the PLA's advance into Tibet was conceived as the last scene of the "Chinese People's War of Liberation," the legitimacy of the central government's authority in Tibet must be embodied in the justifiability of the planned military operation. Therefore, "liberation of Tibet" became the conclusive note of the march played by the CCP's propaganda machine when the PLA advanced to every corner of China. The note turned out to be rather difficult to play. Several different versions of it appeared (emphases added):

> In February 1950, "Directive of the Party Committee of the 18th Army on the Work of Entering Tibet" informed the army's units: "At present *a small group of feudal rulers of Tibet*, under the direction of *British and American imperialists*, was making plots for betraying the motherland. Tibet is part of China's territory, and the Chinese people cannot tolerate any criminal action that will throw the Tibetan compatriots under the long enslavement by imperialism and feudalism. Under the circumstance, liberation of Tibet already becomes an urgent task."
>
> In April, Zhou Enlai told a group of Tibetan cadres receiving training in Beijing: "The PLA must enter Tibet. Its mission is to drive out *the spies of British and American imperialism* and protect the Tibetan people."
>
> In May, when reporting to Beijing about Tibetans' reactions to Beijing's radio broadcasting in the Tibetan language, the Southwest Bureau suggested that the broadcasting made some statements detrimental to the party's effort of winning over the Dalai clique, such as "The Tibetan people are under a dual oppression by *theocracy and autocracy*, and we will come to liberate you." Mao Zedong agreed and ordered Li Weihan to conduct a close review of the content of the broadcasting.
>
> In November, the Southwest Military-Political Council issued a public notice on the PLA's marching toward Tibet, which included these words: "Deeply concerned about the Tibetan people who have endured many years of oppressions by *British and American*

imperialism and Chiang Kai-shek's reactionary regime, Chairman Mao Zedong of the People's Central Government and Commander-in-Chief Zhu De of the PLA issued a special order to this army for entering Tibet and helping the Tibetan people to rid themselves of such oppressions for ever."[8]

As indicated in the documents and statements above, the CCP hesitated among "imperialism," "feudalism," and "KMT reactionaries," unable to decide which among the three enemies should be the target of the struggle to "liberate Tibet." After settled with a policy of winning over the upper strata of the Tibetans, Beijing could certainly no longer target the actual obstacle to the PLA operations, which was the Tibetan government. In the meantime, neither could the KMT government qualify as the main target of the PLA in Tibet. If facts could be stretched and the KMT regime's feeble office in Lhasa before 1949 be named the symbol of the KMT oppression of Tibet, any KMT influence no longer existed in Tibet after Lhasa expelled all Han in July 1949. Under the circumstances, the political logic of "liberating Tibet" could only be articulated through Beijing's objection to alleged "British and American imperialist" conspiracies regarding Tibet. The Cold War theme in Beijing's Tibet policy was hereby created.

As the successor to the British imperial privileges in Tibet, India concluded a series of agreements with China between 1954 and 1955. These agreements terminated those old rights detrimental to Chinese sovereignty. As a result, imperialist influence of the traditional sense did not exist in Tibet any more.[9] In concert with its general foreign policy in the Cold War arena, Beijing began to treat the United States as the main target of its anti-imperialist struggle in Tibet. After the Korean War began, the CCP propaganda asserted that the United States' intention toward Tibet was the same as that toward Korea and Vietnam, which "is to encircle China militarily and to make preparations for a large-scale aggression against China."[10]

In the early 1950s, however, because of the friendly relationship between China and India, it was difficult to establish how the United States could encircle China from the direction of the Himalayas. In 1954, when talking to Indian Prime Minister Jawaharlal Nehru, Mao Zedong stressed that China and India were in the same front against imperialism. He reported some recent developments around Tibet:

> American airplanes dropped agents from the sky to our interiors. These agents acted in groups of seven to ten people and carried transceivers. Until this date several tens of groups of such agents parachuted to our interior provinces. In Sichun and Tibet's neighbor Qinghai, American airplanes airdropped agents and weapons to local bandits. This situation has proved that a handful people in the American government want to harass us whenever they have the opportunities.[11]

What Mao described to Nehru was part of the covert operations against the PRC conducted jointly by the CIA and the KMT authorities in Taiwan. The airlifting and parachuting were mainly carried out by a "Civil Air Transport" organization under the CIA. After landed in China, very few of these agents were able to elude the Chinese authorities.[12] In this game of cat and mouse with the United States, Mao noticeably did not include Tibet in the geographic scope of the contest.

Therefore, the so-called struggle against American imperialism within Tibet was an invisible one that existed mainly in Beijing's threat perception in the Cold War context. After the seventeen-point agreement was concluded, the CCP Tibet Working Committee (TWC) understood the anti-American struggle in the area as a psychological warfare that "uses anti-imperialism and patriotism as the central themes for stabilizing the upper strata and winning the upper strata from imperialism."[13] In this psywar Beijing strived to convince the Dalai Lama and his followers that the United States or any other foreign government could not possibly provide any meaningful assistance to Tibetan separatism, and that the only future for the Dalai clique was to be of one heart and one mind with the Chinese central government.

After 1956 the Tibetan society became nervous because of the reform question. In November the Dalai Lama and the Panchen Lama traveled to India to participate in the memorial service for the 2,500th anniversary of Buddha's nirvana. A group of Tibetan expatriates in India tried to persuade the Dalai Lama to stay. The episode became the first serious crisis for Beijing's political strategy toward Tibet since 1951. Between November and January of next year, in trying to dissuade the Dalai Lama from the idea of staying in India, Zhou Enlai took time from his busy visit in South Asia and talked to the Dalai Lama three times. Aside from reaffirming Beijing's promise for not carrying out in Tibet in the next six years, Zhou pointed out that the Indian government would not allow its territory to be used by activities against China and for Tibetan independence. As for the United States, Zhou told the Dalai Lama: "The so-called American assistance is a lie. It is so far away from Tibet and cannot cross the land of Indian. So the only thing it can do is to brag."[14]

During the Dalai Lama's visit in India, the CIA did try to contact him. It is however interesting to note that at the time the CIA shared Zhou's opinion about the Dalai Lama's travel plan. The Americans also wanted to persuade the Dalai Lama to return to Tibet and take the lead in Tibetan resistance against the CCP. Then, from the Dalai Lama's brother Gyalo Thondup, the CIA learned that the Tibetan leader was contemplating seeking asylum abroad. Because of the obvious distance between the intentions on the two sides, the CIA decided not to contact the Dalai Lama for the time being.[15] In April 1957, the Dalai Lama returned to Tibet, mainly because of Zhou's effort of suasion.

While using the tactic of belittling the ability of the U.S. government in persuading the Dalai Lama, the CCP leaders actually did not see the Americans as a serious threat. The distance between the United States and Tibet mentioned by Zhou reflected Beijing's view on America's geostrategic position in Asia. A few years later, Mao put the view in clear terms when he tried to convince Indian leaders that China would not become India's enemy:

> The Chinese people's enemy is in the east. American imperialism established many military bases in Taiwan, South Korea, Japan, and the Philippines. All these are aimed at China. Therefore, China's principal attention and struggle orientation are directed toward the east and toward the ferocious and aggressive American imperialism in the western Pacific, but not toward India and all the countries in South and Southeast Asia.[16]

Although in military sense CCP leaders regarded the United States as a threat from the Pacific, they still had reasons to worry about America's psychological influence in Tibet. For many people in Tibet's ruling circles did not see American influence along the Himalayas as a mere mirage. Among the leading members of the Tibetan government, Ngapo Ngawang Jigme had the closest relationship with the CCP. When accompanying the Dalai Lama during his visit in India, Ngapo was exposed to all kinds of information and misinformation.

After returning to Tibet, he immediately approached Tan Guansan, political commissar of the CCP's Tibetan Military District, and made two requests. First, he wanted to become a member of the CCP, and secondly, in the event that the PLA was unable to hold its position in Tibet, he and his family wanted to retreat together with the PLA. At the time Phuntso Wangye was the sole Tibetan member of the TWC. Having learned about the episode, Wangye felt that if a person like Ngapo could believe in the possibility of American aid to anti-communist activities in Tibet, it was not hard to imagine how the others thought. Shortly after, Zhou Enlai met with Ngapo in Qingdao. Now he had to reinforce this Tibetan ally's confidence in Beijing, saying that any so-called American assistance to Tibetan independence "could do no more than using some money to keep the Dalai family alive."[17]

Covert Operations

Such a judgment would not have been far off the mark a few years before. When the PRC was just established, the United States did not have the ability to provide material assistance to anti-communist forces in China interior. According to the CIA's estimate at the time, only by airlifting could American materials be distributed to the remnant anti-communist forces scattered in different locations of China. This was unfeasible not only because airlifting was costly but also because the United States did not have a necessary airbase in the mainland that could serve as a transfer station. Furthermore, an overt air operation by America to aid anti-communist forces in China would be tantamount to an open war against the PRC.[18]

The situation changed drastically after the Korean War began. Through close cooperation between the U.S. military and the CIA, the United States successfully developed an ability of carrying out covert airlifting over long distance. As indicated in Mao's conversation with Nehru, American air force became the principal instrument used by Washington to harass the PRC. In 1957, the U.S. government began to implement covert airdrops into Tibet. The Pakistani military provided effective assistance to this endeavor by turning an airfield in East Pakistan to the Americans as a transfer station.[19] In retrospect, Beijing made an erroneous strategic judgment after the mid-1950s in continuing to view the United States only as an oceanic threat. Beijing's continued view of the United States as a shadow adversary in the psywar for Tibet would have serious consequences in its relations with India when the situation in Tibet deteriorated.

Despite the significant increase of American ability to take actions in the Himalayas, the CIA did not manufacture nor could it control the armed rebellions that were unfolding in Tibet after 1956. The root cause of the conflicts in Tibet was a struggle over "sovereignty" between Beijing and Lhasa. Any foreign involvement could only add fuel to a flame that started within Tibet. Although eager to ignite the flame, the CIA was one step behind the developments inside China. In the summer of 1956, the CIA and Gyalo Thondup worked out a plan to train Tibetan commandos. In February 1957, the first class began in Saipan, the western Pacific island. Beginning with May 1958, the training site was relocated to "Camp Hale" in the mountains of Colorado, the United States. The operation would continue in the next six years.[20]

According to the CIA's initial plan, after receiving training, the Tibetan commandos would penetrate into Tibet and start making secret preparations for a "resistance movement." The so-called resistance movement was a form of covert warfare designed by the CIA to sabotage foreign regimes hostile to the United States in the Cold War. As defined by the CIA,

"Resistance is the weapon deployed by oppressed people to overthrow the oppressive government. Resistance runs the gamut from 0 assets to the ultimate (i.e. downfall of the oppressive power)." If unfolding according to the design, the first stage of the course was to stimulate the will of resistance among a small, selected group. Then they would engage in secret agitations, induction of followers, spreading rumors, political assassinations and so on to cause a ruling crisis for the oppressive regime. At a proper moment open rebellions would be held to complete the last phase, numbered the twelfth in the CIA plan, which was to seize power. The CIA did not plan for Tibet an immediate open rebellion, which could be easily crashed. An underground network of secret cells similar to the CCP's pre-1949 underground organizations and guerrilla units should be developed first, which would have the trained commandos as the backbones and would spread from village to village and from town to town. These cells would get ready and wait for directions from the CIA. Then, in coordinating with the need of American foreign policy, the CIA would give the signal at the right moment for a general uprising to begin in Tibet.[21]

Such a textbook model of "resistance movement" was a far cry from the social and political conditions of Tibet. In October 1957, when the CIA dropped the first group of Tibetan agents back to Tibet, the armed conflict between Khampa fighters and the PLA already began and would continue to unfold according to its own logic. Such a situation certainly did not discourage Washington, and the CIA seized the opportunity to wage a covert war against the PRC. In the next twelve years, America's secret war in Tibet included the following activities:

- From 1957 to 1961, 250 tons of military supplies and 49 Tibetan agents were airdropped into Tibet. Among these agents, two were captured alive, ten escaped into India, and the rest died in battles.
- After the Lhasa uprising happened, the CIA monitored the PLA's activities in Tibet and provided informed to the Dalai Lama's group through two Tibetan agents, and helped the group get the Indian government's permission to cross the border and seek asylum in India.
- Between 1961 and 1969, the CIA provided weapons and financial assistance to a Tibetan military base in Mustang of Nepal, and directed the Tibetan fighters to launch raids into Tibet, collect intelligence information, and sabotage China's transportation lines.[22]

American assistance did not change the predicament of the Tibetan rebels. A CIA study dated 1963 estimated that the PLA controlled three transportation lines entering Tibet and on average could send in 1,600 tons of materials per day in a year. The yearly total would be 584,000 tones. These figures overestimated the Chinese authorities' ability of transportation in Tibet. During the entire year of 1959, the Chinese authorities sent 31,410 tons of goods and 10,875 troops and personnel of other categories into Tibet. In that year 1,149 trucks of a total 5,238 tones of carrying capacity were in operation. By 1963 the number of trucks increased to 1,898, with 8,838 tones of capacity. In the meantime, the traditional way of transportation with horses and yaks was also in use. In different years it transported goods ranging from 12% to 30% of those by the trucks. Such ability could not possibly reach the level estimated by the CIA.[23] Still, in comparison, the total tonnage airdropped into Tibet by the CIA was insignificant.

At one point the number of Tibetan rebels reached 30,000. The question as to how to allocate the small amount of American materials often became a cause of factional frictions among the Tibetan fighters. Within the U.S. government an idea was contemplated that America's superior air force be used to interrupt the lifelines of the PLA over land. The idea was soon abandoned because Washington never intended to start a war with the PRC over Tibet.[24] Meanwhile, because American assistance was delivered to the rebels via covert operations, Washington could not take advantage of its involvement in a psywar fashion to frustrate Beijing. To most of the Tibetan fighters, American assistance was an unverifiable rumor and had only a dubious value in enhancing Tibetan morale.[25]

In 1959, the Dalai Lama's exile in India could have been a windfall to Washington's Cold War propaganda. Yet the opportunity did not generate an effect as expected by American leaders. Mindful of its general psywar strategy directed toward all communist countries, the U.S. government hoped that the world public opinion could be led to understand the Tibetan affair as the Tibetan people's completely spontaneous resistance against the communist regime of China. Therefore, after the Lhasa uprising took place, Washington chose to maintain a "strategic silence" about the Tibetan situation. Secretly, the CIA tried to enlist the Dalai Lama's help to America's Cold War effort as a leader of the Buddhists throughout the world. But during his long exile, the Tibetan leader never expressed such an intention.[26]

Even though the CIA did not manufacture a Tibetan resistance movement, its covert operations implicated Washington as the principal foreign influence interfering in Tibet. Strangely, the events in Tibet after the mid-1950s did not cause ripples in the already troubled waters of the Sino–American relationship. Instead, they became the catalysts for the changed dynamics in China's relations with India and the Soviet Union. In the next few years, a "friendly neighbor" in the southwest and a "socialist brotherly state" in the north successively turned into China's enemies. As a result, the international geopolitical relations of South Asia and Eurasia changed drastically, and a cold war of a different kind began. Available CIA documents have so far not indicated the agency's taking credit for causing these changes. In the 1960s, the CIA indeed boasted that the Sino–Soviet split was a byproduct of America's firm policy toward both communist powers. Regarding China, the CIA's view was that American policy prevented the CCP from taking Taiwan and thus frustrated Mao's dream of "carrying the revolution to the end," and that Beijing's frustrations led to its misgivings toward Moscow. Yet, in the CIA analyses of the Sino–Indian and Sino–Soviet relations in this period, it was not even hinted that America's covert operations in Tibet might have an impact on these relations.[27] Having no sense about how the Lhasa uprising vexed Beijing and caused Beijing to change its policy toward India, intelligence analyses by the U.S. government appeared to overlook completely the importance of the Tibetan question to Beijing, and how it affected Beijing's international strategy. To American policy makers, the CIA's Tibetan operation could at most cause some tactical difficulties to Beijing, and therefore the U.S. government was prepared to cut the cost and wash its hands in the involvement anytime.

During the Cold War years, the United States engaged the PRC in overt confrontations along the western Pacific coast and covert operations in the Himalayas. Washington's choices of policy instruments in the two directions indicated that the Cold War did not fundamentally alter the general rules of international competitions. Until 1972, the U.S. government treated Beijing as its principal adversary in the Cold War struggle for Asia, resorting to actions such as containment, blockade, and sabotage. In the meantime, Washington never challenged "China" as an international political entity accepted by the international society since the end of World War II. Whereas the Tibetans were waging a resistance against the China-Han-Communism trinity, Washington never opposed China's sovereignty in Tibet. During the first half of the Cold War, Washington maintained an anti-CCP alliance with the

KMT regime in Taiwan and continued to support a "Nationalist China." In other words, to American leaders, their containment effort against international communism was in concert with their protection of the existent "international relation culture." Such political connotations of the Cold War rendered it unlikely for the U.S. government to oppose in principle the historical transformation of Chinese territoriality, incorporation of Tibet into the PRC being part of the transformation.

From Friends to Foes

Beginning with the mid-1950s, the United States was waging a small proxy war against China along the Himalayas. But America's escalated Cold War in Tibet was not the direct cause of these changes. The CIA's Tibet operation was conducted in utter secrecy. To conceal America's involvement, the weapons airdropped into Tibet were mainly those made by the British in World War I. At the time these were commonly used in South Asian countries. During the four years of the CIA's airlifting, only once an airplane received fire from light weapons on the ground.[28] After 1960 in several occasions the PLA seized airdropped supplies from the rebels and captured a small number of parachuted Tibetan agents. These should sooner or later lead to Beijing's realization of America's covert operations.[29] But until the end of the Cold War the PRC government kept silence about this matter. It remains one of the puzzles in the Cold War history exactly when leaders in Beijing discovered the CIA's operations in Tibet and why they would not utter a word of protest against the United States.

In the meantime, the Tibetan question became a catalyst in changing international dynamics in the Asian Continent. After the Lhasa uprising, Beijing changed its anti-American orientation in Tibet and began to target India, which until the time had maintained a largely friendly relationship with China. This was the first major reorientation in China's Cold War foreign policy, a precedent to Beijing's switching sides between the Soviet Union and the United States more than a decade later.

On July 10, 1958, in a note to the Indian government, the Chinese Ministry of Foreign Affairs pointed out that American and KMT agents were undermining the Sino–Indian friendship in using Kalimpong of India as a base for launching armed rebellion in Tibet. The note asked the Indian government to stop such activities in Kalimpong. A few days later, in a directive to the TWC, the CCP Central Committee revealed that in the light of recently captured evidence, among the leaders of the Tibetan rebellions in Sichuan, Qinghai, and Gansu "there were indeed agents of imperialism, especially American imperialism, and the counterrevolutionary clique in Taiwan." On March 21, 1959, the day after Beijing discovered the Dalai Lama's escape, the General Political Department of the PLA issued a directive on suppressing the Tibetan rebellion. It stated: "The betrayal of the nation committed by the Tibetan reactionary clique was a planned and organized counterrevolutionary action instigated, supported, and supplied by American and other imperialisms and by other foreign reactionary forces."[30] These diplomatic and internal documents indicated that for a while before and after the Lhasa uprising, the CCP maintained its Cold War perception and continued to view the United States as the principal foreign threat as far as Tibet was concerned.

Beijing did harbor unhappiness toward the "Indian friends." During the Lhasa uprising, protesters in the streets handed a "proclamation of independence" to the Indian consulate and asked Indian officials present to make contact with Kalimpong and to notify the United Nations on their behalf.[31] The development caused Zhou Enlai to assert at a politburo meeting of March 17: "This event involved the Indian authorities. The British and American governments were very active behind the scene and pushed the Indian authorities to the forefront. The headquarters of the rebellion is in Kalimpong of India." For the time being, however, Mao Zedong decided that India should not be openly implicated for now and the account would be settled later after India did enough injustice to China. In the following month, therefore, China's propaganda continued to promote Chinese–Indian friendship. At most the Chinese media only expressed some regret that in India certain quarters made "statements very incompatible with the Chinese-Indian friendship."[32]

On April 18, the Dalai Lama issued a written statement at Tezpur, India. The event became a turning point in terms of Beijing's public attitude toward the Indian government. The Dalai Lama now suggested that in 1951 his government accepted China's "suzerainty" under duress but did not enjoy any meaningful autonomy afterwards. He blamed Beijing for the collapse of the seventeen-point agreement, and characterized his exile into India as an act of free will for his personal safety.

A few days later, the Chinese media issued a rebuttal to the Dalai statement in the form of a political commentary by the Xinhua News Agency. The commentary was however revised and finalized by Mao himself. The commentary attacked the Dalai statement as an expression of imperialist aggressors' intention and will. It reasoned that the writing of the statement showed a "European or quasi-European style," and therefore it must not have been drafted by the Dalai Lama himself but by a treacherous group fostered by the British in Tibet. Now, the commentary continued, "Indian expansionists inherited this inglorious British legacy."[33] The next day, Mao declared that it was the time to launch a concentrated propaganda counterattack against India. In a written remark dated April 25, Mao explained the reorientation in propaganda:

> We have used the statement for a long time that "imperialism, Chiang Kai-shek's bandit gang, and foreign reactionaries are instigating rebellions in Tibet and interfering in China's internal affairs." This statement is completely inaccurate and must be immediately changed into, "acting in collusion, British imperialists and Indian expansionists openly interfere in China's domestic politics and attempt to take over Tibet." The whole country should follow the line of the political reporter's commentary on the 18th in making statements, targeting directly Britain and India without equivocation.[34]

In the new line of propaganda, "British imperialism" was named to maintain an anti-imperialist rhetoric, and the real target was "Indian expansionists." In the next two weeks, all China's propaganda apparatuses blasted India. On May 7, Mao called for a time-out. At a politburo conference a few days later, Mao explained that when criticizing the bad side of Nehru, we should also remember his good side and give him a way out. Mao appeared to demonstrate his mastery of propaganda warfare, attacking and retreating at will. But, neither Mao nor other CCP leaders would be able to reverse the course of the Sino–Indian relationship that was going downhill rapidly.

Mao's decision on falling out with India may have been based on these considerations. First, the evidence of Indian inference in the Tibetan affairs seemed clear. Although Beijing always held the United States as the main culprit of inciting troubles in Tibet, aside from some information about American agents in Kalimpong, there was no direct evidence that Washington was involved in the Tibetan rebellion. Before the Lhasa uprising, therefore,

Beijing's allegations about American plots in Tibet mainly reflected CCP leaders' assumptions in the Cold War context. The CIA's effectiveness in ensuring the secrecy of its operations in Tibet and Washington's "strategic silence" after the Lhasa uprising prevented Beijing from factually implicating the United States for causing the collapse of the Tibetan situation. In contrast, Indian media and government officials always openly complained about the developments in Tibet; the Indian consulate in Lhasa did receive antigovernment protestors; and the Indian government also failed to weed out the irregularities in Kalimpong. These facts easily created an impression in Beijing that India was involved in Tibetan affairs. The two CIA-trained Tibetan agents accompanying Dalai's flight into India were identified by Beijing's own intelligence and by foreign press as "Indian telegraph operators."[35] In addition, in the end of 1958 Nehru informed Zhou Enlai that the "McMahon Line," viewed as illegal by the Chinese, should be regarded as the legitimate border between the two countries. To Chinese leaders these facts were enough to prove that the Indian government inherited Britain's imperialist legacies and was behind the Tibetan rebellion for achieving its own territorial ambitions about in Tibet.[36]

Secondly, the statement by the Dalai Lama enraged Beijing. As discussed in Chapter 8, in the years following the seventeen-point agreement, Beijing could neither change the Dalai Lama nor cut the religious-political ties between him and ordinary Tibetans. Beijing's effort to incorporate Tibet into the political obit of the new China stalled for years. Ironically, Beijing's impasse was solved by the Tibetan rebellion. The CCP leadership may have actually expected such a result: since the Dalai Lama could not be reformed, the best solution would be the disappearance of the Dalai factor from the political equation about Tibet, provided that Beijing could be cleared of any responsibility for such occurrence. During the Dalai Lama's visit in India in 1956, Mao said at a party conference that "a couple tied together cannot become husband and wife" and he would not be sad if Dalai did not return. When the Lhasa uprising took place, Mao immediately anticipated the Dalai Lama's exile and almost welcomed such a result.[37]

Before his departure for India, the Dalai Lama exchanged a few letters with Tan Guansan, the top PLA official in Lhasa at the time. In these letters he expressed displeasure about the turmoil in Lhasa and hinted his lack of freedom of movement. After the Dalai Lama went into exile, these letters enabled Beijing to allege that he was abducted by treacherous rebels. The rhetoric proved most useful for Beijing to pacify the Tibetan society in the wake of the upheaval.[38] But when the Dalai Lama's Tespur statement was issued, it seriously undermined Beijing's effort to maintain the story that until his exile the Dalai Lama was on good terms with the CCP. At the time it was already too late to reconsider the wisdom of letting the Dalai Lama out. Neither could Beijing change its official line about his abduction. The Indian government, therefore, had to be blamed for the Tespur statement. In early May, Mao talked to the Panchen Lama and other Tibetan notables. He described the Dalai Lama as a "wise man" caught "in a very bad circumstance." Mao told the Tibetans that the Indian government must assume the responsibility for Dalai's statement because, even if the Indians did not write the document themselves, they approved it.[39] As the situation unfolded in this manner, the Dalai factor became the key issue that tipped the balance of the Chinese–Indian relationship.

The geographic and cultural factors made India the only big country that could exert direct influence on Tibet. Furthermore, history made India the successor of the British imperialist interests in Tibet. These conditions were behind the reasons for Beijing's strong reaction to the Indian government's any criticism about the Tibetan situation. Whatever form the Indian criticism might be, it could not avoid touching a raw nerve of every Chinese central government since the beginning of the twentieth century—the question of Chinese sovereignty. For a moment all the grievances against British imperialism accumulated during China's arduous course of modern transformation were vented out toward India.

Yet, although in respect to the Tibetan situation CCP leaders appeared to let their nationalist temperament overwhelm their Cold War mentality, Beijing's quarrel with India did not diverge far from its general Cold War orientation. Mao and his associates never viewed China's relations with India as merely a bilateral dealing between two national states. Leaders in Beijing believed that a clamorous quarrel with India over Tibet would actually enhance China's international struggle against the United States. This was the third consideration behind Mao's demarche toward India.

In the Mao era, the tactics of the PRC foreign policy grew out of the CCP's seasoned political strategies accumulated in its domestic revolutionary struggles. United front was such a typical stratagem. As perceived by the CCP, because of its Asian identity and colonized past, India was a natural member of the international united front against Western imperialism headed by the United States. In April 1955, at the Bandung Conference the Chinese and the Indian governments co-sponsored the five principles of peaceful coexistence designed for facilitating relations among countries of different political systems. This became the high peak of the two governments' cooperation in uniting Asian and African countries. At the same time the CCP applied its class-analysis approach to political groupings in the international scene. Accordingly, India's international stance was determined by the class identity of the Indian leadership. Mao put Nehru into the category of "Indian bourgeois middle-of-the-roaders." The CCP's established policy toward such wavering "middle-of-the-roaders" was to unite through criticism.

After the Dalai statement appeared in India, Mao suggested that criticism of Nehru must be sharp. There was no need to fear upsetting him or falling out with him. And the struggle against Nehru must be carried to the end in order to achieve unity with him. Such a seemingly self-contradictory "struggle philosophy" had a complete set of inner logic of the CCP thinking. The main reasoning was about the relationship between "part" and "whole" of matters. In May 1959, Mao deployed such logic in finalizing an important letter from the Chinese Ministry of Foreign Affairs to the India government. In the letter, Mao explained to the Indian government that the Sino–Indian disagreement over Tibet involved China's internal affairs and sovereignty, over which China could not make concessions. Yet Mao also appeared conciliatory in suggesting that this disagreement only involved a "temporary" and "partial" problem and should not damage the two nations' overall cooperation in international affairs.[40] If Mao expected that China's "sharp" struggle against India could result in drawing the "middle of the roader" closer to the socialist camp in the Cold War, he completely miscalculated. The Indian government did not receive China's struggle against it calmly, even though this was just a "partial" struggle.

When applied to international relations, Mao's logic proved counterproductive. This was admitted in the 1960 annual report of the Chinese Ministry of Foreign Affairs. The ministry used Mao's idea about "part" and "whole" as the guideline to all China's foreign relations perceived as international struggles. Thus, the report identified separately the United States, the Soviet Union, India, and Indonesia, all having problems with China in different senses, as targets of China's diplomatic struggles in overall, partial, and sub-partial situations. India was the main target of Chinese diplomatic struggle in South and Southeast Asia, and India's anti-China policy was the central focus of Chinese diplomatic struggle during the first half of 1960. In the meantime, the struggle against India must be subordinated to the struggles against the United States and the Soviet Union. In reality, such an orderly, stratified pyramid of international struggles often resulted in confusion. As admitted by the report, in the execution of foreign policies, two recurring mistakes were to confuse the relationship between "struggle" and "unity" and to "see trees only but not the forest."[41]

In the final analysis, the confusion in Beijing's decisions about foreign policy priorities reflected an omnipresent contradiction between the CCP leaders' Cold War mentality informed by ideology and those concrete foreign policy issues that the new Chinese national state had to deal with. When the 1960s began, the Sino–Indian relationship, just like the Sino–Soviet relationship, was suffering from an expanding crack caused by the two sides' conflicting national interests. These long and entrenched interests would eventually ruin the "common welfare" of the Cold War era based on supranational and artificial groupings such as "Asian-African unity" and "socialist camp." After the second Taiwan Strait crisis of 1958 passed, the Sino–American relations entered what Mao called a period of "Cold War coexistence." Except their indirect contest in the Vietnam War, China and the United States engaged each other only in mutual verbal abuses through propaganda. Yet, when China's "overall" Cold War with the United States became stabilized, its "partial" confrontation with India began to escalate rapidly.

From Comrades to Adversaries

Soon after the Tibetan rebellion, the political relationship between China and India deteriorated into armed conflicts along their borders. Since 1954 the Indian government had already established control over territories south of the McMahon line. In April 1959, the CCP Central Military Commission ordered the PLA units in Tibet to "seal the border immediately, control important roads and passages close to the unsettled Chinese-Indian border along the McMahon line, construct defense works, and prevent treacherous bandits from crossing the border in both directions."[42] With these measures, the border between the two new national states of Asia formally became a line of confrontation. Four months later, the first armed conflict between the two sides took place. This so-called Langjiu incident was only the first shot of a much larger border war that would break out in October 1962.

When visiting India in 1954, Zhou Enlai said in a public speech that China and India were connected with a common border of nearly 3,000 kilometers, and that "century after century, history has recorded peaceful cultural dialogues and economic exchanges between our two countries but has never recorded wars and hatred."[43] Zhou's statement ignored the fact that the two countries began to share a common border only as a result of transformation of territoriality that happened to both in the nineteenth and twentieth centuries. Actually, not until 1959 did the cartographic connection between the two countries become substantiated with human contact. But the people involved were soldiers, and the controversial border soon became a witness of hostilities and animosities.

A basic fact in China's international standing in the 1950s was that the PRC was a member of the "socialist camp." To Beijing, this international identity was firmly established when the PRC concluded an alliance with the Soviet Union. Understandably, the deterioration of the Sino–Indian relationship caused concerns in Moscow. "Socialist camp" was a unique product of the international politics of the Cold War era. Members of the camp upheld "leader principle" (the Soviet Union as the head), emphasized the "brotherly inter-party" relationship (common ideology) among them, promoted a new type of interstate relationship (internationalism over nationalism), and understood world affairs from a class-struggle perspective. These features made the socialist camp alien to the larger international community whose members followed the usual norms in their mutual relations. The ruling parties of the socialist countries were convinced that in possessing a superior socio-political system and practicing just and reasonable interstate relations, the socialist camp would eventually supercede the current international system of the "bourgeois nation-states." In practice, however, this ideal for reforming the international order was incompatible with these socialist countries' own ingrained nation-state character. The internal strife within the socialist camp never really stopped, and it was eventually the reason for a fundamental restructuring of the Cold War power relations.

By the time of the first border conflict between China and India, Beijing and Moscow had already experienced their quarrels over the so-called joint fleet and long-wave radio stations.[44] In early October 1959, Nikita Khrushchev led a Soviet delegation to meet with the CCP leadership in Beijing. The two sides engaged each other in tense arguments over the recent Taiwan Strait crisis and the Sino–Indian conflict. The Soviet side accused Beijing for taking a bellicose stand over the Taiwan question and risking the danger of provoking an unnecessary war with the United States. In addition, the Soviets suggested that Beijing made serious mistakes in postponing reforms in Tibet and failing to intercept the Dalai Lama's flight into exile. They also attributed the responsibility to Beijing for causing the Sino–Indian conflict, contending that the CCP's India policy created opportunities for American imperialism.

Not surprisingly, Mao and his associates refused to accept any of these criticisms, reciprocating the Soviets by labeling their attitude as opportunism. The Chinese side stressed that both Taiwan and Tibet were China's internal affairs and China could not possibly retreat from its principled stand. CCP leaders wondered why, as a "big brother," the Soviet Union should make no distinction between right and wrong and take the side of the bourgeois India in the question of the Sino–Indian conflict. During the talks Khrushchev invoked the idea of "the Soviet Union as the head of the socialist camp." He intended to explain why the Soviets "said things ordinary guests would not have said," meaning that the Soviet side criticized Beijing in the "big brother" capacity and on the basis of "communist principled stand."[45]

These exchanges best illustrated the contradiction between the internationalist principles supposedly governing the internal relationships of the socialist camp and the national stands held respectively by Chinese and Soviet leaders. It has been suggested that failing to support Beijing in its 1959 confrontation with India, the Soviets established a precedent of not basing Soviet foreign policies on the "class stand." Three years later, during the Cuban missile crisis, Beijing would reciprocate in not only denying Moscow a firm support but also sharply criticizing Khrushchev's handling of the situation.[46] After these scuffles between Beijing and Moscow, the socialist camp on one side of the Cold War disintegrated.

In view of the tensions between the "internationalist norms" upheld in theory by members of the socialist camp and their "nation-state" behaviors in practice, the Sino–Soviet split could hardly be avoided.[47] Yet, so far as the PRC foreign policy was concerned, the combination between Mao's revolutionary theories and the national temperament of the Chinese state produced rather extreme effects. In the spring of 1962, Wang Jiaxiang, head of the CCP Central Liaison Department, made an effort to change China's situation of facing enemies in all directions. He was especially concerned about the prospect of China's splitting with the Russians and bearing the brunt of American animosities. He proposed that in handling interstate relations, China should avoid falling into a vicious circle of mutual attacks and counter-attacks. Regarding India, Wang suggested that Nehru not be identified as an enemy of the Chinese nation and the border disputes be solved through negotiations. Wang made his proposals at a bad time. Because of the economic difficulties caused by the Great Leap Forward, decline of China's security along the borders, and nervous relationship among CCP's top leaders, a sharp "turn to the left" in Chinese diplomacy was already underway. Wang's proposals only invited personal attacks.[48]

In August, Wang's ideas, characterized as "three kindness [toward imperialism] and one fewness [toward revolutionary movements]" by Mao, was repudiated at a working conference of the CCP Central Committee, which was followed by the Sino–Indian border war in October. Soon after the border war began, in an internal speech Zhou Enlai rejected the opinion that Chinese diplomacy had created enemies in all directions, asserting that the United States remained the main target of China's international struggles. Zhou asserted: "In this struggle against the Indian reactionaries, we still made the United States the most conspicuous [target]." In other words, at the time the distinction between the "partial" struggle against India and the "overall" struggle against the United States no longer existed in Beijing's foreign policy.[49]

As the Sino–Indian conflicts were unfolding, as far as China was concerned, the foreign policies of India and the United States converged. Thus, the difficult historical legacies in the bilateral relations between China and India became intertwined with the Cold War international contests. When the PRC was just founded, Washington complained that India's neutral stand in the Cold War was tantamount to appeasement toward communist countries. After the Sino–Indian war began, the CIA pointed out with satisfaction that a "profound change has taken place in India's outlook." "A conviction of Peiping's [Beijing] fundamental hostility and perfidy has emerged among virtually all levels of Indian opinion in the past few months. . . . At the same time, there is general gratification with the sympathy and support received from the US and the British Commonwealth and a growing realization that the preservation of India's freedom will be heavily dependent on the West." In the Sino–Indian conflict and Sino–Soviet rupture Washington also saw opportunities for the United States to "take a tougher stance" against China and for American–Soviet collaboration in dealing with the PRC. The CIA estimated that as of the end of 1962, the so-called Aid India Club, including the United States and the Soviet Union, had committed totally $2.5 billion for India's economic development in the next two years.[50]

Even before the Sino–Indian border war began, Zhou Enlai lamented that peaceful coexistence between China and India would soon be replaced by a "long armed coexistence."[51] The war certainly dispersed what imagined by the CCP leadership as a cross-Himalaya united front against American imperialism. For a moment, what emerged along the Himalayas was an American–Indian consortium for the purpose of containing China. The Sino–Indian border war would be over shortly, but the Himalayas would remain a second front for China's Cold War in many years to come.

* * *

After the Sino–Soviet split became a fact of life beyond any doubt, a CIA analysis pointed out:

> Relations between the Soviet Union and Communist China have deteriorated so far in the past ten years that we can say with validity that they are now engaged in their own "cold war." . . . The present rupture signifies that Communist ideology has not only failed to overcome nationalism within the bloc, but has indeed aggravated such sentiment.[52]

To policy makers in the West who in the early Cold War years viewed the communist bloc as a monolith, this estimate by the CIA constituted a revolutionary change of perceptions. But what "Chinese nationalism" revealed in Beijing's Cold War diplomacy was much more complex than that demonstrated in the Sino–Soviet rupture. In the historical events discussed in this chapter, Beijing's policies toward Tibet, India, the United States, and the Soviet Union may be understood at once as the CCP's Cold War behavior and as historical steps of China as a national state. In the latter frame of reference, Beijing's Tibetan and Indian problems were about the establishment of China's "domestic sovereignty" and demarcation of China's "geo-body"; its dealings with the United States and the Soviet Union reflected China's normative relationships with two opposing international societies.

Since the nineteenth century, the Chinese state has gone through a process of structural, territorial, and behavioral reorientation replete with contradictions and conflicts. No longer able to sustain its traditional imperial system inconsistent with the dominant Western international relation culture, the weak Qing Empire was compelled to adapt itself to the modern international environment. Once China adopted the prevailing international relation culture, it began to transform into a national state of explicit sovereignty and definite bordered territory, and began to participate in international competitions in the modern sense. As discussed in this chapter, China consolidated its modern sovereignty in Tibet at a special juncture of history, or an era of China's continuous revolution and the world's bipolarization. The process therefore brought about rather violent confrontations and conflicts. The ascendance of a communist movement to power in China, the rise of India as a newly independent national state, the continuation of Tibet's unique culture and medieval systems, and the entry of the United States as a destabilizing foreign influence—all these forces converged on Tibet. The result could only be an extremely complex, confusing, and tangled contest. In this contest the PRC managed to hold its bottom line of preserving sovereignty in Tibet, but in doing so Beijing paid a price in giving up its initial intention of seeking interethnic harmony in the region. The ensuing deterioration of the Sino–Indian relationship seems to have been caused by the two governments' disagreement about how their common borders should be drawn. The dispute actually reflected historical "progress" in the two countries' relations—those vague arrangements over buffer zones of the imperialist age were replaced with sovereign claims over clearly defined boundaries between two national states.

After 1959, in implementing "democratic reforms," Beijing injected communist ideology into the Buddhist Tibetan society. This communist expansion into Tibet, however, did not provoke the United States to act as it did in Korea, Vietnam, and the Taiwan Strait. Leaving aside other reasons, Washington's moderation should be understood against the fact that Beijing's consolidation of "domestic sovereignty" in Tibet did not violate the established international norm of differentiating domestic from foreign affairs. Beijing's abrogation of the Tibetan status quo ended the last historical legacy of the late Qing's "loose-rein" type of "dependency" policy. As a state entity, China hereby accomplished one more stride in nationalizing territoriality and achieved the same qualities as European or American actors in the international scene.

A historical coincident is that China's "becoming national" was completed in a time when enemies and friends in international politics were identified with supranational ideologies. Thus, ironically, it was China's supposed soul mate in the socialist camp, the Soviet Union that openly questioned Beijing's Tibet policy and the anti-Indian consequences. As indicated in the CCP–Soviet quarrels over Tibet and India, the so-called principled basic line of the PRC diplomacy was framed by a national-state temperament that had taken shape since the nineteenth century, not informed by the communist dogmas that became prevalent in China after 1949. In this perspective, it becomes evident that Mao's political adaptability or the CCP's expedient tactics for the sake of the Cold War were only part of the explanation for the PRC's estrangement from the "great socialist family" headed by the Soviet Union in the 1960s and its "tacit alliance" with the United States in the 1970s. Also at work was more profound historical logic—China's normative direction in international relations already afoot long before these events.

This is not to depreciate the role of ideology in Beijing's foreign policy. In the Cold War era, communist ideology indeed loomed large in China's state policies. For instance, a principal difference between the KMT policy toward Tibet before 1949 and Beijing's policy was their different attitudes toward Tibetan Buddhism. Unable to affect the Tibetans with the Three People's Principles or to coerce Lhasa with force, the KMT regime seized Buddhism as a cultural bridge for maintaining its tenuous ties with the Tibetan society. In contrast, in the 1950s the CCP's tolerance of the Tibetan lamaist leadership was temporary and expedient.[53] Other examples of ideological functions were Beijing's "class perception" in understanding the United States and India and its initial illusion about Moscow and the "socialist camp." In studying China's official behavior after 1949, the difficulty is to decide, among China's traditional culture and history, modern nationalism, and communist ideology, which one and in what occasion was predominant. So far as China's Cold War international behavior was concerned, if Chinese culture was an omnipresent "gene," then Chinese nationalism was the fundamental character forged during China's adaptation to the modern international environment, and the communist ideology, which did not influence Chinese diplomacy until 1949, was more instrumental than characteristic in Beijing's coping with the international Cold War climate.

Notes

1. Intelligence Handbook, "The Deterioration of Sino-Soviet Relations 1956–1966," 4/22/1966, CIA FOIA F-2000–01330, http://www.foia.cia.gov; Dai Chaowu, "India's Foreign Policy, Great Power Relations, and the Chinese-Indian Border Wars in 1962", in Niu Dayong and Shen Zhihua, eds., *Lengzhan yu Zhongguo de Zhoubian Guanxi* (The Cold War and China's relations with the neighboring regions) (Beijing: Shijie Zhishi Chubanshe, 2004), 487–556.
2. Group on Composing the History of the Self-Defense and Counter-Offensive Operations along the Chinese-Indian Borders, *Zhong Yin Bianjing Ziwei Fanji Zuozhanshi* (History of the self-defense and counter-offensive operations along the Chinese-Indian borders) (Beijing: Junshi Kexue Chubanshe, 1994), 109, 454; Yang Gongsu, *Zhongguo Fandui Waiguo Qinlue Ganshe Xizang Difangshi* (History of China's opposition to foreign aggressions and interferences in Tibet) (Beijing: Zhongguo Zangxue Chubanshe,), 318; Wang Hongwei, *Ximalayashan Qingjie: Zhong Yin Guanxi Yanjiu* (The Himalayan complex: a study of the Chinese-Indian relations) (Beijing: Zhongguo Zangxue Chubanshe, 1998), 129–151.
3. CIA memorandum, "Historical Sketch of the Sino-Indian Dispute," 12/18/1962, CIA FOIA EO-1997–00408, http://www.foia.cia.gov.
4. Neville Maxwell, *India's China War* (London: Jonathan Cape Limited, 1970), 67.
5. Francine R. Frankel, "Introduction," in Francine R. Frankel and Harry Harding, eds., *The India-China Relationship: What the United States Needs to Know* (New York and

Washington, D.C.: Columbia University Press and Woodrow Wilson Center Press, 2004), 16–17.

6. Zhou Enlai's speech at the forum on the establishment of the Guangxi Zhuang Autonomous Region held by the second committee of the National Political Consultative Conference, March 25, 1957, *Zhou Enlai he Xizang*, 156.
7. Martine Stuart-Fox, *A Short History of China and Southeast Asia: Tribute, Trade and Influence* (Crows Nest, Australia: Allen & Unwin, 2003), 5, suggests that "international relations culture" includes conceptions about values, behavior norms, and expected effects of international interactions commonly endorsed by states involved in such interactions.
8. *Heping Jiefang Xizang*, 59, 105–106; *Zhou Enlai yu Xizang*, 111; *Mao Zedong Xizang* Wenxuan, 14.
9. Yang Gongsu, *Zhongguo Fandui Waiguo Qinlue Ganshe Xizang Difangshi*, 262–270.
10. "Refute America's Conspiracy toward Tibet", *People's Daily*, November 22, 1950, *Heping Jiefang Xizang*, 182–183.
11. Mao Zedong's conversation with Nehru, October 19, 1954, Ministry of Foreign Affairs and CCP Central Office of Documentary Research, *Mao Zedong Waijiao Wenxuan* (Selected manuscripts of Mao Zedong on diplomacy) (Beijing: Zhongyang Wenxian Chubanshe, 1994), 164–165.
12. Kenneth Conboy and James Morrison, *The CIA's Secret War in Tibet* (Lawrence: University Press of Kansas, 2002), 37–38.
13. *Zhonggong Xizang Dangshi Dashiji*, 43.
14. *Zhou Enlai yu Xizang*, 329–330.
15. Conboy and Morrison, *CIA's Secret War in Tibet*, 36.
16. Mao Zedong's added words to the Ministry of Foreign Affairs' written reply to a speech made by an official of the Indian Foreign Ministry, May 13, 1959, *Mao Zedong Waijiao Wenxuan*, 376.
17. Goldstein, Sherap, and Siebenschuh, *A Tibetan Revolutionary*, 216; *Zhonggong Xizang Dangshi Dashiji*, 77.
18. ORE 76–49, "Survival Potential of Residual Non-Communist Regimes in China," 10/19/1949, National Intelligence Council *Tracking the Dragon: National Intelligence Estimates on China During the Era of Mao, 1948–1976* (Pittsburg: Government Printing Office).
19. John Kenneth Knaus, *Orphans of the Cold War: America and the Tibetan Struggle for Survival* (New York: PublicAffairs, 1999), 46; Conboy and Morrison, *The CIA's Secret War in Tibet*, 75; Mikel Dunham, *Buddha's Warriors: The Story of CIA-Backed Tibetan Freedom Fighters, the Chinese Invasion, and the Ultimate Fall of Tibet* (New York: Jeremy P. Tarcher / Penguin, 2004), 221–222.
20. Knaus, *Orphans of the Cold War*, 137–139, 155; Dunham, *Buddha's Warriors*, 197–199.
21. "Letter of Instruction," 12/23/1953, CIA FOIA SS-2003–0002, http://www.foia.cia.gov; Conboy and Morrison, *The CIA's Secret War in Tibet*, 74; Dunham, *Buddha's Warriors*, 242.
22. Knaus, *Orphans of the Cold War*, 153, 168, 233, 246; Dunham, *Buddha's Warriors*, 263, 300–301; Conboy and Morrison, *The CIA's Secret War in Tibet*, 145–163.
23. *Xizang Gonglu Jiaotong Shi* (History of transportation of Tibetan highways), Compilation Committee for *Xizang Jiaotong Shi*, comp. (Beijing: Renmin Jiaotong Chubanshe, 1999), 182, 214; *Xizang Zizhiqu Zhi: Gonglu Jiaotong Zhi* (Annals of the Tibetan Autonomous

Region: annals of highways and transportation), Compilation Committee for *Xizang Zizhiqu Zhi*, comp. (Beijing: Zhongguo Zangxue Chubanshe, 2007), 130–132.

24. Studies in Intelligence, "Tonnage through Tibet," 4/1/1963, CIA FOIA, CSI-2001–00018, http://www.foia.cia.gov; Conboy and Morrison, *CIA's Secret War in Tibet*, 99–100.
25. Dunham, *Buddha's Warriors*, 251, 308, 337–339; Knaus, *Orphans of the Cold War*, 148–149.
26. Knaus, *Orphans of the Cold War*, 179–181; Dunham, *Buddha's Warriors*, 217.
27. NIE 100–3-60, "Sino-Soviet Relations," 8/9/1960, CIA FOIA, F-1997–00812; CIA memo, "Implications of the Sino-Soviet Rupture for the US," 7/18/1963, CIA FOIA, EO-1998–00565; Intelligence Handbook, "The Deterioration of Sino-Soviet Relations, 1956–1966," CIA FOIA, F-2000–01330; SNIE 13/31–2-62, "The Sino-Indian Conflict: Outlook and Implications," 12/14/1962; CIA memo, "Historical Sketch of the Sino-Indian Dispute," 12/18/1962, CIA FOIA, EO-1997–00408.These are from http://www.foia.cia.gov.
28. Conboy and Morrison, *CIA's Secret War in Tibet*, 76–77; Knaus, *Orphans of the Cold War*, 153, 232–233.
29. Committee on Collection of Party History Materials of the Tibetan Autonomous Region, *Pingxi Xizang Panluan* (Pacification of the Tibetan rebellion) (Lhasa: Xizang Renmin Chubanshe, 1995), 183; *Zhonggong Xizang Dangshi Dashiji*, 119, 122, 135, 213; Wang Gui et al., *Xizang Lishi Diwei Bian* (Xizang's historical position defined), 599.
30. "Chinese Foreign Ministry's note that demands the Indian government to abolish the sabotage activities against Tibet conducted by American and Jiang [Taiwan] spies, native agents, and Tibetan reactionaries based in Kalimpong, 10 July 1958," *Pingxi Xizang Panluan*, 125–127; "The center's reply to Tibet on the question of possible rebellions, 14 July 1958," ibid., 64–65; "Directive by the political department of the Chinese People's Liberation Army on the political work for firmly pacifying the Tibetan rebellion, 21 March 1959," ibid., 94.
31. "Ambassador Pan Zili's report on his conversation with the Dalai Lama, 3 January 1957," *Pingxi Xizang Panluan*, 116–117; *Zhou Enlai yu Xizang*, 484; "CCP Working Committee on Tibet's report to the center on the Tibetan upper strata's activities for formally seeking independence, 11 March 1959," *Pingxi Xizang Panluan*, 77–78; *Zhonggong Xizang Dangshi Dashiji*, 90, 93.
32. *Zhou Enlai yu Xizang*, 478, 85–90; Wu Lengxi, *Shi Nian Lunzhan* (Ten-year polemics) (Beijing: Zhongyang Wenxian Chubanshe, 1999), 1: 193.
33. "The Dalai Lama's statement to the press, 18 April 1959," *Pingxi Xizang Panluan*, 149–151; "Comment on the so-called Dalai Lama statement, 21 April 1959", ibid., 143–148.
34. Wu Lengxi, *Shi Nian Lunzhan*, 1: 196–199; Mao Zedong's written comments to Hu Qiaomu, Wu Lengxi, and Peng Zhen, April 25, 1959, *Mao Zedong Xizang Gongzuo Wenxuan*, 186.
35. "A former office worker of the Tibetan office in Jiqiao of Shannan talks about the Dalai Lama group's flight through the area, 21 April 1959," *Pingxi Xizang Panluan*, 201; *Zhong Yin Bianjing Ziwei Fanji Zuozhan Shi*, 82.
36. *Zhong Yin Bianjing Ziwei Fanji Zuozhan Shi*, 451–452; Wang Hongwei, *Ximalayashan Qingjie*, 121; minutes of Chairman Mao Zedong's conversation with the Panchen Lama and others, May 7, 1959, *Pingxi Xizang Panluan*, 157.
37. Mao Zedong's speech at the second plenum of the CCP's eighth central committee, November 15, 1956, *Mao Zedong Xizang Gongzuo Wenxuan*, 152; *Zhonggong Xizang Dangshi Dashiji*, 91.

38. "Public notice of the Tibetan Military District of the Chinese People's Liberation Army, 20 March 1959," *Zhou Enlai yu Xizang*, 79–80.
39. Minutes of Chairman Mao Zedong's conversation with the Panchen Lama and others, May 7, 1959, *Pingxi Xizang Panluan*, 162. Dunham, *Buddha's Warriors*, 172–173, suggests that the Dalai statement was indeed issued with Nehru's endorsement, but that Nehru's interference actually resulted in deleting from the original the harshest words against the Chinese government.
40. Mao Zedong's conversation with the delegations from the Soviet Union and other ten countries, September 6, 1959, *Mao Zedong Xizang Gongzuo Wenxuan*, 193–194; Wu Lengxi, *Shi Nian Lunzhan*, 1: 198–199; Mao Zedong's added words to the written reply of the Ministry of Foreign Affairs to a speech made by an official of the Indian Foreign Ministry, May 13, 1959, 376–377; Wang Hongwei, *Ximalayashan Qingjie*, 148–151.
41. Information Report, "Chinese Communist Ministry of Foreign Affairs Foreign Policy Report," 7/3/1961, CIA FOIA, EO-2001-00347, http://www.fioa.cia.gov. According to the introduction to this document, this is a report disseminated by the Chinese foreign ministry among its missions abroad. The CIA obtained the Chinese original from a defected Chinese diplomat.
42. "The Military Commission of the CCP Central Committee's directive on the rebellion pacification in Shannan of Tibet and the current work, 23 April 1959," *Pingxi Xizang Panluan*, 99.
43. "Zhou Enlai's broadcast speech to the Indian people, 27 June 1959," *Zhou Enlai yu Xizang*, 122.
44. "Document 1: First Conversation of N.S. Khrushchev with Mao Zedong, Hall of Huazhentan [sic][Beijing], 31 July 1958," *Cold War International History Project Bulletin* (Washington, D.C.: Woodrow Wilson International Center for Scholars), Issue 12/13 (Fall/Winter 2001), 250–260.
45. "Document 3: Memorandum of Conversation of N.S. Khrushchev with Mao Zedong, Beijing, 2 October 1959," *Cold War International History Project Bulletin* (Washington, D.C.: Woodrow Wilson International Center for Scholars), Issue 12/13 (Fall/Winter 2001), 262–270.
46. M. Y. Prozumenschikov, "The Sino-Indian Conflict, the Cuban Missile Crisis, and the Sino-Soviet Split, October 1962: New Evidence from the Russian Archives," *Cold War International History Project Bulletin* (Washington, D.C.: Woodrow Wilson International Center for Scholars), Issues 8–9 (Winter 1996/1997), 251–256.
47. Examples of recent studies on the Sino–Soviet split include Dong Wang, "The Quarrelling Brothers: New Chinese Archives and a Reappraisal of the Sino-Soviet Split, 1959–1962," *Cold War International History Project Working Paper No. 49* (Washington, D.C.: Woodrow Wilson International Center for Scholars). Sergey Radchenko's doctoral dissertation at the London School of Economics, *The China Puzzle: Soviet Policy towards the People's Republic of China in the 1960s*, is noteworthy. Hope M. Harrison's *Driving the Soviets Up the Wall: Soviet-East German Relations, 1953–1961* (Princeton: Princeton University Press, 2003) indicates that even in the eastern European bloc controlled tightly by Moscow, the relations between the Soviet Union and its satellites were still affected by their national interests and the balance of international power, and that under certain circumstances the weaker side could prevail.
48. Xu Zehao, *Wang Jiaxiang Zhuan* (Biography of Wang Jiaxiang) (Beijing: Dangdai Zhongguo Chubanshe, 1996), 563. For an informative analysis of the "left turn" by

Chinese diplomacy, see Niu Jun, "1962: The Eve of the Left Turn in China's Foreign Policy," *Cold War International History Project Working Paper No. 48* (Washington, D.C.: Woodrow Wilson International Center for Scholars).

49. Xu Zehao, *Wang Jiaxiang Nianpu, 1906–1974* (Chronology of Wang Jiaxiang's life, 1906–1974) (Beijing: Zhongyang Wenxian Chubanshe, 2001), 491–493; Zhou Enlai, "Ten issues about the counterattack in self-defense along the Chinese-Indian border, 24 November 1962," The CCP Central Office of Documentary Research and the Military Science Academy of the Chinese People's Liberation Army, *Zhou Enlai Junshi Wenxuan* (Selected military writings of Zhou Enlai) (Beijing: Renmin Chubanshe, 1997), 4: 469–470.
50. SNIE 13/31–2-62, "The Sino-Indian Conflict: Outlook and Implications," 12/14/1962, CIA FOIA, EO-1993–00513; CIA memo, "Implications of the Sino-Soviet Rupture for the US," 7/18/1963, CIA FOIA, EO-1998–00565; CIA memo, "India's Economy and the Sino-Indian Conflict," 12/14/1962, CIA FOIA, EO-1997–00577. These are from http://www.foia.cia.gov.
51. *Zhou Enlai yu Xizang*, 517. Zhou Enlai used "long-term armed coexistence" in his telegram, dated July 23, 1962, to the Chinese delegation to the Geneva Conference.
52. SC No. 02684/66, "Intelligence Handbook: The Deterioration of Sino-Soviet Relations, 1956–1966," 4/22/1966, CIA FOIA, F-2000–01330, http://www.foia.cia.gov.
53. For an analysis of the KMT regime's religious policy toward Tibet, see Gray Tuttle, *Tibetan Buddhists in the Making of Modern China* (New York: Columbia University Press, 2005).

Epilogue: Search for a Frontier Theme

In the daily discourse of our time, "frontier" often symbolizes progress such as cutting-edge research in scientific fields, exploration of the outer space, and new realms of economic development. The frontier of a country's homeland, by contrast, tends to indicate backward conditions or "immaturity" of the state by the standard of our nation-state world. The frontier conditions of the United States, for instance, have to be found in a historical time more than a hundred years ago. The case of China is difficult in this regard as in any: whereas "immaturity" can hardly be applied to this country of several thousand years old, its frontier conditions have been present to this date. Yet China of the twentieth century is rarely understood in a frontier perspective either for the reason that its Inner Asian frontiers have been obscured by those astonishing developments in its eastern provinces, or that events associated with the frontiers have been disassociated with the rest of China in most scholarly writings. Hence there is a need to rediscover the frontier of China in order to understand recent Chinese history adequately.

The year of 2009 saw the celebration of the sixtieth anniversary of the New China understood in the political discourse of what John King Fairbank termed "the great Chinese revolution."[1] From the perspective of Chinese frontier history, however, the "new China" began much earlier than 1949. When the People's Republic of China was established, a long and continual historical process just began to see some accumulative results. And, sixty years later, this process is yet to find a conclusion.

China as a "Frontier State"

About seven decades ago, in discussing China's dynastic history, Owen Lattimore characterized China as a "frontier state" by identifying a constant rivalry for mutual control between dynasties found on or beyond the Inner Asian frontier and those within China.[2] Although the so-called rivalry did not necessarily always evolve in violent forms and relatively peaceful coexistence did exist at times, it is unmistakable that such intense contact between dynastic Chinese states and Inner Asian states of various forms constituted a vital condition for historical development on both sides. Since the end of China's dynastic history, neither has such intense contact ceased nor the importance of the frontier has declined for China. In modern times what changed were the forms in which the animosities or amenities between the two sides unfolded. What Lattimore described was an open, imperial frontier of "all under heaven." In modern times it gradually changed into an enclosed, ethnopolitical frontier of the "Chinese Nation," or *Zhonghua Minzu*. The ancient frontier for empire building was replaced in modern times with one for nation building. Despite the change, the frontier has continued in China's successive life cycles.

The open and the enclosed conditions of the Chinese frontier marked the epochal difference between China's traditional and modern ages. Before the twentieth century, a prominent feature of the Chinese frontier was its perpetual openness to contest. In capturing this feature, a poem of the Song Dynasty states, "The Central Plain [China] and the *Yidi* ['barbarians'] rise and fall alternately."[3] Because of such continual competitions on the frontier, the territory

This map of the late 19th century reflects the border demarcation that the Qing Empire went through in the 19th century and the resultant begonia-leaf image of China.

Source: The David Rumsey Map Collection, www.davidrumsey.com. The original was published in *Rand, McNally & Co.'s Indexed Atlas of the World* (Chicago: Rand, McNally & Co., 1897), 106–107.

"Da Qing Diguo" (Great Qing Empire), a reprint of the early edition first published in 1908. The map evidences that before the Qing Dynasty ended in 1911, China already assumed the feature of a bordered "national" state. The begonia-leaf image was also established in the Chinese mind at this time.

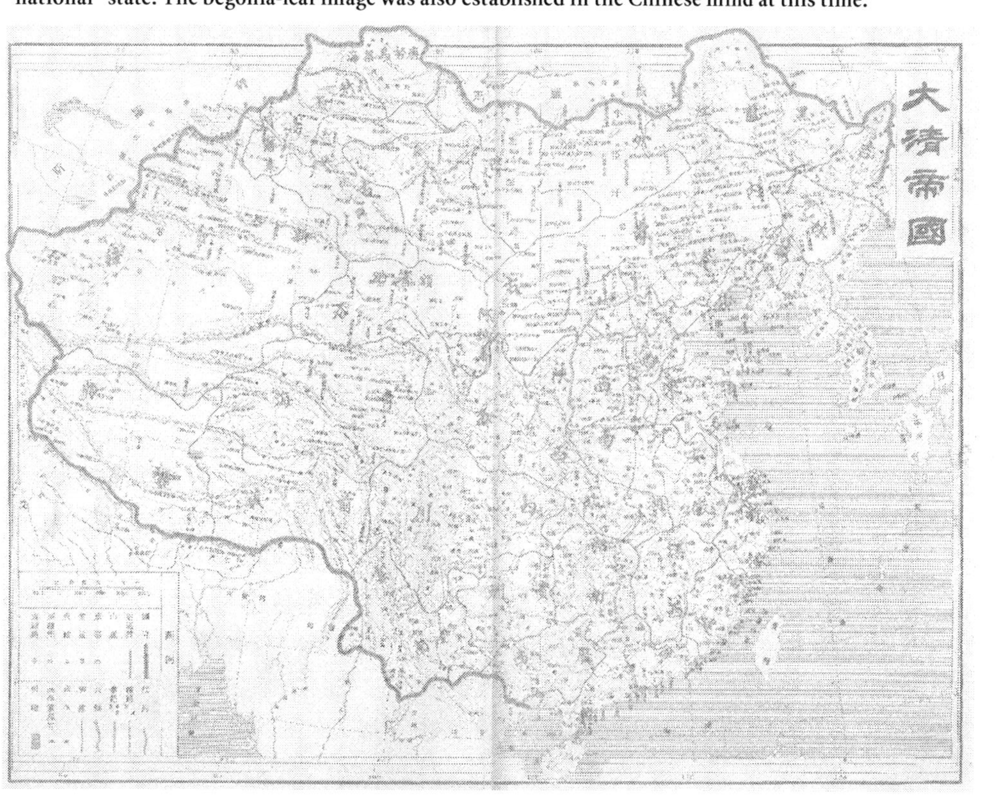

Source: *Da Qing Diguo Quantu* (Complete atlas of the great Qing empire) (Shanghai: Shangwu Yishuguan, 1942).

This map was published in the 1920s. Note the "inner borders" between China proper and the frontier zones. This continues a feature in many 19th-century maps published in the West that marked "China" as a distinctive area within the "Chinese Empire."

Source: The David Rumsey Map Collection, www.davidrumsey.com. The original was published in *Times survey atlas of the world* (London: The Times, 1922), 62.

of historical China was as fluctuant as a seasonal lake, though some of these "territorial seasons" could last for centuries.

This is perhaps the reason why in premodern Chinese history, obsessive conceptions about the shape and size of dynastic territories did not exist. Ancient Chinese used *shanhe* (mountains and rivers) to symbolize their homeland. They also used *jin'ou* (gold goblet) to convey the idea of territorial intactness. The territorial image created by these terms is shapeless and abstract in comparison to today's territorial images conveyed through political maps. Although China has a long history of using maps, ancient Chinese maps did not demarcate China and its neighbors as bordered geo-entities. In the ancient world of China, border demarcation was occasionally practiced but was not institutionalized, for systematic border demarcation would have contradicted the universalistic ideology of "all under heaven" and misrepresented the political reality of China's shifting frontiers.

Comprehensive and systematic border demarcation is therefore a modern phenomenon as far as China is concerned, or an immediate result of the collapse of the Sino-centric interstate order of East Asia. After the mid-nineteenth century, one thing the Western powers did to Asia was to reshape and resize Asian states. After more than a dozen of treaties with foreign powers that involved territorial issues, the Qing Empire lost its tributary dependencies in the east and in the south. Meanwhile, the Qing managed to keep its territorial dependencies in Inner Asia and started to make them into integral parts of its imperial domain. Such drastic transformation of territoriality was reflected in cartographic modernization. During the last decade of the Qing Dynasty, maps published in China were catching up with Western cartography and presented a begonia-leaf image of China's territorial sovereignty.[4] In the image, China's Inner Asian frontiers were enclosed by fixed international boundaries and no longer separated from China proper with inner divides as in nineteenth-century maps of China made in the West.

These developments before 1911 started the process of changing China's open frontier for empire building into an enclosed frontier for nation building. On the New Year's Day of 1912, Sun Yat-sen, in the capacity of Provisional President of the Republic of China, declared:

> People are the essence of the state. To combine the areas of the Han, Manchu, Mongols, Hui, and Tibetans into one state is to combine these races [*zu*] into one nation. This is national unification.[5]

The inclusion of Inner Asian borderlands into the territories of the Chinese republic not only proclaimed the geographic extension but also the multiethnic configuration of a modern Chinese nation.

Sun's statement marked the beginning of China's conscious nation building. His incorporation of the Inner Asian territories into the Republic of China however indicated an ideological development that was divorced from the political reality of the time. Throughout the republic period, a succession of "central" Chinese governments strived for gaining actual centrality in the divisive Chinese politics, none of which was unable to overcome the de facto separation of Tibet and Outer Mongolia from the Chinese state. Nor could these regimes effectively deal with foreign intrigues and local autonomous movements in Inner Mongolia, Manchuria, and Xinjiang. The old contest on the frontier thus continued in the form of a struggle between the centralizing drive of Chinese nationalism and the separatist tendency of Inner Asian peoples, even though in Chinese leaders' political imagination this struggle was internal to China's homeland.

Because the physical identity and inner composition of the "Chinese Nation" was at stake, the internal settlement of the interethnic relationship on China's Inner Asian frontiers was as important as China's external struggle for regaining lost territories and abrogating the unequal treaties that unfolded mainly in the east half of China. By the end of World War II, the Chinese government's efforts in the east had achieved decisive progress. Yet, the efforts in the west would have to continue for many years to come.

During the better part of the Qing Dynasty, the Manchus as the ruling minority based the stability of their empire on the harmonious yet segregated coexistence among the empire's five ethnopolitical constituencies (Manchu, Han, Mongol, Tibetan, and Muslim). During China's national period, the political elites of the Han majority made homogenization between China proper and the ethnic frontiers, which automatically entailed ethnic conflicts, a fundamental condition for China to fare as a "nation." This unfinished agenda was carried over to the People's Republic of China after 1949.

Enclosed Frontiers

Only during its formative years, influenced by the Leninist doctrine on national self-determination, did the Chinese Communist Party disagree seriously with the Chinese Nationalists with regard to the ethnic borderlands. By 1949, the CCP's interethnic experiences in the Long March, in China's eight-year war against Japan, and in the Chinese Civil War had resulted in complete convergence between Chinese Communism and Chinese Nationalism in respect to the fundamentals of China's nationhood.[6]

During the Mao Zedong era, the CCP's effort to end China's frontier condition went through three phases, or a trilogy of "liberation," "regional autonomy," and "socialism." These conceptions assumed specific meanings in the discourse of the CCP history, but they were nevertheless nation-building measures about China's ethnic frontiers that the Chinese Nationalists would have taken under similar or different names if they had prevailed in the Chinese Civil War after 1945. In other words, "liberation" meant extension by military means of the Chinese central authority to the ethnic frontiers. In 1949, whereas people in China's interior provinces understood the conception mainly as a regime change from the Nationalists to the Communists, residents in the borderlands sensed the arrival of the Chinese government more than anything else. The next step, "regional autonomy," was also a shared device between the Chinese Nationalists and the Chinese Communists for restructuring the governance of the frontiers, which will be explained further below. And, finally, "socialism" simply replaced "Three People's Principles" as the official ideology to remold the frontier societies in the image of the rest of China.

There is no need to labor the military process of "liberation" around 1949 here, but "regional autonomy" deserves more words because of existent misconceptions about its history. As a matter of fact, when the two Chinese parties entered the final round of their power struggle after World War II, so far as China's ethnic frontiers were concerned, the only remaining squabble between them was about ethnic minorities' status within China. Whereas the Nationalists defined the ethnic minorities as big and small "branch clans" (*zongzhi*) of the Chinese Nation, the Communists insisted that they were equal member "nationalities" (*minzu*) of the Chinese Nation.[7] The policy implications of these conceptions were not about different political prospects for the ethnic frontiers but how a device of "particularization" should be used for the sake of homogenizing the ethnic frontiers with the rest of China.

At different times before 1949, the Chinese Nationalist Government considered granting Tibet and Outer Mongolia a status of "high-degree self-government" (*gaodu zizhi*) under Chinese sovereignty. The measure was devised to lure Outer Mongolia (before its official independence in August 1945) and Tibet, the two "particularized" areas, back to China. In the meantime, such a treatment was denied to Xinjiang and Inner Mongolia that had already been made into provinces for many years.[8]

When the Chinese Communists adopted the device, differently named as *quyu zizhi* (regional nationality autonomy), it was part of their power-contending strategy against China's official central government controlled by the Nationalists. At one of the crucial moments of the Chinese Civil War, the CCP leadership was convinced that its political and military position in Manchuria and Inner Mongolia could be significantly improved if concessions were made to a powerful third force in the region, the Eastern Mongolian autonomous movement.[9] The CCP thus simply took advantage of the Nationalists' rigidity in Inner Mongolia and supported the Inner Mongols' demand for rolling back the Chinese province system and "re-particularizing" their area, or making Inner Mongolia "ethnic" again.

In May 1947, an Inner Mongolian Autonomous Government was launched as the CCP's ethnic ally against the Nationalists. The two fundamental principles underlying the body were the Inner Mongols', not the CCP's. One was "unified autonomy" that provided a governing body to all Inner Mongols, and another was territorial autonomy that included all "original lands" of Inner Mongolia. It is conventional in the PRC to suggest that the *quyu zizhi* system of the PRC began in Inner Mongolia in 1947. It is more accurate however to say that in 1947 the CCP supported the Inner Mongols' claim to "high-degree self-government" within the Republic of China, the same right that the Nationalist regime had promised to the Tibetans and the Outer Mongols.[10]

The CCP learned a valuable lesson from the Inner Mongolia case: a low-degree particularization could bring about high-degree homogenization. An interesting historical coincidence is that after the Manchus of the seventeenth century used the Mongolian cavalries in establishing their great empire of China, the CCP used the political model of Inner Mongolia to broaden the party-state bequeathed by the Nationalists into a party-nation.

It is in this context we should understand the CCP's decision in September 1949 to apply *quyu zizhi* to all ethnic minority communities of China, and eventually to "identify" 55 ethnic minorities for this purpose.[11] The particularization and "re-ethnicization" of many visible or obscure ethnic groups living inside China in turn contributed significantly to the homogenization of the Inner Asian frontiers. The step effectively reduced the particularizing significance of *quyu zizhi* and enhanced its homogenizing function by way of rolling back the old provincial establishments in Inner Mongolia and Xinjiang between 1949 and the mid-1950s. The homogenizing effect of *quyu zizhi* was even more explicit when the system was applied to Tibet years later.

Initially, the CCP leadership envisioned that *quyu zizhi* at various levels would be established in ten provinces. Today it exists as a four-level system (province, prefecture, county, and township), and *quyu zizhi* at the top three levels is established in twenty of China's thirty-four province-level districts. The area of the system covers about 65% of China's territories.[12] Those "pure" Han provinces without the *quyu zizhi* system now actually become a particular and minority category.

As early as in the end of 1956, the rapid nationwide application of *quyu zizhi* led the Xinhua News Agency to report that the system had been established in nearly all the ethnic minority regions. Inspired by the development, Ulanfu, then director of the National Committee on Nationality Affairs, announced at the CCP's eighth national conference: "[T]he party has victoriously solved the domestic nationality question."[13]

In virtually declaring the closure of the contested condition of China's ethnopolitical frontiers, Ulanfu's 1956 announcement is comparable to the U.S. Census statement in 1890 on the end of America's "pioneer frontiers." The difference between the two cases is that the frontier condition of the United States decisively disappeared after 1890 whereas the Chinese frontier would continue after 1956.

As Ulanfu made the announcement, the interethnic entente cordiale in the early years of the PRC was about to end, similar to what happened to the relations between the CCP and China's "national bourgeoisie" and intellectuals. In view of the CCP's success during the early years of the PRC in incorporating the progressive partisans of Xinjiang and Inner Mongolia into its revolution and in arranging a working relationship with the conservative Tibetan establishment, a counterfactual question emerges easily: Without the frenzied, excessive Maoist revolution after the late 1950s, could the CCP have ended China's antagonistic ethnopolitics and achieved an internally cohesive Chinese Nation? History, of course, does not provide an answer.

In the twentieth century the Chinese Revolution focused the world's attention on events in the eastern half of China and almost erased the frontiers from the historiography about modern China. It is easy to forget that the Chinese Revolution began with an uncompromising ethnopolitical agenda calling for "driving out the [Manchu] barbarians and restoring the Chinese." The first half of this agenda was soon revised into giving the non-Han peoples equal treatment within the Chinese republic. As of 1949, the second half of the agenda had been achieved to such an extent that the Chinese Revolution must incorporate all ethnic groups in China. Consequently, equal treatment to ethnic minorities logically meant that the ethnic frontiers would have to experience every step of the Maoist revolution with the rest of China in the name of "transition to socialism."

After 1949, the CCP leadership never had any doubt that as members of the same "great family," all ethnic groups of the PRC "must enter socialism."[14] All measures of moderation regarding the frontiers in the early years of the PRC anticipated a moment when class struggles of the Maoist style would be fully implemented in the frontiers regardless of their ethnic particularities. Any political compromise or socioeconomic expediency in the frontiers could only be temporary for it indicated incompleteness of Beijing's domestic sovereignty and un-thoroughness of the Chinese Revolution. To leaders of the newly found PRC, the difference between means and goals was murky when it came to asserting their "central authority" in every inch of the land and spreading the Chinese Revolution to every corner of the country. Nation building and revolution making became one.

Thus, as the Anti-Rightist Campaign and the Great Leap Forward movement engulfed China, political frenzies in the PRC rapidly erased the remaining differences between the ethnic frontiers and the Chinese provinces. In late 1957 and early 1958, CCP officials at the provincial and central levels launched attacks against "local nationalism" in Xinjiang, Inner Mongolia, and Guangxi Zhuang Autonomous Region.[15] In the Tibetan areas of western Sichuan, southern Gansu, and Qinghai, local armed resistance against "democratic reforms" broke out between late 1955 and 1958. These were followed by the collapse of the already delicate political balance in Tibet and the Lhasa uprising in March 1959.

According to the constantly triumphant logic of Maoist politics, the frontier antagonisms in the late 1950s could mean nothing but progress of the Chinese Revolution. Entering the 1960s, "socialism" made such big strides in the PRC that Beijing no longer wanted to tolerate the inconvenience of the "national question." In 1964, an authoritative article of the *People's Daily* made an assertion by citing Mao: "The national question and the class question are related, and in essence the national question *is* the class question."[16]

Although the Tibetan situation is best known for illustrating continuously the unstable frontier conditions of the PRC, Inner Mongolia in the Cultural Revolution shows most clearly why Chinese Communism at its height could not bring the Chinese frontier to a closure. Among the Inner Asian frontiers, Inner Mongolia has had the closest affiliation with the ruling center of China since the Manchu conquest of China. In the late 1940s the Inner Mongols again became the first frontier group that rallied to the incoming power center of China, the CCP. They were the only frontier group that directly contributed to the birth of the PRC by participating in the Chinese Civil War on the CCP's side and by setting up the *quyu zizhi* model for the other ethnic frontiers.

So, if any frontier of the PRC could have ended before the Cultural Revolution, it was Inner Mongolia. But, at the very beginning of the Cultural Revolution, Ulanfu, the highest-positioned non-Han CCP official and the first administrator of the *quyu zizhi* system, was attacked, not by grassroots "revolutionary rebels," but by the CCP leadership itself from the top. He became one of the first provincial leaders deposed by the "Cultural Revolution." Significantly, one of Ulanfu's "crimes" was his reissuing in the 1960s of a 1935 statement by the CCP. The statement under Mao's name defined the Inner Mongols as a "nation," asserting that "nation is the most revered and all nations are equal."

During the "Cultural Revolution," the Inner Mongolian Autonomous Region was dismembered, and the Inner Mongols suffered from the largest mass persecution of that period.[17] In the meantime, political homogenization pushed forward ruthlessly. It is revealing that in those years Inner Mongolian herdsmen in the Silingol grassland changed their daily greeting from the Mongolian *sanu* (how are you) to an awkward mimicry of the prevalent Chinese phrase at the time, *Mao zhuxi wanshouwujiang* (wish chairman Mao boundless longevity).[18]

Socialist Frontier with Chinese Characteristics

In the post-Mao era, Beijing's reorientation indicated that Maoist "class struggles" had exhausted the credibility of the Marxist doctrine in the frontiers as well as in the rest of China. Yet, when China's reforms began gingerly in a manner of "wading across a river by feeling the rocks," as far as the ethnic frontiers were concerned, leaders in Beijing seemed convinced that the river ahead was overly treacherous and offered few rocks for them to step on.

Only briefly, before Hu Yaobang was deposed, did the CCP leadership show a degree of audacity. Experimental policies were initiated to treat Tibet as a special ethnopolitical zone, echoing from afar those "special economic zones" along China's southeast coast. Although not intended for the other ethnic frontiers to copy, the Tibetan experiment in the 1980s contained two potentially potent ideas of general significance. One was the salient emphasis on the uniqueness of a particular ethnic frontier in contrast to the homogenizing trend since 1949; another was explicit sensitivity about international criticisms in contrast to the defiance of the Mao era against the outside world.[19] Yet, whereas the economic SEZs along the east coast eventually led to the transformation of the PRC into a different place, the ethnopolitical SEZ along the Himalayas did not go very far.

At the onset of the PRC's reform era, Deng Xiaoping set *xiaokang* (relatively comfortable life) as the initial goal of China's economic reforms. In the meantime, he appeared satisfied with China's ethnopolitical conditions, saying that China "does not have large-scale ethnic conflicts." This may be dubbed as *xiaozhi*, or a "relatively stable order."[20] These criteria were pragmatic for a country that was still recovering from the catastrophic "Cultural Revolution." They however sound insignificant today when China is heading toward a leading status in world affairs.

Until the recent global financial crisis, the PRC maintained an impressive double-digit rate of economic growth. Yet, thirty years after the reform era began, the PRC is yet to achieve a stability index in the ethnic frontiers comparable to its economic feat. The *quyu zizhi* plus economic modernization formula has not been able to shut down inter-ethnic conflicts of the frontier regions. Researchers in China have found out that in the past few decades, "political disturbances," "counterrevolutionary armed rebellions," and "terrorist activities" in Xinjiang have been as frequent as in the 1950s and 1960s. In the meantime, the "leaping development" (*kuayue shi fazhan*) in Tibet promoted by Beijing has not been able to remove the issue of Tibet from the front pages.[21]

Thus, Owen Lattimore's characterization of China as a "frontier state" remains valid for China in the twenty-first century. During China's imperial history, the frontiers were shifting zones that reflected the balance of power between Inner Asian powers and Chinese or non-Chinese dynasties based in China proper. During China's national history, the Inner Asian frontiers became internal to the bordered land of the Chinese state, but old frontier contests continued in new forms. A common theme ran through the late Qing, Republic, and People's Republic periods, which is a confrontation between the centralizing and homogenizing drive of the ruling center and the separatist and particularist aspirations of the ethnic frontiers.

As of today, the frame of national state has managed to confine the ethnic frontiers within the PRC, but a shared ethos is yet to emerge and coordinate the kinetic energies of China proper and these frontiers. The status quo of the Chinese frontier can be described as a "socialist frontier with Chinese characteristics." Inspired by Deng Xiaoping's subterfuge—"socialism with Chinese characteristics," the phrase is nevertheless more honest in suggesting that although the ethnic frontiers and Chinese proper have been homogenized under a supra-ethnic ideology, the homogenization remains Chinese in nature.

Today, the frontier of China is evidence of the country's potential for growth, exotic lure, territorial vastness, security uncertainty, internal weakness, and many other things all at the same time. For those who still harbor a desire to permanently end the frontier of China, a comforting thought may be that it took nearly 120 years for the United States to end its frontier, twice as long as the PRC experience so far.

Notes

1. John King Fairbank, *The Great Chinese Revolution, 1800–1985* (New York: Harper Perennial, 1987).
2. Owen Lattimore, *Inner Asian Frontiers of China* (Boston: Beacon Press, 1940), 409.
3. Li Gang, "a poem of indignation written after reading the March 6th edict on the emperor's abdication and announcement to the troops, expressing concerns about the crisis of the royal family, pity on the people's suffering, sorrow about rejected advice, and outrage against those crafty sycophants who undermined the state," in Wang Qixing and Zhang Hong, eds., *Zhongguo Lidai Aiguo Shici Jingpin* (The best of patriotic poems from the dynasties of China) (Wuhan: Wuhan Daxue Chubanshe, 1994), 93.
4. Two modern maps of the Qing Empire from *Da Qing Diguo Quantu* (Complete atlas of the Great Qing Empire) (Shanghai: Shangwu Yishuguan, 1905) and *Huangchao Zhisheng Ditu* (Provincial maps of the imperial dynasty) (Wuchang: Yaxin Dixuehui, 1903) can be seen in *China in Ancient and Modern Maps* (London: Philip Wilson Publishers Limited, 1998), 261, 267. But one has to go to the Chinese originals to see the complete images.

According to Zou Zhenhuan, *Wan Qing Xifang Dilixue zai Zhongguo* (Western geography in late Qing China) (Shanghai: Shanghai Guji Chubanshe, 2000), 324–330, Chinese cartographer Zou Daijun's *Zhong Wai Yudi Quantu* (Complete atlas of China and foreign countries), published in 1903, had the greatest influence on the new Chinese cartography in the early twentieth century.

5. "Provisional president Sun Wen's [Yat-sun] proclamation, January 1, 1912," in Zhang Yuxin and Zhang Shuangzhi, eds., *Minguo Zangshi Shiliao Huibian* (Collection of historical materials on the Tibetan affairs of the Republic of China) (Beijing: Xueyuan Chubanshe, 2005), 1: 31; "Provisional constitution of the Republic of China, issued on March 11, 1912," ibid., 1: 42.
6. A detailed discussion of the evolvement of the CCP's ethnopolitical stance can be found in my *Frontier Passages: Ethnopolitics and the Rise of Chinese Communism, 1921–1945* (Washington, D.C. and Stanford: Woodrow Wilson Center Press and Stanford University Press, 2004).
7. For the CCP–KMT debate in the war years about the nationality status of China's ethnic groups, see Chiang Kai-shek, *China's Destiny* (New York: Macmillan Company, 1947) and Chen Boda, "On China's Destiny (July 21, 1943)," *Minzu Wenti Wenxian Huibian, Yi Jiu ER Yi. Qi—Yi Jiu Si Jiu. Jiu,* (Collected documents on the nationality question, July 1921–September 1949), the Department of United Front of the Chinese Communist Party Central Committee, comp. (Beijing: Zhongyang Dangxiao Chubanshe, 1991. Hereafter, *MWWH*), 945–949. In Chiang's book ethnic groups having been incorporated into historical China are defined as large or small clan branches (*zongzhi*) of the Chinese nation.
8. Wu Zhongxin's memo for Chiang Kai-shek, "Plan for Recovering the Lost Mongolian Banners and for Postwar Political Establishment in Mongolia and Tibet, August 27, 1944," Zongtongfu Dang'an (Archives of the Presidential Palace, Academia Sinica, Taiwan; hereafter *ZD*), 055/1631; Wu Zhongxin and Luo Jiangjia to Chiang Kai-shek, May 26, 1945, ZD, 055/0501; *Xian Zongtong Jianggong Sixiang Yanlun Zongji* (General collection of the late president Chiang's thoughts and words) (Taipei: Guomindang Dangshi Weiyuanhui, 1984), 21: 170–175; Wang Chonghui, "Supplementary Comments on the Xinjiang Question, September 1, 1941," Jiang Zhongzheng Zongtong Dang'an: Geming Wenxian (Kangzhan Shiqi) (Archives of president Chiang Kai-shek: revolutionary documents [the period of the war of resistance], Academia Sinica, Taiwan), 3: 53–54; "Civil Affairs Desk of the Interior Ministry Transmits the Meeting Minutes Discussing the Suggestion by Masud and others for Granting High-Degree Autonomy to Xinjiang, October 22, 1945," *Waijaobu Dang'an Congshu; Jiewu Lei, Disan Ce: Xinjiang Juan (1)* (Series of foreign ministry archives; border affairs, book three: volume on Xinjiang [1]), Ministry of Foreign Affairs of the Republic of China, comp. (Taipei: Waijiaobu, 2001), 366; The Secretariat of the Executive Yuan to the Ministry of Foreign Affairs, "Chairman Wu of the Xinjiang Province's Opinion about the Provincial Politics, Circulated by the Nationalist Government, April 8, 1946," ibid., 368. A little known yet highly interesting case is the KMT government's negotiations with Kanjud, a tribal state of Kashmir, between 1947 and 1948 for converting the state into an autonomous region of the ROC. See documents in *Waijaobu Dang'an Congshu; Jiewu Lei, Disan Ce: Xinjiang Juan (2)*, 27–30, 102–103.
9. Aside from Tibet, a separatist "Eastern Turkistan Republic" existed in Xinjiang between 1944 and 1949. But, since the CCP influence did not reach these areas until 1949 and

1950, conditions of Tibet and Xinjiang did not have direct impact on the CCP deliberation of the *quyu zizhi* formula in the postwar years.

10. This discussion is based on Xiaoyuan Liu, *Reins of Liberation: An Entangled History of Mongolian Independence, Chinese Territoriality, and Great Power Hegemony, 1911–1950* (Washington, D.C. and Stanford: Woodrow Wilson Center Press and Stanford University Press, 2006), 115–280.
11. "Common Program of the Chinese People's Political Consultative Conference, September 29, 1949," Central Office of Documentary Research, comp., *Jianguo Yilai Zhongyao Wenxian Xuanbian* (Selected important documents issued since the state foundation) (Beijing: Zhongyang Wenxian Chubanshe, 1992), 1: 1–14; Wang Jianmin et al., *Zhongguo Minzuxue Shi* (History of ethnology in China) (Kunming: Yunnan Jiaoyu Chubanshe, 1998), 2: 106–129.
12. Mao Zedong, "Comments on the Issue of Regional Autonomy, September 16, 1950," Mao Zedong, *Jianguo Yilai Mao Zedong Wengao* (Mao Zedong's manuscripts since the foundation of the state) (Beijing: Zhongyang Wenxian Chubanshe, 1987), 1: 518; Xiao Gen, *Zhongguo Shaoshu Minzu Xingzheng Zhidu* (China's administrative systems for the minority nationalities) (Kunming: Yunnan Daxue Chubanshe, 1999), 474–475.
13. Luo Guangwu, *Xin Zhongguo Minzu Gongzuo Dashi Gailan, (1949–1999)* (Survey of important events in the nationality work of the new China, [1949–1999]) (Beijing: Huawen Chubanshe, 2001), 222–223; Ulanfu, "The Party Has Victoriously Solved the Domestic Nationality Question, September 19, 1956," in Ulanfu, *Wulanfu Wenxuan* (Selected writings of Ulanfu) (Beijing: Zhongyang Wenxian Chubanshe, 1999), 1: 408–418.
14. Zhou Enlai, "A Few Questions about the Nationality Policy of Our State, August 4, 1957," *Zhou Enlai yu Xizang* (Zhou Enlai and Tibet), Office of the Party History of the Tibetan Autonomous Region, comp. (Beijing: Zhongguo Zangxue Chubanshe, 1998), 165–187; Ulanhu, "Conclusion at the Qingdao Forum on Nationality Work, August 5, 1957," Ulanhu, *Wulanfu Wenxuan*, 474–483.
15. Luo Guangwu, 274–275, 279–282, 288–290.
16. Luo Guangwu, 274–275, 284–285, 288–292, 388–391.
17. According to Li Sheng, *Zhongguo Xinjiang: Lishi yu Xianzhuang* (Xinjiang of China: history and current situation) (Urumuqi: Xinjiang Renmin Chubanshe, 2003), 344–348, and *Zhonggong Xizang Dangshi Dashiji* (Important events of the CCP history in Tibet), Committee for Collecting Party History Materials of the Tibetan Autonomous Region, comp. (Lahsa: Xizang Renmin Chubanshe, 1995), 187–189, between 1967 and 1970 a secret "Eastern Turkestan People's Revolutionary Party" of nearly 6,000 members was active in Xinjiang, and armed rebellions took place in several locations in Tibet in 1969. For an insightful discussion of the "Cultural Revolution" in Tibet, see Melvyn C. Goldstein, Ben Jiao, and Tanzen Lhundrup, *On the Cultural Revolution in Tibet: The Nyemo Incident of 1969* (Berkeley: University of California Press, 2009). Tumen and Zhu Dongli, *Kang Sheng yu "Nei Ren Dang" Yuan'an* (Kang Sheng and the wrong case of "Inner Mongolian People's Revolutionary Party") (Beijing: Zhonggong Zhongyang Dangxiao Chubanshe, 1995), reflects the main-stream interpretation in China of the "Cultural Revolution" events in Inner Mongolia. It should be balanced with Gao Shuhua and Cheng Tiejun, *Neimeng Wenge Fenglei: Yiwei Zaofanpai Lingiu de Koushu Shi* (The storm of the cultural revolution in Inner Mongolia: an oral history by a rebel leader)

(Carle Place, N.Y.: Mirror Books, 2007). The 1935 statement of the CCP can be found in *MWWH*, 322–324.

18. This is based on the author's own experience who resided in the Eastern Ujumuchin Banner of Inner Mongolia for six years from the late 1960s to the mid-1970s.
19. "Notice by the CCP Central Committee on the Circulation of 'Summary of the Symposium on the Tibetan Work,' April 1, 1984," *Xizang Gongzuo Wenxian Xuanbian* (Selected documents on the Tibet work), Office of Documentary Research of the CCP Central Committee and the CCP Committee of the Tibetan Autonomous Region, comp. (Beijing: Zhongyang Wenxian Chubanshe, 2005. Hereafter *XGWX*), 358–369. For a detailed survey of Beijing's policy toward Tibet and the Dalai Lama in the post-Mao era, see Tashi Rabgey and Tseten Wangchuk Sharlho, *Sino–Tibetan Dialogue in the Post-Mao Era: Lessons and Prospects* (Washington, D.C.: East–West Center Washington, 2004).
20. Deng Xiaoping, "Promote the Common Prosperity of All Nationalities," *XGWX*, 298–299.
21. Ma Dazheng, *Guojia Liyi Gao Yu Yiqie: Xinjiang Wending Wendi de Guancha yu Sikao* (State interest is superior to anything else: reflections and observations on the question of stability in Xinjiang) (Urumqi: Xinjiang Renmin Chubanshe, 2003), 30–136; Li Sheng, 330–377; Jiang Zemin, "Promote the Realization of Leaping Development and Lasting Order and Stability in Tibet, June 25, 2001," *XGWX*, 547–560; Hu Jintao, "Seize the Favorable Moment and Push Leaping Development in Tibet, March 5, 2002," ibid., 612–616.

Bibliography

Manuscript Collections

Joseph W. Ballantine Papers, Hoover Institution on War, Revolution and Peace, Stanford, CA
Chen Kuang-fu. "Reminiscences of Chen Kuang-fu." Oral History Project of Columbia University (1961), Butler Library, Columbia University, New York City
Clark M. Clifford Papers, Harry S. Truman Library, Independence, MO
Matthew J. Connelly Papers, Truman Library
Lauchlin Currie Papers, Hoover Institution
Victor Ch'i-ts'a Hoo (Hu Shize) Papers, Hoover Institution
Stanley K. Hornbeck Papers, Hoover Institution
Harry L. Hopkins Papers, Franklin D. Roosevelt Library, Hyde Park, NY
Harry N. Howard Papers, Truman Library
Hsiung Shihui (Xiong Shihui) Collections, Butler Library
Philip C. Jessup Papers, Library of Congress, Washington, DC
Jiang Zhongzheng Zongtong Dang'an (Archives of President Jiang Zhongzheng [Jiang Jieshi]), Academia Historica, Taiwan: Geming Wenxian (revolutionary documents) / Tejiao Dang'an (specially submitted documents) / Tejiao Wendian (specially submitted telegrams)
V. K. Wellington Koo Papers, Butler Library
Owen Lattimore Papers, Library of Congress
John F. Melby Papers, Truman Library
Franklin D. Roosevelt Papers, Roosevelt Library: Map Room Files / Official Files / President's Personal Files / Secretary's Files
T. V. Soong (Song Ziwen) Papers, Hoover Institution
Harry S. Truman Papers, Truman Library: Intelligence Files, Post-Presidential Memoirs, President's Secretary's Files
Albert C. Wedemeyer Papers, Hoover Institution

Unpublished Government Documents

People's Republic of China

Archives of the Inner Mongolian Autonomous Region, Hohhot:

Quanzonghao 4: Dongmeng Zhengfu (Eastern Mongolian Government)
Quanzonghao 6: Neimenggu Zizhi Yundong Lianhehui (Alliance of the Inner Mongolian Autonomous Movements)

Second Historical Archives of China, Nanjing:

Quanzonghao 1: Guominzhengfu (Nationalist Government)
Quanzonghao 18: Waijaobu (Ministry of Foreign Affairs)
Quanzonghao 141: Meng Zang Shiwu Weiyuanhui (Mongolian and Tibetan Affairs Commission)
Quanzonghao 761: Junshi Weiyuanhui (Military Council)

Taiwan

Guoshiguan (Academia Historica):

Guomin Zhengfu Dang'an (Records of the National Government)
Xingzhengyuan Dang'an (Records of the Executive Yuan)
Zongtonfu Dang'an (Records of the Presidential Palace)

Guomindang Dangshi Weiyuanhui (Historical Council of the GMD):

Guofang Zuigao Weiyuanhui Dang'an (Records of the Supreme Council of National Defense)

Waijiaobu Dang'an Zixunchu (Desk of Archives of the Ministry of Foreign Affairs):

Waijiaobu Yataisi Dang'an (Records of the Asia-Pacific Division of the Ministry of Foreign Affairs)
Waijiaobu Yaxisi Dang'an (Records of the Western Asian Division of the Ministry of Foreign Affairs)

United Kingdom

India Office, London:

L/P&S/12, Political Department, Annual Files

Public Record Office, Kew Gardens, Surrey, England:

FO 371, Foreign Office, Registry Files

United States

National Archives and Federal Records Center, Suitland, MD:

General Records of Chungking Embassy, China, 1943–1945
Records of the China Theater of Operations, United States Army (CT): Records of the Office of the Commanding General (Albert C. Wedemeyer)
Top Secret General Records of Chungking Embassy, China, 1943–1945

National Archives II, College Park, MD:

General Records of the United States Department of State Central Files: China (RG 59) Records of the Division of Chinese Affairs, 1944–1950 (RG 59)
Records of Harley A. Notter (Postwar Planning) (RG 59)
Records of the Joint Chiefs of Staff (RG 165)
Records of the National Security Council (RG 273)
Records of the Office of Chinese Affairs (RG 59)
Records of the Office of Strategic Services (RG 226)

Published Documentary and Manuscript Collections

In English

Chinese Ministry of Information (Taiwan). *The Collected Wartime Messages of Generalissimo Chiang Kai-shek, 1937–1945*. New York: Kraus Reprint Co., 1969.

Cold War International History Project. *Bulletin, Issues 6–7: The Cold War in Asia*. Washington, D.C.: Woodrow Wilson International Center for Scholars, 1995–1996.

—. *Bulletin, Issues 8–9: New East-Bloc Evidence on the Cold War in the Third World and the Collapse of Détente in the 1970s*. Washington, D.C.: Woodrow Wilson International Center for Scholars, 1996–1997.

—. *Bulletin, Issue 10: Leadership Transition in a Fractured Bloc*. Washington, D.C.: Woodrow Wilson International Center for Scholars, 1998.

—. *Bulletin, Issues 11–12: The End of the Cold War*. Washington, D.C.: Woodrow Wilson International Center for Scholars, 2001.

Degras, Jane Degras, ed. *Soviet Documents on Foreign Policy*. 4 vols. New York: Octagon Books, 1978.

U.S. Department of State. *Foreign Relations of the United States: Diplomatic Papers*. Washington, D.C.
1941; IV–V (1956)
China, 1942 (1956)
China, 1943 (1957)
The Conference at Cairo and Teheran, 1943 (1961)
The Conference at Malta and Yalta, 1945 (1955)
1944: VI (1967)
1945: VII (1969)

United States Joint Chiefs of Staff. *Records of the Joint Chiefs of Staff*. Frederick, MD: University Publications of America, 1980–1983. Microfilm.

Zhang Shuguang and Chen Jian, eds. *Chinese Communist Foreign Policy and the Cold War in Asia: New Documentary Evidence, 1944–1950*. Chicago: Imprint Publications, 1996.

In Chinese

Chaoxian Zhanzheng: Eguo Dang'anguan de Jiemi Wenjian (The Korean War: Declassified Documents from the Russian Archives). Compiled by Shen Zhihua. 3 vols. Taipei: Zhongyang Yanjiuyuan Jindaishi Yanjiusuo, 2003.

Daqingshan Kang Ri Youji Genjudi Ziliao Xuanbian (Selected Materials on the Anti-Japanese Guerrilla Base in the Daqingshan Mountain). Compiled by the Committee on the Collection of Party History Materials of the CCP Committee of the Inner Mongolian Autonomous Region and the Archives of the Inner Mongolian Autonomous Region. Hohhot: Neimenggu Renmin Chubanshe, 1987.

Geming Wenxian (Revolutionary Documents). Compiled by Historical Council of the Guomindang. Multivolume. Taipei: Guomindang Dangshi Weiyuanhui, 1976–.

Gongchan Guoji, Liangong (Bu) yu Zhongguo Guomin Keming Dang'an Ziliao Congshu (Series of Archival Materials on the Comintern, the Soviet Communist Party [Bolshevik], and the Chinese Revolution). Translated and compiled by First Research Department of the Research Office on the Party History of the CCP Central Committee. 12 vols. Beijing: Beijing Tushuguan Chubanshe, 1997 (vols 1–6); Beijing: Zhongyang Wenxian Chubanshe, 2002 (vols 7–12).

Heping Jiefang Xizang (Peaceful liberation of Tibet), Committee for Collecting Materials on Party History of the Tibetan Autonomous Region and Leading Group on Colleting Materials on Party History of the Tibetan Military District, comp. Lhasa: Xizang Renmin Chubanshe, 1995.

Jianguo yilai Liu Shaoqi Wengao (Liu Shaoqi's Manuscripts after the Establishment of the State). Beijing: Zhongyang Wenxian Chubanshe, 1998.

Jianguo Yilai Mao Zedong Wengao (Mao Zedong's Manuscripts since the Foundation of the State). Beijing: Zhongyang Wenxian Chubanshe, 1987.

Jianguo Yilai Zhongyao Wenxian Xuanbian (Selection of Important Documents since the Establishment of the State). Compiled by the Documentary Research Office of the CCP Central Committee. Multivolume. Beijing: Zhongyang Wenxian Chubanshe, 1992.

Mao Zedong Junshi Huodong Jishi (Records of Mao Zedong's Military Activities). Compiled by Chinese Military Museum. Beijing: Jiefangjun Chubanshe, 1994.

Mao Zedong Shuxin Xuanji (Selected Correspondence of Mao Zedong). Beijing: Renmin Chubanshe, 1983.

Mao Zedong Waijiao Wenxuan (Selected Diplomatic Works of Mao Zedong). Beijing: Zhongyang Wenxian Chubanshe, 1994.

Mao Zedong Wenji (Manuscripts of Mao Zedong). 5 vols. Beijing: Renmin Chubanshe, 1993–1996.

Mao Zedong Xizang Gongzuo Wenxuan (Selected writings of Mao Zedong on Tibetan work), Office of Document Research of the Central Committee of the Chinese Communist Party et al., comp. Beijing: Zhongyang Wenxian Chubanshe and Zhongguo Zangxue Chubanshe, 2001.

Mao Zedong Zaoqi Wengao (Early Writings of Mao Zedong). Changsha: Hunan Chubanshe, 1995.

Minguo Zangshi Shiliao Huibian (Collection of historical materials on the Tibetan affairs of the Republic of China), Zhang Yuxin and Zhang Shuangzhi, comp. (Beijing: Xueyuan Chubanshe, 2005),

Minzu Wenti Wenxian Huibian (Collected Documents on the Nationality Question). Compiled by United Front Department of the Central Committee of the Chinese Communist Party. Beijing: Zhonggong Zhongyang Dangxiao Chubanshe, 1991 (internal circulation).

Neimenggu Dang'an Shiliao (Archival Materials on Inner Mongolian History). Quarterly. Hohhot: Neimenggu Dang'anguan, 1992–.

Neimenggu Tongzhan Shi: Dang'an Shiliao Xuanbian (History of the United Front in Inner Mongolia: Selected Archival Materials). Compiled by United-Front Department of CCP Committee of Inner Mongolia and Archives of Inner Mongolian Autonomous Region, 1987 (internal circulation).

Neimenggu Zizhi Yundong Lianhehui Dang'an Shiliao Yuanbian (Selected Archival Materials on the Inner Mongolian Autonomous Movement Association). Beijing: Dang'an Chubanshe, 1989.

Pinxi Xizang Panluan (Suppression of the Tibetan rebellion), Committee for Collecting Party History Materials of the Tibetan Autonomous Region and Leading Group on Colleting Party History Materials of the Tibetan Military District, comp. Lhasa: Xizang Renmin Chubanshe, 1995.

Riben Diguozhuyi Duiwai Qinlue Shiliao Xuanbian (Selected Historical Documents on Japanese Imperialist Foreign Aggression). Compiled and translated by Japanese History Group of the History Department of Fudan University. Shanghai: Renmin Chubanshe, 1975.

Suiyuan "Jiu Yi Jiu" Heping Qiyi Dang'an Shiliao Xuanbian (Selected Archival and Historical Materials on the 19 September Peaceful Uprising in Suiyuan). Compiled by Inner Mongolian Archives. Hohhot: Neimonggu Renmin Chubanshe, 1986.

Sulian Gongchandang Zuihou Yige Fandang Jituan (The Last Antiparty Clique in the Soviet Communist Party). Complete minutes of June 1957 conference and October 1964 conference of Soviet Union Communist Party Congress, translated by Zhao Yongmu et al. Beijing: Zhongguo Shehui Chubanshe, 1997.

Sulian Lishi Dang'an Xuanbian (Selected Historical Archives of the Soviet Union). Translated and compiled by Shen Zhihua et al. 34 vols. Bejing: Shehui Kexue Wenxian Chubanshe, 2002.

Woguo Minzu Quyu Zizhi Wenxian Ziliao Huibian (Collected Documents on the Nationality Regional Autonomy of Our Country). Compiled by Nationalities Institute of Chinese Academy of Social Sciences (no pub., n.d.).

Xian Zongtong Jiang Gong Sixiang Yanlun Zongji (Complete Works of the Late President Jiang [Jieshi]). Compiled by Historical Council of the Guomindang. 40 vols. Taipei: Guomindang Dangshi Weiyuanhui, 1984.

Xizang de Minzhu Gaige (Democratic reforms in Tibet), Committee on Collecting Party History Materials of the Tibetan Autonomous Region, comp. Lhasa: Xizang Renmin Chubanshe, 1995.

Xizang Gongzuo Wenxian Xuanbian (1949–2005) (Selected documents on Tibetan work, 1949–2005), Office of Documentary Research of the Central Committee of the Chinese Communist Party and the Committee of the Chinese Communist Party of the Tibetan Autonomous Region, comp. Beijing: Zhongyang Wenxian Chubanshe, 2005.

Xizang Lishi Dang'an Huicui (A collection of historical archives of Tibet), Archives of the Tibetan Autonomous Region, comp. Beijing: Wenwu Chubanshe, 1995.

Zhan Dong Zonghui Wenxian Ziliao Huiyilu (Materials and Recollections on the General Society for Wartime Mobilization). Compiled and published by Party History Research Office of the Chinese Communist Party Shanxi Committee, 1987.

Zhonggong Zhongyang Wenjian Xuanji (Selected Documents of the Chinese Communist Party Central Committee). Compiled by the Central Archives. 18 vols. Beijing: Zhonggong Zhongyang Dangxiao Chubanshe, 1992.

Zhongguo Gongnong Hongjun Disi Fangfianjun Zhanshi Ziliao Xuanbian, Changzheng Shiqi (Selected Materials on the Combat History of the Fourth Front Army of the Chinese Workers' and Peasants' Red Army, the Long March Period). Beijing: Jiefangjun Chubanshe, 1992.

Zhonghua Minguo Zhongyao Shiliao Chubian: Dui Ri Kangzhan Shiqi (Preliminary Compilation of Important Historical Records of the Republic of China: The Period of the War of Resistance against Japan). Historical Council of the Guomindang. 7 vols. Taipei: Guomindang Dangshi Weiyuanhui, 1981.

Zhong Su Guojia Guanxi Ziliao Huibian (Collected Documents on the History of Sino-Soviet Interstate Relations). Compiled by Xue Xiantian et al. Multivolume. Beijing: Zhongguo Shehui Kexue Chubanshe, 1993–.

Zhou Enlai Junshi Wenxuan (Selected Military Works of Zhou Enlai). Beijing: Renmin Chubanshe, 1997.

Zhou Enlai Yijiusiliu Nian Tanpan Wenxuan (Selected Documents on Zhou Enlai's Negotiations in 1946). Compiled by Documentary Research Office of Chinese Communist Party Central Committee and Chinese Communist Party Committee of Nanjing. Beijing: Zhongyang Wenxian Chubanshe, 1996.

Zhou Enlai yu Xizang (Zhou Enlai and Tibet), Party History Office of the Tibetan Autonomous Region, comp. Beijing: Zhongguo Zangxue Chubanshe, 1998.

Internet Search

http://wwics.si.edu
Cold War International History Project Virtue Archive
http://www.foia.cia.gov
CIA FOIA, CSI-2001–00018
CIA FOIA, EO-1993–00513
CIA FOIA, EO-1998–00565
CIA FOIA, EO-1997–00408
CIA FOIA, EO-1997–00577
CIA FOIA, EO-2001–00347
CIA FOIA, F-1997–00812
CIA FOIA, F-2000–01330
CIA FOIA, SS-2003–0002

Selected Reminiscent and Scholarly Works

In English

Adas, Michael. "Imperialism and Colonialism in Comparative Perspective," *International Historical Review* 20(2) (June 1998): 371–388.

Akiner, Shirin, ed. *Mongolia Today*. London: Kegan Paul International, 1991.

Aldrich, Richard J. et al., eds. *The Clandestine Cold War in Asia, 1945–1965: Western Intelligence, Propaganda and Special Operations*. London: Frank Cass, 2000.

Anderson, Benedict. *Imagined Communities: Reflections on the Origin and Spread of Nationalism*. London: Verso, 1991.

Anderson, Malcolm. *Frontiers: Territory and State Formation in the Modern World*. Cambridge: Polity Press, 1996.

Andreyev, Alexandre. *Soviet Russia and Tibet: The Debacle of Secret Diplomacy, 1918–1930s.* Leiden: Brill, 2003.

Armstrong, David. *Revolution and World Order: The Revolutionary State in International Society.* Oxford: Clarendon Press, 1993.

Atwood, Christopher. "A. I. Oshirov (c. 1901–1931): A Buriat Agent in Inner Mongolia." In *Opuscula Altaica: Essays Presented in Honor of Henry Schwarz*, ed. Edward H. Kaplan and Donald W. Whisenhunt. Bellingham: Center for East Asian Studies of Western Washington University, 1994.

—. "East Mongolian Revolution and Chinese Communism," *Mongolian Studies* 15 (1992): 7–82.

—. *Encyclopedia of Mongolia and the Mongol Empire.* New York: Facts on File, 2004.

—. "National Party and Local Politics in Ordos, Inner Mongolia (1926–1935)." *Journal of Asian History* 26(1) (1992): 2–10.

—. *Young Mongols and Vigilantes in Inner Mongolia's Interregnum Decades, 1911–1931.* Leiden: Brill Academic Publishers, 2002.

Banac, Ivo, ed. *The Diary of Georgi Dimitrov, 1933–1949.* New Haven, Conn.: Yale University Press, 2003.

Barany, Zotan. "Soviet Takeovers: The Role of Advisers in Mongolia in the 1920s and in Eastern Europe after World War II." *Eastern European Quarterly* 28(4) (January 1995): 409–433.

Barbar. *Twentieth Century Mongolia.* Cambridge: White Horse Press, 1999.

Barfield, Thomas. *The Perilous Frontier: Nomadic Empires and China.* Cambridge: Basil Blackwell, 1989.

Barmin, Valery. "Xinjiang in the History of Soviet–Chinese Relations from 1937 to 1946." *Far Eastern Affairs (FEA)* 1 (2000): 63–77.

Barnett, A. Doak. *China's Far West: Four Decades of Change.* Boulder: Westview Press, 1993.

Batbayar, Tsedenbambyn. "Stalin's Strategy in Mongolia, 1932–1936," *Mongolian Studies* 22 (1999): 1–17.

Batsaikhan, Ookhnoin. "Issues Concerning Mongolian Independence from the Soviet Union and China: The Attempt to Incorporate Mongolia within the USSR and the Positions of Soviet Leaders, Stalin, Molotov, and Mikoyan." Unpub. paper presented at International Workshop on Mongolia and the Cold War, Ulaanbaatar, March 19–20, 2004.

Bawden, C. R. "A Joint Petition of Grievances Submitted to the Ministry of Justice of Autonomous Mongolia in 1919." *Bulletin of the School of Oriental and African Studies* 30(3) (1967): 548–563.

—. *The Modern History of Mongolia.* London: Kegan Paul International, 1989.

Benson, Linda. *The Ili Rebellion: The Moslem Challenge to Chinese Authority in Xinjiang, 1944–1949.* Armonk: M.E. Sharpe, 1990.

Berezhkov, Valentin M. *At Stalin's Side: His Interpreter's Memoirs from the October Revolution to the Fall of the Dictator's Empire.* Trans. Sergei V. Mikheyev. New York: Carol Publishing Group, 1994.

Bobrick, Benson. *East of the Sun: The Epic Conquest and Tragic History of Siberia.* New York: Poseidon Press, 1992.

Brown, William and Urgunge Onon, trans. *History of the Mongolian People's Republic.* Cambridge: East Asian Research Center of Harvard University, 1976.

Brzezinski, Zbigniew. *The Grand Chessboard: American Primacy and Its Geostrategic Imperatives.* New York: BasicBooks, 1997.

Bukovansky, Mlada. *Legitimacy and Power Politics: The American and French Revolutions in International Political Culture.* Princeton, N.J.: Princeton University Press, 2002.

Bulag, Uradyn E. *The Mongols at China's Edge: History and the Politics of National Unity.* Lanham, Md.: Rowman & Littlefield, 2002.

—. *Nationalism and Hybridity in Mongolia.* Oxford: Oxford University Press, 1998.

Campi, Alicia J. "Perceptions of the Outer Mongols by the United States Government as Reflected in Kalgan (Inner Mongolia) U.S. Consular Records 1920–1927." *Mongolian Studies* 14 (1991): 81–109.

Chen Jian. *Mao's China and the Cold War.* Chapel Hill: University of North Carolina Press, 2001.

Chen, King C. *Vietnam and China, 1938–1954.* Princeton: Princeton University Press, 1969.

Chinese Ministry of Information (Taiwan). *The Collected Wartime Messages of Generalissimo Chiang Kai-shek, 1937–1945*. New York: Kraus Reprint Co., 1969.

Chuev, Felix. *Molotov Remembers: Inside Kremlin Politics, Conversations with Felix Chuev*. Chicago: Ivan R. Dee, 1993.

Chuluun, O. "The Two Phases in Mongolian–Chinese Relations, 1949–1972." *FEA* 1 (1974): 24–32.

Clubb, O. Edmund. *China & Russia: The "Great Game."* New York: Columbia University Press, 1971.

Cohen, Warren I. *East Asia at the Center: Four Thousand Years of Engagement with the World*. New York: Columbia University Press, 2000.

Cold War International History Project. *Bulletin, Issues 6–7: The Cold War in Asia*. Washington, D.C.: Woodrow Wilson International Center for Scholars, 1995–1996.

—. *Bulletin, Issues 8–9: New East-Bloc Evidence on the Cold War in the Third World and the Collapse of Détente in the 1970s*. Washington, D.C.: Woodrow Wilson International Center for Scholars, 1996–1997.

—. *Bulletin, Issue 10: Leadership Transition in a Fractured Bloc*. Washington, D.C.: Woodrow Wilson International Center for Scholars, 1998.

—. *Bulletin, Issues 11–12: The End of the Cold War*. Washington, D.C.: Woodrow Wilson International Center for Scholars, 2001.

Conboy, Kenneth and James Morrison. *The CIA's Secret War in Tibet*. Lawrence: University Press of Kansas, 2002.

Connor, Walker. *Ethnonationalism: The Quest for Understanding*. Princeton, N.J.: Princeton University Press, 1994.

Creveld, Martin van. *The Rise and Decline of the State*. Cambridge: Cambridge University Press, 1999.

Crossley, Pamela Kyle. *A Translucent Mirror: History and Identity in Qing Imperial Ideology*. Berkeley: University of California Press, 1999.

The Dalai Lama. *Freedom in Exile: The Autobiography of the Dalai Lama*. New York: HarperCollins Publishers, 1990.

—. *My Land and My People*. London: Weidenfeld and Nicolson, 1962.

Davies, John Paton Jr. *Dragon by the Tail: American, British, Japanese, and Russian Encounters with China and One Another*. New York: W. W. Norton, 1972.

Degras, Jane Degras, ed. *Soviet Documents on Foreign Policy*. 4 vols. New York: Octagon Books, 1978.

Deriabin, Peter S. *Inside Stalin's Kremlin: An Eyewitness Account of Brutality, Duplicity, and Intrigue*. Washington, D.C.: Brassey's, 1998.

Di Cosmo, Nicola. "Mongolian Topics in the U.S. Military Intelligence Reports." *Mongolian Studies* 10 (1986–1987): 97–106.

—. "Qing Colonial Administration in Inner Asia." *International History Review* 20(2) (June 1998): 287–309.

Dijkink, Gertjan. *National Identity and Geographical Visions: Maps of Pride and Pain*. New York: Routledge, 1996.

Dikotter, Frank. *The Discourse of Race in Modern China*. Stanford, Calif.: Stanford University Press, 1992.

Dower, John W. *War without Mercy: Race and Power in the Pacific War*. New York: Pantheon, 1986.

Duara, Prasenjit. *Sovereignty and Authenticity: Manchukuo and the East Asian Modern*. Lanham, Md.: Rowman & Littlefield, 2003.

Dunham, Mikel. *Buddha's Warriors: The Story of CIA-Backed Tibetan Freedom Fighters, the Chinese Invasion, and the Ultimate Fall of Tibet*. New York: Jeremy P. Tarcher / Penguin, 2004.

Elleman, Bruce A. *Diplomacy and Deception: The Secret History of Sino-Soviet Diplomatic Relations, 1917–1927*. Armonk, N.Y.: M. E. Sharpe, 1997.

—. "Secret Sino-Soviet Negotiations on Outer Mongolia, 1918–1925." *Pacific Affairs* 66 (Winter 1993–1994): 554–558.

—. "Soviet Policy on Outer Mongolia and the Chinese Communist Party." *Journal of Asian History* 28(2) (1994): 108–123.

Elliott, Mark C. *The Manchu Way: The Eight Banners and Ethnic Identity in Late Imperial China*. Stanford, Calif.: Stanford University Press, 2001.

Esherick, Joseph W., ed. *Lost Chance in China: The World War II Dispatches of John S. Service*. New York: Random House, 1974.

Ewing, Thomas E. *Between the Hammer and the Anvil? Chinese and Russian Policies in Outer Mongolia, 1911–1921*. Bloomington: Research Institute for Inner Asian Studies of Indiana University, 1980.

—. "Ch'ing Policies in Outer Mongolia 1900–1911." *Modern Asian Studies* 14(1) (1980): 145–157.

Fitzgerald, John. *Awakening China: Politics, Culture, and Class in the Nationalist Revolution*. Stanford, Calif.: Stanford University Press, 1996.

Fletcher, Joseph. "Ch'ing Inner Asia *c*. 1800." In *The Cambridge History of China, Volume 10: Late Ch'ing, 1800–1911, Part I*. Cambridge: Cambridge University Press, 1978.

—. "Sino-Russian Relations, 1800–62." In *The Cambridge History of China, Volume 10: Late Ch'ing, 1800–1911, Part I*. Cambridge: Cambridge University Press, 1978.

—. "The Heyday of The Ch'ing Order in Mongolia, Sinkiang and Tibet." In *The Cambridge History of China, Volume 10: Late Ch'ing, 1800–1911, Part I*. Cambridge: Cambridge University Press, 1978.

Forbes, Andrew. *Warlords and Muslims in Chinese Central Asia: A Political History of Republican Xinjiang, 1911–1949*. New York: Cambridge University Press, 1996.

Frankel, Francine R. and Harry Harding, eds. *The India-China Relationship: What the United States Needs to Know*. New York and Washington, D.C.: Columbia University Press and Woodrow Wilson Center Press, 2004.

Friters, Gerard M. *Outer Mongolia and Its International Position*. Baltimore: Johns Hopkins University Press, 1949.

—. "The Prelude to Outer Mongolian Independence." *Pacific Affairs* 10 (2) (June 1937): 168–189.

Futaki, Hiroshi. "A Re-Examination of the Establishment of the Mongolian People's Party, Centering on Dogsom's Memoir." *Inner Asia* 2 (2000): 37–61.

Garver, John W. *Chinese–Soviet Relations, 1939–1945: The Diplomacy of Chinese Nationalism*. New York: Oxford University Press, 1988.

Gelber, Harry G. *Nations Out of Empires: European Nationalism and the Transformation of Asia*. New York: Palgrave, 2001.

Gellner, Ernest. *Nations and Nationalism*. Ithaca, N.Y.: Cornell University Press, 1983.

Glantz, David M. *August Storm: The Soviet 1945 Strategic Offensive in Manchuria*. Fort Leavenworth, Kan.: Combat Studies Institute of U.S. Army Command and General Staff College, 1983.

Goldstein, Melvyn. *A History of Modern Tibet, 1913–1951: The Demise of the Lamaist State*. Berkeley: University of California Press, 1989.

—. *A History of Modern Tibet, 1952–1956: Gathering of Storms*. Berkeley: University of California Press, 2007.

—, Ben Jiao, and Tanzen Lhundrup. *On the Cultural Revolution in Tibet: The Nyemo Incident of 1969*. Berkeley: University of California Press, 2009.

—, Dawei Sherap, and William R. Siebenschuh. *A Tibetan Revolutionary: The Political Life and Times of Bapa Phuntso Wangye*. Berkeley: University of California Press, 2004.

Goncharov, Sergei. "The Stalin–Mao Dialogue; Ivan Kovalev, Stalin's Personal Envoy to Mao Zedong, interviewed by historian and sinologist Sergei Goncherov." *FEA* 1 (1992): 100–116.

Goncharov, Sergei N., John W. Lewis, and Xue Litai. *Uncertain Partners: Stalin, Mao, and the Korean War*. Stanford, Calif.: Stanford University Press, 1993.

Grousset, Rene. *Empire of the Steppes: A History of Central Asia*. New Brunswick, N.J.: Rutgers University Press, 1970.

Grunfeld, A. Tom. *The Making of Modern Tibet*. Armonk: M.E. Sharpe, 1996.

Guo Tao-fu (Merse). "Modern Mongolia." *Pacific Affairs* 3(8) (August 1930): 754–762.

Hammond, Thomas T. "The Communist Takeover of Outer Mongolia: Model for Eastern Europe?" *Studies on the Soviet Union* 11(4) (1971): 107–144.

Hayes, Grace P. *The History of the Joint Chiefs of Staff in World War II: The War against Japan*. Annapolis: Naval Institute Press, 1982.

Hechter, Michael. *Containing Nationalism*. Oxford: Oxford University Press, 2000.

Heinzig, Dieter. *The Soviet Union and Communist China, 1945–1950: The Arduous Road to the Alliance*. Armonk, N.Y.: M. E. Sharpe, 2004.

Heuschert, Dorothea. "Legal Pluralism in the Qing Empire: Manchu Legislation for the Mongols." *International History Review* 20(2) (June 1998): 310–324.

Ho, Ping-ti. "In Defense of Sinicization: A Rebuttal of Evelyn Rawski's 'Reenvisioning the Qing.'" *Journal of Asian Studies* 57(1) (February 1998): 123–155.

Hobsbawn, E. J. *Nations and Nationalism since 1780*. Cambridge: Cambridge University Press, 1990.

Hopkirk, Peter. *Setting the East Ablaze: Lenin's Dream of an Empire in Asia*. New York: Kodansha International, 1995.

Hostetler, Laura. *Qing Colonial Enterprise: Ethnography and Cartography in Early Modern China*. Chicago: University of Chicago Press, 2001.

Huang, Ray. *China: A Macro History*. Armonk, N.Y.: M. E. Sharpe, 1990.

Hunt, Michael H. *The Genesis of Chinese Communist Foreign Policy*. New York: Columbia University Press, 1996.

Iriye, Akira. *Power and Culture: The Japanese-American War, 1941–1945*. Cambridge: Harvard University Press, 1981.

Isono, Fujiko. "Soviet Russia and the Mongolian Revolution of 1921." *Past and Present* 83 (March 1979): 116–140.

Jagchid, Sechin. *The Last Mongol Prince: The Life and Times of Demchugdongrob, 1902–1966*. Bellingham: Center for East Asian Studies, Western Washington University, 1999.

Johnson, Chalmers A. *Peasant Nationalism and Communist Power*. Stanford, Calif.: Stanford University Press, 1962.

Kaplonski, Christopher. "Creating National Identity in Socialist Mongolia." *Central Asian Survey* 17(1) (1998): 35–49.

Kennan, George F. *Memoirs, 1925–1950*. New York: Pantheon Books, 1967.

Knaus, John Kenneth. *Orphans of the Cold War: America and the Tibetan Struggle for Survival*. New York: Public Affairs, 1999.

Kotkin, Stephen and Bruce Elleman, eds. *Mongolia in the Twentieth Century: Landlocked Cosmopolitan*. Armonk, N.Y.: M. E. Sharpe, 1999.

Krasner, Stephen D. *Sovereignty: Organized Hypocrisy*. Princeton, N.J.: Princeton University Press, 1999.

—, ed. *Problematic Sovereignty: Contested Rules and Political Possibilities*. New York: Columbia University Press, 2001.

Kriukov, Mikhail. "Once Again about Sun Yatsen's Northwest Plan." *FEA* 5 (2000): 69–84.

Kuznetsov, I. I. "The Soviet Military Advisors in Mongolia, 1921–1939." *Journal of Slavic Military Studies* 12(4) (December 1999): 118–137.

LaFeber, Walter. *The Clash: U.S.–Japanese Relations throughout History*. New York: W. W. Norton, 1997.

Laird, Thomas. *Into Tibet: The CIA's First Atomic Spy and His Secret Expedition to Lhasa*. New York: Grove Press, 2002.

Laitinen, Kauko. *Chinese Nationalism in the Late Qing Dynasty: Zhang Binglin as an Anti-Manchu Propagandist*. London: Curzon Press, 1990.

Lattimore, Owen. *China Memoirs: Chiang Kai-shek and the War against Japan*. Compiled by Fujiko Isono. Tokyo: University of Tokyo Press, 1990.

—. "Mongolia Enters World Affairs." *Pacific Affairs* 7(1) (March 1934): 15–28.

—. *Nationalism and Revolution in Mongolia*. New York: Oxford University Press, 1955.

—. *Nomads and Commissars: Mongolia Revisited*. New York: Oxford University Press, 1962.

—. "Prince, Priest and Herdsman in Mongolia." *Pacific Affairs* 8(1) (March 1935): 35–47.

—. *Studies in Frontier History: Collected Papers 1929–58*. London: Oxford University Press, 1962.

LeDonne, John P. *The Russian Empire and the World, 1700–1917: The Geopolitics of Expansion and Containment.* Oxford: Oxford University Press, 1997.

Ledovsky, Andrei. "Mikoyan's Secret Mission to China in January and February 1949." *FEA* 2 (1995): 72–94.

—. "The Moscow Visit of a Delegation of the Communist Party of China in June to August 1949." *FEA* 4; 5 (1996): 64–86; 84–97.

Leffler, Melvyn P. *A Preponderance of Power: National Security, the Truman Administration, and the Cold War.* Stanford: Stanford University Press, 1992.

Levine, Steven I. *Anvil of Victory: The Communist Revolution in Manchuria, 1945–1948.* New York: Columbia University Press, 1987.

Lieven, Dominic. *Empire: The Russian Empire and Its Rivals.* New Haven, Conn.: Yale University Press, 2000.

Lin Hsiao-ting. *Tibet and Nationalist China's Frontier: Intrigues ad Ethnopolitics, 1928–1949.* Vancouver: British Columbia University Press, 2006.

Litvinov, Maxim. *Notes for a Journal.* New York: William Morrow, 1955.

Liu Xiaohong. *Chinese Ambassadors: The Rise of Professionalism since 1949.* Seattle: University of Washington Press, 2001.

Liu Xiaoyuan. *Frontier Passages: Ethnopolitics and the Rise of Chinese Communism, 1921–1945.* Washington, D.C., and Stanford, Calif.: Woodrow Wilson Center Press and Stanford University Press, 2004.

—. *A Partnership for Disorder: China, the United States, and Their Policies for the Postwar Disposition of the Japanese Empire, 1941–1945.* Cambridge: Cambridge University Press, 1996.

—. *Reins of Liberation: An Entangled History of Chinese Territoriality, Mongolian Autonomy, and Great Power Hegemony, 1921–1950.* Washington, D.C., and Stanford, Calif.: Woodrow Wilson Center Press and Stanford University Press, 2006.

Lkhagva, Togoochiyn. "What Was Stalin's Real Attitude to [sic] the Mongols." *FER* 4 (1991): 117–136.

Louis, Wm. Roger. *Imperialism at Bay: The United States and the Decolonization of the British Empire, 1941—1945.* New York: Oxford University Press, 1978.

Ludden, David. "Presidential Address: Maps in the Mind and the Mobility of Asia," *Journal of Asian Studies*, 62 (4) (November 2003): 1057–1078.

Luzianin, Sergei. "Mongolia: Between China and Soviet Russia." *FEA* 2 (1995): 53–70.

—. *Rossiia–Mongoliia–Kitaii v pervoii polovine XX v: Politicheskie vzaimootnosheniia v 1911–1946 g.* (Russia, Mongolia, and China in the first half of the twentieth century: Political relations, 1911–1946). Moscow: Far Eastern Institute of Russian Academy of Sciences, 2000.

—. "The Yalta Conference and Mongolia in International Law before and during the Second World War." *FEA* 6 (1995): 34–45.

Maier, Charles S. "Consigning the Twentieth Century to History: Alternative Narratives for the Modern Era." *American Historical Review* 105(3) (June 2000): 807–831.

Manela, Erez. *The Wilsonian Moment: Self-Determination and the International Origins of Anticolonial Nationalism.* Oxford: Oxford University Press, 2007.

March, G. Patrick. *Eastern Destiny: Russia in Asia and the North Pacific.* Westport, Conn.: Praeger, 1996.

Mastny, Vojtech. *The Cold War and Soviet Insecurity: The Stalin Years.* New York: Oxford University Press, 1996.

Maxwell, Neville. *India's China War.* London: Jonathan Cape Limited, 1970.

Mayers, David Allan. *Crack the Monolith: U.S. Policy against the Sino-Soviet Alliance, 1949–1955.* Baton Rouge: Louisiana State University Press, 1986.

Melby, John F. *The Mandate of Heaven: Record of a Civil War, China 1945–49.* New York: Doubleday, 1971.

Memmi, Albert. *The Colonizer and the Colonized.* Boston: Beacon Press, 1991.

Morley, James W., ed. *The China Quagmire: Japan's Expansion on the Asian Continent, 1933–1941.* New York: Columbia University Press, 1983.

Morozova, Irina Y. *The Comintern and Revolution in Mongolia*. Cambridge: White Horse Press, 2002.

Murphy, George G. S. *Soviet Mongolia: A Study of the Oldest Political Satellite*. Berkeley: University of California Press, 1966.

Nagai, Yonosuke and Akira Iriye, eds. *The Origins of the Cold War in Asia*. New York: Columbia University Press, 1977.

Newman, Robert P. *Owen Lattimore and the "Loss" of China*. Berkeley: University of California Press, 1992.

O'Connor, Timothy Edward. *Diplomacy and Revolution: G. V. Chicherin and Soviet Foreign Affairs, 1918–1930*. Ames: Iowa State University Press, 1988.

Onon, Urgunge and Derrick Pritchatt. *Asia's First Modern Revolution: Mongolia Proclaims Its Independence in 1911*. Leiden: E. J. Brill, 1989.

Paine, S. C. M. *Imperial Rivals: China, Russia, and Their Disputed Frontier*. Armonk, N.Y.: M. E. Sharpe, 1996.

Pechatnov, Vladimir O. *The Big Three after World War II: New Documents on Soviet Thinking about Postwar Relations with the United States and Great Britain*. Cold War International History Project Working Paper 13. Washington, D.C.: Cold War International History Project, Woodrow Wilson International Center for Scholars, 1995.

Perdue, Peter C. "Boundaries, Maps, and Movement: Chinese, Russian, and Mongolian Empires in Early Modern Central Eurasia." *International History Review* 20(2) (June 1998): 263–286.

—. *China Marches West: The Qing Conquest of Central Eurasia*. Cambridge: Belknap Press of Harvard University Press, 2005.

—. "Comparing Empires: Manchu Colonialism." *International History Review* 20(2) (June 1998): 255–261.

—. "Military Mobilization in Seventeenth and Eighteenth-Century China, Russia, and Mongolia." *Modern Asian Studies* 30(4) (1996): 757–793.

Persits, Moisei. "A New Collection of Documents on Soviet Policy in the Far East in 1920–1922." *FEA* 5 (1997): 79–93.

Pipes, Richard, ed. *The Unknown Lenin: From the Secret Archive*. New Haven, Conn.: Yale University Press, 1996.

Purenvdorzh, Ch. "Soviet–Mongolian Cooperation during the Second World War." *FEA* 4 (1985): 35–43.

Qing Simei. *From Allies to Enemies: Visions of Modernity, Identity, and U.S.-China Diplomacy, 1945–1960*. Cambridge: Harvard University Press, 2007.

Rabgey, Tashi and Tseten Wangchuk Sharlho. *Sino–Tibetan Dialogue in the Post-Mao Era: Lessons and Prospects*. Washington, D.C.: East–West Center Washington, 2004.

Radchenko, Sergey S. *The Soviets' Best Friends in Asia: The Mongolian Dimension of the Sino-Soviet Split*. Cold War International History Project Working Paper 42. Washington, D.C.: Woodrow Wilson International Center for Scholars, 2003.

Radchenko, Sergey. *Two Suns in the Heaven: The Sino-Soviet Struggle for Supremacy, 1962–1967*. Stanford and Washington, D.C.: Stanford University Press and Wilson Center Press, 2009.

Rawski, Evelyn S. "Presidential Address: Reenvisioning the Qing: The Significance of the Qing Period in Chinese History." *Journal of Asian Studies* 55(4) (November 1996): 829–850.

Rupen, Robert. *How Mongolia Is Really Ruled: A Political History of the Mongolian People's Republic*. Stanford, Calif.: Stanford University Press, 1979.

Sandag, Shagdariin and Harry H. Kendall. *Poisoned Arrows: The Stalin–Choibalsan Mongolian Massacres, 1921–1941*. Boulder, Colo.: Westview Press, 2000.

Santman, Barry and June Teufel Dreyer, eds., *Contemporary Tibet: Politics, Development, and Society in a Disputed Region*. Armonk: M.E. Sharpe, 2006.

Schaller, Michael. *The U.S. Crusade in China, 1938–1945*. New York: Columbia University Press, 1979.

Selden, Mark. *The Yenan Way in Revolutionary China*. Cambridge: Harvard University Press, 1971.

Serruys, Henry. "Documents from Ordos on the 'Revolutionary Circles,' Part I." *Journal of the American Oriental Society* 97(4) (October–December 1977): 482–507.

Service, Robert. *Lenin: A Biography*. Cambridge, Mass.: Harvard University Press, 2000.

Shakya, Tsering. *The Dragon in the Land of Snow: A History of Modern Tibet since 1947.* London: Pimlico, 1999.
Shen Zhihua. "Clashes of Interests and Their Settlement during Negotiations on the Chinese–Soviet Treaty of 1950." *FEA* 3 (2002): 97–112.
Shirendev, Bazaryn. *Through the Ocean Waves: The Autobiography of Bazaryn Shirendev.* Bellingham: Western Washington University Press, 1997.
Shlapentokh, Vladimir. "The World Revolution as a Geographic Instrument of the Soviet Leadership." *Russian History / Historire Russe* 26(3) (Fall 1999): 315–334.
Smith, Anthony D. *The Ethnic Origins of Nations.* Oxford: Basil Blackwell, 1988.
Smith, Warren W. Jr. *Tibetan Nation: A History of Tibetan Nationalism and Sino-Tibetan Relations.* Boulder: Westview, 1996.
Sneath, David. *Changing Inner Mongolia: Pastoral Mongolian Society and the Chinese State.* Oxford: Oxford University Press, 2000.
Starr, S. Frederick, ed., *Xinjiang: China's Muslim Borderland.* Armonk: M.E. Sharpe, 2004.
Stephan, John. *The Russian Far East: A History.* Stanford, Calif.: Stanford University Press, 1994.
Stueck, William. *The Wedemeyer Mission: American Politics and Foreign Policy during the Cold War.* Athens: University of Georgia Press, 1984.
Tang, Peter S. H. *Russian and Soviet Policy in Manchuria and Outer Mongolia, 1911–1931.* Durham, N.C.: Duke University Press, 1959.
Taylor, Jay. *The Generalissimo: Chiang Kai-shek and the Struggle for Modern China.* Cambridge: The Belknap Press of Harvard University Press, 2009.
Thaxton, Ralph A. *Salt of the Earth: The Political Origins of Peasant Protest and Communist Revolution in China.* Berkeley: University of California Press, 1997.
Thorne, Christopher. *Allies of a Kind: The United States, Britain and the War against Japan, 1941–1945.* Oxford: Oxford University Press, 1978.
Tikhvinsky, S. "China in My Life." *FEA* 4 (1989): 88–105.
Tønnesson, Stein. *The Vietnamese Revolution of 1945: Roosevelt, Ho Chi Minh and de Gaulle in a World at War.* London: Sage, 1991.
Totrov, Yuri. "American Intelligence in China." *FEA* 2 (2002): 100–116.
Trachtenberg, Marc. *A Constructed Peace: The Making of the European Settlement, 1945–1963.* Princeton, N.J.: Princeton University Press, 1999.
Trenin, Dmitri. *The End of Eurasia: Russia on the Border between Geopolitics and Globalization.* Washington, D.C.: Carnegie Endowment for International Peace, 2002.
Tuttle, Gray. *Tibetan Buddhists in the Making of Modern China.* New York: Columbia University Press, 2005.
Volkogonov, Dmitri. *Stalin: Triumph and Tragedy.* Trans. Harold Shukman. New York: Grove Weidenfeld, 1991.
Wakeman, Frederic, Jr. *The Great Enterprise: The Manchu Reconstruction of Imperial Order in Seventeenth-Century China.* Berkeley: University of California Press, 1985.
Wang, David D. *Under the Soviet Shadow: The Yining Incident: Ethnic Conflicts and International Rivalry in Xinjiang, 1944–1949.* Hong Kong: Chinese University Press, 1999.
Wedemeyer, Albert C. *Wedemeyer Reports!* New York: Henry Holt, 1958.
Westad, Odd Arne. *Cold War and Revolution: Soviet–American Rivalry and the Origins of the Chinese Civil War, 1944–1946.* New York: Columbia University Press, 1993.
—. *Decisive Encounters: The Chinese Civil War, 1946–1950.* Stanford, Calif.: Stanford University Press, 2003.
Winichakul, Thongchai. *Siam Mapped: A History of the Geo-Body of a Nation.* Honolulu: University of Hawaii Press, 1994.
Wong, R. Bin. *China Transformed: Historical Change and the Limits of European Experience.* Ithaca: Cornell University Press, 1997.
Xiang Lanxin. *Recasting the Imperial Far East: Britain and America in China, 1945–1950.* Armonk, N.Y.: M. E. Sharpe, 1995.

Yakhontoff, Victor A. "Mongolia: Target or Screen?" *Pacific Affairs* 9(1) (March 1936): 13–23.
Yu Maochun. *OSS in China: Prelude to Cold War.* New Haven, Conn.: Yale University Press, 1996.
Zhang Shuguang. *Economic Cold War: America's Embargo against China and the Sino-Soviet Alliance, 1949–1963.* Stanford and Washington, D.C.: Stanford University Press and Wilson Center Press, 2001.
Zhang Shuguang and Chen Jian, eds. *Chinese Communist Foreign Policy and the Cold War in Asia: New Documentary Evidence, 1944–1950.* Chicago: Imprint Publications, 1996.
Zhang Yongjin. *China in the International System, 1918–1920: The Middle Kingdom at the Periphery.* London: Macmillan, 1991.
Zubok, Vladislav and Constantine Pleshakov. *Inside the Kremlin's Cold War: From Stalin to Khrushchev.* Cambridge, Mass.: Harvard University Press, 1996.

In Chinese

Bai Zhen. "Recollection of Making Contact with the Soviet–Mongolian Army." *Zhangbei Wenshi Ziliao* (Literary and Historical Materials of Zhangbei) 1 (n.d.): 47–49.
Balgud. "The Rebellions in the Zasagtu and Zhenguogong Banners." *Neimenggu Wenshi Ziliao* (Literary and Historical Materials of Inner Mongolia) 1 (1962): 63–82.
Bayanbulag. "Soviet–Mongolian Red Army Passed through Sunid Right Banner." *Sunite Youqi Wenshi Ziliao* (Historical and Literary Materials of Sunid Right Banner) 1–2 (1985): 33–34.
Bayantu. "Awakening before Dawn: August 11 Uprising Remembered." *Xing'an Geming Shihua* (Historical Record of the Revolution in Xing'an) 3 (1990): 192–201.
Bei Xiaoyan. "The Birth of the Inner Mongolian Autonomous Government." *NWZ* 50 (1997): 278–311.
Budebara. "Recollections and Memories." *Xilinguole Shi Wenshi Ziliao* (Literary and Historical Materials of the Shilingol Municipality) 1 (1985): 46–72.
Bukhe. "The Struggle of Suppressing Bandits and Opposing Local Tyrants in West Khorchin Central Banner." *Xing'an Dangshi Wenji* (Collected Essays on the Party History of Xing'an) 2 (1993): 278–302.
Bukhe and Sayin. *Boyanmandu Shengping Shilue* (Buyanmandukhu's Life and Time). Hohhot: Neimenggu Daxue Tushuguan, 1999 (internal circulation).
Butegechi. *Fengyu Jiancheng Wushinian* (Advance in Trials and Hardships for Fifty Years). Hohhot: Neimenggu Renmin Chubanshe, 1997.
Buyantu. "Awakening before Dawn: August 11 Uprising Remembered." *Xing'an Geming Shihua* 3 (1990): 185–202.
—. "Brief Chronicle of Wandannima's Career." *NWZ* 19 (1985): 36–43.
Committee for Collecting Party History Materials of the Tibetan Autonomous Region, *Zhonggong Xizang Dangshi Dashiji 1949–1994* (Chronicle of important events in the CCP history in Tibet). Lhasa: Xizang Renmin Chubanshe, 1995.
Dalizhaya ji Furen Jin Yuncheng Shiliao Zhuanji (Special Issue on Historical Materials about Darijahyaga and Wife Jin Yuncheng). *Bayanno'er Wenshi Ziliao* (Literary and Historical Materials of Buyannuur) 9 (1988).
Dangdai Zhongguo de Neimenggu (Inner Mongolia of Contemporary China). Beijing: Dangdai Zhongguo Chubanshe, 1992.
Dawa-ochir. "My Experiences." *NWZ* 31 (1988): 104–185.
Delgerchogtu. "The 'Inner Mongolian Youth Party' as I Knew It." *Wulanchabu Wenshi Ziliao* (Historical and Literary Materials of Ulachab) 2 (1984): 89–115.
Demchugdongrob. "Demuchukedonglupu Zishu" (Autobiography of Demchugdongrob). *Neimenggu Wenshi Ziliao* (Literary and Historical Materials of Inner Mongolia) 13, 1984.
Documentary Research Office of the Chinese Communist Party Central Committee. *Liu Shaoqi Nianpu* (Chronicle of Liu Shaoqi's Life). Beijing: Zhongyang Wenxian Chubanshe, 1996.
—. *Mao Zedong Nianpu* (The Chronicle of Mao Zedong's Life). Beijing: Zhongyang Wenxian Chubanshe, 1993.

—. *Zhou Enlai Nianpu* (The Chronicle of Zhou Enlai's Life). Beijing: Zhongyang Wenxian Chubanshe, 1989.

Gan Fengling. "Brief Biography of the Eleven Members of the Political Council of Inner Mongolia." *NWZ* 50 (1997): 335–345.

Gao Shuhua and Cheng Tiejun. *Neimeng Wenge Fenglei: Yiwei Zaofanpai Lingiu de Koushu Shi* (The storm of the cultural revolution in Inner Mongolia: an oral history by a rebel leader). Carle Place, N.Y.: Mirror Books, 2007.

Geng Binying, ed. *Shuguang Zhaoyao Zhelimu* (Dawn upon Jerim). Beijing: Minzu Chubanshe, 1988.

Gu Jigang and Shi Nianhai. *Zhongguo Jiangyu Yange Shi* (History of China's Changing Territories). Beijing: Shangwu Yanshuguan, 2000.

Gu Weijun (Wellington Koo). *Gu Weijun Huiyilu* (Memoirs of Gu Weijun). 12 vols. Beijing: Zhonghua Shuju, 1983–1993.

Hao Yufeng. *Wulanfu Zhuan* (Biography of Ulanfu). Hohhot: Neimenggu Renmin Chubanshe, 1990.

Hu Shaoheng. "Excerpts from Hu Shaoheng's Diary." *Xing'an Geming Shihua* 3 (1990): 213–294.

Huang Xiurong, ed. *Sulian, Gongchan Guoji yu Zhongguo Geming de Guanxi Xintan* (New Studies of the Relationship between the Soviet Union, Comintern, and Chinese Revolution). Beijing: Zhonggong Dangshi Chubanshe, 1995.

Jiang Kefu. *Minguo Junshishi Luegao* (Brief Military History of the Chinese Republic). 4 vols. Beijing: Zhonghua Shuju, 1991.

Jiang Mingsheng. "Brief biography of Temurbagana." *Xing'an Dangshi Wenji* (Collected Essays on the Party History of Xing'an) 1 (1993): 226–236.

Jiang Shuchen. *Fu Zuoyi Zhuanlue* (Biography of Fu Zuoyi). Beining: Zhongguo Qingnian Chubanshe, 1990.

Jin Chongji. *Zhou Enlai Zhuan, 1949–1976* (Biography of Zhou Enlai, 1949–1976). Beijing: Zhongyang Wenxian Chubanshe, 1998.

Kho'erge. "Recollections of the Unification of Inner Mongolian Autonomous Movement." *NWZ* 50 (1997): 143–155.

Layi. "Recollection of the Political Situation in Hailar after September 3." *Hulunbei'er Wenshi Ziliao* (Historical and Literary Materials of Hulunbuir) 3 (1985): 1–6.

Ledovsky, Andrei. *Sidalin yu Zhongguo* (Stalin and China). Trans. Chen Chunhua and Liu Cunkuan. Beijing: Xinhua Chubanshe, 2001.

Li Haiwen. "The Inaccuracies in Kovalev's Reminiscences: An Interview with Shi Zhe." *Guoshi Yanjiu Cankao Ziliao* (Reference Materials for the Study of State History) 1 (1993): 91–94.

Li Sheng. *Zhongguo Xinjiang: Lishi yu Xianzhuang* (Xinjiang of China: history and current situation). Urumuqi: Xinjiang Renmin Chubanshe, 2003.

Li Shouxin. *Li Shouxin Zishu* (Autobiography of Li Shouxin). *NWZ* 20 (1985).

Liu Chun. "Remembrance of Work in Inner Mongolia." *NWZ* 50 (1997): 33–98.

Liu Xiao. *Chushi Sulian Banian* (Eight-Year Ambassadorship in the Soviet Union). Beijing: Zhonggong Dangshi Ziliao Chubanshe, 1986.

Lu Minghui. *Menggu "Zizhi Yundong" Shimo* (The Beginning and End of the Mongolian "Autonomous Movement"). Beijing: Zhonghua Shuju, 1980.

Luo Guangwu. *Xin Zhongguo Minzu Gongzuo Dashi Gailan, (1949–1999)* (Survey of important events in the nationality work of the new China, [1949–1999]). Beijing: Huawen Chubanshe, 2001.

Ma Dazheng, *Guojia Liyi Gao Yu Yiqie: Xinjiang Wending Wendi de Guancha yu Sikao* (State interest is superior to anything else: reflections and observations on the question of stability in Xinjiang). Urumqi: Xinjiang Renmin Chubanshe, 2003.

Mongolian History Compiling Group. *Mengguzu Jianshi* (Brief History of the Mongolian Nationality). Hohhot: Neimenggu Renmin Chubanshe, 1985.

Niu Dayong and Shen Zhihua, eds., *Lengzhan yu Zhongguo de Zhoubian Guanxi* (The Cold War and China's relations with the neighboring regions). Beijing: Shijie Zhishi Chubanshe, 2004.

Office of Diplomatic History of the Ministry of Foreign Affairs. *Xin Zhongguo Waijiao Fengyun* (New China's Diplomatic Storms). Beijing: Shijie Zhishi Chubanshe, 1990.

Office for Party History Research of the Chinese Communist Party Committee of Inner Mongolia. *Neimenggu Dang de Lishi he Dang de Gongzuo* (The Party's History and Works in Inner Mongolia). Hohhot: Neimenggu Renmin Chubanshe, 1994.

Oljeinaren. "In the Mighty Torrent of Inner Mongolia's Liberation Movement." *NWZ* 50 (1997): 193–206.

Pei Jianzhang. *Zhonghua Renmin Gongheguo Waijiao Shi, 1949–1956* (Diplomatic History of the People's Republic of China, 1949–1956). Beijing: Shijie Zhishi Chubanshe, 1994.

Qian Linbao. *Jiefang Zhanzheng Shiqi Neimenggu Qibing* (Inner Mongolian Cavalries during the War of Liberation). Hohhot: Neimenggu Daxue Chubanshe, 1989.

Second Historical Archives of China. *Jiang Jieshi Nianpu Chugao* (Preliminary Draft of the Chronicle of Jiang Jieshi's Life). Beijing: Dang'an Chubanshe, 1992.

Shen Zhihua. *Mao Zedong, Sidalin yu Chaoxian Zhanzheng* (Mao Zedong, Stalin and the Korean War). Guangzhou: Guangdong Renmin Chubanshe, 2003.

Shi Bo. *Waimenggu Duli Neimu* (Inside Story of Outer Mongolian Independence). Beijing: Renmin Zhongguo Chubanshe, 1993.

Shi Zhe. *Feng yu Gu: Shi Zhe Huiyilu* (Peaks and Valleys: Memoirs of Shi Zhe). Beijing: Hongqi Chubanshe, 1997.

—. *Wo de Yisheng: Shi Zhe Zishu* (My Life: In Shi Zhe's Own Words). Beijing: Renmin Chubanshe, 2001.

—. *Zai Lishi Juren Shenbian: Shi Zhe Huiyilu* (At the Side of Historical Giants: Memoirs of Shi Zhe). Beijing: Zhongyang Wenxian Chubanshe, 1995.

Tegus. "The May First Conference as I Knew." *Xing'an Dangshi Wenji* (Collected Essays on the Party History of Xing'an) 1 (1993): 10–19.

Temle. *Jianguo qian Neimenggu Difang Baokan Kaolu* (Investigation and Classifications of Newspapers and Journals in the Area of Inner Mongolia before the Foundation of the State). Hohhot: Neimenggu Tushuguan, 1987.

Tumen and Zhu Dongli. *Kang Shen yu Neirendang Yuan'an* (Kang Sheng and the Unjust Case of the IMPRP). Beijing: Zhongyang Dangxiao Chubanshe, 1995.

Ulanfu. *Wulanfu Huiyilu* (Memoirs of Ulanfu). Beijing: Zhonggong Dangshi Ziliao Chubanshe, 1989.

Wang Dongxing. *Wang Dongxing Huiyi Mao Zedong yu Lin Biao Fangeming Jiduan de Douzheng* (Mao Zedong's Struggle with the Lin Biao Counterrevolutionary Clique as Remembered by Wang Dongxing). Beijing: Dangdai Zhongguo Chubanshe, 2004.

—. *Wang Dongxing Riji* (Wang Dongxing's Diaries) (Beijing: Zhongguo Shehui Kexue Chubanshe, 1993.

Wang Duo. *Wushi Chunqiu* (Fifty Eventful Years). Hohhot: Neimenggu Renmin Chubanshe, 1992.

Wang Hongwei. *Ximalayashan Qingjie: Zhong Yin Guanxi Yanjiu* (The Himalayan complex: a study of the Chinese-Indian relations). Beijing: Zhongguo Zangxue Chubanshe, 1998.

Wang Jianmin et al. *Zhongguo Minzuxue Shi* (History of ethnology in China). Kunming: Yunnan Jiaoyu Chubanshe, 1998.

Wang Lixiong. *Tianzang: Xizang de Mingyun* (Sky burial: the destiny of Tibet). Carle Place, NY: Mirror Books, 1998.

Wang Shijie. *Wang Shijie Riji* (Wang Shijie's Diaries). Taipei: Zhongyang Yanjiuyuan Jidaishi Yanjiusuo, 1990.

Wang Shusheng and Hao Yufeng. *Wulanfu Nianpu* (Chronicle of Ulanfu's Life). Beijing: Zhonggong Dangshi Ziliao Chubanshe, 1989.

Wulanfu Jinian Wenji (Memorial Essays on Ulanfu). Hohhot: Neimenggu Renmin Chubanshe, 1990.

Wulanfu Yanjiu Lunwenji (Essays on Ulanfu Studies). Compiled by Inner Mongolia Society of Ulanfu Studies. Hohhot: Neimenggu Wenhua Chubanshe, 1994.

Wu Lengxi. *Shinian Lunzhan, 1956–1966: Zhongsu Guanxi Huiyilu* (Ten Years of Debates, 1956–1966: A Memoir of Sino-Soviet Relations). Beijing: Zhongyang Wenxian Chubanshe, 1999.

Wu Xiuquan. *Wo de Jingli* (My Experience). Beijing: Jiefangjun Chubanshe, 1984.

Xu Zehao. *Wang Jiaxiang Zhuan* (Biography of Wang Jiaxiang). Beijing: Dangdai Zhongguo Chubanshe, 1996.

Yang Gongsu. *Zhongguo Fandui Waiguo Qinlue Ganshe Xizang Difangshi* (History of China's opposition to foreign aggressions and interferences in Tibet). Beijing: Zhongguo Zangxue Chubanshe, 1992.

Yang Kuisong. *Mao Zedong yu Mosike de En En Yuan Yuan* (Gratitude and Grievances between Mao Zedong and Moscow). Nanchang: Jiangxi Renmin Chubanshe, 1999.

—. *Xi'an Shibian Xintan* (New Study of the Xi'an Incident). Taipei: Dongda Tushu, 1995.

—. *Zhonggong yu Mosike de Guanxi, 1920–1960* (The Chinese Communist Party's Relationship with Moscow, 1920–1960). Taipei: Dongda Tushu Gongsi, 1997.

Yun Shiying and Chao Luomeng. "Recollections of Works of the Shilingol League." *NWZ* 50 (1997): 156–175.

Zai Jiang Jieshi Shenbian Ba Nian: Shicongshi Gaoji MuliaoTang Zong Riji (With Jiang Jieshi for Eight Years: Senior Member of the Aides' Office Tang Zong's Diary). Compiled by the Ministry of Public Security Archives. Beijing: Qunzhong Chubanshe, 1992.

Zhahalofu (M. B. Zakharov). *Jieju: 1945 Nian Dabai Riben Diguozhuyi Lishi Huiyilu* (The Finale: A Historical Memoir of the Defeat of Japanese Imperialism in 1945). Translated from Russian by Jun Qing. Shanghai: Shanghai Yiwen Chubanshe, 1978.

Zhang Ce. "My Onerous Lifetime." *Xing'an Geming Shihua* 3 (1990): 1–184.

Zhang Ce, Hu Shaoheng, and Fang Zhida. "Some Events from the Time of the Eastern Mongolian Autonomous Government to the Establishment of the Inner Mongolian Autonomous Government." *Xing'an Dangshi Wenji* (Collected Essays on the Party History of Xing'an) 1 (1993): 1–9.

Zhang Qixiong. *Shoufu Waimeng Zhuquan, 1917–1920* (Restoration of Sovereignty in Outer Mongolia, 1917–1920). Taipei: Meng Zang Weiyuanhui, 1998.

—. *Waimeng Zhuquan Jiaoshe* (Negotiations over Sovereignty in Outer Mongolia). Taipei: Zhongyang Yanjiuyuan Jindaishi Yanjiusuo, 1995.

Zhonghua Minguo Shi Neizheng Zhi (Chugao) (History of the Republic of China: A Chronicle of Domestic Administration). Compiled by Academia Historica. Taipei: Guoshiguan, 1992.

Zhou Qingshu. *Neimenggu Lishi Dili* (Historical Geography of Inner Mongolia). Hohhot: Neimengu Daxue Chubanshe, 1993.

Zhou Wending and Chu Liangru. *Teshu er Fuzai de Keti: Gongchan Guoji, Sulian he Zhongguo Gongchandang Guanxi Biannianshi, 1919–1991* (A Unique and Complex Subject: The Chronicle of the Relationship between the Comintern, the Soviet Union and the Chinese Communist Party). Wuhan: Hubei Renmin Chubanshe, 1993.

Zhu Peimin. "Changes in the Soviet Policy in Xinjiang from 1943 to 1949." *Zhonggong Dangshi Yanjiu* (Studies in the Chinese Communist Party's History), supplementary issue (December 1990): 87–92.

Index

Made in the USA
Lexington, KY
16 August 2012